AMERICAN WOMEN'S AUTOBIOGRAPHY

Wisconsin Studies in American Autobiography

WILLIAM L. ANDREWS
General Editor

American Women's Autobiography
Fea(s)ts of Memory

Edited, with an Introduction, by

MARGO CULLEY

The University of Wisconsin Press

The University of Wisconsin Press
114 North Murray Street
Madison, Wisconsin 53715

3 Henrietta Street
London WC2E 8LU, England

5   4   3   2   1

Printed in the United States of America

Library of Congress Cataloging-in-Publication Data
American women's autobiography : fea(s)ts of memory / edited with an
   introduction by Margo Culley.
      348 pp.   cm. — (Wisconsin studies in American autobiography)
      Includes bibliographical references and index.
      ISBN 0-299-13290-0   ISBN 0-299-13294-3 (pbk.)
      1. American prose literature—Women authors—History and
   criticism.   2. Women authors, American—Biography—History and
   criticism.   3. Women—United States—Biography—History and
   criticism.   4. Autobiography—Women authors.   I. Culley, Margo.
   II. Series.
   PS366.A88A48   1992
   810.9′49272—dc20   91-46700

For Lee, Arlyn, Joe, and Kath—comrades true

Contents

Acknowledgments

I am grateful to Dorothy Johnson and Doris Abramson of the Common Reader Bookshop in New Salem, Massachusetts, who allowed me to rummage among their shelves of women's autobiographies. I am also in debt to my students at the University of Massachusetts in Amherst who sustained my enthusiasm for this project. My thanks go to the patient contributors to the volume without whom the book would not exist. Particular gratitude goes to the one contributor (you know who you are) who met the original deadline for essays. To the two friends and contributors (you know who you are) who never met the final, final deadline for essays, all is forgiven. To my in-home editor, an editor's editor, thanks for everything.

Contributors

LYNN Z. BLOOM is Professor of English and Aetna Chair of Writing at the University of Connecticut. Her concentration on biography and autobiography of women, children, and families has resulted in such works as *Dr. Spock: Biography of a Conservative Radical*, editions of Natalie Crouter's *Forbidden Diary: A Record of Wartime Internment, 1941–1945* and Margaret Sams's *Forbidden Family: A Wartime Memoir of the Philippines, 1941–1945*, and *American Autobiography, 1945–1980: A Bibliography*, with M. L. Briscoe and B. Tobias. Much of her research has been supported by grants from the National Endowment for the Humanities.

MARGO CULLEY is the editor of *A Day at a Time: Diary Literature of American Women* and the Norton edition of Kate Chopin's *The Awakening* and co-editor, with Catherine Portuges, of *Gendered Subjects: The Dynamics of Feminist Teaching* and, with Leonore Hoffmann, *Women's Personal Narratives*. She maintains large perennial gardens and is the first woman elected to the Selectboard in the town of Wendell, Massachusetts, population 900.

ARLYN DIAMOND is a medievalist, feminist, and union activist. With Lee R. Edwards she edited *American Voices, American Women* and *The Authority of Experience: Essays in Feminist Criticism*. She is currently working on narratives of courtly love, and, of course, going to lots of meetings.

ANN D. GORDON is co-editor of the *Papers of Elizabeth Cady Stanton and Susan B. Anthony*. She earned her Ph.D. from the University of Wisconsin–Madison and has published numerous articles in women's history. She is at work on a history of how women attained school suffrage in the United States during the nineteenth century.

JANIS GREVE is a doctoral candidate in English at the University of Massachusetts in Amherst with specializations in Emily Dickinson, Women's Autobiography and Photography, and Southern Women Writers. Her most consuming and immediately gratifying interest is her three-year-old daughter, Stefana.

C. MARGOT HENNESSY teaches courses on African-American women writers, women's autobiography, contemporary women's literature, literary criticism, and feminist theory at Clark University. She is currently completing a booklength study on postmodern theories of identity and feminist politics.

SHIRLEY GEOK-LIN LIM has published a collection of short stories and three books of poetry, most recently *Modern Secrets* (1989). Winner of the 1980 Commonwealth Poetry Prize, she has received Wien, Fulbright, Mellon, NEH, ISEAS and other fellowships. She has published essays in *Feminist Studies* and *Women's Studies,* is co-editor of *The Forbidden Stitch: An Asian American Women's Anthology,* and is currently working on a novel and a book of memoirs. She is a professor of Asian American Studies at the University of California at Santa Barbara.

MARY G. MASON is Professor of English at Emmanuel College. She has published articles and reviews on nineteenth-century literature, on women writers, and especially on women's autobiographical writing. She co-edited, with Carol Hurd Green, *Journeys: Autobiographical Writings by Women* and published the only essay on women's autobiography in the James Olney anthology *Autobiography: Essays Theoretical and Critical.* She is working on a booklength study of women's autobiography.

KATHLEEN MULLEN SANDS is a professor in the English Department at Arizona State College where she teaches American Indian literatures, folklore, autobiography, Western American literature, and cross-cultural writing. She is the co-author, with Gretchen Bataille, of *American Indian Women, Telling Their Lives* and the editor of *Circle of Motion: An Anthology of Contemporary Arizona Indian Literature, The Autobiography of a Yaqui Poet,* and is a co-editor of *People of Pascua.* She has also written numerous articles on American Indian oral traditions and contemporary fiction and co-directs the Arizona Heritage Fair, an annual folklife festival in Phoenix.

SIDONIE SMITH is Professor of English and Women's Studies at the State University of New York at Binghamton. She is the author of *Where I'm Bound: Patterns of Slavery and Freedom in Black American Autobiography* and *A Poetics of Women's Autobiography: Marginality and the Fictions of Self-Representation,* and co-editor with Julia Watson of *De/Colonizing the Subject: Politics and Gender in Women's Autobiography.* She has just completed a study of twentieth-century women's autobiographical practice, entitled *Subjectivity, Identity, and the Body.*

CATHARINE R. STIMPSON is a University Professor at Rutgers University where she has recently served as Dean of the Graduate School. She is the author of both fiction and nonfiction. A selection of her essays, *Where the Meanings Are,* appeared in 1988. She was the founding editor of *Signs: Journal of Women in Culture and Society* and served as President of the Modern Language Association in 1990.

KATHLEEN M. SWAIM, a specialist in the poetry of John Milton, has also published on Spenser, Herbert, Bunyan, and Swift. Her books include *Before and After the Fall: Contrasting Modes in Paradise Lost* and *Pilgrim's Progress, Puritan Progress: Discourses and Contexts* (forthcoming). Her recent interests have turned to the literary place and productions of seventeenth-century women in England and, with her contribution to this volume, in America as well. She is a professor of English at the University of Massachusetts—Amherst.

ANN TAVES is Associate Professor of American Religious History at the School of Theology at Claremont and Co-Director of the Program in Women's Studies in Religion at Claremont Graduate School. Her current research interest is the relationship between theology and the psychosocial order as viewed through the lens of women's autobiography. She is the editor of *Religion and Domestic Violence in Early New England: The Memoirs of Abigail Bailey* and the author of several articles on women and/or gender issues in American religious history.

NANCY WALKER is Director of Women's Studies and Associate Professor of English at Vanderbilt University. She is the author of *A Very Serious Thing: Women's Humor and American Culture* and the co-editor of *Redressing the Balance: American Women's Humorous Writing from Colonial Times to the 1980s.* Her book *Feminist Alternatives: Irony and Fantasy in the Contemporary Novel by Women* won the first Annual Eudora Welty Prize awarded by the University of Mississippi Press. She is currently working on a book on Fanny Fern and editing a critical edition of Kate Chopin's *The Awakening.*

AMERICAN WOMEN'S AUTOBIOGRAPHY

CHAPTER 1

What a Piece of Work is "Woman"! An Introduction

MARGO CULLEY

I

It would be hard to point to a field of contemporary literary studies more vibrant than autobiography studies. Where else does one find a wealth of primary material still mostly unread and unranked? Complicated, self-conscious texts in which the subject stands at once naked and veiled — inspiring and annoying texts, generous and cranky ones, modest and bombastic ones written in plainstyle or baroque — all draw us as surely as we are drawn to the pages of *People* magazine in the dentist's waiting room. And if this is not enticing enough, autobiography theory today is an international playground where strenuous mental gymnastics keep all at the top of their form. The most pressing concerns of contemporary scholars — genre and gender as culturally inscribed; the construction of the self within language systems; the referentiality of language itself; the nature of subjectivity, authority, and agency; the problematics of making meaning and making history; theories of time, memory, and narrative — all absorb critics of autobiography. And the final delight is that these critics have permission to indulge the pleasure of talking about themselves performing their aerial feats ("Look, Ma!"), for criticism is, after all, autobiography.

Though little more than a decade old, theory and criticism of women's autobiography already has its own history. Feminist critics with diverse perspectives and methodologies have found within women's personal narratives a rich mother lode. Those whom Elaine Showalter has called *gynocritics* ("Women's Time, Women's Space" 37), by which she means those with an Anglo-American bent, eager to retrieve lost texts and challenge the canon, find in autobiography rich unexplored territory. Those whose intellectual roots are in European philosophy, psychology, and linguistics, whose in-

3

terest in the inscription of gender within texts Alice Jardine calls *gynesis* (25–26), are also powerfully drawn to the literature whose subject is the self. Indeed, autobiographical studies is one arena where the differences in feminist criticisms seem most fruitfully negotiated as, for example, in Françoise Lionnet's book on women's autobiography that begins with chapters on Augustine and Nietzsche before turning to the work of five women writers, two African American and three Francophone writers of the so-called Third World.

Debates within feminist theory, and within literary theory more broadly, have shaped the criticism of women's autobiography. One group of critics has focused on the question of how women's autobiography might be essentially different from men's. They argue, for example, that women's autobiography displays unique narrative discontinuity (Jelinek), writes the self through the Other (Mason), tests boundaries between the public and the private spheres (Smith), exhibits a collective consciousness (Friedman). And because one simply cannot engage the subject of autobiography without confronting philosophical issues of the self and textuality, important work on women's autobiography has been done by those trained in the continental tradition: Germaine Brée, Elaine Marks, Domna Stanton, and Nancy Miller. Though for a moment, Domna Stanton removed the "bio" in coining the term "autogynography," most feminist critics of autobiography (Stanton included) exhibit a reluctance to indulge in fashionable extremes of skepticism about self, authorizing, and referentiality. As Nancy Miller writes, "the post-modern decision that the Author is Dead and the subject along with him does not . . . necessarily hold for women, and prematurely forecloses the question of agency for them" (106). Critics exploring autobiographical traditions outside the dominant Anglo-American tradition, such as Elizabeth Fox-Genovese working on African American women's narratives and Doris Sommer working on Latin American women's *testimonios,* have been quick to agree (Fox-Genovese 66–67; Sommer 120).

In addition to debates about unique features of women's autobiography and about the connections between *auto*(self)/*bio*(life)/*graphy*(writing), the engagement of "WOMAN" with "women" finds rich grounding in autobiography studies. In a kind of sea change away from those who in the 1970s demonstrated how MAN erased WOMAN, influential feminist theory now argues that WOMAN (in both its American and French constructions) has erased the historical specificity of many women. The danger of earlier "essentialist feminism" was that it represented only some women thinking about some women, and also that it was in danger of reinscribing patriarchal structures in valorizing the differences between Woman and Man. Most fully articulated in Elizabeth Spelman's *Inessential Woman,* the call has gone out to find theoretical apparatus that will affirm the differences among women and the multiplicity of voices within individual women.

In her work on autobiography, Lionnet uses the concept of *métissage* to signal this multiplicity, particularly the plural realities of postcolonial subjects. Her method of reading women's autobiographies charts a way of "perceiving difference while emphasizing similarities in the process of cultural encoding from which none of us can escape" (248). Women's autobiography, in offering a field of radical heterogeneity, indeed a *mondo bizzarro* of textual difference, offers rich grounding for critics working on these issues.

This *mondo bizzarro* is immediately apparent if we look at the range of what has been published as autobiography in America. The four major bibliographies of American autobiography—Louis Kaplan, *A Bibliography of American Autobiography*, with 6,377 entries published in America before 1945; Mary Louise Briscoe et al., *American Autobiography 1945–1980*, with 5,008 entries; Russell C. Brignano, *Black Americans in Autobiography*, with 710 entries; and Patricia K. Addis, *Through a Woman's I: American Women's Autobiography 1946–1976*, with 2,217 entries including collections of letters and travel narratives—are themselves texts to be "read." Granted that the pleasures of narrative here are minimal, these volumes do yield some telling insights and raise a number of teasing questions. What would we see if we made the eccentric choice in fact to "read" these bibliographies?

First we would see that although contemporary autobiography studies looks like a free-form competition, a counter-canon anarchy, it has in fact dealt with only a tiny, tiny fraction of what has been published as autobiography. While repeating the truism that autobiography is the most democratic of genres, and making occasional gestures that autobiography indeed might include precontact Indian cave drawings, photo albums, narrative quilts, and cookbooks, most critics have focused on a narrow group of highly "literary" texts and/or texts of writers known for their public achievements. Part of the reason for that selectivity is the sheer volume of what has been published—5,000 volumes in America between 1945 and 1980 as Briscoe demonstrates. But a more adequate explanation is that critics simply do not know what to do with, or perhaps do not even want to see, the radical heterogeneity of texts. Writing as early as 1923, Kate Douglas Wiggin asked toward the end of her autobiography:

And what shall we say of that horde of uncatalogued autobiographies that has arisen in our time and of which this very page is another? You may any day see in the newspapers that a man who holds a swimming or boxing record, or a woman who weighs five hundred pounds and travels with a circus, will either of them write down their memories if they can find a publisher. (436)

Indeed, what shall we say of all the famous-men-I-have-known and/or -married boasts, all the living-with-or-cured-from-a-fatal-illness testimonies, all the "as told to" life stories with clear commercial purposes? The corpus of American women's autobiography includes the well-known texts of Harriet Jacobs, Elizabeth Cady Stanton, Gertrude Stein, Mary McCarthy, Margaret Mead, and Lillian Hellman but also the original *Out on a Limb* which is about Louise Baker's life with one leg; Kipp Washington (pseud.), *Some Like It Dark: The Intimate Autobiography of a Negro Call Girl;* Josephine Earp, *I Married Wyatt Earp;* Netfa Enzinga, *I Was Kidnapped by Idi Amin;* Cleo Birdwell, *Amazons, An Intimate Memoir by the First Woman Ever to Play in the National Hockey League;* and Nancy Reagan's *My Turn.*

A second observation about this most democratic of genres is that American women publish significantly fewer autobiographies than American men. Whether they *write* fewer cannot be determined here, and bibliographical practices may, of course, shape the evidence. But less than twenty percent of the entries in Louis Kaplan's and Russell Brignano's bibliographies are autobiographies by American women; slightly over twenty percent of the entries in Briscoe are by women. (Working in roughly the same period, Addis records more items by women than Briscoe but she includes collections of letters and travel narratives and does not document men's texts for comparison.) And as Tillie Olsen reminds us in "One Out of Twelve: Writers Who Are Women in Our Century": "Any figure but one to one would insist on query: Why? What not true for men but *only for women,* makes this enormous difference? (Thus, class — economic circumstance — and color, those other traditional silencers of humanity, can be relevant only in the special ways that they affect the half of their numbers who are women)" (24). What is it, we must ask, that leads American women as individuals and as a group to conclude that their lives are less remark-able than the lives of men?

A third observation gleaned from "reading" bibliographies is that in most cases our naming practices signal the sex of the author. The figures above can be recited with confidence because we can easily distinguish between most male-authored and female-authored autobiographies in any list. Occasionally we will be fooled (perhaps deliberately) as with Leslie Lacy's *Native Daughter,* by a black male social worker with female clients in an antipoverty program in New York. But in most cases the name on the title page accurately signals the sex of the author and bears out Paul de Man's observation in another context that "any book with a readable title-page is, to some extent, autobiographical" (922).

In addition to telling us one crucial autobiographical "fact" about its author, the gendered name on the title page may determine who buys and reads which books as well as how they are read. As the first issue of Addison's *Spectator* observed, "a reader seldom peruses a Book with Pleasure, untill he knows whether the Writer of it be a black or a fair Man, of a mild or choleric Disposition, Married or a Bachelor, with other Particulars of the like nature, that conduce very much to the right understanding of an Author." It would be asking a lot for the signature on the title page to convey all this, and theorists who write about signature have argued that the name on the title page cannot represent any "real" self and remind us of mystifying devices such as the use of pen names or initials, or outright ruses like *The Autobiography of Alice B. Toklas.* But in most autobiographical texts where the subject is the self, gendered authorship is doubly inscribed. It is here, in the match between the signature on the title page and the subject within its pages, that Philip Lejeune has argued that the "autobiographical pact" is sealed (4). And if, as Lejeune extends his argument elsewhere, the autobiographical pact is a mode of *reading* (29), then the gendered name on the title page shapes the reading experience in foundational ways.

Even more complicated are the ways in which the gendered signature, that is to say the gendered self, has shaped the *generation* of the text. Elizabeth Fox-Genovese's statement that "more often than not" African American women's autobiographies "have been written from within the cage" (64) can be applied to the "cage" of gender as well as race. The touchstone of contemporary criticism that we cannot conceptualize or utter anything except within heavily ideological conceptual and language systems ("cages") may be confirmed with another piece of data from the title pages. It is startling to see how often white women autobiographers *re*inscribe their gender in the title of their texts despite the redundancy of that act. (One cannot determine except in particular cases whether any given title originates with an author, editor, or publisher, but my point about cultural practices is the same whatever the origin of the title, though it would become more intriguing if we could know who has chosen a particular title.) In the modern period one out of five white women either repeats her name in the title of her autobiography or uses some other sign of gender. We can think of well-known examples like *Memories of a Catholic Girlhood* and *Unfinished Woman,* and beyond these are scores and scores of books with titles like *Wyoming Wife, Daddy's Girl, "What's a Woman Doing Here?"* and *Lady Lawyer.* White American women represent themselves in the titles of their autobiographies by their relationships to others: wife, mother, sister, daughter, widow, stepmother, and aunt. (When male autobiographers represent themselves as "father" it is as in *Father of the Blues* or *Father of the Highway Diesel.*) From *All the Brave Promises: Memories of an Aircraft Woman 2nd Class—2146431* to *Woodswoman,* women writers use the sign "woman" to qualify other self-designations: *Bowery to Bellevue: The Story of New York's First Woman Ambulance Surgeon; Through the Flower: My Struggle as a Woman Artist; Washington*

By-Line, The Personal History of a Newspaper Woman; The Making of a Woman Cop; Notes from a Woman Psychiatrist. From *Woman with Arthritis: The True Story of a Recovery* to *"Mo": A Woman's View of Watergate,* they signal a special perspective grounded in gender. With an ingenious array of sex-specific signals, white women announce themselves as brides and belles, nuns and nurses, schoolmistresses and stewardesses, prostitutes and witches. At least three autobiographies published since 1946 have the word "breast" in the title (and are about dealing with cancer).

I have been writing "white women" because the sign of race seems to override the sign of gender in the titles of black women's autobiographies. From the evidence in Brignano's bibliography, we see that approximately twenty-five percent of black autobiographers, male and female, signal race in the titles of their texts. (Here the origin of the titles is also a vexed question with an editor/publisher who may not be black.) About a dozen black women signal both race and gender in their titles as in Mary Church Terrell's *A Colored Woman in a Black World* or Alice Dunnigan's *A Black Woman's Experience from School House to White House,* and only a very few signal gender alone (I know of only five) as in Maya Angelou's *The Heart of a Woman* or Era Bell Thompson's *American Daughter.* Much more common than either of these models is for black women autobiographers to signal race alone as in Elizabeth Adams, *Dark Symphony;* Annie Burton, *Memories of Childhood's Slavery Days;* Helen Caldwell Day, *Color, Ebony;* or Nikki Giovanni, *Gemini: An Extended Autobiographical Statement on My First Twenty Five Years of Being a Black Poet.*

American male autobiographers, black and white, inscribe gender in the titles of texts much less often than do women (a ratio of one to ten), and white American autobiographers, male and female, inscribe race in their titles virtually not at all. This is by no means to argue that race and gender are not essential elements in the construction of the self for members of the dominant culture, but only that race and gender are not the necessary categories with which the writer must begin when the white and/or male subject takes itself as object of scrutiny. We come to understand their priority to every other category only in noticing their absence.

To make matters even more complicated, Elizabeth Spelman argues (drawing from Aristotle and broad patterns of Western thought including white feminist) that for women to have a gender identity is itself a "race" privilege (55). That is, for white women who need not think of themselves in racial terms, gender becomes the foundational category for self-organization. For most black women, as for most black men, the foundational category is race. This is not to deny the reality of multiple or plural subjectivities, but only to argue that all subjectivities may not be created equal. Some women autobiographers have explicitly resisted the categories within which the culture grounds the construction of self. Zora Neale Hurston's *Dust Tracks on a Road* is a famous example of resistance to racialist categories, and Anna Arnold Hedgeman addresses the same issue in *The Trumpet Sounds: A Memoir of Negro Leadership:*

Another white woman asked what I personally had to complain about. She said, "You are accepted and respected. You have status." She was a little taken aback when I told her that I had been forced to spend my whole lifetime discussing the implication of color and that this was to me a waste of time and of whatever talent I had. I added that the opportunities I really wanted were closed to me. (198)

All of this bibliographical evidence is simply to argue the obvious point that the construction of self in the American context (and any other one) begins *within* one or more given and heavily ideological categories. In a culture such as ours where gender and racial divisions are so sharply drawn, white women's autobiography, while it may do other things as well, exhibits — even in its very being — women in contestation with the content of the dominant culture's sign "WOMAN." Black autobiography, and by extension ethnic autobiography, while it may do other things as well, including contesting the sign of WOMAN, exhibits — even in its very being — black people in contestation with the content of the dominant culture's sign "BLACK."

We may "see" this more clearly if we move from the image of the "cage" to the image of the mirror so often invoked in identity theory (Lacan), feminist theory (Beauvoir, Rowbotham, and others), and autobiography theory (Gusdorf, Barthes, and others). No woman, as we know, truly sees herself in a mirror; she sees herself through the imagined (or real) gaze of another. And to the extent that the autobiographical text can be thought of as a mirror, it is a mirror gazed at in public. Any woman can tell you of the difference (in degree at least) between viewing her image in the privacy of a bathroom or bedroom mirror and catching a glimpse of herself in a mirror in public, a store window or mirror placed strategically in a department store. For women, all mirrors in public are two-way mirrors behind which invisible security guards convict her of her failures or her crimes. And here she is surrounded not only by the public gaze but by the paraphernalia — in the store window doubly exposed on her image, or framed within her grasp in the department store mirror — that will help her expiate her crimes. An Ernie Barnes print called "Window Wishing" captures some of this dynamic. A group of pleasantly lumpen women of various shades with their backs to the viewer stare up at emaciated, pale mannequins wearing diaphanous garments in a store window. The window, well above the street, separates the women who seem to have lives and work ("sensible" shoes, heavy packages, muscular arms and legs) from the lifeless forms. The word SALE in large letters appears in three places across the scene within the window. The vision of the black male artist is primarily ironic. I would wager that the feelings within the hearts of the women caught gazing at the impossible ideals are a good deal more conflicted.

Women's autobiography is, among other things, that mirror glimpsed at, gazed into, and negotiated with in public.

II

Most of the important work in women's autobiography has been international in scope scanning centuries and diverse cultures with the lens of "Woman"; but as the essays that follow demonstrate, we may also trace with profit the development of a tradition of women's life-writing within historically and socially specific contexts. Particular cultural forms and practices shape American women's autobiography as do certain persistent literary conventions, some of which American women share with their countrymen. I will argue here, and the essays that follow will further develop the evidence, that the dominant tradition of American women's autobiography has roots in Puritan beliefs about the self and the Puritan practice of conversion narratives; and that even in periods when autobiography has become a thoroughly secular enterprise its forms and purposes can be traced to these earlier traditions.

While professing explicit self-denial, the Puritans engaged in obsessive self-absorption, believing that one's life was a text to be read, read for evidences of God's dealings with the soul. "Reading the self" in the Puritan context was actually an intertextual event, as the self was read in relation to the scriptural metatext and widely apprehended morphologies of the conversion experience. While "reading the self" was a constant individual discipline, it was also a communal event. Puritan churches "gathered" their membership with the practice of conversion narratives in which aspiring members of the community rendered in public a formulaic account of God's saving grace in their lives. The congregation, whose task was to judge the fitness of the speaker for full communion within the parameters of the metatexts, was at the same time to be strengthened in its own faith by hearing the recitation. Thus, the individual autobiographical act was ultimately an act of community building. The focus on as well as the ambivalence about the first person singular; the articulation of the self within given belief structures; the positioning of the autobiographical act within a social context in the expectation that one will be judged but also in the hope that one's life story will be useful to others and will strengthen the community, all have their roots in the earliest practice of autobiography in America.

With the emergence of secular autobiography, the most famous early example of which is Benjamin Franklin's *Autobiography,* scriptural paradigms and formulas of conversion which had had a certain gender-neutral character yield to equally powerful metatexts, among them the commonly apprehended ideas of gender difference. No longer tracing their journeys as Christian pilgrims, women begin writing *as women* and expect to be judged as such. The autobiographical act continues to be socially positioned as women begin to write explicitly for other women. Just as the Puritan self-absorption stands in paradoxical relationship to their belief in self-denial, so too the act of writing for a public audience stands in some tension with the prevailing idea of woman. In defying the traditional injunction to silence for women, the autobiographical act itself contests WOMAN, something of which many autobiographers are aware as they await the judgment of their community of readers. With both Puritan narratives and women's secular autobiography, these contradictions are negotiated by arguing the edifying potential of autobiography and its utility in view of the felt need to build community. But as we shall see, the purposefulness of women's autobiography does not entirely obscure the frank pleasures women writers take in constructing a text from a life.

If we turn to three mid-nineteenth-century secular autobiographies by American women, *The Autobiography of an Actress* by Anna Cora Mowatt, *Memories of a Grandmother By a Lady of Massachusetts* by A. M. Richards, and *Incidents in the Life of a Slave Girl* by Harriet Jacobs, we will see the writers wrestling with these issues. Here we find "woman writing" negotiating with "woman reading" over the term they share in common. Their expectations and fears that they will be judged as women are moderated by hopes that their life stories will be *useful* to audiences like themselves. Like so many of their nineteenth-century counterparts, Mowatt, Richards, and Jacobs are writing *as women* aware that they will be so judged and that in the very act of writing for the public they may offend. Though Anna Cora Mowatt had behind her a triumphant career as an actress on stage and had weathered many storms about the propriety of women in the theater, she begins and ends her autobiography with apologies: "In an autobiography, there seems a degree of egotism in the constant use of the first person singular, from which I have in vain sought some method of escape. For any consequent trenching upon the borders of good taste, I hope to be pardoned as for an unavoidable literary trespass." Her escape from egotism, ironically enough, is found in the metaphor of the theater: "I have endeavored to divest myself from all remembrance of the reader, in the same way that I should mentally abstract myself while interpreting a character upon the stage" (448). Casting herself as a character in a play she has written and is directing, Mowatt empties herself of self-centeredness.

But this splitting of the subject is not enough. As her introduction indicates, the real defense against unseemly egotism is the social positioning of the text. Family members (her husband) have urged her to write her life story and she earnestly hopes it will be of use to others: "If one struggling sister in the great human family, while listening to the history of my life, gain courage to meet and brave the severest trials; if she learn to look upon them as blessings in disguise: if she be strengthened in the performance of her 'daily duties,' however 'hardly paid'; if she be inspired with faith in the power imparted to a strong will, whose end is good, then I am amply rewarded for my labor" (3–4).

Published anonymously by A. M. Richards in 1854, *Memories of a Grandmother By a Lady of Massachusetts* embodies similar strategies for dealing with the public gaze. Its editor apologizes, "At the risk of 'suffering the private I' to be considered 'too much in the public eye,' the following veritable Auto-biography is given, as originally written, *In the first person* . . ." (1). Though published anonymously, the text is socially positioned, dedicated "To My Dear Children . . . as the Younger Offspring of a Mother's Production and Care" (n.p.). In her introduction, this "Lady" and "Grandmother" explains why she has not included a picture of herself as a frontispiece in her volume: "I dare not smile upon you, dear and respected Public, on opening my Book, as my *heart with tears in its eyes is smiling,* anxiously awaiting your verdict of pleasing or not pleasing" (13). What follows is a witty and complex discussion of silence and female portraiture. In an era when the daguerreotype was replacing the painted portrait, Richards—having sat for both—debates which medium captures the superior likeness. She chooses the painted portrait because the artist engaged her in conversation "so full of wit and spirit, it infused a life and likeness into the painting that has never been caught since" (13). The daguerreotype, on the other hand, required utter stillness of the subject for its execution, and "gave an expression of gravity to my face never since removed" (14). The photographer attributed his failure to his subject's silence, saying, "I hadn't a bit of expression in my face when I wasn't talking!" (14). Raised by a grandmother who intoned, "Little girls should be seen and not heard," the autobiographer candidly admits, "I wished to indulge in both privileges at once."

The autobiography IS that indulgence, both portrait and voice, but it does not absolve her from being judged for speaking in public, an issue she returns to at the end of her book:

in presenting this little volume to the world. . . . My heart sinks as I fear its judgement. . . . I court its notice, yet I dread its contact; for after all the changes of an eventful life, even with these white lines upon my temples, there yet lingers but timidly now the one ambition, the desire of early days—I still wish to be beloved. (140)

Alas for our anxious author, one "reader response" is inscribed in the copy of the book I own: "J. H. S. read this book in Aug. 1879 but didn't think it amounted to much."

Much has been written about Harriet Jacobs' negotiation with her imagined reader over the idea of WOMAN and the fear of judgment. Complicated by the gulf between the fugitive slave and her northern white readers, the issues between author and reader become even more acute. Like Mowatt and Richards she writes *as a woman* and dreads one consequence of the autobiographical act—unfavorable judgment by the woman reader. In the convention of nineteenth-century fiction, she addresses the reader directly, "But, O, ye happy women, whose purity has been sheltered from childhood, who have been free to choose the objects of your affection, whose homes are protected by law, do not judge the desolate slave girl too severely!" And "Pity me, and pardon me, O virtuous reader. . . . I feel that the slave woman ought not to be judged by the same standards as others" (55–56). Like Mowatt and Richards, she has been urged to write her life story by others and she denies any egotistical motives: "I have not written my experiences in order to attract attention to myself; on the contrary, it would have been more pleasant to me to have been silent about my own history" (1). She overcomes her reluctance in the hope that her life story may be *useful* to others: "But I do earnestly desire to arouse the women of the North to a realizing sense of the two millions of women at the South, still in bondage, suffering what I suffered, and most of them far worse. I want to add my testimony to that of abler pens to convince the people of the Free States what Slavery really is" (1–2). Jacobs' reluctance to expose the details of her history is grounded in fears of real consequences for her and her children, but her protestations are also broadly similar to the conventional gestures made in many, many women's autobiographies of the period.

These conventions of women's secular autobiography in the nineteenth century—writing as a woman and expecting to be judged as such, writing for other women in the hopes that one's narrative might be useful to them —remain so strong that Mary Hunter Austin is able to parody them in her 1912 novel cast as autobiography, *Woman of Genius*. The narrator begins, "It is strange that I can never think of writing any account of my life without thinking of Pauline Mills and wondering what she will say of it" (3). Pauline Mills embodies all the attitudes of Main Street, in this case, Main Street, "Taylorsville, Ohio." In reading autobiographies, Mrs. Mills searches for "the advertisement of that true womanliness which Pauline loves to pluck from every feminine bush" (3). The first-person narrator continues,

> I thought then of writing the life of an accomplished woman, not so much of the accomplishment as of the woman; and I have never been able to make a start at it without thinking of Pauline Mills and that curious social warp which obligates us most to impeach the validity of woman's opinion at the points where it is most supported by experience. From the earliest I have been rendered highly suspicious of the social estimate of women, by the general social conspiracy against telling the truth about herself. (4)

At the end of the novel Pauline Mills has appeared in person to be directly rebuked and summarily dismissed by the author who has overcome her dread of the Pauline Millses of the world and has undertaken her autobiography at her sister's insistence that her book will help others. "It is the fact of your telling, whether they believe you or not, of your not being ashamed to tell that is going to help them. . . . At any rate it will help other women to speak out what they think, unashamed. Most women are not thinking at all what they are very willing to be thought of as thinking" (503).

This appeal to the *utility* of one's life story is the most persistent of the conventions of autobiography, and it survives well into the twentieth century. The appeal to utility rests on a number of prior assumptions: that the wish to be useful to others is morally superior to indulging a variety of selfish pleasures; but also that one's experience is generalizable, that common ground exists or can be forged between writer and reader, and that through that common ground knowledge or wisdom may be transmitted. It also means that autobiography, to borrow Jane Tompkins' insight about nineteenth-century women's fiction, has *designs* upon the reader, and those designs are often very explicit. There is no very great distance between the religious sentiment recorded by the "Colored Evangelist" Amanda Smith in 1893, "my whole object and wish is that God will make it a blessing to all who may read it" (505), and the wish to affect, change, influence, shape, help the reader in a variety of secular ways. While the design of a life may remain a figure in the carpet, the designs upon the reader may be as aggressive as Carry Nation's axe. With her life's work near its end, Nation took up the pen:

> I represent the distracted, suffering, loving motherhood of the World. Who, becoming aroused with a righteous fury rebelled at this torture. . . . This book is a statement of facts, proving the super-human engrafted into the human, and will bring to confusion the infidel and sceptic and never will there arise in this nation a contradiction of the facts in this book. This thing was not done in a corner and IT IS WRITTEN. (n.p.)

Elaine Showalter may be correct that "the female witness, sensitive or not, is still not accepted as first-person universal" ("Women Who Write Are Women" 33), but scores and scores of women autobiographers certainly feel confident that the first-person female can be generalized and that they are writing as part of a community. As Lucy Larcom states in *A New England Girlhood,* "None of us can think of ourselves as entirely separate beings. Even an autobiographer has to say 'we' much oftener than 'I'" (6). Lucy Larcom's "we" is explicitly grounded in gender: "My audience is understood to be composed of girls of all ages, and of women who have not forgotten their girlhood. Such as have a friendly appreciation of girls — are also welcome to listen to as much of my narrative as they choose. All others are eavesdroppers, and, of course, have no right to criticize" (5). By the twentieth century, the idea of WOMAN becomes only one of a number of ways women autobiographers may construct the community or communities of their audience(s). And it is not unusual for women to negotiate multiple "we's" in a single text. Black women's "we" usually has its foundation in race as in Ruby Berkley Goodwin's assertion "I sincerely believe that the lives of many Negro children follow the same pattern as mine" (7), and Ossie Guffy's address to the white reader: "Your TV screens are showing more black faces, and you're reading about us in your papers, but you ain't getting any picture of what we're really like, 'cause most of us ain't got any voices speaking for us" (ix–x).

Other women, particularly immigrant women, generalize their experience as women on the basis of national culture. If they sound a bit like Benjamin Franklin, it is because they, like him, have substituted "American" for "Christian" but remain, as he did, very much in the Puritan tradition of constructing autobiography in and for a community.

For I am writing not only of myself . . . I am writing this for myself and those who, like me, are America's foster children . . . I am writing to those sons and daughters of immigrant fathers and mothers who are now in America. (E. G. Stern 11–12) . . . It is the story of an American Jewish family in the past half-century, which I know and love and as such it is the story about America (Edna Ferber 6) . . . But I dare to hope . . . I have so managed to transcend my own particularity that, for better or worse, it becomes an American story. (Virgilia Peterson n.p.)

It is through the construction of such common ground that the anxiety about *transmission* of a message to a community, at the heart of so many women's autobiographies, may be resolved. Often women's desire for such transmission is expressed in familial and/or generational terms — sometimes to children or "the next generation," and in an intriguing number of cases, to mothers. With a variety of strategies, the writers submerge the personal in some "larger" purposes in order to become the vehicle for conveying a message about history: for example, Jane Addams in the founding of the settlement movement in Chicago (vii), or Ida B. Wells in "agitation against civil lynching" (4). Some wish to communicate to their readers "what their privileges have cost their early mothers," as do the pioneer physician B. A. Owens-Adair (n.p.) and the black activist Ellen Tarry (viii). Others feel their life stories illustrate very particular lessons. Lucy Larcom insists to her readers, "the meaning of life is education" (273); Agnes Newton Keith wants to impress "the horror of war" (n.p.); Lynda Huey organizes her narrative around "the problem women face in their attempt to be serious athletes" (x); Margaret Mead says she writes "to throw what light it may upon how children can be brought up" (1), as does Mary Casal whose concern is parents' openness about sexuality, particularly homosexuality (6). Numerous women frame their personal histories within calls for tolerance (*Log Cabin Lady* 108), human rights (King 29), justice (Hedgeman 202). Others have more concrete purposes—to tell "why I entered the management field" (Sawyer 1) or to demystify, especially for women, international politics (Davis 3).

The strong hortative cast of some American women's autobiography does not entirely obscure, indeed it may be the obverse side of, the pleasures of the autobiographical act. Purposefulness seems to give permission for the pleasures of indulgence in egotism, language (the dangers of which the Puritans well knew), narrative, and reminiscence. When Kate Douglas Wiggin asks a friend, "Just why is it that all these autobiographies are written?" he replies, "Because all you quill-drawers like to talk about yourselves! You can never get in so many words on that special topic in any other way. You'd have to die before a biographer did it, and then you'd miss the fun, if the public liked his book about you" (1). Edna Ferber seems to concur:

Who doesn't think his own life dramatic? In the day's miscellany of mail every professional writer finds a letter or two saying:

> . . . it is an idea for a great book, but I do not feel I can write it myself because I am too busy. It is the story of my life. All of my friends say that if I would just write down the story of my life it would make a wonderful book.

Well, you think (though you toss the letter in the wastebasket), and so it doubtless would. The story of any life, told with truth, selection, and dramatic sense, would make an arresting book. (4)

For some who do write down the stories of their own lives, the pleasures of autobiography are the pleasures of language and narrative. "I love to tell stories," declares Fleur Cowles (11) who is one of those Anne Morrow Lindbergh describes as "the people who like to recount their adventures, the diary-keepers, the story-tellers, the letter-writers, a strange race of people who feel half cheated of an experience unless it is retold. It does not really exist until it is put into words" (8–9).

For others the pleasures of autobiography are the pleasures of reminiscence. Ruth Painter Randall admits, "It has been a deeply emotional experience in the past months to live my life over again in these diaries" (ix). Gladys Brooks concurs: "There is a poignant pleasure that comes in the writing of one's past" (3). Indulging her memories, Mabel Osgood Wright delights in "the pleasant company that was beginning to gather" (3). And for many the pleasure of the company is the company of an earlier self:

I can see very distinctly the child that I was, and I know how the world looked to her, far off as she is now. . . . I have enjoyed bringing her back, and letting her tell her story, almost as if she were somebody else. I like her better than I did when I was a child, and I hope I never have to part company with her. (Lucy Larcom 12)

. . . It has been a good deal like renewing acquaintance with a friend I had not seen since childhood. (Ida Tarbell 399)

Agnes Meyer describes her "satisfaction" in the text of her life with curiously androgynous metaphors of birth: "It would never have occurred to me to write an autobiography. Nor would my full share of interest in what Paul Claudel called 'that terrible path toward oneself' have held me to its description for two years. But since I now feel the same satisfaction over the completion of this ordeal which mothers feel after the birth of a lusty infant, it is only just to declare the paternity of this child of my old age." Anne Morrow Lindbergh finds her satisfaction in the conventional victory of the autobiographical text over time:

There is, of course, always the personal satisfaction of writing down one's experiences so they may be saved, hoarded against the winter of forgetfulness. Time has been cheated a little, at least in one's own life, and a personal, trivial immortality of an old self assured. (8)

For others, the pleasures of autobiography are more primal, total, even euphoric (*jouissance?*). Mabel Dodge Luhan writes:

Here I begin, as they say, to give myself away. But this is the way anyone must do who writes a true history of himself—and I feel a gladness rising in me at the thought of it—of giving myself away whole, all of me, to the world, my world.

And Mary MacLane, who always pushes self-consciousness and theatricality to its limits, writes: "My mind is fairly bursting with egotism and pain, and in writing this I find a merciful outlet. Often I lay my head and my lips caressingly upon the pages" (*The Story of Mary MacLane* 282). When MacLane reminds us elsewhere, "I write this book for my own reading," (*I, Mary MacLane* 282) we see clearly that for many women writers the feats of memory become feasts for reader and writer alike.

III

As we can see in the above discussion of the shaping traditions of American women's autobiography, one feature that distinguishes autobiography from fiction is the persistence, indeed the insistence, with which autobiography talks explicitly about itself. Forewords, afterwords, and a variety of direct addresses to the reader within the texts—all established conventions of nineteenth-century fiction—persist in autobiography long after they have been abandoned in most novels. Again, when Mary Hunter Austin wants to *imitate* autobiography in her novel *Woman of Genius,* she achieves her effect with many such self-referential passages: "The first notion of an obligation I had in writing this part of my story, was that if it is to be serviceable, no lingering sentiment should render it less literal, and none of that egotism turned inside out which makes a kind of sanctity of the personal experience, prevent me from offering it whole" (115). And it is in the "real" discussions of the autobiographical process, usually in the prefaces and afterwords of American women's autobiographies, that we find women writers individually and collectively aware of most of the commonplaces of contemporary theory and criticism of autobiography. They understand that defining the nature of autobiography is a seductive but ultimately elusive task. They interrogate the nature of autobiographical "truth" and the adequacy of both memory and language in its service. They dismiss static and unitary notions of the self and remain skeptical of any totalizing "self-knowledge." They know that the autobiographical process *creates* truth even as it attempts to recover and record it. And mirabile dictu, they address these issues without recourse to theoryspeak, conveying ideas as complex as the Chinese knotmaker's knot (Kingston 190) with one well-chosen image.

American women autobiographers know, for example, that the lines between fact and fiction blur. As with Mary McCarthy, the word that comes to mind for many is "lies." Kate Douglas Wiggin ends the foreword to her autobiography with the comment of a friend, "blood tells, but remember it sometimes tells lies" (xxv). Mary Casal concurs: "Oh yes, we are [liars], and you know it, and we have been all our lives" (8). Margaret Anderson prefers the word "fiction" in passing on the observation of a friend: "Someone asked her, 'What is Margaret's book about?' Jane, with a loud laugh, 'Herself—fiction!'" (27). Tricks of time and memory blur the distinctions between fact and fancy for Helen Keller who knows that the present writes the past: "When I try to classify my earliest impressions, I find that fact and fancy look alike across the years that link the past with the present. The woman paints the child's experiences with her own fantasy" (11). For Mary MacLane, it is the audience that is the source of her dissimulations:

"I am in no small degree, I find, a sham—a player to the gallery" (*The Story of Mary MacLane* 133).

Others know that the source of lies, fiction, or fancy may be the limits of self-knowledge. Septima Clark concludes her journey toward the self with "I wonder if anybody knows himself. Can any man read his own face? Can any man judge his own heart? I truly wonder" (234). Mary MacLane's expressed intention is to "tell all":

I am trying my utmost to show everything—to reveal every petty vanity and weakness, every phase of feeling, every desire. It is a remarkably hard thing to do, I find, to probe my soul to its depths, to expose its shades and half lights. (*The Story of Mary MacLane* 75)

But even she admits defeat:

I know what I am. Another may know who he is. But I can't tell Me to Another and Another can't tell Himself to Me. I can tell Me to Myself and write it. Another if he reads will see Me: but not as I see Me. Instead, through many veils—curtains and glasses, very darkly. (*I, Mary MacLane* 165)

By the end of this, her second autobiographical book, MacLane has given up on fully telling "Me to Myself":

Something, and it may be that MIST, makes one's view of everything—everything in life—a little blurred. It may even blur one's view of oneself. So it may be I do not see myself with entire clearness—I only know I write Me as clearly as I see Me, considering the MIST. (196)

MacLane would have understood Gertrude Stein's conundrum in *Everybody's Autobiography:*

And identity is funny being yourself is funny as you are never yourself to yourself except as you remember yourself and then of course you do not believe yourself. That is really the trouble with an autobiography you do not of course you do not really believe yourself why should you, you know so well so very well that it is not yourself, it could not be yourself because you cannot remember right and of course if you do remember right it does not sound right and of course it does not sound right because it is not right. You are of course never yourself. . . . (53)

A contemporary comment also dismisses unitary notions of self-knowledge and confronts new challenges: "This account is told from my point of view but sometimes the ground on which I stand shifts. . . . I speak in different voices" (King 24–25).

For others, it is not the limits to self-knowledge but the limits of language itself ("it does not sound right") that stand between the writer and "truth." From the early and formulaic expression of Abigail Bailey, "No language could now express the sorrow and grief of my soul" (36), to the

modern reflection of Mary MacLane, autobiographers agree that words
are not adequate to the task:

I fail remarkably. I write Eye where I mean Tooth. I write Fornicate when I mean
Caress. I write Wine when I mean Blood. For no better reason than that my hand
is not sufficiently dextrous: the little flashing shutters open and shut so quickly
that the second ones are shut and the third ones open before I have got written
the things I saw through the first ones. Only not always. (*I, Mary MacLane* 192)

In another place MacLane admits that the "bio" and the "graphy" entirely interpenetrate one another: "I don't know whether I write this because I wear two plain dresses or whether I wear two plain dresses because
I write it" (*I, Mary MacLane* 189). Along with MacLane, many other
women autobiographers concur with the assertion that the autobiographical process may *create* truth. As I. A. R. Wylie observes, "if you write about
yourself, as I have observed in other people's autobiographies, you produce a person you didn't know existed and you may wish you hadn't. . . .
I realize that by the time I have finished this book some stranger will have
emerged with whom, for better or worse, I shall have to live for the rest
of my days" (7–8). Wylie is very specific about the truths she has created:
"We have discovered, for instance, that we no longer detest our father as
we did and are, in fact, rather amused by him" (351). Ida Tarbell has had
the same experience: "This explains why telling my story has been so full
of surprises. 'I did not realize I felt that way,' I have told myself more than
once. 'I had forgotten I did that.' 'I cannot imagine why I thought that'"
(399). Lillian Smith, one of an intriguing few women who have *revised*
their autobiographies, writes in the preface to the second edition of *Killers
of the Dream:* "I wrote it because I had to find out what life in a segregated culture had done to me, one person. I had to put down on paper
these experiences so that I could see their meaning for me. I was in dialogue with myself as I wrote . . ." (13). The twelve years that have elapsed
between the first and second editions of her book have changed her perspective on her life and times, but she also argues that it was the writing
act itself that changed her:

For I have changed since writing it. I am different. Because I wrote it. In the writing
I explore layers of my nature which I had never touched before . . . my beliefs
changed as I wrote them down. As is true of any writing that comes out of one's
own existence, the experiences themselves were transformed during the act of writing by awareness of new meaning which settled down on them. (14)

For Eudora Welty, discoveries about the personal past never stop: "the
time as we know it subjectively . . . it is the continuous thread of revelation" (75). What she writes about her fiction surely applies as well to her
autobiographical essays in which these comments appear:

Writing . . . is one way of discovering *sequence,* of stumbling upon cause and effect in the happenings of a writer's own life. This has been the case with me. Connections slowly emerge. Like distant landmarks you are approaching, cause and effect begin to align themselves, draw closer together. Experiences too indefinite of outline in themselves to be recognized for themselves connect and are identified as a larger shape. And suddenly light is thrown back, as when your train makes a curve, showing there has been a mountain of meaning rising behind you on the way you've come, is rising there still, proven now through retrospect. (98)

The train ride is one of Welty's favorite images for her journeys of discovery—"I could look back on them and see them bringing me news, discoveries, premonitions, promises—I still can; they still do" (75). Other American women writers use an array of images to describe the autobiographical process—drawing aside a veil (Larcom 6), spring cleaning (Wylie 338), weaving (Clark 233), building a statue (Hurston 34), editing a film (Mead 2). Their images of the autobiographical product variously suggest design, sequence, and movement—a chain (Stern 11), a string of beads (Tietjens 332), a dance (Kirkland 308), a tapestry (Clapper 8; Mead 2), photographs (Sneller vii; Wright 2). Lillian Hellman's discussion of "pentimento" in old paintings is one of the more intriguing images of both the autobiographical process and its product. Another used by Laura Z. Hobson also suggests the full complexity of the autobiographical act. In her second autobiographical volume, Hobson concludes, "Having now reached the end of this second volume I find myself remembering that maternal grandmother of mine, carrying messages in invisible ink on snippets of cloth tucked into peaches, plums and apples—still carrying fruit inside to the political prisoners of Russia" (298). Here we see, among other things, full acknowledgment of the coding of messages, the instability of the text, the problematic relationship between the maternal writer (who feeds) and the reader who consumes, the anxiety of transmission, and the political context of women's autobiography.

IV

The essays that follow develop more fully the themes hinted at in Laura Hobson's rich recollection of her grandmother and introduce others as well. Dealing indeed with "snippets of cloth," Kathleen Swaim in "'Come and Hear': Women's Puritan Evidences" looks at Puritan women's conversion narratives collected by Thomas Shepard which run in length from 6 to 128 lines of printed text. Swaim elaborates the religious context within which the autobiographical act in America took its earliest form. She reminds us that in the context of the biblical injunction to silence for women "the best conversion narrative would be no story at all," but demonstrates that women nonetheless found voice within strict formulaic norms and even made occasional gestures toward suggestively idiosyncratic narratives. It is in these narratives that Swaim finds the first hints of the "celebration of individuation and the extraordinary self" that is to become full-blown American autobiography.

In "Self and God in the Early Published Memoirs of New England Women," Ann Taves explores some of the tensions and contradictions that emerge in the more extended spiritual memoirs of women in the early national period. Here we continue to find a "self-in-relation-to-God," but with a focus on the issues of affliction and vocation in women's writing, Taves finds the self pushing the limits of both permitted behavior and expression. In response to severe affliction in their lives, women writers gave passionate vent to feelings of anger and resistance before achieving submission to the patriarchal will. And in their desire for more visible and public lives, they explained the pull toward autonomy with the language of vocation, a call to greater usefulness in the world. In the period she is studying, Taves finds support for these emerging voices in networks of women's friendships and more formal female academies and societies.

Sidonie Smith, in "Resisting the Gaze of Embodiment: Women's Autobiography in the Nineteenth Century," demonstrates how the West's romance with the self and devotion to epistemological certitudes about selfhood dominate the cultural landscape in that century. She traces the philosophical split between two essentialist and sex-specific views of selfhood—the (male) self of essences, the unencumbered metaphysical self, and the (female) embodied self specularized as Other. The century's ideology of irreducible racial differences further codified the categories within which the self might be imagined. In her readings of Elizabeth Cady Stanton and Harriet Jacobs, Smith demonstrates the ambiguities at the core of any essentialist selfhood and shows the women to be "creative sign makers in the discursive economy of the century." Stanton's and Jacobs' negotiations between "metaphysical" and "essentialist" polarities and the consequent multiplicities of their positionings, Smith argues, disturb cultural configurations and render their self-imaginings elastic and dynamic.

As a historian of the suffrage movement, Ann Gordon in "The Political is the Personal: Two Autobiographies of Woman Suffragists" gives us a different reading of Elizabeth Cady Stanton's *Eighty Years and More*. Situating this autobiography and Abigail Scott Duniway's *Pathbreaking* within the context of the publicly contested issues of the suffrage campaign, Gordon shows how as outsiders to the mainstream of the women's movement at the time they wrote their life histories, both women use their narratives to vindicate their beliefs and strategies. Gordon shows how the writers organize their treatments of childhood, marriage, the conversion to politics, and subsequent public careers around dominant themes in their lives. Stanton's rebellion against religious authorities in her youth led to a questioning of all authority and placed her profoundly at odds with the movement that survived her; and Duniway's understanding of herself as a "frontier feminist" shaped her ideology and tactics and distinguished her from her "eastern" sisters.

Lynn Z. Bloom introduces a generally less well known group of "frontier feminists" in "Utopia and Anti-Utopia in Twentieth-Century Women's Frontier Autobiographies." From the energetic boosterism of Elinor Stewart's *Letters of a Woman Homesteader* to the dark vision of Annie Pike Greenwood's *We Sagebrush Folk,* Bloom demonstrates how these writers reconcile the dreams that drew them west with the harsh realities of their lives. Double voices, narrative and/or pictorial frames allow them to balance the romance and the realism, the utopian and anti-utopian visions. The farther removed the reality of their frontier experience is from the utopian ideal, Bloom argues, the more forceful the voices of the women autobiographers become. Though circumstances may defeat aspirations, autobiography becomes a "powerful way of reshaping their lives . . . of gaining control of their past through re-inventing it in their works."

Hard as it is to credit, in roughly the same period that these women are writing of carving a life on the western frontier, Gertrude Stein is exploring frontiers of art, language, and life-style in Paris. Just as they seem to inhabit different planetary orbs of experience, so too their approaches to autobiography contrast markedly. The former texts, abounding in the literal detail of physical hardship and challenge, offer direct address to the reader that is above all *sincere* in its message. Stein's well-known *The Autobiography of Alice B. Toklas,* as Catharine Stimpson deftly demonstrates in "Gertrude Stein and the Lesbian Lie," is a "ludic romp," playing with mixed messages about sexuality, ultimately ironic in its gap between promise and delivery. Her plain style, "to write as though she were incapable of lying," becomes a form of homosexual dissimulation, a game to whose rules some readers are privy, some are not. Subverting generic, linguistic, and sexual codes, Stein "lies" both to distract and to divert her critics and also to "strengthen the community of liars."

Looking at another highly self-conscious, literary autobiography, Janis Greve connects Mary McCarthy's orphanhood with her use of photographs and "photo-portraiture" in *Memories of a Catholic Girlhood.* McCarthy, Greve argues, counters her persistent fear of self-obliteration with an attempt to capture and "frame" images of her ancestors. But here McCarthy confronts the ironic paradox that in preserving their images, she is also "killing" them. Greve connects this tension in the autobiographic/photographic act with stages in ego formation and object relations as elaborated by Melanie Klein to show how McCarthy's early loss of her mother trapped her in the dilemmas of her autobiographical project.

In "Dorothy Day and Women's Spiritual Autobiography," Mary Mason explores four autobiographical texts of this twentieth-century radical activist, texts that abound in other forms of mixed messages about sexuality. Best known for her leadership of the Catholic Worker Movement, its hospitality houses for the destitute, its work farms and its newspaper, Dorothy Day was also a militant pacifist whose long life also embraced the civil rights movement, the anti–Vietnam War movement, and the labor struggles of the United Farm Workers. Mason places Day's lifework in the context of American radical women such as Elizabeth Gurley Flynn, Emma Goldman, and Mother Jones, and her life-writing within the tradition of the conversion narrative. In contrast to her radical social vision, Mason argues, Day articulates an increasingly conservative view of womanhood as she creates and re-creates her life. She moves from an ideology of bohemianism and independence in which she celebrates unmarried love and natural motherhood to a place where she understands that period in her life as her "preconversion" self. As a "converted sinner," she changes her view of sexuality, adopts strict notions of sex-role differences, and expresses increasingly didactic views of domesticity and motherhood. Day comes, then, to speak in the double voice Mason finds characteristic of women's autobiography, full of the costs and contradictions of abandoning her domestic roles as she understood them for her public life's work for peace and social justice.

Arlyn Diamond looks at the autobiographies of six women, black and white, who enacted their commitment to social justice in the civil rights movement of the 1960s. Here, too, Diamond finds the enmeshing of the personal with the social, the historical, and the political; and she argues that "the myth of the autonomous individual which characterizes the dominant American discourse of the self erases the brutal intrusions of history in the construction of personal being." Reminding us that "privilege is as real as the oppression that enables it," she sketches the broad social formation of daughter-of-the-Confederacy turned social activist Virginia Foster Durr, as well as the forces in Anne Moody's Mississippi childhood that led to the murder of Emmett Till. Taken together, these narratives give us, in contrast to the "official" histories, a picture of the civil rights movement with women at its center. The six women share a vision of a "beloved community" despite the conflicts, contradictions, and sheer drudge of real-world politics. Diamond argues that women's role in the struggle for human and civil rights has yet to be written. These autobiographical narratives and Diamond's essay about them make important contributions to the writing of that history.

In *"No Laughing Matter:* The WASPs Climb Down," Nancy Walker illuminates yet another configuration of the public/private thematics in a woman's autobiography. Margaret Halsey, prolific author and acute critic of American values, anticipated most of her peers with a focus on race relations in the 1940s, materialism and consumerism in the 1950s, and ethics in public politics ten years before Watergate. In her autobiography, Halsey's target is the dominant culture and its ideologies, particularly its sense of privilege and self-importance, qualities she sees in herself and attributes to her WASP background. In contrast to traditional American autobiographers who celebrate in Franklin fashion personal achievements as at one with national aspiration, Halsey understands her personal *failures* as illustrative of failures in the American character. Halsey struggled with alcoholism and agoraphobia and became estranged from most of those close to her including her mother, sister, daughter, and two husbands. Sadly and ironically, though Halsey embraced progressive causes throughout her life, she never addressed the issue of gender or looked to the women's movement for understanding of the isolation and despair that marked her life.

The final three essays in the book take us beyond the dominant traditions of Anglo-American women's autobiography. In her essay, Shirley Geoklin Lim reads the well-known *The Woman Warrior* by Maxine Hong Kingston within the context of women's life stories well established in the early twentieth century in Chinese-American literature. Contrasting *The Woman Warrior* with Jade Snow Wong's *Fifth Chinese Daughter,* Lim shows that while both books are "daughterly texts" addressing issues of race, male power, and female sexuality, Wong's focus on fathers and daughters contrasts with Kingston's interest in mothers and daughters. Beyond these contrasting thematics, Wong's text, written in the third person, remains linear in structure, has a unitary (or singly split) notion of consciousness and a view of culture built on polarities. Kingston, on the other hand, uses a first-person narrator able to move through all the pronouns, constructs her narrative in "unstructured circularities," and understands subjectivity and culture to be multiply conflictual. In these ways and in its view of language, *The Woman Warrior,* Lim argues, is marked as an "overwritten" and "literary" text and represents in relation to its predecessors a "breathtaking leap in female consciousness."

Autobiography is not an indigenous form of literature for American Indian peoples, Kathleen Sands argues in her essay "Indian Women's Personal Narrative: Voices Past and Present." Traditional Indian literature is communal and oral, expressive of a culture that did not and does not place particular value on the individual. Nevertheless, Sands identifies three forms of personal narrative that have evolved since the nineteenth century in the conjunctions of tribal and Euro-American traditions: the written, the composite, and the multigenre. Sands gives us examples of each and shows how, in different ways, each form is a bicultural event either in its generation as an "as-told-to" ethnography or in its address to and reception by non-Indian audiences. The multigenre autobiography practiced today by writers such as Leslie Silko and Paula Gunn Allen may use a combination of tribal and family stories and myth, personal reminiscences, fiction, poetry, and photography. Sands expects more Indian women to experiment with autobiography in the form of "cultural composite" as Indian autobiography "adapts to new needs, accommodates non-Western ways of knowing, generates new concepts of text, and expands the definition of what is literary."

Margot Hennessy's essay "Listening to the Secret Mother" shifts our focus to the reader of autobiography. As a white woman reading a black man's autobiography, *Brothers and Keepers* by John Edgar Wideman, Hennessy challenges assumptions about the singularity of female and male experience. Insisting on multiple subjectivities, Hennessy explores how the text is "engendered" by both writer and reader. Through an examination of Wideman's construction of his mother in the text, Hennessy shows how Wideman's learning from his mother to listen to his brother Robby models in the text what the reader of autobiography must learn as well, a process that encodes gender within it. If Hennessy makes us look again at gender in relation to the categories used in all the other essays in this book—writer, reader, text—if her essay makes one feel that the earlier essays must be read again, then placing her essay last in this volume will have achieved its purpose.

Autobiography studies continues to be that vital space where those challenging the constraints of canonicity and those intoxicated by *haute theorie* fruitfully meet. The essays in this book, grounded in the cross-cultural history that is America, reflect both impulses—in some cases simultaneously. Taken together, these essays celebrate women's lives, women's autobiographical writing including criticism, and finally the fea(s)ts of reading women's writing. Enjoy.

WORKS CITED

Abrecht, Mary Ellen. *The Making of a Woman Cop.* New York: William Morrow, 1976.

Adams, Elizabeth Laura. *Dark Symphony.* New York: Sheed and Ward, 1942.

Addams, Jane. *Twenty Years at Hull House.* New York: Macmillan, 1910.

Addis, Patricia K. *Through a Woman's I: An Annotated Bibliography of American*

Women's Autobiographical Writings, 1946–1976. Metuchen, NJ, and London: Scarecrow Press, 1983.

Addison, Joseph. *The Spectator.* Vol. 1, no. 1. March 1, 1711.

Allen, Charlotte Vale. *Daddy's Girl: A Memoir.* New York: Wyndham Books, 1980.

Anderson, Margaret. *The Strange Necessity.* New York: Horizon Press, 1969.

Angelou, Maya. *The Heart of a Woman.* New York: Random House, 1981.

Austin, Mary. *A Woman of Genius.* Garden City: Doubleday, 1912.

Bailey, Abigail. *Memoirs of Mrs. Abigail Bailey. . . .* Ed. Ethan Smith. Boston: Samuel T. Armstrong, 1815.

Baker, Louise. *Out on a Limb.* New York: McGraw Hill, 1946.

Barringer, Emily Dunning. *Bowery to Bellevue: The Story of New York's First Woman Ambulance Surgeon.* New York: W. W. Norton, 1950.

Barthes, Roland. *Roland Barthes by Roland Barthes.* Trans. Richard Howard. New York: Hill and Wang, 1977.

Beauvoir, Simone de. *The Second Sex.* Trans. H. M. Parshley. New York: Bantam, 1970.

Benetar, Judith. *Admissions: Notes from a Woman Psychiatrist.* New York: Charterhouse, 1974.

Benstock, Shari, ed. *The Private Self: Theory and Practice of Women's Autobiographical Writings.* Chapel Hill: University of North Carolina Press, 1988.

Birdwell, Cleo. *Amazons, An Intimate Memoir by the First Woman Ever to Play in the National Hockey League.* New York: Holt, Rinehart, 1980.

Brée, Germaine. "The Fictions of Autobiography." *Nineteenth-Century French Studies,* 4 (Summer 1976), 43–49.

Brignano, Russell C. *Black Americans in Autobiography.* 2d ed. Durham, NC: Duke University Press, 1984.

Briscoe, Mary Louise, et al., eds. *American Autobiography 1945–1980: A Bibliography.* Madison: University of Wisconsin Press, 1982.

Brodzki, Bella, and Celeste Schenck, eds. *Life/Lines: Theorizing Women's Autobiography.* Ithaca: Cornell University Press, 1988.

Brooks, Gladys Rice. *Boston and Return.* New York: Atheneum, 1962.

Burton, Annie L. *Memories of Childhood's Slavery Days.* Boston: Ross Publishing, 1909.

Casal, Mary. *The Stone Wall, An Autobiography.* Chicago: Eyncourt Press, 1930.

Chapelle, Dickey. *What's a Woman Doing Here?* New York: William Morrow, 1962.

Chicago, Judy. *Through the Flower: My Struggle as a Woman Artist.* Garden City: Doubleday, 1977.

Clapper, Olive. *One Lucky Woman.* Garden City: Doubleday, 1961.

Clark, Septima Poinsette. *Echo in My Soul.* New York: E. P. Dutton, 1962.

Cowles, Fleur. *Friends and Memories.* New York: Reynal with William Morrow, 1978.

Cummins, Clessie Lyle. *My Days with the Diesel: The Memoirs of Clessie L. Cummins, Father of the Highway Diesel.* Philadelphia: Chilton Books, 1967.

Davis, Harriet Eager. *World on My Doorstep: A Venture in International Living*. New York: Simon and Schuster, 1947.

Day, Helen Caldwell. *Color, Ebony*. New York: Sheed and Ward, 1951.

Dean, Maureen. *"Mo": A Woman's View of Watergate*. New York: Bantam, 1976.

de Man, Paul. "Autobiography as De-Facement." *Modern Language Notes*, 94 (December 1979), 919–930.

Dunnigan, Alice Allison. *A Black Woman's Experience: From Schoolhouse to White House*. Philadelphia: Dorrance, 1974.

Earp, Josephine. *I Married Wyatt Earp: The Recollection of Josephine Sarah Marcus Earp*. Tucson: University of Arizona Press, 1976.

Enzinga, Netfa. *I Was Kidnapped by Idi Amin*. Los Angeles: Holloway House, 1979.

Ferber, Edna. *A Peculiar Treasure*. New York: Literary Guild of America, 1939.

Fox-Genovese, Elizabeth. "My Statue, My Self: Autobiographical Writings of Afro-American Women." In Benstock 63–89.

Franklin, Benjamin. *The Autobiography of Benjamin Franklin*. Ed. Leonard W. Labree et al. New Haven: Yale University Press, 1964.

Friedman, Susan Stanford. "Women's Autobiographical Selves: Theory and Practice." In Benstock 34–64.

Frooks, Dorothy. *Lady Lawyer*. New York: Robert Speller and Sons, 1975.

Furman, Bess. *Washington By-line: The Personal History of a Newspaper Woman*. New York: Alfred Knopf, 1949.

Giovanni, Nikki. *Gemini: An Extended Autobiographical Statement on My First Twenty-Five Years of Being a Black Poet*. Indianapolis: Bobbs-Merrill, 1971.

Goodwin, Ruby Berkley. *It's Good to Be Black*. Garden City: Doubleday, 1953.

Guffy, Ossie. *Ossie: The Autobiography of a Black Woman*. New York: W. W. Norton, 1971.

Gusdorf, Georges. "Conditions and Limits of Autobiography." In Olney 28–48.

Handy, William Christopher. *Father of the Blues: An Autobiography*. Ed. Arna Bontemps. New York: Macmillan, 1941.

Hedgeman, Anna Arnold. *The Trumpet Sounds: A Memoir of Negro Leadership*. New York: Holt, Rinehart and Winston, 1964.

Hellman, Lillian. *Pentimento, A Book of Portraits*. Boston: Little, Brown, 1973.

Hellman, Lillian. *Unfinished Woman—A Memoir*. Boston: Little, Brown, 1969.

Hobson, Laura Z. *Laura Z: A Life, Years of Fulfillment*. New York: Donald I. Fine, 1986.

Huey, Lynda. *A Running Start: An Athlete, A Woman*. New York: Quadrangle, New York Times, 1976.

Hunter, Rodello. *Wyoming Wife*. New York: Alfred A. Knopf, 1969.

Hurston, Zora Neale. *Dust Tracks on a Road, An Autobiography*. Philadelphia: Lippincott, 1942.

Jacobs, Harriet. *Incidents in the Life of a Slave Girl, Written by Herself*. Ed. Jean Fagan Yellin. Cambridge: Harvard University Press, 1987.

Jardine, Alice A. *Gynesis: Configurations of Woman and Modernity*. Ithaca: Cornell University Press, 1985.

Jelinek, Estelle. *The Tradition of Women's Autobiography from Antiquity to the Present.* Boston: Twayne, 1986.

Jelinek, Estelle, ed. *Women's Autobiography: Essays in Criticism.* Bloomington: Indiana University Press, 1980.

Kaplan, Louis. *A Bibliography of American Autobiographies.* Madison: University of Wisconsin Press, 1962.

Keith, Agnes Newton. *Three Came Home.* Boston: Little, Brown, 1947.

Keller, Helen. *The Story of My Life.* Garden City: Doubleday, 1954.

King, Mary. *Freedom Song: A Personal Story of the 1960s Civil Rights Movement.* New York: William Morrow, 1987.

Kingston, Maxine Hong. *The Woman Warrior: Memoirs of a Girlhood among Ghosts.* New York: Vintage, 1977.

Kirkland, Caroline. *A New Home, Or Life in the Clearings.* New York: Putnam, 1953.

LaBastille, Anne. *Woodswoman.* New York: Dutton, 1976.

Lacan, Jacques. *Ecrits: A Selection.* Trans. Alan Sheridan. London: Tavistock, 1977.

Lacy, Leslie Alexander. *Native Daughter.* New York: Macmillan, 1974.

Larcom, Lucy. *A New England Girlhood, Outlined from Memory.* Boston and New York: Houghton Mifflin, 1892.

Lejeune, Philippe. *On Autobiography.* Ed. John Paul Eakin. Minneapolis: University of Minnesota Press, 1989.

Lindbergh, Anne Morrow. *North to the Orient.* New York: Harcourt Brace, 1935.

Lionnet, Françoise. *Autobiographical Voices: Race, Gender, Self-Portraiture.* Ithaca: Cornell University Press, 1989.

The Log-Cabin Lady: An Anonymous Autobiography. Boston: Little, Brown, 1922.

Luhan, Mabel Dodge. *Intimate Memoirs.* New York: Harcourt Brace, 1933.

McCarthy, Mary. *Memories of a Catholic Girlhool.* New York: Harcourt Brace and World, 1972.

MacLane, Mary. *I, Mary MacLane, By Herself. A Diary of Human Days.* New York: Frederick A. Stokes, 1917.

MacLane, Mary. *The Story of Mary MacLane.* Chicago: Herbert S. Stone, 1902.

Marks, Elaine. "'I Am My Own Heroine': Some Thoughts about Women and Autobiography in France." In *Teaching about Women in the Foreign Languages,* ed. Sidonie Cassierer. Old Westbury: Feminist Press, 1975.

Mason, Mary. "The Other Voice: Autobiographies of Women Writers." In Olney 207–35.

Mead, Margaret. *Blackberry Winter: My Early Years.* New York: William Morrow, 1972.

Meyer, Agnes E. *Out of These Roots: The Autobiography of an American Woman.* Boston: Little, Brown, 1953.

Miller, Nancy. *Subject to Change: Reading Feminist Writing.* New York: Columbia University Press, 1988.

Mowatt, Anna Cora. *Autobiography of an Actress; or, Eight Years on the Stage.* Boston: Ticknor, Reed and Fields, 1854.

Nation, Carry A. *The Use and Need of the Life of Carry A. Nation.* Topeka, KS: F. M. Steves, 1909.

Olney, James, ed. *Autobiography: Essays Theoretical and Critical.* Princeton: Princeton University Press, 1980.

Olsen, Tillie. "One Out of Twelve: Writers Who Are Women in Our Century." In *Silences* 22–46. New York: Delacourt Press, 1978.

Owens-Adair, B. A. *Dr. Owens-Adair: Some of Her Life Experiences.* Portland, OR: Mann and Beach, n.d.

Peterson, Virgilia. *A Matter of Life and Death.* New York: Atheneum, 1961.

Randall, Ruth Painter. *I Ruth. An Autobiography of a Marriage.* Boston: Little, Brown, 1968.

Reagan, Nancy. *My Turn: The Memoirs of Nancy Reagan.* New York: Random House, 1989.

[Richards, A. M.]. *Memories of a Grandmother, By a Lady of Massachusetts.* Boston: Gould and Lincoln, 1854.

Rowbotham, Sheila. *Woman's Consciousness, Man's World.* London: Penguin, 1973.

Sawyer, Antonia. *Songs at Twilight.* New York: Devin-Adair, 1939.

Scott, Ann [psued.]. *Woman with Arthritis: The True Story of a Recovery.* New York: Abelard-Schuman, 1957.

Settle, Mary Lee. *All the Brave Promises: Memories of an Aircraft Woman 2nd Class — 2146431.* New York: Delacourt, 1966.

Showalter, Elaine. "Women's Time, Women's Space: Writing the History of Feminist Criticism." In *Feminist Issues in Literary Scholarship,* ed. Shari Benstock, 30–44. Bloomington: Indiana University Press, 1987.

Showalter, Elaine. "Women Who Write Are Women." *New York Times Book Review,* December 16, 1984.

Smith, Amanda Berry. *The Story of the Lord's Dealing with Mrs. Amanda Smith, the Colored Evangelist.* . . . Chicago: Meyer and Brother, 1893.

Smith, Lillian. *Killers of the Dream.* 2d ed. New York: W. W. Norton, 1961.

Smith, Sidonie. *A Poetics of Women's Autobiography: Marginality and the Fictions of Self-Representation.* Bloomington: Indiana University Press, 1987.

Sneller, Anne Gertrude. *A Vanished World.* Syracuse: Syracuse University Press, 1964.

Sommer, Doris. "'Not Just a Personal Story': Women's *Testimonios* and the Plural Self." In Brodzki and Schenck 107–30.

Spelman, Elizabeth V. *Inessential Woman: Problems of Exclusion in Feminist Thought.* Boston: Beacon Press, 1988.

Stanton, Domna. "Autogynography: Is the Subject Different?" In *The Female Autograph: Theory and Practice of Autobiography from the Tenth to the Twentieth Century* 3–20. Chicago: University of Chicago Press, 1987.

Stanton, Elizabeth Cady. *Eighty Years and More (1815–1897): Reminiscences of Elizabeth Cady Stanton.* New York: European Publishing Company, 1898.

Stein, Gertrude. *The Autobiography of Alice B. Toklas.* New York: Random House, 1933.

Stein, Gertrude. *Everybody's Autobiography.* New York: Random House, 1937.

Stern, E. G. *My Mother and I.* New York: Macmillan, 1931.

Tarbell, Ida. *All in the Day's Work: An Autobiography.* New York: Macmillan, 1939.

Tarry, Ellen. *The Third Door: The Autobiography of an American Negro Woman.* New York: David McKay, 1955.

Terrell, Mary Church. *A Colored Woman in a White World.* Washington, DC: Ransdell, 1940.

Thompson, Era Bell. *American Daughter.* Chicago: University of Chicago Press, 1946.

Tietjens, Eunice. *The World at My Shoulder.* New York: Macmillan, 1938.

Tompkins, Jane. *Sensational Designs: The Cultural Work of American Fiction, 1790–1860.* New York: Oxford University Press, 1985.

Washington, Kipp [pseud.]. *Some Like It Dark: The Intimate Autobiography of a Negro Call Girl.* As Told to Leo Guild. Los Angeles: Holloway House, 1966.

Wells-Barnett, Ida B. *Crusade for Justice: The Autobiography of Ida B. Wells.* Chicago: University of Chicago Press, 1970.

Welty, Eudora. *One Writer's Beginnings.* New York: Warner, 1984.

Wiggin, Kate Douglas. *My Garden of Memory: An Autobiography.* Boston and New York: Houghton Mifflin, 1923.

Wright, Mabel Osgood. *My New York.* New York: Macmillan, 1926.

Wylie, I. A. R. *My Life with George: An Unconventional Autobiography.* New York: Random House, 1940.

CHAPTER 2

"Come and Hear":
Women's Puritan Evidences

KATHLEEN M. SWAIM

American autobiography is precisely coeval with Puritan colonization because early New England churches required candidates for membership to recite their spiritual histories before the congregations they hoped to join. In Massachusetts' first decades, churches took shape as godly applicants offered public professions admitting them to fellowship with the group of at least seven citizens of an original covenant. These earliest inscriptions of self differ markedly from modern norms of autobiography, but do nonetheless lay the foundations upon which later envisionings could be built. They themselves took shape from traditions of Puritan meditation upon the occasions and providences of this life and of grace and from Reformation enhancements of individuality growing out of Luther's principle of the priesthood of all believers.

What follows is a study of a collection of the public professions of spiritual experience and belief presented for membership in Thomas Shepard's church in Newtown [later Cambridge], Massachusetts, between 1638 and 1645, "gathered" under the title *The Confessions of Diverse Propounded to be Received and Were Entertained as Members.* Through an analytical contrast of Shepard's twenty-two female narratives and twenty-eight male narratives, this study addresses the history and discourse of the earliest of American women's autobiographical acts. A series of Shepard's other writings — an *Autobiography,* a *Journal,* a series of sermons on Matthew 25.1–13, the specifically female parable of the Ten Virgins, and *The Sound Believer,* a treatise on church membership as he understood it and taught it to his flock[1] — provides full contexts for inquiries into relevant issues of theology, gender, and genre. Shepard is also an especially welcome collector for our purposes for unlike many of his fellow ministers, and in despite of 1 Corinthians 14.34 and 1 Timothy 2.11–12, he expected women as well as men to recount publicly to the congregation the work of grace in their souls.

I

Early seventeenth-century immigrants to the American colonies expected — and were expected — to participate fully in the life of the Puritan church, the most comprehensive social, political, and cultural institution of the times as well as the most formative personal influence. New England churches offered cultural stability in an alien, often hostile land thousands of ocean miles from the comforts, family securities, and familiar mores, landscape, and institutions of Old England. The New World citizens with whom we are concerned had made the dangerous journey at least in part, and mostly in very large part, in order to practice freely the strict and "purified" form of Protestant Christianity they brought with them. They left behind a parochially organized religion, by definition inclusive of all neighborhood residents, in favor of a separatist, independent, congregationally organized system requiring that its members freely choose, actively earn, and daily prove their worthiness for membership among — what they called themselves — the Visible Saints.

Clearly set off from the more worldly European society they had left behind and from any "openly profane" society on this side of the Atlantic, Puritans committed themselves to and required of each other fellowship, freely made religious commitment, and proven fitness for the holy life. Despite its being such a time-intensive and labor-intensive activity, church membership is the Puritan sine qua non. One earned it after intense introspection and extensive discussions with the minister, elders, and others, as well as through careful Bible reading and attention to sermons. Its achievement meant participating in such public church activities as sermons, prayers, prophesyings, Bible readings, church disciplinings, alms, covenant makings and renewals, and other church ordinances. It meant also associating intimately and continuously with other believers in smaller social and family devotional exercises, in conferences, counsels, and godly conversations with peers, advisors, and potential or lapsed converts. At the private level, Puritans also regularly practiced "closet" devotions, meditations, and diary keeping. In honoring 1 Corinthians 14.26, "let all things be done unto edifying," they covenanted with each other, professed faith, and demonstrated an understanding of doctrines, good behavior, and submission to the discipline of the church.[2] They drew regularly upon biblical texts and ideals in various formal and informal advisories of their friends and enemies, such discourse being authorized by Ephesians 4.29: "Let no corrupt communication proceed out of your mouth, but that which is good to the use of edifying, that it may minister grace unto the hearers." As Charles Cohen puts it "to be a puritan meant living a life distinctively ardent"— ardent and distinctly arduous!

These people did not merely search their consciences for actual sins, for failures in such matters as moderation, chastity, humility and vigilance; they scrutinized their whole range of capabilities and talents, their weaknesses, shortcomings and their whole temperamental make-up; they studied the reactions of their souls to certain impressions, the strength of their powers of resistance. They used every means to form a just estimate of themselves. (4)

When one is locked into a searching and tireless preoccupation with the self, such traits can go beyond excess to obsession, and as Alan Simpson remarks of the typical Puritan: "Taught to expect [sin] everywhere, and to magnify it where he found it, he easily fell into the habit of inventing it" (91).

Under the shadow of predestinate damnation, Puritans honored Calvin's insistence upon a scrupulous examination of conscience for signs and proofs of salvation or damnation, by eagerly studying, recording, and reinterpreting the details of their spiritual lives. Especially did they require as well as enjoy telling and hearing tell of the details of their own and each others' achievements, falterings, and strengthenings in the arena of saving grace. With an eye always on the heavenly goal, they measured their spiritual progress and prospects against clearly defined and sequenced models. They expected to enfold individual careers and erase idiosyncrasies within codified schemes of character, study, and expression. Through disciplined self-study they examined events in their own lives against biblical doctrine and norms, measured their progress and lapses against the exemplary histories of the most visible of the Visible Saints, and in general progressively sought to build unified rational wholes out of their lives. As with the study of the Word, such self-examinations, at once exhaustive and never-ending, looked for both sudden and progressive illuminations.

Besides treasuring personal experience for its evidences of election, Puritans valued their life histories as texts inscribing divine doctrine and imperatives. They continuously sought to interread the Bible and the larger patterns and smallest details of their lives on the assumption that the Word and experience were reciprocally illuminating, and they understood their "interpreted" life experience to be a secondary Scripture or *logos,* a de facto authority by contrast with the de jure authority of the biblical Word (Kaufmann 201–9). John Bunyan speaks for the Puritan tradition more generally in claiming that a Christian "cannot, will not, dare not be contented until he find his soul and Scripture together, with the things contained therein, to embrace each other, and a sweet correspondency and agreement between them" (*Miscellaneous Works* I 358).

Elsewhere Bunyan calls the study of past sins "a soul-humbling, a Christ-advancing, and a creature-emptying consideration" (*Works* I 617), and as Owen Watkins remarks, "A man was what he was through the process of being remade" (238). Between the rude beginnings in original sin and the ultimate goal of salvation lies a progressive edifying present in which the principal endeavor is living a godly life, especially by analyzing and applying gospel principles and texts to every part of existence. Committed to growth and to understanding the patterns of that growth, Puritans pursued self-definition through a range of relationships "to God, the Father, Son, and indwelling Spirit; to fellow believers, deviant groups, persecutors, and potential converts; to family, friends, and society at large; to one's own past, present, and ideal self as discerned in the act of writing about them" (Watkins 238).

A good number of the public professions offered as credentials for church membership survive as brief expressions of such self-study. Sometimes called *Relations, Evidences, Narrations,* or *Experiences,* these self-histories align an individual's life with the grids of conversion morphology, they lay claims to the greatest sinfulness, and they document the "experimental" proofs of God's providences or the particular works of grace in the soul. Sometimes also called *Confessions* (i.e., of experience) and sometimes *Professions* (i.e., of faith), such narratives were expected to express "saving faith," to demonstrate an understanding of Christian doctrine, and to be reinforced by the living of a godly life. These "original" stories of inner turmoil and deliverance from sin are characteristically intense, confessional, and introspective, but also distinctly formulaic and short on specifics of time, place, and person. They generally rehearse definitive convictions of sin and comings to Christ. Their status as at once a personal and a public profession predetermines their content, form, audience, and purpose, reducing "the autobiographical act . . . to testifying that one's experience has conformed, with allowable variations, to a certain pattern of feeling and behavior." This initiation rite proves a newcomer's compatibility with the group through "a declaration of deep spiritual affinity, not just the wish to join a club."[3]

The chief biblical authority for church Evidences is Psalm 66.16: "Come and hear, all ye that fear God, and I will declare what he hath done for my soul," supported by 1 Peter 3.15–16:

But sanctify the Lord God in your hearts: and be ready always to give an answer to every man that asketh you a reason of the hope that is in you with meekness and fear: Having a good conscience; that, whereas they speak evil of you, as of evildoers, they may be ashamed that falsely accuse your good conversation in Christ.

The biblical models for such narrations are David in the Psalms and Paul describing his sinful past and sudden enlightenment and election on the road to Damascus in Acts 22. Like Saint Paul, a number of Puritan autobiographers claim to be "the chief of sinners," echoing 1 Timothy 1.15 ("sinners, of whom I am chief," and similarly Ephesians 3.8, "Less than the least of all Saints").

Church Evidences provided the grounds upon which a separatist congregation, exercising "the judgment of charity," voted to include or exclude candidates for membership. The multiplication of such narrations, reflecting collectively and in retrospect the spiritual conditions of all its members, is the essential and constituting factor for the separatist church. This means, as Patricia Caldwell argues, that the unique communal nature of the congregational way depends upon the verbal skills of believers and upon complex linguistic and rhetorical interactions among the community members.

The full-fledged relation made up a three-sided figure: for the speaker, it was meant to be not a set of doctrines intellectually assented to but a living experience of the heart voluntarily told in his or her own words; for the audience, it was meant to be not just a passive absorption of information but a spiritual act—of hearing, of rendering the "judgment of charity," and of receiving (sometimes rejecting) a "living stone" for the temple; and for the "Militant-visible church," it was the closest thing in this world to a guarantee of the purest possible membership. (108, 46–47)

Puritan assumptions of everyman as storyteller and everyman as contributing reader and interpreter of others' stories fostered close observation of detail and developed speaking, listening, and interpreting skills in the community, encouraging a continuous consciousness of the intimate relation between human event and divine cause (Hunter 83). The audience's responsive understanding of such narrations, like the events and articulation of the stories themselves, signaled infusions of grace in all participants.

II

For the purposes of a literary inquiry, Puritan models of personality, of sequential spiritual action, and of appropriate expression readily translate into the literary categories of character, plot, and style. To a modern eye, what is most striking about Puritanism are the extent to which its members and discourses are governed by paradigms and rules and the extent to which their biblically derived and variously codified rules became so thoroughly internalized in all members of the society. Given the mutual interaction of doctrine and experience in the believer's life, each autobiographical act at once expresses both the Puritan tradition in general and also a personal response to it.

Puritanism fostered a standardized rather than individualized personality model and defined self-knowledge as "th[e] anxiety to determine whether one's every experience fits the proper pattern (or, more accurately speaking, th[e] zealous effort to make all experiences fit)" (Webber 137). The Puritan character model for both men and women compounds sobriety, humility, godliness, righteousness, efficiency, religious scruple, meticulous reasoning, intense introspection, strong self-awareness, and energetic self-mastery and self-reform (Schucking 9). Anne Bradstreet's epitaph on her mother translates these theoretical virtues into a specifically female outline of normative character and conduct.

> Here lyes,
> A worthy Matron of unspotted life,
> A loving Mother and obedient wife,
> A friendly Neighbor, pitiful to poor,
> Whom oft she fed, and clothed with her store;
> To Servants wisely aweful, but yet kind,
> And as they did, so they reward did find:
> A true Instructer of her Family,
> The which she ordered with dexterity.
> The publick meetings ever did frequent,
> And in her Closet constant hours she spent;
> Religious in all her words and wayes,
> Preparing still for death, till end of dayes:
> Of all her Children, Children, liv'd to see,
> Then dying, left a blessed memory.[4]

Men's expected activities and roles are also regularly idealized in comparable funereal portraits.

The Puritan model narrative, also clearly codified, puts such character into motion. William Haller outlines the prescribed plot in *The Rise of Puritanism*:

The story was characteristically supposed to begin with an account of the horrid sins or scarcely less deplorable dry indifference from which the soul destined to be saved was called and after terrific struggle converted, generally by the reading of some godly book or by the influence of some powerful preacher. Then followed the chronicle, which might be more or less extended according to the circumstances, of the saint's lifelong war against the temptation to despair and the other abominations of his heart, lightened by the encouragements vouchsafed to him by God in the form of good fortune and of worldly and spiritual success. The last scene was the deathbed, one last terrific bout with Satan and then triumph and glory forever after. (108)

Whether one's life story was written by others in the forms of funeral sermons or biographies, or written by oneself in the forms of conversion narratives, diaries, meditations on the self, or formal autobiographies, the pattern was basically a progress from sin to grace, the compound of precept and example translating life into *logos,* pious legend, edifying example. Categorizing these genres as "spiritual gossip," Haller discovers their origins in the universal concern for salvation, a natural interest in the daily struggles and adventures of the inner life, a generally accepted psychological profile and standard of measurement, and thence opportunities for the most minute comparisons of one's own history with the paradigm and with other converts' inspiring successes and comforting failures.

Edmund Morgan has dubbed this expected Puritan plot or life pattern "the Morphology of Conversion." Its often codified stages include Effectual Calling, Justification, Sanctification, and Glorification. Awakening from an initial indifference, converts gradually leave behind blind confidence in the Covenant of Works and progress to humiliation at their self-deception and depravity. Moving through intensifications and alternations of self-consciousness, self-deception, moral sensitivity, terror, alienation, and despair, they arrive at moments of comfort and assurance and an overwhelming sense of God's benevolence, technically through Imputed Righteousness and Justification by Faith. Despite renewed fears and temptations, thereafter they persevere in promise and hope, though never achieving the comfort of secure, permanent assurance. A denial of such climax and closure constantly forces converts to return to and review the origins of their hopes. Sequential progress toward assurance of personal salvation is both logical and psychological, at once biblically rooted, universally prescribed, and uniquely enacted by the individual who felt that his or her destiny, as Dean Ebner remarks, "depended upon his ability to recognize this pattern of divine illumination within his own mind."[5]

Although its dramatic quality makes it loom large, in fact conversion constituted only a brief prelude to what would normally be an extended postconversion spiritual life. After the initial startled awakening, the convert was steadily alert to signs of saving grace and of backsliding, always questioning the genuineness of the former and fearing false security. The believer went round and round in a regular rhythm of perplexity, quest for assurance, diligent self-examination, and moral dissection, but also of remembering God's mercies and promises. Assurance, of course, like joy, grief, or fatigue, generates its own other set of dangers such as pride, despair, or complacency. Each achievement can thus spark another cycle of guilt and self-testing. Church Confessions, to which we shall return in a moment, emphasizing the initial stages of conversion morphology schemes, necessarily renounce the self and seek out formulaic expression. More inclusive, full-scale autobiographies, however, usually involve more complex inquiry and achieve sufficient distancing to recognize both patterns of alternation and progress among a number of these stages.

In style, as in character and plot, Puritans tend to embrace an undecorated manner as well as a simple narrative line. They aim for a simple, sincere "transparency" between expression and truth. This is especially true for candidates for church admission, where the content is necessarily subjective and where unsuccessful narrations could result in a refusal or postponement of membership. Peter J. Carlton explains the stylistic governors in terms of the larger system:

The pattern they were taught, they sought for; the pattern they sought, they experienced; the pattern they expressed, they narrated to those who taught it to them, so that they might be accepted and teach the pattern to others in their turn.

Carlton develops the corollary, that the validity of conversion utterances hinges upon obedience to the conventions they operate out of. The only measure of sincerity is thus replication: an "inspired" utterance can be seen to be so only if it sounds like all other "inspired" utterances. The only proof of originality emerges as conformity to type (29). While theoretically at least, Puritans considered rote recitations anathema, in practice they thought of "extraordinary" experiences, those that deviated in unexpected ways from the orthodox pattern, as dangerously antinomian. Autobiographical writing with no touches of individuality is, of course, rare, but contrary to modern thinking and practice, such deviations are here accidental rather than prioritized. The models serve to structure experience but also to obliterate differences and resistance. They intensify the individual's guilt even as they transmute collective anxiety into a kind of shared security.[6]

III

The members of Thomas Shepard's Newtown/Cambridge congregation were generally modest, youthful laypersons of the middle rank, although four were at least temporarily servants. All had, of course, emigrated from England and were in the process of establishing themselves in a new land and a new society. Many came, quite explicitly, in order to practice their religion freely, and, as their wills show, they prospered financially in the new land. At least seventeen of the total of fifty-one are related by marriage and by blood, as seven sets of husbands and wives and one mother with two of her children. About one-third speak of their ability to read.

Shepard's congregation was less severe and less elaborate in its admissions practices than many Bay Colony churches. It did follow the practice usual to contemporary churches of requiring candidates to declare the work of grace that the Lord had wrought in them, but where some churches required two professions—one of experience and one of faith—Shepard's professions cover both categories at once. His church also sometimes practiced testimonies on behalf of candidates and question-and-answer exchanges on points of doctrine and church polity, but the records do not show elaborate series of interviews, inquiries into offenses, and testimonials that attended propoundings in many other congregation. And, as noted earlier, Shepard treated his female applicants as he did his male ones, not excusing women from full public profession as some other ministers did.

Shepard's *Confessions* appear to be his shorthand record of the speeches candidates actually delivered before the entire congregation rather than notes of proposed—and therefore edited or assisted—speeches. Such transmission builds into his record some awkwardnesses of expression but also flavor, variety and, of course, immediacy. Whether from Shepard's shorthand or the candidates' deliveries, the stories' syntax and even sense are sometimes cryptic, tangled, and incomplete, the more so because Shepard's handwriting is very difficult to decipher. Shepard's record shifts freely between first and third persons, between the speaker's narration and his own distanced representation. As their spiritual leader, Shepard, of course, had a stake in candidates' success, as they were necessarily invested in honoring his instruction. Perhaps, too, some leveling is inseparable from a single and interested transcriber filtering a variety of parallel items.

The basics of Shepard's instruction survive in his *The Sound Believer: A Treatise of Evangelical Conversion, Discovering the Work of Christ's Spirit in Reconciling of a Sinner to God,* a text that develops variations upon the traditional conversion morphology scheme. Shepard imposes a firm division between an initial four stages and a later six salvation stages.[7] Church Evidences take up the initial group only—Conviction of sin, Compunction for sin, Humiliation or self-abasement, and Faith. These four modes of Christ's action reverse Shepard's earlier set of the four chief means by which people ruin themselves:

1. Ignorance of their own misery; 2. Security and unsensibleness of it; 3. Carnal confidence in their own duties; 4. Presumption or resting upon the mercy of God by a Faith of their own forging. (*Works* I 116)

These positive and negative lists map virtually all the content of the Narrations of Shepard's congregation, especially because "the Lord brings in a convicting evidence of the particulars," that is, "the remembrance and consideration of some one great, if not a man's special and most beloved sin; and thereby the Spirit discovers, gradually, all the rest" (I 119, 120).

As examples of a genre essentially about spiritual birth, the *Confessions* necessarily privilege beginnings at the expense of narrative middles and endings, and what dramatics there are in the genre find their scope here, at the locus of the most important of spiritual conflicts, the moment of reversal, the achievement of "that gracious work of the Spirit, whereby a humbled sinner receiveth Christ" (*Works* I 190). Most of Shepard's confessors speak of their reception of—or resistance to—ministers, sermon texts, and Bible or other theological readings and their unspecified "afflictions" and fears of sickness and death. They often describe secret impulses both salvational and damnational and lament merely going through religious motions without real engagement. Typically, one of Shepard's converts found herself "affected but afterward left of a dead blockish frame" while later the "Lord melted [her] heart in private" (*Confessions* 121).

The Relation's central and longest sections review biblical and sermonic effects (especially promissory ones), often through a sort of dialogue with the Bible. Although authors regularly vacillate among tantalizing hopes, coolness of responses, resistances or rebellions, and secret anxieties, their texts and anxieties do not sort themselves into progressive sequences. Indeed their pattern, if it can be called that, is circular rather than linear. Speakers go over and over the same grounds of anxious doubt and fragile hope without apparent relief. In traditional literature, narrative middles very often trace out battles and journeys, but the wrestlings among these Confessions do not really present themselves as definable conflicts. Even more surprising, although nearly every one of these testifiers makes specific reference to the journey from England to the New World, that travel is not made metaphoric or even spiritually transitional. Some speakers focus on personal insufficiency or a particular sin—pride, sloth, Sabbath breaking, rebellion, acting against a specific commandment—but these too tend to be repeated rather than sequentially processed. The chief kind of change involves painful silences giving way to speaking or discovering oneself to religious friends or leaders. But in general, the middles of these narratives reiterate the same issue, even quite explicitly, until the author's pride or resistance has been broken.

Shepard's histories display most of what Patricia Caldwell finds characteristic of the genre: conciseness, exclusive focus on those experiences exhibiting the work of grace in the author's soul, orderly arrangement, a certain amount of objective examination, and heavy reliance on scriptural reinforcement. But in general, except for invoking the formulae "taking hold of Christ," "closing with Christ," "laying hold on the promise," and "laying under the Lord," they do not show what Caldwell also claims, formal conclusions with recitals of principles and numbered "evidences" of faith (5–7). The regeneration that presumably floods upon the convert receives surprisingly little attention in the endings of these narratives. Indeed, authors are much more likely to trail off than to put forward a breakthrough of fresh light or energy so that their final sentences often do not warrant the name of ending at all. Several speak simply of "hearing of God's mercy and that it might be for me." Stronger endings are unwarranted in a system crediting the working of the Spirit upon humbled and passive receivers of Christ's grace, especially in view of Shepard's definition of Humiliation as "that work of the Spirit whereby the soul, being broken off from self-conceit and self-confidence in any good it hath or doth, submitteth unto, or lieth under, God, to be disposed of as he pleaseth" (*Works* I 175). Entrance into the full Christian life requires that those destined for the promised kingdom must become as little children.

This confessional genre precisely targets the moment of transition between negative selfhood and positive selfhood, and the convert's narrative and even expressional dissolutions render that event mimetically. Calvinist theology presumes a desperately needy self totally unable, through its own efforts, to bring about its own relief, a self defined by its need of external grace or, as they would put it, in need of Imputed or Justifying Righteousness, obliging the believer to lose himself or herself in order to find a new reborn selfhood in God. When the autobiographical discourse is the outward and visible sign of the achieved annihilation of self, the genre necessarily differs radically from what we usually think of as autobiography.

Given the strong leveling, and even silencing, pressures of the genre, we should not be surprised that only modest differences distinguish the church Evidences of men and women, a condition biblically authorized by Galatians 3.26–29:

For ye are all the children of God by faith in Christ Jesus. For as many of you as have been baptized into Christ have put on Christ. There is neither Jew nor Greek, there is neither bond nor free, there is neither male nor female: for ye are all one in Christ Jesus.

Shepard identifies only two of his twenty-two women by both first and last names rather than by marital or social status designations, while first and last names designate twenty-four of the twenty-eight men. By all standards of measurement, the women's are shorter than the men's samples, averaging 52.7 lines in a modern edition as opposed to 73.[8] Among other gendered differences, we may note that some of the men in Shepard's sample present a highly confident sense of self through their use of personal pronouns. Even the most humble are on the whole less tremulous than some of the women. Several are subjected to question-and-answer exercises after their Professions as no women are. The men prefer less emotional and familial Scriptures and have read greater numbers of pious books. As sinners, they claim disobedience to parents, unruliness, drunkenness, gluttony, lust, and covetousness as women do not. John Stansby seems more than merely formulaic in calling himself "a child of hell and if ever any a child of the devil, I" and one guilty of "enticing and haling others to sin" (*Confessions* 86).

Charles Cohen's study of this genre notes that women mention their children and men mention Satan more frequently and that men confess more freely to pride while women confess to sloth (222), but such findings are only relative. Four of Shepard's women, including two servants, call attention to Matthew 11.28 — "Come unto me, all ye that labour and are heavy laden, and I will give you rest." Given the tremendous labors of carving a life and home out of what was recently a wilderness, the temptation to sloth, or the promise of relief from weariness, would indeed be a powerful call. But six of Shepard's men also claim this text and failure, while the women regularly admit to dangerous pride. Shepard's women specify such prideful faults as worldliness, vanities, neglect of duties and means, Sabbath breaking, and blasphemous thought. Appropriately Christian, but also characteristically feminine, is the tendency to wait for the Lord to make things happen.

In a context discrediting selfhood, the best conversion Narration would be no story at all, and two of Shepard's female candidates approach that condition with narrations of only 6 and 8 lines. In the case of Mrs. Greene, Shepard records "Testimonies carried it" (*Confessions* 118), and the proof of her and Hannah Brewer's worthiness resides in the whole of their lives and even their silence. In an interesting gendered difference, Robert Daniel's Profession covers just 12 lines, but it is extended through 27 lines of questions and answers. In women's cases, the encouragements to speak of faith in Psalm 66.16 and 1 Peter 3.15–16 are qualified by the stern injunction of 1 Corinthians 14.34: "Let your women keep silence in the churches: for it is not permitted unto them to speak; but they are commanded to be under obedience, as also saith the law." 1 Timothy 2.11–12 similarly insists: "Let the woman learn in silence with all subjection. But I suffer not a woman to teach, nor to usurp authority over the man, but to be in silence."

One of the most fascinating gender differences is the women's preference for certain specifically women's Bible texts. Mary Angier cites "the woman that had the bloody issue" (Mark 5.25, Luke 8.43–48, Matthew 9.20–22; *Confessions* 67); Jane Winship "Woman, great is thy faith" (Matthew 15.28; *Confessions* 148); and Jane Holmes "bad women lewd with lusts" (2 Timothy 3.6; *Confessions* 79). Brother Jackson's maid reads the deity in terms of betrothal and marriage (Hosea 2.19), determining that "Christ would be better than earthly husband. No fear there of widowhood" (*Confessions* 120). Seven out of twenty-two women specifically credit some part of Matthew 25.1–13, the parable of the Ten Virgins, sometimes citing Christ as Bridegroom, but mostly zeroing in on the foolishness of half of them. The preference for this parable reflects Shepard's copious instruction surviving as a 635-page compilation of sermons on this text (*Works* II). In view of the sheer bulk of this instruction, it is surprising that only three of the twenty-eight men mention its influence, and then only in abstract, and, except for John Fessenden, not at all in familiar or emotional terms (and see *Confessions* 88, 195). In a related point, although they are not gender-specific texts, four of the women—Mary Parish, Jane Winship, Joanna Sill, and Mary Angier—claim the importance of Hosea 14.3, 51, and 52 for their emphasis on God as father and read themselves as fatherless. Typically, the only male to cite this text (Richard Eccles) does not mention fatherhood or fatherlessness but only the numbers of chapter and verse. The emphasis upon familial relationships in these textual preferences reflects what some modern feminist scholarship has noted, that women's sense of self is organized around making and maintaining affiliations with others rather than self-enhancement.[9]

The Evidences of Elizabeth Cutter and two of her three children enforce similar gender differences. Barbary, the daughter, shows a very tidy mind in regularly enumerating lessons, memories, and arguments. Although numbering is a constant sermonic practice, Barbary's insistent use of the practice is unique among Shepard's women. Her quality of mind is reinforced by a preference for Scriptures having to do with cleaning. She looks to the Lord for cleansing those he finds worthy and cites the washing of robes from Revelation 7.14 and Christ's washing the disciples' feet from John 13.4–17. Her brother Richard also cites John 13.8 as a convicting passage. Because he had to be readmitted to the fellowship on a second occasion, he was probably a backslider, and his assertion, "I saw I had done as much evil as I could" (*Confessions* 179), may record more than the usual formulaic claims to excessive sinfulness. All three family members cite the parable of the Ten Virgins (Matthew 25). Where Barbary responds to Christ as a glorious Bridegroom, "And there know Lord means me" (91), and his mother responds to the foolish virgins as unloved and cast off (145), however, what matters for Richard are the radical distinctions between people and response, the misery of not knowing Christ, and the need to accept Christ when offered (*Confessions* 180, 181). For him, that is, the parable of the virgins is not a gendered text.

As a test case for gender differences among the narrations, the one anonymous Confession among Shepard's collection proves difficult to assign confidently to either a male or a female author. This Evidence credits a mother's awakening influence and shows interest in interpersonal relations, as Shepard's women tend to do, but its length of over a hundred lines, even after the loss of its opening, is more usual for a male than a female convert. Neither the sins it claims nor its biblical texts provide distinctly feminine signals, and the very fact of nongendered Scriptures may itself be evidence of male authorship. Because its pronominal presentation of self bespeaks the confidence often found in male Narrations and because this speaker is queried after the telling, my guess is for a male author, but the matter is not susceptible of proof.

IV

For modern readers, self-writing necessarily grows out of a celebration of unique selfhood and individuation, and autobiography absolutely requires a self, indeed a valued self, to be examined, interpreted, and projected. For seventeenth-century Puritans, however, these narratives served other kinds of theological and social expectations, and they would have worried about rather than approved even such minimal clues to identity as we have discovered.

It is not as if the seventeenth-century lives were without remarkable events as recorded in history if not in the Evidences themselves. Elizabeth Olbon (Luxford), for example, found that her husband was a bigamist when she had one child and another on the way. The Newtown/Cambridge authorities voided the marriage, fined Luxford, and ordered him to provide for her and return to England. A few months later, however, still in the area, he was found guilty of forgery, lying, and other offenses, and sentenced to whipping, having his ears cut off, and deportation. Mrs. Luxford's Narration had earlier claimed pride as her great sin (*Confessions* 39). Even before these scandals broke upon her, she resolved her Evidence with the insight "how vain a thing it was to put confidence in any creature" (41) and concluded with the philosophical principle: "Sometimes a heart to run and sometimes to sit still in the Lord's way" (41). Five years later, according to the Cambridge records, she married a Mr. Cole.

Sometimes complexity of character and character interactions unwittingly escapes even from behind the strictly formulaic. A welter of events and feelings, for example, underwrites the history of Martha Collins' journey:

And so my husband's heart was inclined to come to New England, but when I came to quickening means, then I secretly desired it but yet opposite I was to it by looking upon my miseries here. And yet I saw miseries there toward me and

my children and very unwilling and discontent when I was at it to come. Yet I thought
if the Lord should bring me here it would be a great mercy I was alive. And when
I came on shore and seeing people living otherwise than I looked for, I was affected.
But meeting with sorrows and feeling no life in ordinances I thought I was sealed
up. Then one child was struck with me and then I struggled with God and so then
pulled down. And then Lord struck my heart and I thought it was for my sin and
so let the Lord do with me what He will. (131)

We sense that hers is a restless rather than a comfortable nature, but because the hopes and fears, resistances and submissions of her domestic life
are so tangled, we cannot guess *how* the sights of New England affected
her, and whether she had anticipated the paradise or the wilderness of colonial propaganda (Carroll 5, 9, 14). Her husband, whose Relation also
occurs in the collection, appears to have been a serene, godly, and as it
happened a wealthy man and honored Cambridge citizen. Mrs. Collins
herself lived to great age (d. 1700).

From our modern vantage, two of Shepard's Evidences point beyond
the embryonic genre and toward the individuated story of a secular selfhood. They participate in what is for us a metaphoric discourse and linear
narrative; in short, they show a developing autobiography ready to escape
the strictures of its present form.[10] The Confession of Brother Crackbone's
wife runs to just a single page, but in that brief space shadows forth external and internal dramas with solid narrative potential. Initially, it follows
the usual format of guilt for unspecified sin and encouragements from specific reading and sermons, but it takes on distinctive humanizing touches
when she loses a child to affliction and death and blames herself for not
having prayed, or prayed sufficiently, to save it. Thereafter a few brief
sentences collapse a complex of emotions and events into the barest of salvational transactions:

And so came to New England. I forgot the Lord as the Israelites did and when
I had a new house yet I thought I had no new heart. And means did not profit
me and so doubted of all Lord had done, yet hearing when Lord will do good He
takes away all ornaments. . . . and heard Lord will break the will of His last work.
And seeing house burned down, I thought it was just and mercy to save life of
the child and that I saw not after again my children there. And as my spirit was
fiery so to burn all I had, and hence prayed Lord would send fire of wood, baptize
me with fire. And since the Lord hath set my heart at liberty. (*Confessions* 140;
see also Mary Parish, *Confessions* 136)

Typically, Mrs. Crackbone aligns her thought with the Israelites and with
baptism by fire from Matthew 3.11 and Luke 3.16. Quite untypically, for
Shepard's flock, she "realizes" her experience by interrelating texts with
powerful external realities. Typically, she lacerates herself with guilt, but
less typically her real caring for her children and, less innocently by Puri-

tan standards, her pride and joy in her new dwelling and its ornamentation show through. Quite untypically, she transmutes her affliction into transcending vision and elemental expression. Her final sentence here, the last of her narration, enfolds her preceding pain into a striking resolution of freedom and spiritual achievement.

By a curious coincidence, Anne Bradstreet translated her similar ordeal into an alternative discourse that allows for narrative advance without sacrificing immediacy or spiritual application. She reviews the lost furnishings, social circumstances, and ultimate priorities of her burned house, indeed its way of life, from a perspective at once tellingly immediate and distanced.

> When by the Ruines oft I past
> My sorrowing eyes aside did cast
> And here and there ye places spye
> Where oft I sate and long did lye,
> Here stood that Trunk, and there yt chest
> There lay that store I covnted best
> My pleasant things in ashes lye
> And them behold no more shall I.
> Vnder thy roof no gvest shall sitt,
> Nor at thy Table eat a bitt.
> No pleasant tale shall 'ere be told
> Nor things recovnted done of old.
> No Candle 'ere shall shine in Thee
> Nor bridegroom's voice ere heard shall bee.
> In silence ever shalt thou lye
> Adeiu, Adeiu, All's Vanity.

Bradstreet proceeds to place this review of a woman's most valued things, activities, and associations into a perspective that Puritanism would fully applaud:

> Then streight I 'gin my heart to chide,
> And did thy wealth on earth abide,
> Didst fix thy hope on mouldring dvst,
> The arm of flesh didst make thy trvst?
> Raise vp thy thovghts above the skye
> That dunghill mists away may flie.
> Thou hast an house on high erect
> Fram'd by that mighty Architect,
> With glory richly furnished
> Stands permanent tho: this bee fled.
> 'Its purchased + paid for too
> By him who hath Enovgh to doe.
> A prise so vast as is vnknown

Yet by his Gift is made thine own.
Ther's wealth enovgh I need no more,
Farewell my pelf, farewell my Store.
The world no longer let me Love
My hope, and Treasure lyes Above.
(236–37)

Like the earlier author, Bradstreet attaches her afflictions to a larger destiny, but not before giving them full and memorable expression.

Jane Holmes's Confession glances at the typical romance plot of later fiction, despite compressing its more striking narrative details. Her earliest awakening occurred at a young age, and she soon inquired after the Puritan way and sought Christ's righteousness. In England she was sometimes wholly charmed, sometimes deeply disillusioned by local ministers, judging one local vicar an Arminian and unholy liver, but thinking another "an angel of light" and that she could not live without his ministry. On the ship to America, she severely judges the false teaching of a minister on board, only to find that "that wretch. . . . began to insinuate himself into [her] company." After a variety of theological argument and sermons, welcomed and resisted, he tells her of his earlier sexual temptations, of "at last [getting] his desire" and "enjoy[ing] her three or four times a day" (*Confessions* 78, 79). His story of seducing another woman soon turns into a seduction of Holmes herself. He turns aside the biblical texts through which she tries to help him (e.g., 1 Timothy 3.6). Even though Holmes tries to resist by reaffirming her spiritual commitment, what she later calls "my ship entanglements" follow the usual pattern of seduction stories:

So I thought shall I leave this way for him? So I would seek, yet he by insinuation got within me and I would not leave him which I speak it to horror of that which it left me. I had been the vilest wretch. (79)

When Holmes says, "and so, my condition being discovered, I went and told him [a Roxbury minister] my condition," the first *condition* I believe describes a pregnancy (similarly 191), while the second carries the meaning usual in this collection, that is, spiritual state, in her case "back-sliding." In keeping with the biblically based discourse of this culture, Holmes casts her history into the tokens of Tamar's seduction by Judah in Genesis 38 with the simple sentence: "So I" (80). Her full awakening comes about with the striking "admiration at God's mercy to deliver one from such a wretch and errors," and she arrives at her present presentation of herself for church membership through Christ's cleansing of the leper in Mark 1.40–41. At the time of giving her Evidence, aged twenty-five, she is the wife of Robert Holmes of Brattle Street, whose Evidence also occurs in

Shepard's collection. She bore nine children, perhaps dying in the birth of the ninth in 1653.

Narratives such as these do not as a rule peep through the texts of men's Evidences. John Sills's repeated resistance to Shepard's ministry while both were still in England hints at some clash of character or principles, but it may be that as a concerned party Shepard just reports the matter with special fullness. Only one of Shepard's male speakers finds a way to present a fully realized self, if not history, and a glance at his story will make our review more comprehensive. The speaker is Henry Dunster (1609–1659) who succeeded Shepard as pastor, served as president of Harvard College, developed Anabaptist views, and was even tried and found guilty of disturbing the ordinances of the Cambridge church (*Confessions* 156). His telling may perhaps be called a *Profession* of belief, and a professional and hortatory one at that, but not really a *Confession* of emotional and spiritual history. It is very long, twice as long as the longest woman's story and three times as long as the male average. Its first half is deliberately oratorical, didactic, conscious of instructing an audience, offering much enumeration, much use of the second person, and much material on how he thinks the church should operate. Its second half calls attention to his precocity, his education and teaching experience, his courage in standing up for his religious beliefs, and his excessive love of learning (162). Dunster's concluding advice may variously reflect upon himself: "I desire you to be careful what scholars enter to your churches and pray for humility of spirit" (164).

Dunster shows strong narrative control and development and a forceful and descriptive, particular style, a grasp of causes and effects, a sense of principles in conflict, and a teleological argument. Because of his education or professional training, he grasps the principles of audience and of the presentation of self as persona. By containing the generic formulae within his other purposes, he moves beyond the scope of the genre of Evidences. He exploits the occasion to set himself up as heroic exemplar of the culture of which he is a somewhat pompous by-product. He also forecasts future generic developments.[11]

From beneath the trappings of the very restrictive genre of church Evidences, in at least these samples, there are a vital, individuated, even fascinating life and life story poised to emerge. In a Puritan commonplace, experience is the proving ground of the Word, and *experience* means both the accumulation of an individual's deeds and thoughts and also the public telling or record of such accumulations. An "Experience" is such a story as we have been reviewing, but in a secondary meaning, the *experience meeting* (*OED* 4.b) signifies those exercises through which church members shared with each other their continuing and additional graces and providences, their slips and backslidings, but especially their accumulating insights into the meaning and pattern of their lives. When set narrations open up to dialogic sharing, it is no longer a matter of initial minimal stirrings of grace but a demonstration of a new redeemed epistemology and didactics in action, what Shepard calls "renewed conversions" by contrast with the original traumatic one (*God's Plot* 25; and see Caldwell 76–78). This practice marks an advanced stage of understanding and articulateness in the individual and also a more cohesive social and spiritual community. It paves the way too for a more richly envisioned and more fully articulated life story.

Stories incorporating such enriched relations of speaker and audience constitute proper seventeenth-century Puritan spiritual autobiography, a genre that differs from church Relations most obviously in covering all or most of the author's specifically spiritual life, not just conversion, and in targeting a larger occasion than church entrance and a larger audience. Such autobiography is necessarily also notably longer. N. H. Keeble summarizes the principles through which personal writing advances toward a more realized Puritan discourse of self:

Faith does not put our mental faculties into retirement: it is by reflective attentiveness that we grow in grace. An individual who does not meditate on what has happened to him has, in fact, had no experiences. He has no history. And it . . . is only the human mind, alert and waiting on the guidance of the Spirit, which can, by recollecting, comparing and assessing experience, give purpose and order to life. (224)

Full-scale Puritan autobiography provides a distanced and perspectived review of the past and shows the soul gradually rather than suddenly transformed. Its greater temporal distance from its events makes possible

a long-range assessment of past experiences, a shaping of the past, as it were, into a coherent pattern with stages and with self-consistency of character. It superimposes upon the welter of remembered facts, in other words, the unity and order of a present mental attitude. (Ebner 19)

By contrast, church Evidences transfer the most private of feelings and events into the public arena usually without benefit of realistic specifics, or persona, or temporal distancing—a situation especially complicated when the speakers are relatively unsophisticated people, when the genre is new, and when the speaking self is only at best in the process of becoming an articulated personality. When the genre of autobiography becomes fully formed, the medium itself serves as a device for the formation of self, of a studied and thus stabilized self. It harnesses reflection, memory, cumulative retrospections, and the quest for spiritual illuminations and design to build a fully functioning self-knowledge and self-image and a fully shaped and directed narrative.

William C. Spengemann's three distinct but overlapping modes of auto-biography—"historical self-recollection, philosophical self-exploration, and poetic self-expression"—capture the progress and differences within the generic line. Building his model on Saint Augustine's *Confessions,* Spengemann anatomizes his first category, the *confession* of historical self-recollection, into "at once a conceptual act (the arrangement of tempo-rally scattered events into their one, true, eternal design), a penitential act (the painful recollection of old errors), and an act of thanksgiving to God" for guidance and deliverance. When it serves the purposes of philosophi-cal self-exploration, however, *confession* becomes "no longer a revelation of the self to God, who already knows everything, but a revelation of the self to the self, an act of self-knowledge, a process of discovering the true meaning of one's life." The first of these autobiographical modes treats con-version as an achievement of the past, but in the second, conversion marks only the beginning of a continuous process to be worked out through the medium of the autobiography itself (32, 5, 4).

Clearly church Evidences participate, and that only partially, in the first of these categories, historical self-recollection. Their authors are tremu-lous, hopeful recent converts facing a panel of judges in a matter believed to be of the greatest importance. The writer of autobiography, on the other hand, is at once both the agitated protagonist and the enlightened nar-rator, both "the recreated self of the past (the protagonist) and the authorial self of the present (the narrator-teacher)." The shift from a profession of achieved knowledge to a mode of inquiry coincides with an adjustment of audience from a church gathering and purpose to interview with the self over time. Self-writing thus moves from putting forward a static model of truth to recording "the dynamic process of experience through which the truth becomes known" (Spengemann 4, 6, 44; Newey 195).

In related distinctions, Mason Lowance contrasts life-reckoning and life-chronicling (75), and William Matthews describes two modes of seven-teenth-century autobiography, the first an instrument of religious witness, the second a private record (3–4). Shepard's own *Autobiography* follows the second term in these pairs, not so much recording divine intervention in human affairs as expressing human personality, while Shepard's *Journal* is very much a life-reckoning, literally a day-by-day accounting of spiritual "considerations" between November 1640 and March 1644. Both the *Jour-nal* with all its immediacy and the *Autobiography* with all its retrospec-tion are the only documents of their kind known to have survived from this earliest Puritan era. Shepard's *Autobiography,* addressed to his son and running to thirty-eight pages in its modern edition, clearly looks forward to the genre as we know it, with a self-conscious narrator selecting and editing materials from a much larger time frame, providing a shaped narrative with double attitudes and points of view that reveal an interior self as well as external events, and participating in a tension between the cultural paradigm and a recalcitrant human and natural self. Although Shepard has much to say of his spiritual history, vacillations, beneficial ministries and tests, fears and stubborn resistances, he also provides copious details and assessments and opinions about his education, career, marriage, travel, society, individuals, housing, geography, history, politics, and feelings. He is clearly a theologically learned and pious man, but his autobiography nonetheless teems with life and fully credited external realities.

Full-scale autobiography, like Shepard's, embraces a very different didactics from those of church Evidences, most often targeting an audience of the author's children or comparably conceptualized parishioners. This longer autobiography functions not just as confession, but as epistle, chronicle, catharsis, devotion, and propaganda. Its pious content translates sinful beginnings into an exemplary life, and thus into a memorial stimulus and guidebook. It both expresses a personal retrospective exercise and provides an instrument for others to use in their spiritual and memory exercises (Shea 111–12). Such self-study projects exemplary personal history as what U. Milo Kaufmann calls "parabolic drama," that is, the elevation of individual history into public parable (83).

These earliest examples of American personal history both do and do not anticipate the larger genre they precede. The life writings Shepard collected of others do not yet embrace autobiography's full possibilities, but they do construct the frames by means of which progressive self-study, structured interpretation of one's own life, and participation in temporal continuity can proceed toward a celebration of individuation and the extraordinary self. Church Evidences take the initial but transforming step of translating one's own life into a text, of stabilizing the flux of experience within verbal containers. They have not yet developed the key attitudes toward the self and the audience that will allow for narrative shaping and authorial inquiry and growth. But at the most basic level, church Evidences can offer a discourse for inscribing and then, as Brother Crackbone's wife may have discovered, for freeing the self.

NOTES

1   Six additional but later Confessions from Shepard's Cambridge church — only one by a woman (Mrs. Wigglesworth) — occur at the end of *The Diary of Michael Wigglesworth*. The two dozen church Relations in *The Notebook of the*

Reverend John Fiske, 1644–1675 also do not provide comparable evidence for the present purposes. Fiske's Wenham church grows through transfers from other congregations — hence second Relations — and by the addition of numerous children of members, but while the earlier Narrations (1644–48) are preponderantly by women, by 1656 the church has formalized the practice of a male officer delivering women's Narrations for them (106).

2 Hambrick-Stowe 93–94, 103–4, 136; Walzer 223; Nuttall viii; and similarly Morgan 34–35, 88–93. Hambrick-Stowe (86–90) discusses Shepard's *Confessions*. Shepard defines church membership as cleaving to Christ through faith and as cleaving to one another through brotherly love strengthened and confirmed by a solemn covenant (*Works* I 350).

3 Morgan 41–43, 113; Caldwell 72, 67–68; Watkins 37, 51; Damrosch 21. The term "saints" has its backgrounds in the invocations of Pauline epistles. Romans 1.7, for example, addresses "All that be in Rome, beloved of God, called to be saints," and similarly 1 Corinthians 1.2 calls upon "them that are sanctified in Christ Jesus, called to be saints." For "saints" in references to community and agents of good works see also Rom. 12.13, 1 Cor. 16.15, 2 Cor. 8.4, 1 Tim. 5.10, and Eph. 1.18, 2.19, and 14.12. Such passages also background the Puritan word *calling*.

4 Bradstreet 167. On Puritanism as containing a women's movement, see Hambrick-Stowe 47–48, 140.

5 Morgan 66, detailed 91; Ebner 48. Starr in *Defoe and Spiritual Autobiography* lays down a general law for spiritual autobiographies: "The greater attention paid to events before conversion, the less emphasis given to what happens afterwards, and vice versa" (46–47).

6 Damrosch 39, 24; Leverenz 109. McGiffert speaks of the great Puritan paradox of balancing anxiety and assurance: "The sound believer could measure his assurance by his anxiety: the less assured he felt, the more assurance he actually had" (in Shepard, *God's Plot* 19–20). On Puritan conflicting selves, see Damrosch 24–25, 36–37. Hambrick-Stowe backgrounds the issue in *The Practice of Piety:* "In Puritan theology the word 'ordinarily' carried a stronger meaning than modern usage conveys, for the Puritans believed that since the close of the apostolic age God had ceased to work in 'extraordinary' ways. He continued to work in remarkable ways (and the recording of one's 'own remarkable providences' was an important part of Puritan devotion), but not in extraordinary ways that defied the order of nature" (95–96).

7 Shepard, *Works* I 116–17. In the Introduction to Shepard's *Confessions,* Selement and Woolley schematize and discuss what they call his "intricate ideas on conversion" based not just on *The Sound Believer* but all of his sermons (14–18).

8 The male median is 65.5 lines, the female 46.5. The longest male story is 220, the longest female 128. Eight male testimonies run to more than 100 lines, as do two female ones. The briefest male story is 12 lines, the briefest female is 6 lines.

9 This branch of feminist theory is represented by the work of Jean Baker Miller, Nancy Chodorow, Carol Gilligan, and Mary Field Belenky, *et al.* In an interesting analogue, Juster's study of nineteenth-century Evangelical narrations

finds women portraying God as a family member, close friend, lover, or concerned loving parent (40–41) and men portraying God in terms of legislation,
legal proceedings, government, and contracts, always with emphasis on reason and justice. She finds love and its betrayal the key to female evaluation
and finds sin for them attaching to failed or flawed relationships, while her
men understand religious authority to attach to abstract systems and rules (50).
Overall, Juster discovers "the enfeebling selflessness of women, and the over-
bearing selfishness of men in the unregenerate state," with their religion encouraging men to cast off the excess baggage of self that encumbers their search
for salvation, and encouraging women to reduce their dependence on friends
and family and enlarge their sense of self (56–57).

10   The example Caldwell takes as her norm of the genre, *The Experiences of
God's Gracious Dealing with Mrs. Elizabeth White,* develops a full narrative
line with relatively temperate proportions of texts and sermon debts to be paid.
Because White's narration, first published half a century later and running
to fourteen printed pages of Confession followed by five pages of Profession,
far exceeds the Shepard samples in size and is probably of English rather than
American origin, it does not share the genre of Shepard's *Confessions.* Instead,
it outlines some larger prospects that the form was to go on to realize, especially in its subtext translating the biological stages of White's life as a woman
—her girlhood, marriage, pregnancy, "delivery," nursing and weaning—into
a female parable or extended metaphor. A late dream forecasts her death from
childbirth—accurately as it turned out. Caldwell finds in White's narrative
generally orthodox Puritan doctrine, but also "a mood, an atmosphere, a complex of feelings, an undercurrent of desire." White accepts the New Testament
injunction to become as little children in order to enter the kingdom of heaven,
and generally leaves behind energetic, urgent involvement in favor of the otherworldly, the resigned, and the melancholy. She also leaves behind verbs of action in favor of verbs of perception and leaves behind too "a condition of
doing" in favor of "a condition of being or abiding." Clearly, White's telling
of her story is longer, more fully structured, and more strikingly and provoca-
tively concluded than the norms of the church Narrations of our sample (Caldwell 8, 23, 24, 17, 28). On White as British not American, see Hambrick-
Stowe 5 n. 2.

11   Nathaniel Eaton offers an explicit contrast with Dunster among Shepard's
Evidences. Although he is also a teacher and deeply learned, and was Dunster's
predecessor as head of Harvard College, his testimony stays well within the
self-denying norms of the genre. By standards other than the rhetorical, however, Dunster emerges as the better man, for Eaton had to be dismissed from
his Harvard post for cruelty to students, for avariciousness, and "other wan-
tonness" (123). Shepard's *Autobiography* speaks of Eaton as "professing eminently yet falsely and most deceitfully the fear of God" and of Dunster as "a
man pious, painful, and fit to teach, and very fit to lay the foundations of
the domestical affairs of the college, whom God hath much honored and
blessed" (*God's Plot* 68).

WORKS CITED

Belenky, Mary Field, Blythe McVicker Clinchy, Nancy Rule Goldberger, and Jill
    Mattuck Tarule, *Women's Ways of Knowing: The Development of Self, Voice
    and Mind.* New York: Basic Books, 1986.
Bradstreet, Anne. *Complete Works of Anne Bradstreet.* Ed. Joseph R. McElrath,
    Jr., and Allan P. Robb. Boston: Twayne Publishers, 1981.
Bunyan, John. *The Miscellaneous Works of John Bunyan.* 13 vols. Gen. ed. Roger
    Sharrock. Oxford: Clarendon Press, 1976–.
Bunyan, John. *The Works of John Bunyan.* 3 vols. Ed. George Offor. Glasgow:
    Blackie and Son, 1853.
Caldwell, Patricia. *The Puritan Conversion Narrative: The Beginnings of Ameri-
    can Expression.* Cambridge: Cambridge University Press, 1983.
Carlton, Peter J. "Bunyan: Language, Convention, Authority." *English Literary
    History,* 51, (1984), 17–32.
Carroll, Peter N. *Puritanism and the Wilderness: The Intellectual Significance of
    the New England Frontier, 1629–1700.* New York: Columbia University Press,
    1969.
Chodorow, Nancy. *The Reproduction of Mothering.* Berkeley: University of Cali-
    fornia Press, 1978.
Cohen, Charles L. *God's Caress: The Psychology of Puritan Religious Experience.*
    New York: Oxford University Press, 1986.
Damrosch, Leopold, Jr. *God's Plot and Man's Stories: Studies in the Fictional Imagi-
    nation from Milton to Fielding.* Chicago: University of Chicago Press, 1985.
Ebner, Dean. *Autobiography in Seventeenth-Century England.* The Hague: Mouton,
    1971.
Fiske, John. *The Notebook of the Reverend John Fiske, 1644–1675.* Ed. Robert G.
    Pope. Publications of the Colonial Society of Massachusetts, 47. Boston: The
    Society, 1974.
Gilligan, Carol. *In a Different Voice: Psychological Theory and Women's Develop-
    ment.* Cambridge: Harvard University Press, 1982.
Haller, William. *The Rise of Puritanism, Or, the Way to the New Jerusalem as
    Set Forth in Pulpit and Press from Thomas Cartwright to John Lilburne and
    John Milton, 1570–1643.* Reprint. New York: Harper Torchbooks, 1957.
Hambrick-Stowe, Charles E. *The Practice of Piety: Puritan Devotional Disciplines
    in Seventeenth-Century New England.* Chapel Hill: University of North Caro-
    lina Press, 1982.
Hunter, J. Paul. *The Reluctant Pilgrim: Defoe's Emblematic Method and Quest for
    Form in Robinson Crusoe.* Baltimore: Johns Hopkins University Press, 1966.
Juster, Susan. "'In a Different Voice': Male and Female Narratives of Religious Conver-
    sion in Post-Revolutionary America." *American Quarterly,* 41 (1989), 34–62.
Kaufmann, U. Milo. *The Pilgrim's Progress and Traditions in Puritan Meditation.*
    New Haven: Yale University Press, 1966.
Keeble, N. H. *The Literary Culture of Nonconformity in Later Seventeenth-Century
    England.* Leicester: Leicester University Press, 1987.

Leverenz, David. *The Language of Puritan Feeling: An Exploration in Literature, Psychology, and Social History.* New Brunswick: Rutgers University Press, 1980.

Lowance, Mason I. "Biography and Autobiography." *Columbia Literary History of the United States,* gen. ed. Emory Elliott, 67–82. New York: Columbia University Press, 1988.

Matthews, William. "Seventeenth-Century Autobiography." In *Autobiography, Biography, and the Novel: Papers Read at a Clark Library Seminar,* by William Matthews and Ralph W. Rader. Los Angeles: William Andrews Clark Memorial Library, 1973.

Miller, Jean Baker. *Toward a New Psychology of Women.* Boston: Beacon Press, 1976.

Morgan, Edmund S. *Visible Saints: The History of a Puritan Idea.* New York: New York University Press, 1963.

Newey, Vincent. "'With the Eyes of my understanding': Bunyan, Experience, and Acts of Interpretation." In *John Bunyan: Conventicle and Parnassus: Tercentenary Essays,* ed. N. H. Keeble, 189–216. Oxford: Clarendon Press, 1988.

Nuttall, Geoffrey. *Visible Saints: The Congregational Way, 1640–1660.* Oxford: Basil Blackwell, 1957.

Schucking, Levin L. *The Puritan Family: A Social Study from the Literary Sources.* London: Routledge and Kegan Paul, 1969.

Shea, Daniel B., Jr. *Spiritual Autobiography in Early America.* Princeton: Princeton University Press, 1968.

Shepard, Thomas. *God's Plot: The Paradoxes of Puritan Piety, Being the Autobiography and Journal of Thomas Shepard.* Ed. Michael McGiffert. Amherst: University of Massachusetts Press, 1972.

Shepard, Thomas. *Thomas Shepard's Confessions.* Ed. George Selement and Bruce C. Woolley. Publications of the Colonial Society of Massachusetts Collections, 58. Boston: The Society, 1981.

Shepard, Thomas. *The Works of Thomas Shepard.* 3 vols. Boston: Doctrinal Tract and Book Society, 1853.

Simpson, Alan. *Puritanism in Old and New England.* Chicago: University of Chicago Press, 1955.

Spengemann, William C. *The Forms of Autobiography: Episodes in the History of a Literary Genre.* New Haven: Yale University Press, 1980.

Starr, G. A. *Defoe and Spiritual Autobiography.* Princeton: Princeton University Press, 1965.

Walzer, Michael. *The Revolution of the Saints: A Study in the Origins of Radical Politics.* Cambridge: Harvard University Press, 1965.

Watkins, Owen C. *The Puritan Experience.* London: Routledge and Kegan Paul, 1972.

Webber, Joan. *The Eloquent "I": Style and Self in Seventeenth-Century Prose.* Madison: University of Wisconsin Press, 1968.

Wigglesworth, Michael. *The Diary of Michael Wigglesworth, 1653–1657: The Conscience of a Puritan.* Ed. Edmund S. Morgan. Reprint. New York: Harper Torchbooks, 1965.

CHAPTER 3

Self and God in the Early Published Memoirs of New England Women

ANN TAVES

Although it was not uncommon for Puritan New Englanders and their descendants[1] to write memoirs based on diaries, published memoirs of New England women do not begin to appear until the early national period. Edited by Congregationalist clergy and published by devout Congregationalist laymen after the women in question had died,[2] these early published memoirs highlight the importance of such volumes in the eyes of the clergy and the key role which religion played both in the emergence of women's autobiography and in the definition of the exemplary female life.

Of the five texts to be discussed here, only one, *The Memoirs of Mrs. Abigail Bailey* (1815), is a full-length autobiographical memoir. Two of the others, *The Memoirs of the Life of Mrs. Sarah Osborn* (1799) and *The Life and Character of Miss Susanna Anthony* (1796), include autobiographical memoirs along with substantial extracts from the women's diaries and correspondence. The *Writings of Miss Fanny Woodbury* (Emerson, ed., 1815) and the *Memoirs of Mrs. Harriet Newell* (Woods, ed., 1814) include biographical memoirs and extensive "extracts" from the women's diaries and correspondence.

Although the ministers who edited the volumes were not all of the same generation, they and the laymen who published them were all heirs of Jonathan Edwards and, like him, tended toward a more evangelical or outwardly oriented and active form of Congregationalism which emphasized the importance of revivals of religion among baptized New Englanders and missionary work among the "heathen" at home and abroad.[3] Given the common theological orientation and interests of the editors and publishers, it is not surprising that the women shared a similar religious outlook. Their lives, however, differed markedly from one another. Sarah Osborn

57

(b. 1711), Susanna Anthony (b. 1726), and Abigail Abbot Bailey (b. 1746) lived most if not all of their lives during the eighteenth century; Anthony and Osborn lived in the relatively cosmopolitan city of Newport, Rhode Island, and Bailey in isolated towns on the northern New England frontier. Fanny Woodbury (b. 1791) and Harriet Atwood Newell (b. 1793) were contemporaries and friends; both lived in small towns in northeastern Massachusetts, attended Bradford Academy as teenagers, and died young.

These writings clearly demonstrate the growing importance of female friendship and the empowering character of evangelicalism in creating expanded opportunities for women. Sarah Osborn founded "a religious, female society" in 1741[4] which Susanna Anthony joined at the age of sixteen. The friendship and support of women in the women's society and particularly the close friendship between Anthony and Osborn were extremely important to both. Samuel Hopkins, the well-known Congregationalist theologian and minister who edited the writings of both Anthony and Osborn, said of the latter:

She had a number of intimate friends, with whom she conversed with great openness, freedom and pleasure, finding, on acquaintance, that she could safely rely on their candor, friendship, prudence, and fidelity. Among these Miss Susa Anthony, whose life has lately been published, was the first, and her greatest intimate, whom she highly esteemed and loved, as an eminent christian, of uncommon discerning and judgment; and whom she found to be a most faithful, prudent friend, at all times. There was a distinguished and eminently christian and happy friendship enjoyed and cultivated between them, for about fifty years, without any interruption, and to their great mutual comfort and helpfulness.—They were truly, and in a distinguished degree, of one heart and one soul, and during the whole time loved each other with a pure heart, fervently. It is not known or believed that there is to be found, or has been in the century such a union and happy christian friendship between two such eminent christians, for so long a time, as took place in this instance. (Osborn 371–72)

Female friendship played a critical role in the lives of the other three women as well. Abigail Bailey's devout relatives and her church friends (mostly women) played an important role in helping her to get out of her marriage to an abusive husband (Taves 19–24). Fanny Woodbury and Harriet Atwood met at Bradford Academy, and their correspondence with their many school friends makes up much of their respective published writings.

Evangelicalism not only provided the opportunity for these women to gather within female societies and academies, it also called some of them to take on new "unfeminine" roles. Sarah Osborn's role in the Newport revival of 1766–67 was highly unusual, and the large meetings in her home provoked criticism that she was stepping "beyond [her] line." Tavern keepers looked askance on Abigail Bailey when she broke with custom by traveling the 270 miles from New York to New Hampshire alone. While most of Harriet Atwood's friends encouraged her to marry Samuel Newell, others questioned her motives in becoming one of the first Protestant missionaries' wives sent overseas.

In one of the few studies of the memoirs of devout Protestant women, Joanna Gillespie argues that such writing "was important in the creation of women's emerging autonomy" (199). Susan Juster comes to a similar conclusion in a recent study of published conversion narratives. Drawing on Carol Gilligan's theory of female development, she argues that the "experience of grace [in conversion] implicitly strengthened women's sense of autonomy and moral agency" and "empowered [them] by [enabling them to] recover[] their sense of self through the assertion of independence from others" (53). The emphasis on autonomy and independence in these studies obscures the contradictions implicit in a form of empowerment explicitly grounded in subordination to and dependence on God. Within the Puritan tradition the self that was empowered was a self-in-relation-with-God, not a modern "autonomous" self.

Moreover, for the Puritans and their heirs, the relationship of the self to God was problematic. As a result of original sin humans were not, in their view, simply born into a relationship with God. The self in its "natural" form was typically characterized as "selfish" and "willful" and believed to be inherently antagonistic toward God. Conversion was the process whereby the "natural" self was brought into a proper, that is, a subordinate and dependent, relationship with God. The self empowered in this religious system was thus, by definition, a self-denying self whose autonomy and agency were inseparably linked to the will of a God who empowered human beings so that they might serve *his* purposes. This complex notion of the self, with its paradoxical relationship between explicit self-denial and implicit self-assertion or individualism, infused Puritan and later Congregationalist autobiography.[5] Given this understanding of the self, any discussion of the autonomy, independence, or empowerment of women in this tradition must begin with the recognition that their lives were shaped, undergirded, and bounded by a socially constructed reading of God's will.

The way these women interpreted their emotional responses to two important life circumstances — affliction and the narrow range of religious opportunities open to them as women — provides a means of examining the relationship between these women's sense of self and their understanding of God's will. Affliction was an old issue for New Englanders and one which elicited fairly predictable responses from the devout. Nonetheless in the face of unusual afflictions, such as the domestic violence experienced by Abigail Bailey, discernment of God's will could become a major preoccupation. The desire of some of these women for "usefulness" beyond the role of wife and mother was a newer issue. With few approved precedents for such involvement, such desires generated considerable anxiety and, as in the case of unusual afflictions, the discernment of God's will was a major issue.

While a general understanding of God's will for humanity could be presumed by a devout believer, the determination of God's will in new or unusual situations was fraught with complexity. The process of discernment (or interpretation), and following that the attempt to live in accordance with God's will as discerned, inevitably stood in some relation to cultural assumptions about God, the self, and the social order and played a pivotal role in either reproducing or transforming theologically grounded assumptions about where authority should be located and how the self and society ought to be structured. A focus on sociological aspects of the interpretative process suggests that changes in social relations during the early national period led to shifts in the social context of discernment with significant implications for women.

Affliction was an issue for each of the women under consideration here. Sarah Osborn was widowed early in life, and with a second husband who could not work, her financial situation was always precarious. Susanna Anthony, who never married and supported herself primarily as a seamstress, suffered from physical disabilities and internal conflicts. Fanny Woodbury also had health problems and suffered from a substantial loss of hearing from the time she was three. Harriet Atwood gave up family, friends, and home to follow her missionary husband overseas. Abigail Bailey was forced to dissolve her marriage and give up her home after she discovered that her husband was incestuously involved with one of their teenage daughters.

Although born somewhat later than either Osborn or Anthony, Abigail Abbot Bailey's life was in many ways more traditional than the others. Compared to Newport, Rhode Island, towns on the northern New England frontier were fairly homogeneous, and devout women, such as Abigail Bailey, could reasonably look forward to a life in which the ideologies and structures of family life were reinforced by the ideologies and structures of church and township in much the way they had been in the Puritan towns of Massachusetts a hundred years earlier.[6] Raised by devout parents, Abigail Abbot was converted at eighteen, and married at twenty-two to Asa Bailey, a socially respected yet emotionally volatile (and "unconverted") man. Asa began physically abusing Abigail within a month of their marriage, had an affair with one hired woman and attempted to rape another within the next decade, and, after twenty-one years of marriage and the birth of fourteen children, began sexually abusing their sixteen-year-old daughter Phebe. When the evidence of incest became undeniable, Abigail pressured her husband to divide their property and leave the state. Asa resisted her efforts, tricking her into traveling with him to New York State to sell their property. Realizing that she had been deceived, Abigail returned to New Hampshire on her own and, with considerable community support, used legal means to force her husband to make a settlement and leave town. After his departure she successfully obtained a divorce. Most of her memoir is devoted to determining and then acting upon God's will in the face of so startling an affliction.

Based on long-standing Puritan, and indeed Calvinist, tradition, Abigail Bailey knew that it was her duty to submit to any affliction which God might bring to pass in her life. Since God's action was seen in all events, it was assumed that God, not chance, was ultimately responsible for everything that occurred, and thus anything that occurred was in effect God's will. Submission, however, did not necessarily mean passive acceptance. First and foremost, it meant emotional acceptance of the *goodness* and *justice* of God's action. Beyond that it meant determining what response (whether active or passive) God would have the believer make to the affliction.

Initially, Abigail Bailey found it almost impossible to submit and accept the incest as the will of God. For some time, she says, she was unable to "obtain a comforting view that those unusual afflictions were in mercy, and not in judgment; for the rod seemed so severe." Finding it difficult to conform her will to the will of God, she compared her situation to that of those "who were mourning the loss of dear companions, or parents, and children" and concluded that "their little drops of grief would soon be lost in the more extensive flood of sorrow, in which [she] was overwhelmed." During this period, Bailey confesses that she was "tempted to . . . abandon [her]self to grief." She states that at times her grief so overwhelmed her that she thought her "distress must soon finish [her] days, and bring [her] down with sorrow to the grave" (Taves 73–74).

Eventually, however, she began "to suppress, as far as possible, the anguish under which [her] heart was tortured and broken." Feeling that she "ought to obey the voice of the Most High," she told herself that "God kn[e]w best what [she] need[ed], and what will be for his own glory." Concluding that "it was not for [her] to say what trouble God should send" and "that it was as much [her] duty to submit to God under one trial as under another," she "quieted [her]self as a weaned child." Thus calming herself, she was able to "cast [her] burdens on the Lord" and receive sustenance from him. With this, her whole outlook was transformed; where initially she had doubted God's mercy, she "now thought God dealt mercifully with [her], in sustaining and comforting her under [her] affliction."

This is one of the most immediate descriptions of the process of submitting to affliction in these memoirs. Similar descriptions written by Congregationalist women whose family members or friends have just died can be found in unpublished letters and diaries of the period. Thus, for example, Sarah Prince wrote on April 21, 1758, soon after the death of her friend, Esther Edwards Burr:

God in Holy but awfull severity has Again struck at one of My Principle springs of Earthly Comfort. . . . This is the heaviest Affliction next to the Death of My dear Sister *Mercy* I ever met with. . . . My Earthly joy is gone! Not only so but My God hides his Face! Can't see Love in this dispensation! All seems anger yea Wrath to me! What shall I do. Whither shall I turn, Not to Creatures for there is none to comfort me! And I do not find Comfort from God—O Wretched Me. God Points his Arrows at me and I'm ready to say My Way is hid from the Lord. My judgment is passed over from My God and that he has set me as a Mark for his Arrows! I'm ready to sink and I cant find my wonted Comfort! O how shall I drag thro' Life—If God supports not, I shall inevitably sink. (Karlsen and Crumpacker 307–8)

While Sarah Prince describes herself as sinking under the weight of her affliction, Esther Burr, writing on November 2, 1757, after the death of one of her children, emphasized the comfort she ultimately obtained through submission.

I was innabled to Resighn the Ch[ild] (after a severe strugle with Nature) with the gre[at]est freedom—God shewed me that the Child w[as] not my own but His, and that he had a right to recall what he had lent when ever he thought fit, and I had no reason to complain or say God was hard with me. This silenced me. But O how good is God! He not only kept me from complaining but comforted me by ennabling me to offer up the Child by Faith. (295)

The grieving process, as recounted by these women, took on a particular form. Each went through an initial period in which their emotions were unchecked. During this period, they internalized responsibility for their loss, struggling all the while with what theologians have referred to as the problem of theodicy, that is, with the question of how a good, just, and merciful God could allow them to be afflicted. In their grief they allowed themselves to question the justice of God's action and to doubt whether God was in fact as merciful and just as they had been taught that he was.

Their doubts and complaints often left them feeling isolated and without support. Although Abigail Bailey was "in the habit of flying to God in trouble," she was initially "left . . . for a season to mourn in darkness [without] . . . those comforting views of the light of God's countenance, which at other times God had graciously afforded for [her] support" (Taves 74). The sense that she could not survive without God's support is apparent in her fear that her distress would bring her to her grave. Likewise Sarah Prince found no comfort anywhere during the initial period of mourning, and isolated on all sides, she felt that she would "inevitably sink" without God's support. After her husband died, Esther Burr indicates that had God not enabled her "to follow him beyound the Grave into the Eternal World [in a vision] and there [to view] him in unspeakable glory and happyness freed from all sin and sorrow," she would have "long before this have been sunk amongst the dead and covered with the Clods of the vally" (Karlsen and Crumpacker 300).

The comfort and sense of communion with God that these women craved came with the "silencing" or "suppression" of their feelings of anguish and despair. This act of submission was fraught with presuppositions. In Abigail Bailey's case, the suppression of her anguish was linked to an acknowledgment that God knew "best what she needed," and this in turn implied that in questioning God's wisdom she had taken on authority which was not rightly hers. Allowing her anguish to overwhelm her was thus an act of insubordination relative to God. In submitting to God by acknowledging that he knew what was best for her, she submitted her will to God's, relinquished the authority she had (wrongly) assumed, and accepted her place as God's "child." Esther Burr was able to silence her complaints against God when she was reminded that her child was not her own, but God's, and thus that her complaints were "unreasonable." Although she assumed that her inability to resign herself to her child's death was natural, since humans often desired things that were not their own, its naturalness did not make it any less selfish or sinful.

Fanny Woodbury's writings suggest an ongoing struggle for submission of a somewhat different sort. In her journal entry for October 3, 1807, she acknowledges that she was "easily susceptible of that hateful, that detestable sin, anger." Though she "abhor[red] it, yet it remain[ed] in [her] depraved heart" (Emerson 15). The cause of her anger may well have been her hearing loss, an affliction which she refers to repeatedly in her diary and which she found especially hard to bear during church services. In one particularly revealing entry she wrote:

While my dear friends are assembled in the house of God, to hear glorious and animating truths, I am denied the precious privilege, "while I am hungry for the bread of life." But thus it is. *God knows I need affliction* [emphasis added]; and he has therefore touched me in a tender part. But I feel it most acutely, when present in the house of prayer. There I often sit as a mere spectator—not a word for me, while others are fed and nourished. But I would not complain. (15; see also 13–14, 25, 45)

Here her anger, resentment, and self-pity are only lightly veiled. The volatility of her emotions undoubtedly contributed to her feelings of sinfulness and thus in turn helped to convince her that she deserved further affliction. During the hours she spent in private prayer she examined her feelings and used her writing as a means of transforming, or at least suppressing, her anger, internalizing the idea that she "needed" affliction and should not complain, and in the end accepting her deafness as God's will.

In each of these cases, the women understood their affliction as "willed" by God and their duty as one of submission to God's will. In each case this involved putting aside strong feelings of grief, anger, or resentment in the face of God's superior "reason" and "wisdom." In a book entitled *Welcome to Affliction,* Samuel Shaw, an English Puritan minister, acknowledged that such feelings (or "passions") were particularly hard to resist in the midst of affliction. Indeed, he says, the tendency "to indulge our own private and selfish passions, care, fear, sorrow, complaining, &c. is [particularly marked] when the afflicting hand of God is upon us, pressing and grieving us, and taking our beloved comforts from us." At those times, he says, we willingly "suffer ourselves to be carried down the stream of our own passions, which at other times we should think it our duty to resist" (42).

To resist such passionate feelings was to resist sin and simultaneously to internalize basic structuring assumptions about the nature of the self and God and the proper relationship between the two. To submit within this theological system was to accept the idea that God is good and just as well as omnipotent (and thus the ultimate source of all affliction). These ideas cohered logically only if individuals concluded that they in some sense deserved to be afflicted. This set of ideas was frequently translated into an image of God as a divine "father" who simultaneously "afflicted" and "comforted" his devout "children."[7] In her reaction to her twelve-year-old son's death, an event in which she saw "No[thing], but the kind chastisement of [her] indulgent Father," Sarah Osborn brings out the paternal metaphor underlying this conception of God quite explicitly. Her feelings about her son's death were calmed, she says, by the Scripture passage that insisted that "without chastisement, . . . then are ye bastards, and not sons. For whom the Lord loveth, he chasteneth" (68–69).

The primary model for understanding affliction was thus a domestic one in which affliction was understood as chastisement by a father and thus as a sign of love. Use of this model emphasized the idea that affliction was the result of wrongdoing (sin) and that the role of humans vis-à-vis God was that of children submitting to patriarchal authority. The price of comfort and communion in the patriarchal family of God was subordination of the self to God the father, and more specifically the subordination of one's rebellious feelings to the conviction that God knows best what is good for the human family as a whole.

As Stephanie Coontz points out, this idea of subordination structured virtually all relationships in colonial New England.

Patriarchy led to a social acceptance of inequality and rank that extended far beyond relations between father and child or husband and wife. Servants deferred to masters and masters deferred to their social superiors with words that emphasized their humility, their weakness, their unworthiness. Greater men condescended to less, with no sense on either side that this was insulting. (80)

While God was at the head of this system, people were expected to relate to God in much the same way that they were to relate to others above them in the social hierarchy. God, in other words, was conceptualized anthropomorphically as the ultimate lord and master in a hierarchical social order.

This meant that relative to God, women and men were in the same dependent and subordinate position; while, relative to their wives, husbands, like God, could expect deference and submission. The congruence between the role of God with respect to his people and the male head of a household with respect to his family meant that while men and women were spiritually equal, their social roles were not. Like God, men were presumed to act in the best interests of their family as a whole. Wives were expected to contribute to the overall good of the family by being helpmeets, companions, and alter egos to their husbands. "Godly men," in the words of Carol Karlsen, "needed wives who were faithful and loyal; who assisted them in their piety, in their vocations, and in the government of their families; who revered them and acknowledged them as 'Lord'" (164–65). In Puritan New England, "women who failed to serve men failed to serve God. To be numbered among God's elected, women had to acknowledge this service as their calling and *believe* they were created for this purpose" (166).

The passions (emotions) were expected to relate to the soul (reason) in much the same way wives were expected to relate to husbands. As Shaw points out, "passions" were not believed to be sinful in and of themselves. They became sinful only when a "willful" soul "fix[ed] upon and cherish[ed]" them (108). Thus, just as socially wives were to be subordinated to husbands who were subordinated to God, so psychologically the passions were to be subordinated to souls which were subordinated to God. Thus, all relationships whether psychological or social were arranged in hierarchical patterns of domination and subordination and undergirded by theological beliefs which associated this sort of arrangement with an understanding of the "common good" to which, and in keeping with the overall pattern, it was believed the needs and desires of the individual must be subordinated.

The fact that the entire system revolved around not "the needs of the individual but the requirements of church or community" did not preclude what we might view as considerable independence or autonomy on the part of women (Coontz 84–85). It did mean, however, that such independence was not the point in and of itself, but rather a by-product of circumstances, in many cases circumstances (i.e., afflictions) involving the male head of the household. Because her first husband was lost at sea and her second husband was unable to work, Sarah Osborn broke with convention by supporting herself and her husband by teaching school for about forty years. She apparently felt some shame in this regard, but predictably saw God's hand at work in her affliction. Thus, she reflects:

I have often thought that God has so ordered it through out my days hitherto, that I should be in an afflicted, low condition, as to worldly circumstances, and inclined the hearts of others to relieve me in all my distresses, on purpose to suppress that pride of my nature, which doubtless would have been acted out greatly to his dishonor, had I enjoyed good health, and had prosperity, so as to live independent of others. (55)

It is significant to note, given the modern propensity to see work outside the home as a sign of female independence or autonomy, that Osborn herself did not see it this way. Good health and prosperity in the form of a working husband would have allowed her to "live *independent* of others," while poor health and her husband's inability to work forced her to depend on others for her support. In his commentary on her writing, Samuel Hopkins sees her "high taste for a genteel independent way of living" and her "aversion to . . . poverty and dependence" as the sin or character flaw which her affliction was designed to correct. Thus, he says:

God was pleased to order things so in his providence respecting her, as most effectually to cross and mortify this strong propensity; which was the occasion of much pain, hard struggles and sore conflicts, until she was brought to a settled and abiding submission, and constant acquiescence in the will of God, in ordering and fixing her outward circumstances; in consequence of which she enjoyed great and constant calmness and serenity of mind the last twenty years of her life, when she was brought to such poverty as to have nothing of her own on which she could live, and was wholly dependent on others for daily support; and yet wanted nothing, in a happy contentment with her lot. (55–56)

Abigail Bailey's situation was similar in many ways. In the wake of the incest, she became by modern standards far more autonomous; she learned to stand up to her husband's anger, to make judgments independent of her husband, and in the end thwarted his plans for preserving their marriage and obtained a divorce by undertaking a 270-mile journey on her own. Nonetheless, like Osborn, Bailey portrayed her ability to separate from her husband as the result of her increasing *dependence* on God (Taves 19–24).

Bailey was not eager to do without a husband and explicitly states her desire for one whom she can depend on as "a head, a kind friend, a comforter, a guide, to protect us from the thousand evils, to which we were exposed." But given her belief that to stay with a husband who clearly had not reformed would be contrary to God's will, she chose to end her marriage and rely on God for support. As she described it:

I hoped God would provide for us; and that he would enable me to take heed to choose suffering rather than sin; and to cast my burden on the Lord, and trust in him, who has ever shewn the most tender care for the widow, the fatherless, and such as have no helper. (100)

To give in to her need for a husband was, in her eyes, to give in to sin; to depend on God was to suffer (and become independent of her husband). The fact that she had a choice, given Asa's relentless attempts to preserve their marriage, meant that she was constantly tempted to choose sin over suffering. As she indicates late in the memoirs, she "was sure [that 'the fear of *dishonoring God*' by staying too long with her husband] had been among [her] greatest trials and fears" (163).

Although Sarah Osborn and Abigail Bailey were both able to break with the conventional behaviors expected of women, especially in their roles as wives and mothers, and thus, from a contemporary viewpoint, able to demonstrate considerable autonomy and independence, *they* emphasized their increasing *dependence* on God and people other than their husbands and saw that dependence as a virtue. Moreover, neither enjoyed breaking with convention and each implied that it was only through God's help that she was able to overcome the difficulties involved in doing so. In both cases their increased autonomy was an *unintended* and largely unrecognized (because unvalued) consequence of remaining faithful to God's will in the midst of affliction. As such it was much like the role of the "deputy husband" in colonial New England, a role open to women when their husbands were absent or otherwise incapacitated. This role flexibility, far from undermining women's basic position of subordination, was possible, according to Laurel Thatcher Ulrich, only because of the very strength of patriarchal institutions (Ulrich 37; Coontz 98–102).

Alongside the recurrent theme of affliction lay the more unusual problem of women's desire for new fields of "usefulness." Susanna Anthony wrote that after her conversion she "felt some disposition to study what [she]

could render to the Lord for all his benefits." The most conventional of
the women searching for new ways to serve God, she decided to "devote
[her]self to the service of the sanctuary." Despite this rather modest aim,
she "soon found great conflicts; and it [was] suggested to [her] mind, that
[she] should never have any rest, so long as [she] persisted in this way."
She did persist, but when the conflicts became extremely strong, she began
to fear that it was the "pride and naughtiness of [her] heart" that led her
on. Only after communicating her fears to a "particular friend" was she
reassured that these conflicts were from "the invisible tempter, who hates
prayer," rather than an indication from God that she had taken on too much
(10–11).

Sarah Osborn and Harriet Atwood longed for larger opportunities as
well. After the evangelist Gilbert Tennant visited Newport, Sarah Osborn's
"longings to be made useful in the world returned, and [she] earnestly
pleaded with God that he would not suffer [her] to live any longer an unprofitable servant; but would point out some way, in which [she] might
be useful." It was, she believed, in response to these prayers that the "young
women, who were awakened to a concern for their souls, came to [her],
and desired [her] advice and assistance, and proposed to join in a society,
provided [she] would take care of them" (49–50).

After reading "Law's Serious Call to a holy life," Harriet Atwood concluded that she was "as much obligated to yield [her]self a willing soldier
to Christ . . . as he who ministers at the altar, and performs the office of
preacher." Clearly in anguish, she asked: "Why then, am I not employed
in his service? Why stand I here *idle,* all the day?" (Woods 66). Given her
longing to do something, Samuel Newell's "long dreaded" letter asking her
to leave her family, friends, and homeland to help him promote "the gospel
among the heathen" threw her into an agony of indecision. But, as she
wrote a friend, "at length from a firm persuasion of duty, and a willingness
to comply, after much examination and prayer, I answered in the affirmative" (80–81).

Sarah Osborn and Harriet Atwood moved into these new roles because
they felt that God asked it of them. Like Susanna Anthony, they agonized
over their motives with each step, wondering if it was truly God calling
them to new activities or only their own selfish desires. When she began
teaching again after her husband's bankruptcy, Osborn agonized over
whether or not she should lead her students in prayer at the beginning and
the end of the school day:

I am afraid of ostentation, afraid of doing any thing to be seen of men. I am afraid
of neglecting it, on account of what others will say or think, lest that should be
being ashamed of Christ and his ways, in this wicked generation; and yet, I am

afraid of bringing religion into contempt. O Lord, direct me to do, in this case, as will most consist with thy glory. (62)

Similarly, Hopkins indicates that when "numbers [of people began] resorting to her house [during the revival of 1766–67], . . . she was at a great loss what to do."

She trembled with fear that if she encouraged their meeting at her house, it would be going beyond her sphere, offend some of her christian friends, and give occasion to some not friendly to religion, to speak evil of her and of religion, and so do much more hurt than good. On the other hand, she was afraid to discourage them, and refuse to let them come to her and meet at her house, when under apparent concern about their souls, lest, by this, their attention and concern should abate and cease. (77–78)

Harriet Atwood clearly *wanted* to accompany Samuel Newell to India. She wrote one friend that if she "could prevent distress from ever entering the heart of a widowed, beloved parent, and the dearest brothers and sisters, . . . [she] thought [she] could quit America without reluctance, and even *rejoice* to spend [her] life among the benighted heathen" (Woods 77). But she feared that Newell was displacing God in her affections and worried that she was "in great danger of being actuated by a strong attachment . . . and misled by earthly objects" (78). Indeed some of her friends "accuse[d her] of the love of novelty, of an invincible attachment to a fellow creature, of superstition and of wanting a great name" (89). In the end, in accordance with evangelical convention, she disavowed any selfish motives and emphasized the pain of leaving her "affectionate friends, [her] pleasant home, [her] much loved country" for a life of "self-denials, hardships, privations, and sorrows." Concluding that "this [was] the path, which [her] Heavenly Father ha[d] selected for [her], . . . an ardent desire for the salvation of the benighted Heathen, constrain[ed her] to cry, Here am I, Lord, sent me where thou wilt" (88–89).

Similarly, correspondence between Sarah Osborn and the Reverend Joseph Fish from the time of the revival suggests that he attempted to dissuade Osborn from her course. In the face of Fish's objections, as Mary Beth Norton points out, while Osborn "attempted to minimize both the importance of her role in the revival and its social implications, she was nevertheless tenacious in her refusal to abandon that role." Citing Osborn's statement that the nightly meetings "refresh[ed] and recruit[ed] and enliven[ed her] Exhausted spirits," Norton suggests that "behind these words one can discern a lifetime of drudgery, dutiful wifely submission, and feminine inconsequentiality suddenly transformed by God's miraculous will into a life of leadership, purpose, and social importance." When Osborn asks Fish if he would "advise [her] to shut up [her] Mouth and doors and creep into obscurity," her desire for a more visible and public life seems quite evident (Norton 520–21).

These memoirs make clear that ascertaining God's will was a complex interpretive process in which humans, texts (the Bible and other devotional books), and diary keeping all played critical roles. Abigail Bailey kept silent about her marital problems for many years. She took "refuge" in God and gave "vent to [her] private grief" in the pages of her diary. At its most concrete, "taking refuge in God" meant retiring for private prayer, reading the Bible, and meditative diary writing. This meant that for much of her married life, Bailey interpreted God's will with respect to her husband (as "revealed" in the biblical text) in isolation. The process was limited to an inner dialogue (prayer) between herself and God (via the Bible) as set down in her diaries. As she struggled to separate from her husband in the wake of the incest, the interpretive dialogue widened to include her relatives and friends at church. Although they distrusted her husband and felt she should use legal means to effect an immediate separation, she rejected their advice and attempted to obtain an informal settlement. After being deceived repeatedly by her husband, she finally concluded that "trusting in God implies the due use of all proper means" and that she "had greatly erred, in not having opened [her] mind more fully [to her 'familiar connexions'] and sought their advice in everything" (Taves 10, 20, 23).

The other women considered here were less isolated than Bailey, and the networks of family, friends, and ministers who participated with them in the interpretive process were more apparent from the start. Sarah Osborn talked to Reverend Clap about whether or not she should pray with her students, and "he rejoiced much in the proposal; and advised me, by all means to proceed, and let nothing discourage me, and fear no scoffs; for it was God's cause, and he who put it into my heart to do it, would take care of his own glory" (63). Likewise, when unsure whether or not to allow people to meet for instruction in her home during the revival, Osborn "advised with her christian friends, and some ministers; and upon their advising her to encourage them and attend to them, she granted them liberty to come" (77–78). Although some of Harriet Atwood's friends questioned her motives, most of them encouraged her to go. Probably most important, her "widowed, beloved" mother, after an initial period of resistance, released her to make her own decision, saying: "If a conviction of duty and love to the souls of the perishing heathen lead you to India, as much as I love you, Harriet, I can only say, *Go*" (Woods 79).

The memoirs of these women, comprised as they are of excerpts from a variety of types of documents including diary entries, letters, autobiographical reflections, and ministerial commentary, provide insight into the social process through which God's will was ascertained. Although the goal was to shape the self in accordance with God's will, the interactive way in which God's will was discerned meant that the process was not an idiosyncratic one. These women, in keeping with the religious tradition of which they were a part, were selves-in-relation, first of all, they would have said, in relation to God (but, I would add, a God understood communally) and second, in relation to other people. Virtually all these relationships, both with God and with other people, were structured hierarchically and took relationships of dependence and subordination for granted. Private devotions were an occasion for reflection on the self in its relation to God and often, through meditative writing, an occasion for bringing the "passions" into their proper subordinate relation to the soul and ultimately to the will of God.

These memoirs, thus, point to an underlying devotional process in which "desire" was scrutinized. Desires to evade the will of God were suppressed, and desires to conform to the will of God were encouraged. Neither Sarah Osborn nor Abigail Bailey wanted to take on the responsibilities of a "deputy husband," yet both felt that it was the will of God that they do so. There the tension between "selfish" desire and the will of God resulted in a struggle to subdue the "selfish" desires and eventual submission to the will of God. The desire for greater "usefulness" on the part of Susanna Anthony, Sarah Osborn, and Harriet Atwood was deemed in accordance with the will of God and therefore to be encouraged.

In each of these cases, the interactive, and often conflictual, character of the interpretive process makes it clear that the interpretation of God's will, while bounded by group norms, was not rigidly fixed, and thus that changes in group norms or in the nature of the group doing the interpreting could have a significant impact on the interpretation. Abigail Bailey consulted with her relatives (all of whom were church members) and a circle of friends from a newly formed congregation as well as those ministers who were available. In contrast to Bailey with her strongly familio-congregational orientation which hearkened back to an earlier New England, the others were part of more specialized and, in some cases, less localized networks of consultation. Osborn and Anthony consulted not only with their minister and each other, but also with the other members of their women's society. Woodbury and Atwood consulted among a network of friends from different towns all of whom had attended school together, as well as with their families and ministers.

By the early national period, organizations were forming which reflected the emergence of "horizontal solidarities" within what was still an essentially hierarchical society (Coontz 80). Women's societies and female academies fostered the development of peer relations and gave rise to new consultative networks, and as such Osborn's friends in the female society and Atwood's friends from Bradford Academy played a critical role in supporting their movement into new activities. Such movement, however, was bounded by the exclusively male clergy's privileged role in the interpretive process within the Congregationalist tradition. The boundedness of the interpretive process was reflected not only in these women's relations with the clergy during their lives, but also quite graphically in the published texts—the earliest published memoirs of Congregationalist women—all selected for publication, edited, and commented on by the women's ministers after their death. This boundedness limited what could be desired within the evangelical world and resulted, as Martha Vicinus has pointed out for a later generation of evangelicals, in women who could only with "extreme difficulty . . . be brought to express openly [their] personal needs; the vocabulary for such an action simply did not exist" (190). Unable to create organizations and institutions to serve "selfish" needs they could not articulate without feelings of sin, evangelical women opted for indirect, religiously sanctioned means of empowerment. In doing so, they were able to push the limits of what was possible and maintain their respectability without ever challenging the limits themselves.

NOTES

1 Denominationally, this would mean Congregationalists, Presbyterians, and Baptists, and, within New England, primarily Congregationalists. A number of Quaker women did publish autobiographies during this period.

2 The ministers usually added some sort of commentary on the women's own writings: Samuel Hopkins introduced the volumes by Osborn and Anthony with general sketches of their lives and concluded the volumes with his own observations on their lives; Ethan Smith wrote an introduction and an appendix for the Bailey memoirs in which he included selections from her diaries and correspondence; Fanny Woodbury's minister, Joseph Emerson, wrote a preface and the biographical memoir; and Harriet Newell's minister, Leonard Woods, included the funeral sermon he preached for her as well as organizing the extracts from her journal and correspondence so that they would read like a memoir.

3 Jonathan Edwards published the journal of David Brainard, an early missionary to the Indians; Samuel Hopkins had an interest in training African American missionaries for work in Africa; Leonard Woods was a founding member of the American Board of Commissioners for Foreign Missions; Joseph Emerson married Rebecca Hasseltine, sister of Ann Hasseltine Judson, an early missionary wife. Samuel T. Armstrong, publisher of the memoirs of Newell, Bailey,

and Woodbury, was a member of the ABCFM; Leonard Worcester, publisher of the memoirs of Anthony and Osborn, was later in life to preach at his son's ordination as a missionary. In addition, Joseph Emerson was an early advocate of education for young women and an early influence on women educators, such as Zilpah Grant and Mary Lyon (*Dictionary of American Biography,* s.v. Samuel T. Armstrong, Joseph Emerson, Samuel Hopkins, Leonard Woods; Conforti).

4 Hopkins' description appears in Osborn 70ff.; Osborn's own description on 49.

5 See, for example: Bercovitch 17–20; Lang 92; and Cott 140–41.

6 Stephanie Coontz (88) indicates that "family, church, and government all taught roughly the same things and demanded roughly the same commitments, though perhaps in different degrees; relationships in each area did not require qualitatively different ways of behaving or feeling."

7 For a discussion of the parallels between the devout believer in this kind of God and the abused child, see Taves 32–33.

WORKS CITED

Anthony, Susanna. *The Life and Character of Miss Susanna Anthony.* Ed. Samuel Hopkins. Worcester, MA: Leonard Worcester, 1796.

Bailey, Abigail. *The Memoirs of Mrs. Abigail Bailey.* Ed. Ethan Smith. Boston: Samuel T. Armstrong, 1815.

Bercovitch, Sacvan. *The Puritan Origins of the American Self.* New Haven and London: Yale University Press, 1975.

Conforti, Joseph. *Samuel Hopkins and the New Divinity Movement.* Grand Rapids: Christian University Press, 1981.

Coontz, Stephanie. *The Social Origins of Private Life: A History of American Families, 1600–1900.* London and New York: Verso, 1988.

Cott, Nancy F. *The Bonds of Womanhood: "Woman's Sphere" in New England, 1780–1835.* New Haven and London: Yale University Press, 1977.

Emerson, Joseph. *Writings of Miss Fanny Woodbury who Died at Beverly, Nov. 15, 1814, Aged 23 Years.* Boston: Samuel T. Armstrong, 1815.

Gillespie, Joanna Bowen. "'The Clear Leadings of Providence': Pious Memoirs and the Problems of Self-Realization for Women in the Early Nineteenth Century." *Journal of the Early Republic,* 5 (Summer 1985), 197–221.

Juster, Susan. "'In a Different Voice': Male and Female Narratives of Religious Conversion in Post-Revolutionary America." *American Quarterly,* 41/1 (March 1989), 34–62.

Karlsen, Carol F. *The Devil in the Shape of a Woman: Witchcraft in Colonial New England.* New York and London: Norton, 1987.

Karlsen, Carol F., and Laurie Crumpacker, eds. *The Journal of Esther Edwards Burr, 1754–57.* New Haven: Yale University Press, 1984.

Lang, Amy Schrager. *Prophetic Woman: Anne Hutchinson and the Problem of Dis-*

sent in the Literature of New England. Berkeley: University of California Press, 1987.

Norton, Mary Beth. "'My Resting Reaping Times': Sarah Osborn's Defense of Her 'Unfeminine' Activities, 1767." *Signs,* 2/2 (1976), 515–29.

Osborn, Sarah. *The Memoirs of the Life of Mrs. Sarah Osborn.* Ed. Samuel Hopkins. Worcester, MA: Leonard Worcester, 1799.

Shaw, Samuel. *Welcome to Affliction.* London, 1665; rpt. London: Religious Tract Society, 1848.

Taves, Ann, ed. *Religion and Domestic Violence in Early New England: The Memoirs of Abigail Abbot Bailey.* Bloomington and Indianapolis: Indiana University Press, 1989.

Ulrich, Laurel Thatcher. *Good Wives: Image and Reality in the Lives of Women in Northern New England, 1650–1750.* New York: Oxford University Press, 1983.

Vicinus, Martha. *Independent Women: Work and Community for Single Women, 1850–1920.* London: Virago, 1985.

Woods, Leonard. *A Sermon Preached at Haverhill, Mass., in Remembrance of Mrs. Harriet Newell, Wife of the Rev. Samuel Newell, Missionary to India, who Died at the Isle of France, Nov. 30, 1812, Aged 19 Years, to which are added Memoirs of her Life.* Boston: Samuel T. Armstrong, 1814.

CHAPTER 4

Resisting the Gaze of Embodiment: Women's Autobiography in the Nineteenth Century

SIDONIE SMITH

> People are beginning to inquire how far public sentiment should sanction or tolerate these unsexed women, who would step out from the true sphere of the mother, the wife, and the daughter, and taking upon themselves the duties and the business of men, stalk into the public gaze, and, by engaging in the politics, the rough controversies and trafficking of the world, upheave existing institutions, and overrun all the social relations of life.
>
> "Woman's Rights in the Legislature,"
> *Albany Register,* March 7, 1854

> In an autobiography, there seems a degree of egotism in the constant use of the first person singular, from which I have in vain sought some method of escape. For any consequent trenching upon the borders of good taste, I hope to be pardoned as for an unavoidable literary trespass.
>
> Anna Cora Mowatt, *Autobiography of an Actress; or,*
> *Eight Years on the Stage* (1854)

The literature of the "self" is various; but its most obvious generic manifestation is "autobiography," a genre that achieved its status as one of the West's master discourses in the nineteenth century when actual and fictional autobiographies filled the bookshelves. Readers became preoccupied with the literature of individual education and achievement, literature which, suggests J. Hillis Miller, "presupposes and powerfully presents the existence of spiritual entities called selves" (101). Indeed, "selfhood" and "autobiography" mutually implied one another.

Terry Eagleton notes that "certain meanings are elevated by social ide-

75

ologies to a privileged position, or made the centres around which other meanings are forced to turn" (131). The meaning of Western "selfhood" was one such meaning of privilege in the nineteenth century; and it secured its privileges by means of specific historical phenomena, specific ideological interpellations. The inaugural moment of the West's romance with "selfhood" lay of course in the dawn of the Renaissance, during which time the notion of an "individual" emerged.[1] Subsequently pressed through the mills of eighteenth-century enlightenment, early nineteenth-century romanticism, expanding bourgeois capitalism, Victorian optimism, the "individual" came by mid-nineteenth century to be conceptualized as a "fixed, extralinguistic" entity consciously pursuing its unique destiny (Miller 102).[2]

From this ideological perspective, every "self," as Miller remarks, "has its own sharp configuration, different from all others. Each is present to itself and to other such spiritual entities as force, as presence" (101). The "sharp configuration" to which Miller alludes suggests the certitudes of stable boundaries around a singular, unified, and irreducible core, the unequivocal delineation of insides and outsides. Separated from that which is external to it, the "metaphysical self" as isolato constantly asserts its place outside, beside, aside from other clearly configured selves.

Consequently, the "self of essences" is an "unencumbered subject" (Benhabib and Cornell 12). Its resistance to encumbrance derives from the particular positioning of the "individual" in relation to the "social," an orientation concomitant with the gradual separation of "self" from the external or social world. Francis Barker suggests that throughout the seventeenth and eighteenth centuries, "the modern subject is constructed as the bearer of naturalism, the facticity of things and their weightless transcription in discourse" and as such "is contrasted to an outer world which, although 'social,' becomes for it a kind of nature." As a result of this division between "self" and outer world, "for the first time it is possible to speak with some certainty of society—the associative name we give to lived isolation—when it has been effectively desocialized, its humane production elided by the separation from it of the constitution of the human subject" (53). Independent of the outer world, the "self" is neither constituted by nor coextensive with its social roles and private attachments. Social and communal roles with their elaborate masks of meaning may be inevitabilities; but however integumentary they do not entirely absorb the "self of essences." Encroachments, disturbances, occasional detours, they do not determine but rather remain tangential to the central drama of an unembedded "selfhood."

Unique, unitary, unencumbered, the "self" also escapes embodiment. Barker attributes the profound change in consciousness in the eighteenth century not only to the disassociation of the subject from the outer world;

he notes also that, with the move toward "the newly interiorated subjectivity," the body itself as "object" is disassociated from "mind" and resituated elsewhere: "Neither wholly present, nor wholly absent, the body is confined, ignored, exscribed from discourse, and yet remains at the edge of visibility, troubling the space from which it has been banished" (63). The banishment (or splitting off) of the "supplementary body" to the margins of "self" and text invites the "self-censoring" that functions to contain, control, and coopt the body's "dangerous passions." Yet, since the body always persists in that elsewhere at the horizon of experience and meaning, it can never be "jettisoned entirely" nor wholly contained (64, 59).

Disjoined from the body, the "self" becomes a governing consciousness synonymous, as Stanley Corngold contends, with the "Cartesian subject, the *res cogitans,* a substantial self identified uniformly with the thinking subject and cited in 'philosophies of consciousness,' where it is erected into the foundation of an epistemology" (3).[3] Its predominant mode of epistemological engagement with the world is through the agency of reason; and its powers encompass the authorization to theorize and thereby transcend the contingencies of "desire, affectivity, and the body," those constraining particularities of human existence (Young 62). While emotional life is not denied the "metaphysical self," it remains publicly suspect: linked as it is to the only partially repressed body, it is subordinated to and by reason.

With the body subordinated, the "Enlightenment self" pursues "a form of reason capable of privileged insight into its own processes and into the 'laws of nature'" (Flax 624). Reflecting on its essential nature, abstracting its patterns of development, delineating its coherent boundaries of experience, the "metaphysical self" presumes the possibility of self-knowledge. Then through the lens of a coherent self-knowledge, this "self" that "sees" turns toward the world and elaborates through reason that "transcends all situation, context and perspective," a universalizing, unifying vision characterized as "impartial."[4] The very words used to describe the rational practices of autonomous "selfhood" suggest the degree to which "vision" as "truth" or "enlightenment" predominates. "The notion of truth involved here," writes Lang in her discussion of romantic personhood, "remains a fundamentally Platonic one, that of an abstract eternal essence to be glimpsed in a dazzling vision or a brilliant insight; which is to say that seeing (what is hidden behind a veil of appearance) remains the only valid mode of knowing" (62). Thus as subjectivity metamorphoses into objectivity, the "self" becomes the privileged "origin" of meaning, knowledge, truth. "The Cartesian ego founding modern philosophy," writes Iris Marion Young, "realizes the totalizing project. This cogito itself expresses the idea of pure identity as the reflective self-presence of consciousness to itself.

Launched from this point of transcendental subjectivity, thought now more boldly than ever seeks to comprehend all entities in unity with itself and in a unified system with each other" (61).

Imperial interpreter, provocateur of totalization, the "self of essences" is likewise a "free" agent, exercizing self-determination over meaning, personal destiny, desire. Neither powerless nor passive, it assumes and celebrates agency. Its movement through time and history is purposeful, consistent, coherent, hence teleological. Typically "metaphysical selfhood" develops in two directions. The "self" may move consecutively through stages of growth, expanding the horizons of "self" and boundaries of experience through accretion, but always carrying forward through new growth that globe of an irreducible, unified core. This direction we might call horizontal. Or the "self" may proceed vertically, delving downward into itself to find the irreducible core, stripping away mask after mask of false "selves" in search of that hard core at the center, that pure, unique "self." Launched on a romantic journey, the "self" steams into the interior of itself, through lake after lake, layer after layer of circumstance to an unencumbered center of quiet water, pure being or essence.

Politically, the "metaphysical self" is individualistic in its desires and liberal in its philosophical perspective. The French Revolution with its cry for liberty, equality, fraternity; the philosophical systems of Locke and Rousseau with their emphases on empiricism and the experience of the individual's senses as originary loci of knowledge; the self-absorption of romanticism and its preoccupation with subjective experience; the economic and political shift from aristocratic to bourgeois power; the progressive tendencies of Darwinism, particularly social Darwinism; the consolidation of Protestant ideology with its emphasis on the accessibility of God to individual prayer and intercession; all these phenomena coalesced to privilege the self-determing individuality of desire and destiny. Thus every person could autograph history, could mark the times. "Individual effort," notes Mary Poovey, "became the mark of past accomplishments and the guarantor of future success; this was the era of the 'self-made man,' when aristocratic privilege could finally be challenged on a wide scale by individuals possessed of talent, opportunity, and the capacity for hard work" (27).

Finally, a certain ideology of language accompanies this notion of "selfhood." The "self" so understood is both "prelinguistic" and "extralinguistic." Constituted neither in nor by language, it exists prior to and independent of a language conceived as transparent and mimetic. Consequently, this "specular self" appears "well-composed, presentable," "well-defined and firm" (Gallop 80–81). If "selves," as Miller argues, "are merely mediated, described, or interpreted by language," then the life of any particular "self" can be "represented," chronicled from its origins through its teleo-logical course (101). And "representation" itself operates as another total-izing practice, "the sorting out of identity and difference," the naming, forming, and controlling of interpretations (Jardine 118). Like the "self," then, representation is "coherent, unified," the appropriative practice of a "self" that has "privileged insight" and authority (Gallop 57).

The ideology of "metaphysical selfhood" promoted and informed the emergence of autobiography in the West, engendering a certain idea of "Man" as an agent of his own destiny, the bearer, discoverer, and narrator of his particular, unencumbered "self," the origin of controlling knowl-edge about the objective world separable from the "self." From its roots in the Augustinian notion of the soul in search of God to its flowering in nineteenth-century realism, autobiography flourished because there seemed to be a "self" to represent, a unique and unified story to tell which bore common ground with the reader, a mimetic medium for self-representation that guaranteed the epistemological correspondence between "narrative" and "lived life," a self-consciousness capable of discovering, uncovering, recapturing that hard core at the center.[5] All these certitudes of traditional autobiography follow, as Lang suggests, upon "the conviction that 'I,' the speaking subject, has a single, stable referent" (72). They also follow from what Lang describes as "the development of the concept of the author as the sole authority, or single individual responsible for (and therefore ex-pressed through) his writings" (73). Yet conversely, they follow from the way in which the autobiographical text's discursive "life" effectively con-structs the subject of the text as a unitary and wholesome "self." Given these epistemological certitudes, the century assumed the efficacy of pur-suing and representing the "truth" of "metaphysical selfhood," an orienta-tion captured in Rousseau's confident assertion: "I have shown myself such as I was . . . I have unveiled my inmost self such as You Yourself have seen it. Eternal Being . . ." (5). Autobiography itself functioned as guarantor of "metaphysical selfhood."

The "I" of autobiography is the marker of the "self of essences." Speak-ing in the authority, conviction, and power of knowledge, it presents itself, Virginia Woolf noted, as "a most respectable 'I'; honest and logical; as hard as a nut, and polished for centuries by good teaching and good feeding" (104). Dominating the sentence as it delivers totalizing sentences, the "I" takes up its position on the page (of the text, of history) and marks every-thing in and between the lines of its appropriative interpretations. Single letter, single sound, the "I" appears unitary, bold, indivisible. In its very calligraphy and enunciation (in English at least) it defies destabilization, dissemination, diffusion. But that "I" is gendered and it is male. Fundamentally, the "metaphysical self" is what Alice A. Jardine describes as the "self" of the "paternally conceived ego" (229–30), or what Jane Gallop describes as "the self of the same, that is of man" (58).[6] And I would add that this hegemonic, monadic "I" is also unabashedly "white," Eurocentric, colonizing in its deployment.

Product of patriarchy's binarism, the architecture of the "self of essences" rests upon and reinforces the specularization of "woman" as the Other through whom "man" constructs his stature, status, and significance. As Woolf so astutely recognized, woman has functioned as "the looking-glass possessing the magic and delicious power of reflecting the figure of man at twice its natural size" (35). Turned in the theorizing gaze of the "metaphysical self," she is universalized as "woman," fashioned into that-which-man-is-not. To "woman" "man" attributes another kind of "self," a self of essences to be sure, but not a "metaphysical" one.

And so who is this "woman" interpellated in the discursive economies of patriarchy? And what does she know of "selfhood" or "selfhood" know of her? "Technologies of gender," to use Teresa de Lauretis' phrase, hypostasized an ideology of sexually marked "selfhood" in the nineteenth century that rigidly construed and partitioned masculine and feminine spheres of desire, fate, and discourse (chap. 1). The autonomous, monadic "self" of "man," assuming reciprocities of "self" and "soul" and governing the discursive fields of meaning, banishes the "tremulous private body" to the margins of consciousness. The female-marked "self," specularized as Other, is assigned habitation in that very margin. Thus "female selfhood," technologized as biologically determined, inheres in "woman's" embodiment as procreator and nurturer. The dynamics of such partitioning reveal the degree to which, as Judith Butler argues in her critique of Simone de Beauvoir's analysis of the body,

masculine disembodiment is only possible on the condition that women occupy their bodies as their essential and enslaving identities. . . . By defining women as 'Other,' men are able through the shortcut of definition to dispose of their bodies, to make themselves other than their bodies — a symbol potentially of human decay and transience, of limitation generally — and to make their bodies other than themselves. From this belief that the body is Other, it is not a far leap to the conclusion that others are their bodies, while the masculine 'I' is the noncorporeal soul. The body rendered as Other — the body repressed or denied and, then, projected — reemerges for this 'I' as the view of others as essentially body. Hence, women become the Other; they come to embody corporeality itself. This redundancy becomes their essence. (133)[7]

For "woman," "anatomy is destiny," a deterministic indictment attributable to both Napoleon and Freud, those male giants who towered over the beginning and end of the century with equally fateful albeit different kinds of swagger. Culturally charged with constraining meanings, anatomy becomes the irreducible "granite" at the core of "woman's" being.

Embodiment also marks "woman" as an "encumbered self," identified almost entirely by the social roles concomitant with her biological destiny. Affiliated physically, socially, psychologically in relationships to others, "her individuality [is] sacrificed to the 'constitutive definitions' of her identity as member of a family, as someone's daughter, someone's wife and someone's mother" (Benhabib and Cornell 12). The "unified self" disperses, radiating outward until its fragments disappear altogether inside "social and communal" masks. Thus "woman's" destiny cannot be self-determined, her agency cannot be exercised. At best she can only wait, a fate acknowledged by the narrator of Henry James's *The Portrait of a Lady:* "Most women did with themselves nothing at all; they waited, in attitudes more or less gracefully passive, for a man to come that way and furnish them with a destiny" (64).

Furthermore, by the nineteenth century, the very soul of "woman" surrenders to embodiment, signaling a radical shift away from the salvational equality of an earlier Christianity. Augustine and Aquinas, whatever their differences, both held the soul to be a neutral ground and as such unsexed. While "woman's" subordinate status in creation and her less than fully human "moral apparatus" may have prohibited her full participation in the spiritual life of this realm, such inequality did not characterize the relationship of her soul to "man's" soul and thus did not preclude her sharing equal access to grace (Maclean 27). Throughout the seventeenth and eighteenth centuries, however, a newly sexualized soul gradually displaces the theologically unsexed soul of the medieval period and the Renaissance. "The gradual processes of secularisation and theological revision," argues Denise Riley, "were accompanied by an increasing sexualisation which crowded out the autonomous soul—while at the same time a particularly feminised conception of Nature began to develop" (18). As a result, Riley contends, "the associations of 'women' with the natural were magnified to a point of mutual implication" (36). "Femininity" gradually fills the soul until, by the beginning of the nineteenth century, "no neutral enclave of the person remains unfilled and unoccupied by [it]" (36).

The sexualization of her mind continued to mark her epistemological practices in Western discursive regimes. In thrall to her body and to the affections and behavior associated with her encumbrances, "woman" remains "naturally" less rational than man. Rather than working logically, her mind works from the margins of logic: her way of knowing and interpreting is less abstract, less integrative, less transcendant, less impartial, and less self-conscious than the interpretive mode of "metaphysical man."

Inhabiting domesticating space (a space located closer to nature and necessity, a space of immanence and immediacy), she exhibits a less authoritative "feminine" mode of engagement with the world, one characterized as
intuitive, irrational, particularistic, and practical.[8] Consequently "woman"
cannot theorize, cannot universalize, a limitation that Hannah More elaborated in the late eighteenth century when she claimed that women

seem not to possess in equal measure the faculty of comparing, combining, ana-
lysing, and separating these ideas; that deep and patient thinking which goes to
the bottom of a subject; nor that power of arrangement which knows how to link
a thousand connected ideas in one dependent train, without losing sight of the
original idea out of which the rest grow, and on which they all hang. (367; see
also Peterson 127)

Effectively "woman" goes incognito before the Cartesian *cogito* as self-
consciousness evades her, a disadvantage that George Eliot trenchantly acknowledged when she wrote that "women have not to prove that they can
be emotional, and rhapsodic, and spiritualistic; every one believes that
already. They have to prove that they are capable of accurate thought, severe study, and continuous self-command" (334; quoted in Sukenick 33).
And yet, claiming her own equal powers of self-conscious reasoning im-
plicates "woman" in postures of monstrosity; for, as Lynn Sukenick notes,
"not only has this capacity been regarded as not innate in women, it has
been seen by some—by those who posit an opposition between mind and
'sheer being'—as a distinct threat to woman's 'basic' nature" (38). "Woman"
functions best as a "receptacle of feeling" or a "non-reflective bios" (Sukenick 37).[9] The woman who would reason like a man becomes "unwomanly,"
a kind of monstrous creature or lusus naturae.[10]

The surrender of "woman's" reason before embodiment also contaminates
her relationship to the word. Allying her still with the seductive Eve and
the serpent, words return her via yet another route to her biological essence. Cultural practices of the early nineteenth century reaffirmed this
association of the hole in her face and the hole between her legs. Women
could not preach publicly; nor could they recite poetry before mixed groups
of people and maintain their reputation; nor could they participate in formal education. With only limited access to education and to public activity, they could not take advantage of the full play of words with their
powers to name, control, authorize. Without the power of words and public discourse, without the power to theorize on and from her own, "woman"
and women remain silenced, unrepresented, subject always to the theorizing and fictionalizing of man. And theorizing maintained its androcentric
prerogatives.[11]

Fixed in this appropriative gaze, the bourgeois "woman" in the nineteenth century remains subject to man's authority and theorizing because, unmanned, she will subvert the structures of society. To the extent that "woman" represses "the body," erasing her sexual desire and individual identity while embracing encumbering identities in service to family, community, country, she positions herself as a "proper lady" who surmounts her negative identification with the body through selflessness.[12] To the degree that "woman" contests such roles and postures by pursuing her own desire and independence from men, she becomes a monster. For the identification of "female selfhood" with the body is nowhere more prominent than in the fear of woman that permeates nineteenth-century discursive culture: "As the soul of the woman shrinks and is made gender-specific," suggests Riley, "so vice swells in her body; not, of course, with any novelty, except that, crucially, the territorial powers of the body are at the same time enlarged" (41). The "fallen" woman who succumbs to her "true nature" to become sexual, narcissistic, and venal, self-absorbed and self-promoting, acts too much the "woman," thereby reaffirming what Mary Poovey calls "the fundamental paradox that pervades all discussions of women" in the eighteenth and nineteenth centuries: "At the heart of the explicit description of 'feminine,' Angelic women, superior to all physical appetite, resides the 'female' sexuality that was automatically assumed to be the defining characteristic of female nature" (19). Because "the tremulous private body" always threatens to "overflood its walls" and return from the margins, it threatens to disrupt the central places of consciousness and power.[13]

The ideology of the nineteenth century stranded a woman between the granite core of "metaphysical selfhood" and the material surfaces of "embodied selfhood." How then could she position herself toward autobiographical self-representation? Traditional (male) autobiography reaffirmed, reproduced, and celebrated the agentive autonomy and disembodiment of "metaphysical selfhood," valorizing individuality and separateness while erasing personal and communal interdependencies. Asserting arrival in the phallic order and ordering, traditional autobiography reenacted the erasure of "woman" that facilitates male entrance into the public realm of words, power, and meaning. Woman, mother, the feminine, functioned in the text of traditional autobiography to signal the place of lost innocence, the forces of desire pressing upon the individual, or the source of salvation. Always, "she" remained specularized, the reflective medium through which the autobiographer pursued his "metaphysical selfhood."

How could a bourgeois woman see through the gaze of embodiment and its social encumbrances to some granite of "selfhood" at the core when she had to embrace those very encumbrances, sacrificing her "self" to others, to children, family, husband, to God? How could she find "selfhood" as "metaphysical man" did in his romantic journey inward to the core, except inside those very social masks questing "man" would penetrate, expose, and discard? How could she who was situated on the margins of "metaphysical selfhood," always distanced from any core outside of embodiment, discover a unified, monadic "self"? How could she boldly pronounce the "I" of autobiographical discourse when, in order to escape the drag of her body and the potential for evil associated with it, she had to erase her "self" and renounce that "I" through the posture of selflessness and silence? And how could she make that sacrifice in an age that privileged the hard nut of "metaphysical selfhood" as the prevailing ideology of human possibility, desire, and meaning, in an age that celebrated autobiography?

Had she maintained the posture of that specular "self" and resisted the autobiographical "I," the nineteenth-century woman would have remained silenced, unwritten and unread. Yet, despite the fact that traditional autobiography suppressed female subjectivity unmediated by male representation and thereby denied to "woman" the "metaphysical selfhood" prerequisite to entry into culture's "master narratives," actual women wrote autobiographies in increasing numbers, especially middle-class women. They too pursued the discursive economies of self-representation. And they did so because they were not merely overdetermined products of but also creative sign makers in the discursive economies of the century, not merely "subjects" of ideology interpellated inside discourse but agents of contestation.[14] As theorists such as Joan Kelly-Gadol, Toril Moi, and Jane Gallop remind us, patriarchal ideology with its controlling idea of "man" and his possibilities, like any ideology, is not totalized, is not, as Moi notes, "homogeneous and all-encompassing in its effects" (65). In fact, there are "the paradoxically productive aspects of patriarchal ideology" (Moi 64), moments when the phallic order does not work "neatly and efficiently" since "phantoms always lurk, messing up" (Gallop 81). Bourgeois ideologies of gender may attempt to script sexual difference according to "natural" or "God-given" distinctions, but those "cultural" distinctions remain vulnerable to destabilizations that rupture their coherence and hegemony. Thus actual women writing had access to fissures in the figuration of "woman," opened as competing ideologies chafed against one another, generating contradictions.

For instance, the very obstinacy with which androcentric discourse named "woman" in its essentialist terms of embodiment and thereby worked to repress, oppress, and suppress her unmasks the more fundamental apprehension that "woman" is ultimately full of elusive and uncontainable power.[15] A much more magical figure than "man," "she" derives her meaning from both her energizing and her enervating powers, her mutability, her fluidity of form and substance. Precisely this threat of infinite possibility spawned images of closure and containment that condemned "woman" to her embodied, materially based mold. Thus as the imaginative figurine enabling his "metaphysical selfhood," "woman" stood both larger and smaller than man, capacious and mobile yet simultaneously circumscribed and inert. The very complexity of this nexus of dependency and elusiveness means that real women had some spaces in which to maneuver as they contested the power to discipline and identify them, including the spaces of self-representation. It means they had some spaces into which to insert the dynamic specificities of their own personal histories.

Thus actual women could experiment, whether consciously or unconsciously, with the discursive elasticities inherent in self-imagining. For a woman such elasticity accompanied her dynamic positioning between two essentialist "selfhoods"—that of the "metaphysical man" and that of "embodied woman." In daring to write about herself for public consumption, the autobiographer already transgressed cultural boundaries, straying beyond the boundaries of a "selfhood" situated at the very margins of cultural action, meaning, and discourse into another's territory at the center of culture. As she wrote, she traveled discursively between these two territories, sometimes straying further into one territory, sometimes staying longer, but always weaving in and out of them in the complex dance of displacement and redeployment. Resisting silence, she told her story; but the silences persisted, and the story she told was qualified by her ambivalence toward female storytelling, inflected with the conflictual impulses she experienced in her position as a subject in drift between "feminine" and "masculine" domains of "selfhood." But the multiplicity of her positionings in actual life (of class, race, nationality, religion, ethnicity) and in discourse guaranteed her a modicum of agency and, as Paul Smith argues, "the possibility of resistance through a recognition of the simultaneous non-unity and non-consistency of subject-positions" (118).

Such situating of the bourgeois autobiographer within the complexities and contradictions of patriarchal ideologies of gender and the speaking positions they invoke accounts for the oscillations in woman's autobiographical posture and grounds the poetics of resistance characterizing her autobiographical practice in the nineteenth century. To sketch this problematic, I would like now to turn to two nineteenth-century autobiographies by Americans, the first by a white woman of convenient means and the second by an escaped slave.

Elizabeth Cady Stanton announces in the preface to *Eighty Years and More, 1815–1897* that the story of her life is actually split, doubly inscribed: "The story of my private life as the wife of an earnest reformer, as an enthusiastic housekeeper, proud of my skill in every department of domestic economy, and as the mother of seven children, may amuse and benefit the reader. The incidents of my public career as a leader in the most momentous reform yet launched upon the world — the emancipation of woman — will be found in 'The History of Woman Suffrage'" (v). Textually splitting both story and "selfhood" into the dual spheres of private ("feminine") and public ("masculine") activity, Stanton gestures to the "commonplaces"[16] of female identity in the nineteenth century. She apparently positions the public achievements of "metaphysical selfhood" in an elsewhere distant from her autobiographical project, thereby banishing to the margins of her "woman's" text the story of agency and autonomy. In that textual elsewhere she claims her place as a "leader" in "the most momentous reform yet launched upon the world," no small claim to notoriety. Yet even there, in that elsewhere, public achievement is displaced into "self"-less history as her centrifugal role disperses into a "communal" rather than "personal" story of the suffrage movement. Refusing to make "unwomanly" or monstrous claims to publicity, Stanton signals at the gateway to her narrative her resistance to self-promotion. Even her purposes in writing are conventionally "feminine" ones: she writes self-sacrificially for the amusement and the edification of her reader.

Stanton at first appears to embrace the cultural figuration of "woman" by positioning herself squarely inside the enclosure of domestic space, the territory of "embodied selfhood." As she traces her childhood, youth, courtship, and marriage through the opening chapters of the text, she attends to the teleological pattern of "embodied selfhood," those defining moments of the female life cycle. Moreover, she wraps the commonplaces of "woman's" story of courtship in the language and figures of sentimental fiction: "When walking slowly through a beautiful grove, he laid his hand on the horn of the saddle and, to my surprise, made one of those charming revelations of human feeling which brave knights have always found eloquent words to utter, and to which fair ladies have always listened with mingled emotions of pleasure and astonishment" (60). Representing herself as the desirable and decorous heroine of "romance," Stanton invokes the idealized script of young "womanhood." Once past this point in the text she appears to fulfill her opening promise to focus on her life as wife, mother, and housekeeper, invoking the idealized script of nurturant self-sacrifice. Sometimes she invests commentary about motherhood in similarly sentimental garb. Talking of young women whose singing is much remarked she announces: "One has since married, and is now pouring out her richest melodies in the opera of lullaby in her own nursery" (414). More often in talking about motherhood she assumes the posture of the experienced grandmother, practical, authoritative, aggressive in her concern for the welfare of children. In the discourse of housewifery, the older woman offers advice on such domestic concerns as healthy ventilation, stoves, child-rearing practices.

However, the representation of Stanton the wife and mother is disturbed and destabilized throughout the text in a variety of ways.[17] The narrative of "embodied selfhood" ends fairly early when the roles have been fulfilled, when the courtship and romance culminate in marriage and childbearing. Henry Stanton appears in the early pages and then disappears almost entirely once he has married her and fathered her first children. Stanton erases him so effectively that the reader is not really clear whether he has died when she concludes her narrative. Nor do her children assume much prominence in the text. They are noted when she talks about the early trials of marriage and housekeeping, but then they too disappear until the end when they reappear, woven in and out of the text, given as much narrative space as the hundreds of other friends she visits.

Nonetheless the shadow existence of both husband and children in the text serves the function of legitimizing Stanton's "excessive" narrative. Since her cultural authority and readability depend upon her fulfillment of that generic contract whereby she presents herself as a "woman," husband and children establish her identity and credibility as a narrating woman. No virgin spinster (like Susan B. Anthony) Stanton assures her reader that female "embodiment" has operated in culturally respectable and expected ways. All parts having assumed their proper places, her body has fulfilled its destiny. Having positioned herself toward the body in this way, Stanton achieves at least two effects. She diffuses the lurking threat of the monstrous female body, which always threatens to return from the margins of "woman's" text to disrupt the processes and practices of patriarchal culture. Second, she provides herself with a strategic counter: she can use brief, fleeting references to husband and children to reinforce her legitimacy again and again in a text that quickly begins to contest the institution of marriage itself.

For the preface and sentimental posturings notwithstanding, the thrust of Stanton's narrative contests the sanctity of marriage and even the motherhood Stanton would promote. To the roles of wife and mother and their attendant responsibilities she traces her profound dissatisfaction with the fate of "woman" and the constraints of female embodiment. Her domestic life in Seneca Falls she presents as drudgery, isolating, hard, dulling. Parenting she constantly assesses as constricting, brutalizing. Describing her experience as a young mother she writes:

I now fully understood the practical difficulties most women had to contend with in the isolated household, and the impossibility of woman's best development if in contact, the chief part of her life, with servants and children. . . . The general discontent I felt with woman's portion as wife, mother, housekeeper, physician, and spiritual guide, the chaotic conditions into which everything fell without her constant supervision, and the wearied, anxious look of the majority of women impressed me with a strong feeling that some active measures should be taken to remedy the wrongs of society in general, and of women in particular. (147–48)

Throughout her text she interjects commentary on the pettiness, tyranny, and brutality of men and their victimization of women, emotional, physical, political, economic.

Moreover, Stanton locates mutual understanding and comradeship in her relationship with Susan B. Anthony (and with women generally) rather than in her relationship to men, whether husband or father. Pointedly she does not dedicate her narrative to either husband or children but to Anthony, "my steadfast friend for half a century." Textually, Anthony takes the place of the marriage partner, displacing Henry Stanton as source of inspiration. In offering a brief biography of Anthony, Stanton draws upon a rhetoric that celebrates the complementarity traditionally identified with the marriage partner:

So entirely one are we that, in all our associations, ever side by side on the same platform, not one feeling of envy or jealousy has ever shadowed our lives. . . . To the world we always seem to agree and uniformly reflect each other. Like husband and wife, each has the feeling that we must have no differences in public. . . . So closely interwoven have been our lives, our purposes, and experiences that, separated, we have a feeling of incompleteness — united, such strength of self-assertion that no ordinary obstacles, difficulties, or dangers ever appear to us insurmountable. (166, 184)

Stanton spends considerable narrative time weaving Anthony's presence into the text, testifying to the priority of female friendship over wifehood and motherhood.

And whatever lip service she might give to the centrality of the "home" for women, the text constantly displays a kind of homelessness, albeit a wealthy homelessness, not one of poverty but one of constant travel. Stanton describes her travels across the West, back and forth to Europe, from one home to another, one friend to another, one public speaking engagement to another. In her mobile existence even the home to which she returns constantly shifts from place to place.

For a narrative which purports to be about the stable roles of wife, mother, housekeeper, this one incessantly frays, breaks apart, goes off in pursuit of another kind of "selfhood" as Stanton seeks to escape the confinement of "embodied selfhood," to escape enclosure in "woman's place," to escape encoding in "woman's" life script, that narrative marginal to the contractual expectations of autobiography. Thus, Stanton pursues another story, albeit one that is sketchy, not prominently linear but suggestively so. Through the barest shell of an alternative teleology, she locates the originary moments of her developmental "selfhood." First she recalls her experience at the death of her brother when her father refuses to acknowledge her as the substitute son she would be. Then she describes her experience in her father's law office listening to the wives, mothers, and widows who find themselves powerless economically. From there she proceeds to track her involvement in first the abolitionist and then the suffrage movements with their various and complex stages of development.

Charting the course of her education and public involvement, Stanton reifies the liberal humanism and individualism that served as cornerstones of the ideology of "metaphysical selfhood" in the nineteenth century. Effectively, she figures herself as a kind of "unembodied" and "self-made man," fiercely rational, intellectually keen, independent, agentive, mobile, outspoken, tenacious, combative. Again and again she describes her engagements with men, in the process claiming her place alongside them, even claiming a superiority of position. For instance, she confidently denounces the advice of the doctors attending her after her first delivery and describes how ineffective they were, how she assumed their place, determining her own solution to the problem of the baby's health. Recalling how she sparred with various clergy, she dismisses them as reactionary conservatives, arguing her own position on the Bible and on biblical interpretation. Toward the conclusion of the text she discusses her very rewriting of the Bible itself as *The Woman's Bible.*

Textually, Stanton enacts her pledge to her father—"I will try to be all my brother was" (21)—by assuming the position of "son," figuring herself as pseudo-lawyer, reformer, politician, interpreter. In what she claims to be a personal and domestic narrative, Stanton stakes her claim to an empowered "metaphysical selfhood" for herself and for women generally. Resisting the position of "woman" which allows her only a vague "influence," she emphasizes in the text her exercise of "direct power": "A direct power over one's own person and property, an individual opinion to be counted, on all questions of public interest, are better than indirect influence, be that ever so far reaching" (376). Stanton travels from the territory of the margins, travels from the shadow of influence, to the territory of direct action, analysis, and speech. Thus, she appropriates for herself the fiction of "man," reproducing the culturally valued story of "metaphysical selfhood" with its powers of self-reflectiveness and self-fabrication and its preoccupation with quest. In this way Stanton "unsexes" herself, uncouples her "selfhood" from embodiment. In this way she legitimates her desire (and the desire of women in the suffrage movement) to achieve equal political rights with men, to achieve the status of "voter" alongside men.

But lest, in her ventriloquization of "man," she become a lusus naturae, a truly powerful but truly monstrous "woman," Stanton heeds the cultural injunction against unremitting self-assertion in "woman." Rhetorically she tries to maintain a posture of "feminine" self-effacement. For instance, she mutes the agency inherent in her decision to engage in political activism in response to her experience of motherhood by the claim of external determinacy: "My experience at the World's Anti-slavery Convention, all I had read of the legal status of women, and the oppression I saw everywhere, together swept across my soul, intensified now by many personal experiences. It seemed as if *all the elements had conspired to impel me* to some onward step" (148; emphasis mine). Manifesting resistance to the appearance of aggressive self-assertion, she invests the story of her purposeful life quest with the conventions of the "romance of the calling." In doing so she displays what Carolyn G. Heilbrun, in discussing the autobiographies of public women of the late nineteenth century in America, suggests is the etiology of bourgeois woman's activity: "The only script for women's life insisted that work discover and pursue them, like the conventional romantic lover" (17).[18] She also emphasizes, throughout the descriptions of her various journeys to promote the suffrage cause, the physical discomforts and tribulations of her self-sacrificing activities. Moreover, as Jelinek suggests, even as she represents herself as the exceptional "woman," as the "son," she insists on her identification with a broad range of women, even the lonely, isolated, impoverished plainswoman (87–90). Effectively, Stanton uses her position as wife and mother to screen her self-asserting presentation of herself as "individual," as "man," as "metaphysical self." This double-positioning underwrites the tensions, points of opposition, and contradictions of and in the text.

What remains unspoken in Stanton's narrative is the plight of the black woman, as slave, ex-slave, and domestic servant. Stanton acknowledged the aims of the abolitionist and reconstructionist causes to broaden the boundaries establishing the Republican "individual" to incorporate the freed black male. She chose to give priority to another argument for extension of the boundaries: she wanted equal access for bourgeois women. But in this triangulated schema whereby one either calls for bringing bourgeois women into the territory of the "(male) individual" or the black man into the space of the "(white) individual," the missing subject of both arguments is the black woman.[19] Yet if the black female subject is an unspoken in Stanton's narrative, she is not silent in the century. And so, I want also to explore in more detail a nineteenth-century slave narrative published in 1861, some thirty-seven years earlier than Stanton's autobiography. This exploration has its implicit and explicit intentions. Implicitly, it exposes the racialized nature of Stanton's autobiographical practice by specifying the ideological bases upon which the architecture of "white womanhood" rested. Explicitly, it elaborates the problematic relationship of "race" to the ideology of gender inherent in "metaphysical" and "embodied" conceptions of selfhood.

Exploring the significance of the cultural notion of "race" in recent Western history, Henry Louis Gates, Jr., notes that there existed in the mid-nineteenth-century environment a "shared assumption among intellectuals that race was a 'thing,' an ineffaceable quantity, which irresistibly determined the shape and contour of thought and feeling as surely as it did the shape and contour of human anatomy" (3). Consequently, the identifying marker of "race," continues Gates, served as "a trope of ultimate, irreducible difference between cultures, linguistic groups, or adherents of specific belief systems which — more often than not — also have fundamentally opposed economic interests" (5). Encoding the figuration of the Other, "race" cast difference in fixed, essentialist terms (of skin color, anatomy, physiognomy, intelligence, ideas, traditions).

The ideology of race supporting the system of slavery in the southern states (like the ideology of race supporting colonial expansion in Africa, Asia, and South America) fixed "Africans" on the bottom rung of what Gates calls the "minutely calibrated" evolutionary ladder. Blending with vestigial remnants of an earlier discursive "ladder," the Renaissance's great chain of being, the century's "scientific" discourses — of Darwinism, social Darwinism, medical anthropology, ethnography — established a hierarchy of races ranging from the "atavistic" to the "civilized." In the position of hierarchical ordination, white, Western culture stood at the apex of evolutionary achievement, far removed from the "Africans," identified with primitive impulses, ideas, social institutions, religious practices, with uninhibited sexual practices.[20] The very "humanity" of "Africans" remained problematic. For without a written language, "Africans" appeared deficient in memory, mature reason, vision, and, critically, history. Since the century inherited from the Enlightenment its privileging of reason as the fundamental cornerstone supporting the architecture of "metaphysical selfhood," and since the century privileged knowledge of the arts and sciences as the highest achievement of reason and writing as the evidentiary scene of reason, absence of written language signified absence of full humanity.[21] Indeed, Africans were accorded fractional humanity, signified by their status as three-fifths of a human being in the discussions of the "founding fathers." Fixed in their essential racial difference, they were denied "metaphysical selfhood" and relegated instead to the realm of the body as the system's beast of burden.

To write the "self" into history thus served as an oppositional gesture, at once "humanizing" and "individualizing" the "Africans" through recourse to the very "technology of reason" that would dehumanize them.[22] Slave narratives contested the claims of slavery's advocates that "Africans" were primitive, uneducable, outside history and culture. As Frederick Douglass acknowledged in the preface of his narrative, "not only is slavery on trial, but unfortunately, the enslaved people are also on trial. It is alleged, that they are, naturally, inferior; that they are *so low* on the scale of humanity, and so utterly stupid, that they are unconscious of their wrongs, and do not apprehend their rights" (vii). The narratives established the legitimacy of the "Africans'" desire for full political, economic, and intellectual participation. Further, writing autobiography, ex-slaves appropriated a Western generic contract promoting the primacy of "individual selfhood" and proclaimed that "selfhood" publicly. "Text created author," Gates argues,

and black authors, it was hoped, would create, or re-create, the image of the race in European discourse. . . . The recording of an authentic black voice—a voice of deliverance from the deafening discursive silence which an enlightened Europe cited to prove the absence of the African's humanity—was the millennial instrument of transformation through which the African would become the European, the slave become the ex-slave, brute animal become the human being. (11–12)

Combining personal histories with a cultural history of the slave system, the narratives became powerful weapons in the abolitionist cause, especially after 1831 when the crusade gained momentum through widespread organization. Widely read and circulated throughout the northern states, they were written to enlighten potential supporters of the antislavery crusade about the horrors of the "peculiar institution" which would reduce "human beings" to such degradation.[23] As Frederick Douglass wrote to his editor: "Any facts, either from slaves, slaveholders, or by-standers calculated to enlighten the public mind, by revealing the true nature, character, and tendency of the slave system, are in order, and can scarcely be innocently withheld" (vii). Personalizing the story of slavery, the diverse materials incorporated in slave narratives accumulated to render an immediate rather than abstract elaboration of systemic dehumanization and evil and thus to strike "right to the hearts of men" (Boston *Chronotype,* quoted in Andrews 5).

And yet as William L. Andrews argues, the "white" readers of black slave narratives did not necessarily privilege the individuality of the narrator. Rather, "American aesthetic standards of the time made a black narrative that exposed the institutional facts of slavery preferable to one that expressed the subjective views of an individual slave." As a result, the narrator entered a scene of writing that, like the scene of slavery itself, required the erasure of individual history and of "self": "To follow this agenda was to alienate oneself from one's past and to banish oneself in the most fundamental ways from one's own autobiography. Yet speaking too revealingly of the individual self, particularly if this did not correspond to white notions of the facts of black experience or the nature of the Negro, risked alienating white sponsors and readers, too." Andrews suggests that the most sophisticated of the slave narratives reveal a complex resistance to this contradictory set of personal and public expectations, that "they resisted the fragmenting nature of objective autobiography, which demanded that a black narractor achieve credence by objectifying himself and passivizing his voice" (6–7). Harriet Jacobs' narrative is one of those texts that subvert generic expectations in multiple ways.

Making herself into a "talking book" entitled *Incidents in the Life of a Slave Girl, Written by Herself,* Jacobs engaged the mythology of "race" in order to give "voice" to herself and "face" to her people through alternative myths of empowerment (Gates 11–12). In the process she struggled to break the chains of slavery by breaking the chain of being which would relegate her as an "African" to the lowest rung of the ladder and by intervening in the constraints of generic expectations which would reappropriate her "life" in narrative. Engaging the conventions of self-mastery and authority, she staked her claim in the territory of the "human." The black woman, however, had a far more complex struggle for "selfhood" on her hands than either the white woman or the black man. Doubly the site of Western culture's totalizing representations, doubly "embodied" as "African" and "woman," doubly colonized in the territory of rape and enforced concubinage, the slave woman confronted conflated destinies, discourses, and identifications. Marginalized vis-à-vis both "metaphysical" and "embodied [white]" selfhoods, Jacobs travels arduously toward both territories as she narrates a paradigmatic tale of spiritual and rhetorical as well as physical journeys from bondage to "freedom."

Unwilling to accept the conditions of slavery, "Linda Brent" (the name of Jacobs' protagonist) determines to escape her circumstances, eluding her master by hiding in her grandmother's attic for seven years and then fleeing north to New York where she finds work, regains her children, and achieves freedom, not through self-agency but through the agency of her employer. At the center of Jacobs' escape story is "Brent's" will, her determination to figure life on her own terms. Agency functions as the sign of her resistance to her status as slave, subjected always to another's will. Describing her struggle with her master, Doctor Flint, "Brent" foregrounds this agency, figuring the struggle in metaphors of warfare, that quintessential masculine domain: "The war of my life had begun; and though one of God's most powerless creatures, I resolved never to be conquered" (Jacobs 19).[24] Through this "hand-to-hand" combat, "Brent" literally and figuratively wrests agency from the master as her prerogative, beating the master at his own game, outwitting "the man." The narrative presents "Brent" as

an avatar of the "self-made man," bent on achieving freedom by means
of iron will, intelligence, courage, self-sacrifice, and perseverance as well
as moral purposefulness. Both story and text affirm her "individuality" and
"metaphysical selfhood" despite her qualified achievement in the North
and her continuing struggle "to affirm the self in a hostile, or indifferent,
environment" (Genovese 172).

As a narrative of self-determining agency, Jacobs' text participates in the
tradition of the male slave narrative. But other positionings toward "selfhood" in the text cause Jacobs' narrative to deviate from that androcentric
paradigm. For unlike the male slave narrator Jacobs has to attend as she
writes to another story of "selfhood." Not only does she confront "Brent's"
estrangement from "metaphysical selfhood"; she confronts synchronously
her estrangement from "true [white] womanhood" and its sentimental narrative frames. The ideology of "true womanhood" elaborated by feminist
historians looking at the nineteenth century, assigned to the "true woman"
what Barbara Welter has described as "four cardinal virtues—piety, purity, submissiveness and domesticity" (Welter 21).[25] But that assignment implied another assignment—one directed at unprivileged women, women
of color and working-class women. Hazel V. Carby argues that while the
establishment of "what constituted a woman and womanhood" may have
brought "coherence and order to the contradictory material circumstances
of the lives of women," it did so by "balancing opposing definitions of
womanhood and motherhood [for white and black women], each dependent on the other for its existence" (Carby, *Reconstructing Black Womanhood* 24, 25). For instance, the fragile physique characteristic of the "true
woman" contrasted markedly to the bodily strength desirable in the black
female slave.[26] Moreover, the fierce purposefulness of a slave woman's efforts to escape her bondage violated the code of submissiveness so central
to "true womanhood." Any effort by a black woman to establish her con-
sonance with "true womanhood" involved a crossing over from one definitional territory to another's definitional territory, a crossing over to a place
whose boundaries depended on keeping black women in their place.[27]

Inevitably, black and white women experienced differing relationships
to their bodies. A white woman exercized some control over her body. Despite the discourse labeling her naturally lustful, despite the implicit fear
of her sexuality evidenced in the most elaborate defenses of her goodness
and purity, she could achieve some modicum of power by resisting the temptations of the flesh and keeping her body clean, chaste. By maintaining
her virginity and her "reputation," she could secure marriage and with it
social legitimacy. After marriage she could fulfill her duty by bearing legitimate children for the patrilineage. Or she could maintain her virginity
and serve her family as dutiful daughter or her cause as selfless evangelist.

Enshrined in her "separate sphere," she could secure a certain cultural status and currency (literally and figuratively).

While neither male nor female slaves had control over their own bodies, the female slave suffered physical violation of her body beyond what the male slave suffered, a reality to which Jacobs painfully alludes: "When they told me my new-born babe was a girl, my heart was heavier than it had ever been before. Slavery is terrible for men; but it is far more terrible for women. Superadded to the burden common to all, they have wrongs, and sufferings, and mortifications peculiarly their own" (77). Within that "peculiar institution" the fate of woman was itself "peculiar." If in the discursive regimes of "embodied selfhood" the white woman always carried in her the potential for illicit and disruptive sexuality, the black woman lived in that crawlspace of sexual lasciviousness by virtue of the mark that was her skin color. Her black body condemned her to an inescapable essentialism since in the mythology of "race," it served as her defining characteristic, the very sign of her unrepressed and unrepressible sexuality, her licentiousness and insatiability. From the less authoritative discourse of the chain of being to the more scientifically respectable discourse of medical pathology, black female sexuality became synonymous with abnormal sexual appetite.[28] Effectively, her body stood as an invitation to white male desire. And so the white master satisfied his "prurient" sexual desire and his desire for human capital on the female slave's body in one act. In this way her body functioned as the vessel for reproducing "chattel" for the system (since children followed the mother) and for shielding the white woman from "uninhibited" sexual practices; both uses maintained colonial relationships of power.

Despite these apparently intractable cultural obstacles, Jacobs seeks to establish in her narrative some relationship (albeit partially contestatory as I will argue later) to "true womanhood" by situating "Brent" inside shared boundaries with white women. Perhaps the recognition of a shared community with white northern women was abetted by the feminist politics of the two women with whom she worked and corresponded during the writing of her narrative, Lydia Maria Child and Amy Post. "The publication of Jacobs's autobiography," suggests Andrews, "constituted a double opportunity, for as woman and slave, Jacobs dramatized the feminist analysis of the parallel slavery of race and sex. . . . From the feminist point of view, which labeled true womanhood white slavery and submissive wifehood prostitution, Jacobs's multiply marginal identity qualified her amply as one of the most truly representative women of her time" (247–48). And yet her "representative" status was undermined by other positionings. She was after all, as Andrews reminds us, a domestic servant, a woman on the margins of the domestic domain of woman. And the narrative inevitably revealed certain postures antithetical to the postures of the "true woman": her wilfullness noted above, her not always suppressed anger, her independent critique of both southern and northern society, and her revelation of sexual concubinage.

In response to the great irony of her situation—"the more enormous the crimes committed against her, the less receptive people are to hearing about them, especially from the victim herself"—Jacobs, according to Andrews, seeks to "forestall the wrong kind of reading of her book" by constituting in her text a "woman-identified reader" and "remodeling" through the text the kind of enlightened community that would "offer a truly familial kind of fellowship" (Andrews 249, 253). To this end "Brent" speaks directly to white middle-class northern women, comfortable in their status as "true women." Speaking as a woman to other women whose sympathy, understanding, and action she would enlist in the antislavery crusade, she asks that they identify with her sufferings as a woman who shares their concerns for home and children. This desire to gain common ground with her reader determines the emphases in the narrative on the struggle to achieve control over her body and the related struggle to establish a home for the children of that body.

In tracing the former struggle, however, Jacobs reveals not only her determination to escape sexual exploitation but also her surrender to concubinage, confessing that in resisting her master's will she entered deliberately into liaison with another white man by whom she bore two children. Thus the narrator must position herself as the "fallen" woman whose very utterances, because unspeakable, threaten the sanctity of that protected space of "true womanhood." The reality of this threat is acknowledged by Lydia Maria Child in her introduction:

I am well aware that many will accuse me of indecorum for presenting these pages to the public; for the experiences of this intelligent and much injured woman belong to a class which some call delicate subjects, and others indelicate. This peculiar phase of Slavery has generally been kept veiled; but the public ought to be made acquainted with its monstrous features, and I willingly take the responsibility of presenting them with the veil withdrawn. I do this for the sake of my sisters in bondage, who are suffering wrongs so foul, that our ears are too delicate to listen to them. (4)

There is no room for Jacobs' experience as a black woman inside the borders of "true womanhood." Since "silence" surrounds the "indecorous" subject matter and marginalized speaking position of the narrator—"It would have been more pleasant to me to have been silent about my own history" (2)—Jacobs/"Brent" risks rejection by her reader in order to tell the story of her fall from virginity into concubinage, in order to insist on the legitimacy of her experience.

The narrative strategies Jacobs/"Brent" uses to stake her claim as a black woman to a place within the community of "true women" are fascinating and provocative. In tracing her struggle for physical self-determination she appeals rhetorically to her audience by appropriating the very language and narrative conventions of popular fiction, most particularly invoking (and rewriting) the tale of seduction.[29] Presenting herself as a resisting victim of Doctor Flint's sexual aggression, "Brent" figures a story about the forced loss of innocence and the long, anguished struggle to achieve bodily integrity in the face of unremitting emotional and physical abuse. Chronicling her experiences in slavery and out, she foregrounds especially the emotional and physical consequences of her decision to resist sexual victimization, the superhuman self-sacrifice necessary. She suffers separation from her children. Harassed, exhausted, feverish, infected, contorted by the seven-year enclosure inside her grandmother's attic, her body bears the marks of the master's brutality, bares the price of "virtue." At the same time that she testifes to the horrors of that "peculiar institution," therefore, she positions herself as victimized heroine inside the narrative space of "white" fiction.

Jacobs also appeals to white women as mothers by creating "Brent" as the heroic mother whose steel purpose is to achieve freedom and a home for her children and by figuring her story in the rhetoric of domestic fiction with its celebration of the domestic virtues. Presenting herself in what Jean Fagan Yellin reminds us was "the most valued 'feminine' role" of the century" (xxvi), Jacobs emphasizes how hard fought the achievement must be for the female slave, precisely because "motherhood" posed significant problems for the black woman caught in a system that intervened ruthlessly and purposefully in family relationships.[30] Amassing detailed accounts of the difficulties of motherhood in slavery, Jacobs insists on "Brent's" total commitment to her children, to the point of self-sacrifice: "My friends feared I should become a cripple for life; and I was so weary of my long imprisonment that, had it not been for the hope of serving my children, I should have been thankful to die; but, for their sakes, I was willing to bear on" (127). Moreover, Jacobs surrounds "Brent's" struggle as a mother with the struggle of her larger family, a family whose members—grandmother, father, mother, aunts, uncles—she figures as powerful, physically resilient, spiritually hearty, loving, courageous, loyal. She thereby places herself in a noble family lineage, a lineage embodying the highest values of a civilized society, a lineage characterized by spiritual, moral, and social heroism despite the degrading circumstances of slavery. And even as she concludes with an acknowledgment that she can never achieve that "separate sphere" available to white women, she maintains the legitimacy of her desire for equal access: "I still long for a hearthstone of my own, however humble," she concludes, "I wish it for my children's sake far more than for my own" (201).

Finally, "Brent" assumes the narrative posture of the "true woman" who sacrifices herself and her privacy by telling her tale to others for the benefit of her people and their cause, as she earlier sacrifices herself and her comfort for her children and their freedom. Moreover, as Andrews argues, she sacrifices her privacy to benefit her readers: "Jacobs approaches her woman-identified reader with a personal history of secrets whose revelation, she hopes, will initiate that reader into the community of confidence and support that nineteenth-century women needed in order to speak out above a whisper against their oppression" (254).[31]

The closing reference to her failed effort to gain her own "home" underscores the grim reality of Jacobs'/"Brent's" status as exile in her own country and in the country of "ideal [white] womanhood." Ex-slaves, however much they celebrated their freedom, remained second-class citizens, remained strangers in their own land, variously homeless. Pointedly, "Brent" is not even "free" to claim the legitimacy of her experience for herself. Rather she is dependent upon the testimony of Lydia Maria Child, the white abolitionist whose necessary authorization of Jacobs' text points to the ex-slave's reinscription within certain appropriative structures.[32] Moreover, she is dependent upon Child for the editing and marketing of her narrative. As Alice A. Deck suggests, Child's imprint upon the narrative is multiple (33–40). Child herself wrote to Jacobs that she "transpos[ed] sentences and pages, so as to bring the story into continuous order, and the remarks into *appropriate* places"; she requested that Jacobs send her more materials about "the outrages committed on the colored people, in Nat Turner's time," thus emphasizing dramatic details even when they were not a part of Jacobs' personal story: she deleted a last chapter on John Brown because "it does not naturally come into your story and the M.S. is already too long" (quoted in Meltzer and Holland 357). Like other ex-slave narrators, Jacobs finds her narrative and her self-representation subject to and subject of a certain amount of white "paternalistic" control.[33] Yet despite this editorial colonization, the narrative maintains the fierce intregrity of an oppositional vision.

Literally as well as figuratively homeless, Jacobs/"Brent" speaks from a position very different from the one Elizabeth Cady Stanton achieves at the conclusion of her narrative. Indeed, she stands in the speaking position of the "deterritorialized," to use the current phrase of Gilles Deleuze and Felix Guattari (17).[34] From her position on the margins, however, Jacobs can "see" both inside and outside white culture, inside and outside "true womanhood" and its supporting ideology. She can "see" the reality of both margin and center more vividly than Stanton who vis-à-vis Jacobs remains in the center of her culture. She has what bell hooks calls a kind of doubled sight.[35]

This doubled sight characterizes Jacobs' stance toward the culturally legitimated discursive regimes she invokes to gain credibility for the "truth" of her tale: those of the seduction novel, domestic fiction, the more common male slave narrative, biblical tropes, picaresque narratives, and the spiritual narrative of the movement of the soul toward salvation and freedom. Since these loci of authority are white and/or male-identified, she engages them from her oppositional position at the margins, often uncomfortably. Negotiating the intersections of multivalent discourses, Jacobs effectively troubles all these centering rhetorics simultaneously. For her deterritorialized vision leads her to probe, unconsciously and consciously, certain gaps in those conventions, certain disturbances in the surfaces of narrative.

From the perspective of the homeless, Jacobs interrogates even as she imitates the ideology of true womanhood, foregrounding its inherent racialized nature. As Carby argues, "*Incidents* demystified a convention that appeared as the obvious, commonsense rules of behavior and revealed the concept of true womanhood to be an ideology, not a lived set of social relations as she exposed its inherent contradictions and inapplicability to her life" (*Reconstructing Black Womanhood* 49). She does so through her figuration of both the northern women whom she addresses and the southern women whom she describes. On the one hand, she suggests that certain white southern women transcend the privileges of their class and status in identifying with her plight and flight, giving her shelter and support. She challenges thereby the totalized vision of white southern women as proslavery. On the other, she condemns the complacency and indifference of northern women, even those associated with the abolitionist cause, revealing her perception of the absence of sisterly concern among them by quoting from the Bible: "Rise up, ye women that are at ease! Hear my voice, ye careless daughters! Give ear unto my speech" (Isaiah 32.9). Or she manifests, albeit mutedly, a certain bitterness toward her northern reader in her comparisons of their life with hers.

But more directly, she unmasks the ideology of "true womanhood" as a fiction in her characterization of southern women who collude in the degradation of other women and deny the primacy of conjugal bonds: "The qualities of delicacy of constitution and heightened sensitivity, attributes of the Southern lady, appear as a corrupt and superficial veneer that covers an underlying strength and power in cruelty and brutality" (Carby, *Recon-structing Black Womanhood* 53–54). In contrast to the ruthless and un-civilized familial relationships of whites, she creates a world of nurturing, supportive black women, a world of strong black relationships. Incor-porating episodes that make of white men sexual profligates and moral pigmies, that make of white women uncaring, jealous, petty tyrants, this slave narrator provides a contrast of cultures that reverses ideological no-tions of "civilized" and "uncivilized," hierarchized as white and black.

Jacobs/"Brent" also challenges the very notion of American "freedom" and "democracy" and in doing so contests the presence of the agency and autonomy associated with American notions of bourgeois individuality. For instance, in a passage cited for its unveiled, assertive voice (Washing-ton 12), "Brent" comments directly on the fact that her "freedom" has been bought for her by a white woman:

So I was *sold* at last! A human being *sold* in the free city of New York! The bill of sale is on record, and future generations will learn from it that women were articles of traffic in New York, late in the nineteenth century of the Christian reli-gion. It may hereafter prove a useful document to antiquaries, who are seeking to measure the progress of civilization in the United States. I well know the value of that bit of paper; but much as I love freedom I do not like to look upon it. I am deeply grateful to the generous friend who procured it, but I despise the miscreant who demanded payment for what never rightfully belonged to him or his. (200)

Assuming the authoritative stance of a biblical prophet, Jacobs ("Brent") defiantly, unsentimentally, scorns the hypocrisy of the nation and its found-ing documents.[36]

Contrary to the conventional figuration and fate of the antagonist of the seduction tale, Jacobs presents her seducer not as any kind of Byronic figure whose power is attractive and redeemable if lethal but rather as a dehumanized pervert, brutalizing and bestial.[37] Turning the tables on the ideology supporting the slave system, Jacobs renders the white man as less than fully human and assigns him a position low on the chain of being. Moreover, she presents herself not as the passive victim but as the iron-willed antagonist who fights her victimization with bravado. "Jacobs' narrator," suggests Yellin, "asserts that—even when young and a slave— she was an effective moral agent" who "takes full responsibility for her actions" (xxx). And she further differentiates between a "selfhood" syn-onymous simply with bodily chastity and a "selfhood" emanating from self-esteem and integrity as she "abandon[s] her attempt to avoid sexual involvements in an effort to assert her autonomy as a human being" (Yellin xxx; Carby, *Reconstructing Black Womanhood* 60). For instance, she makes a careful distinction between being forcibly raped by her master and choosing her lover: "It seems less degrading to give one's self, than to submit to compulsion" (55). Ironically, she inverts the tale of seduction; the passive victim chooses her lover, chooses her fall. Moreover, and obviously, her tale of seduction does not end conventionally in death. It ends in a rise to moral integrity and freedom as she transforms her fall into the story of real integrity, persistence, and a moral vision that challenges the simplistic notions of morality associated with "true womanhood." "Still, in looking back, calmly, on the events of my life," she reflects, "I feel that the slave woman ought not to be judged by the same standard as others" (56). Later, when she describes how "Brent" reveals the truth of her past to her daughter Ellen and wins Ellen's acceptance, Jacobs reveals her own narrative priorities: she cares more for a daughter's forgiveness than for the reader's (and larger culture's) forgiveness. As Carby suggests, Jacobs places slavery on trial rather than "Brent's" social deviancy (*Reconstructing Black Womanhood* 61). For these reasons, argues Yellin, Jacobs might be calling for "a new definition of female morality grounded in her own sexual experience in a brutal and corrupt patriarchal racist society" (xxxi). Such a notion of morality would be dependent not solely upon woman's sexual purity but on more complicated, contextual grounds. Such morality would be morality historicized rather than essentialized.

Jacobs/"Brent" rewrites every narrative convention that shadows her text. She rewrites the fiction of domesticity by calling for direct political action and intervention rather than the more limited "influence" of domesticated feminism being promoted by certain white feminists of the period. As a "homeless" woman she sees the self-satisfied complacencies of a feminism that would limit its area of concern to reform and celebration of that separate sphere when political, economic, and social forces limited the access to that sphere to white middle-class women.[38] She rewrites the conventions of sentimental fiction whose heroine's fate is marriage, celebrating instead her achievement of "freedom." She rewrites that other scenario of sentimental fiction, the narrative of death by seduction or captivity, by critiquing the platitudes of a morality that erases the specificities of the slave woman's experience. She also rewrites the conventions of the "male" slave narrative which assumes the representative privilege of the male slave's experience of bondage and escape. Unlike a Frederick Douglass who in his several narratives acknowledges neither the woman who helped him escape (and who later became his wife) nor other networks assisting him as he fled, Jacobs/"Brent" eschews the representation of herself as the isolato, self-contained in her rebellion, figuring herself instead as dependent always on the support of family and friends, particularly her grandmother (see Andrews 253–58; Foster, "'In Respect to Females'" 66–70; McKay 177; Washington 3–15).

Finally, Jacob contests the notion of "selfhood's" fixedness. "I was born a slave; but I never knew it till six years of happy childhood had passed away" (3), writes "Brent" in opening her narrative. Early in the narrative Jacobs introduces the distinction between a "fixed" idea of "selfhood" and a culturally and historically contextual notion of "selfhood" (Genovese 170). By doing so she challenges the mythology of "racial" identity as an essentialized phenomenon. Providing character, nobility, full humanity to her black family, and complex humanity to herself, she deconstructs the stereotypes of black identity spawned in the ideology of "race." Refusing to be figured as the sexually unrepressed primitive black woman whose body constitutes her identity, refusing to be figured as the "mammy" of white children, refusing to be figured as morally and spiritually bankrupt, refusing therefore to be figured as less than fully human, she destabilizes colonial notions of "African-ness."

Moreover, Jacobs foregrounds throughout her text not only the intertextualities of self-representation but also the discursive staging of identity. The discourse of the text resists the finalizing impact of the history in the text. The mutual constitution of "reader" and "narrator" marks the text and its self-representational project as simultaneously fluid and contextual. Novelistic passages introduce the dialogic nature of "self-representation," the indeterminacies of role-playing and multiple voicings (Andrews 280). Life-storytelling becomes the site of "selfhood," now understood as discursive, contextual, communicative, and ultimately "fictive." Thus Jacobs' narrative testifies to the ambiguities of any core of irreducible, essentialist "selfhood."

From her position of "homelessness" at the margins of both slave and white societies, Jacobs interrogates in more complex ways than does Stanton conventional pieties of woman's "embodied selfhood" in the nineteenth century as well as conventional empowerments of "metaphysical selfhood." Out of the friction generated as she engages competing and contradictory discourses that never quite fit the parameters of her historically specific experience in slavery, Jacobs experiments with the elasticities of "self"-representation. Hers is a particularly provocative narrative, one which adumbrates those disturbances of the territorial boundaries of both "metaphysical" and "embodied" "selfhood" characterizing autobiographies written by women in the twentieth century.

NOTES

1   Candace D. Lang suggests that the notion of individuality that emerged during the Renaissance was "favored by both socioeconomic and technological developments: the decline of the feudal system and concomitant increase in

capitalist endeavor" (14). Lang argues further that the technology of the printing press, "which would enhance the notion of authorship by saving the text from the relative anonymity of oral tradition," helped foster the emergent notion of individuality. By the nineteenth century, Lang continues, "the notion of the author reached maturity under the aegis of capitalism, with the institution of the copyright, by which the writer acquired sole authority over and responsibility for his works. Historically, that development coincided with the rise of romanticism, which glorified the unique and ineffable self." See also Sidonie Smith, *Poetics of Women's Autobiography* chap. 2.

2 Miller's description of the fixed self itself assumes certain male privileges of power, language, and desire. For instance, his statement assumes that women and men experienced the same access to empowerment through language and its figures of speech. The androcentric nature of this metaphysical "self" will be addressed later in this essay.

3 Corngold quotes from Benoist 184.

4 "Only by expelling desire, affectivity and the body from reason can impartiality achieve its unity" (Young 62). See also 60–70.

5 See Miller for a discussion of the relationship of nineteenth-century realism to the ideology of selfhood which operated from "the presupposition that each man or woman has a fixed character with definite hieroglyphic outlines which may be figured truly, for example in his or her physiognomy or in the figures of speech with which he or she may be described in language" (102). Miller argues further that "the double assumption on which that aspect of realism which involves the mimesis in language of states of mind rests is the following: that there is a prelinguistic self or character and that this in its modes may be expressed, mirrored, or copied without distortion in language" (107).

6 I should note that Gallop is "reading" Luce Irigaray's *Speculum of the Other Woman* at this point in her text.

7 Butler is here glossing Simone de Beauvoir's analysis of gender difference.

8 For a stimulating if flawed analysis of woman's relationship to nature, the private sphere, and to a more personal and particularistic psychological orientation to the world, see Ortner 67–87. For a more recent discussion of the ways in which "liberal conceptions of reason and rationality have rendered the women's point of view either irrational or particularist . . . or concretistic and trivial," see Benhabib and Cornell 11. The authors are summarizing feminist challenges to "liberal" conceptions mounted by Young 56–76; and by Benhabib 77–95.

9 Sukenick explores in some detail nineteenth-century notions of male and female epistemological differences.

10 For a nineteenth-century exposition of sexual difference see Horace Mann in *A Few Thoughts on the Power and Duties of Woman: Two Lectures:* "Between the sexes, then, I hold there are innate and connate distinctions, which nature never loses sight of, unless occasionally in the production of a monster or a lusus. They are not alike, but there is a mutuality of superiority. As a general law, the man surpasses the woman in stature, in physical strength, and in those

groups or combinations of the intellectual faculties where causality plays a part; but the woman surpasses the man in beauty, in taste, in grace, in faith, in affection, in purity. His better nature tends more to science and wisdom; hers, to love and the sympathies. He delights more in the worldly uses of truth; she, more in its immortal beauty; or, as Swedenborg somewhere oddly expresses it: 'Man was created to be the understanding of truth, and woman the affection of good'" (23).

11   "Every theory of the 'subject,'" argues Luce Irigaray, "will always have been appropriate[d] to the 'masculine'" (165).

12   For an extended discussion of the ideology of the proper lady in the eighteenth and nineteenth centuries, see Poovey, esp. chap. 1.

13   For an exploration of Enlightenment notions of the feminine and the identification of the feminine with disruptive cultural forces, see Salvaggio.

14   Joan Kelly-Gadol makes a similar point when she discusses the influence of the new humanism on feminists such as Christine de Pisan: "Feminist theorizing arose in the fifteenth century, in intimate association with and in reaction to the new secular culture of the modern European state. It emerged as the voice of literate women who felt themselves and all women maligned and newly oppressed by that culture, but who were empowered by it at the same time to speak out in their defense" (5). Jardine also refers to Kelly-Gadol's analysis in *Gynesis* (95). At any historical moment, women are influenced by heterogeneous, contradictory forces of culture rather than only those discourses and practices specifically defining their selfhood and life scripts. And even the latter discourses and practices are riddled with contradiction.

15   Nina Auerbach has compellingly argued the case for the power of woman in the nineteenth century in her provocative and splendidly-written *Woman and the Demon: The Life of a Victorian Myth*.

16   The phrase is borrowed from Felicity A. Nussbaum's provocative study "Eighteenth-Century Women's Autobiographical Commonplaces."

17   Estelle Jelinek also notes this resistance in "The Paradox and Success of Elizabeth Cady Stanton" (72).

18   Heilbrun is reviewing at this point in her essay a study by Jill Conway, "Paper on Autobiographies of Women of the Progressive Era," delivered at Workshop on New Approaches to Women's Biography and Autobiography, Smith College Project on Women and Social Change, June 12–17, 1983.

19   For discussions of the negation of "the other of the other," see Michele Wallace (52–67), and Barbara Johnson (166–71).

20   See Sander Gilman's (223–61) analysis of black and white bodies in the art and medicine of the nineteenth century; and see also Andrews 3.

21   "Without writing," summarizes Gates, "no *repeatable* sign of the workings of reason, of mind, could exist. Without memory or mind, no history could exist. Without history, no humanity, as defined consistently from Vico to Hegel, could exist" (11).

22   "Making the book speak . . . constituted a motivated and political engagement with and condemnation of Europe's fundamental sign of domination, the commodity of writing, the text and technology of reason" (Gates 12).

23 For statistics on the sales of slave narratives, see Nichols xiv–xv. For further discussions of slave narratives, see Butterfield; Davis and Gates; Foster, *Witnessing Slavery*; Sekora and Turner; Starling; S. Smith, *Where I'm Bound*; and Stepto.

24 Elizabeth Fox-Genovese (171) explores Jacobs' struggle of wills.

25 For further discussions of "true womanhood," see Spruill; Scott; Clinton; Berg.

26 "Strength and ability to bear fatigue, argued to be so distasteful a presence in a white woman, were positive features to be emphasized in the promotion and selling of a black female field hand at a slave auction" (Carby, *Reconstructing Black Womanhood* 25).

27 What Carby claims for black women after the Civil War applies even more certainly to female slaves before emancipation: "Black women were relegated to a place outside the ideological construction of 'womanhood.' That term included only white women; therefore the rape of black women was of no consequence outside the black community" ("On the Threshold of Woman's Era" 308–9). Carby is elaborating the theories of the black feminist Ida B. Wells who explored the politics of lynching at the end of the nineteenth century. See, for instance, Wells, *On Lynching* (New York, 1969), for a collection of her essays. Carby also explores the politics of the black female body in *Reconstructing Black Womanhood* (26–32).

28 "In the nineteenth century," writes Gilman, "the black female was widely perceived as possessing not only a 'primitive' sexual appetite but also the external signs of this temperament—'primitive' genitalia" (232). Fascination with this phenomenon of physical and physiognomic abnormality reveals itself in the century's preoccupation with the "Hottentot Venus" whose visual characteristics—large buttocks, flat nose, strange labia—function as signs of her phylogenetic place. The critical significance of establishing the difference of black female anatomy lay, according to Gilman, in the following rationalization: "If their sexual parts could be shown to be inherently different, this would be a sufficient sign that the blacks were a separate (and, needless to say, lower) race, as different from the European as the proverbial orangutan" (235). In the catalogue of defining physical characteristics of the female Hottentot, the century read the signs of regression to an earlier state of human evolution. Moreover, in identifying some of those same characteristics as markers of prostitutes (the most sexualized of white women) and in describing the sexual practices of primitive tribes as forms of prostitution, medical anthropologists linked black sexuality and prostitution as two sources of social corruption and disease (syphilis in particular). Sexuality as the dark force in civilized "man" was thus identified with, projected onto, the prostitute and the black female (240–57).

29 Jean Fagan Yellin explores Jacobs' use of the conventions of sentimental fiction in her Introduction (xxix–xxx).

30 Slave marriages were not legally valid. The indiscriminate use of the slave woman's body by white men made fatherhood an absence. Moreover, the subjection of the female body to the will of the white master, functioning as an effective means of "unmanning" the black male, in one more way destabilized

the family and, as Elizabeth Fox-Genovese suggests, left black women with "no satisfactory social definition of themselves as women" (169).

31 See Andrews' extended discussion of the thematics of secrecy in the narrative (254–59).

32 The history of the text's fate at the hands of white abolitionists, critics, and literary historians, however, adds yet another story to her story. The text is legitimized by Lydia Maria Child's attestation that it is the authentic story of the author. Recognizing that "it will naturally excite surprise that a woman reared in Slavery should be able to write so well" (Jacobs 3), Child both explains the author's circumstances and assures the reader that she has acted as editor only. This attestation notwithstanding, the text was labeled fictional by subsequent generations until Jean Fagan Yellin recently verified the authenticity of the places, people, and experiences narrated by "Linda Brent." Ironically, the text as "technology of reason" spoke against itself. See Yellin's Introduction to the text (xiii–xxxv).

33 Deck (34–36) explores the formulaic patterns imposed by white abolitionists on the experiences and narratives of ex-slaves. See also Yellin, *Intricate Knot;* and Stepto.

34 For an elaboration of the deterritorialized nature of women's autobiographical writing, see Kaplan.

35 "Living as we did — on the edge — we developed a particular way of seeing reality. We looked both from the outside in and from the inside out. We focused our attention on the center as well as the margin. We understood both" (hooks preface).

36 See Mary Helen Washington's comments on Jacobs' empowered and assertive voice (11–12).

37 See Andrews (251); and Niemtzow (106). Andrews takes issue with Niemtzow's analysis.

38 Yellin argues that "instead of dramatizing the idea that the private sphere is women's appropriate area of concern . . . *Incidents* embodies a social analysis asserting that the denial of domestic and familial values by chattel slavery is a social issue that its female readers should address in the public arena" (Introduction xxxii). For a discussion of nineteenth-century versions of "domestic feminism" see Baym.

WORKS CITED

Andrews, William L. *To Tell a Free Story: The First Century of Afro-American Autobiography, 1760–1865.* Urbana: University of Illinois Press, 1986.

Auerbach, Nina. *Woman and the Demon: The Life of a Victorian Myth.* Cambridge: Harvard University Press, 1982.

Barker, Francis. *The Tremulous Private Body: Essays on Subjection.* London and New York: Methuen, 1984.

Baym, Nina. *Woman's Fiction: a Guide to Novels by and about Women in America, 1820–1870.* Ithaca: Cornell University Press, 1978.

Benhabib, Seyla. "The Generalized and the Concrete Other: The Kohlberg-Gilligan Controversy and Feminist Theory." In *Feminism as Critique: On the Politics of Gender,* 77–95. Minneapolis: University of Minnesota Press, 1987.

Benhabib, Seyla, and Drucilla Cornell. "Introduction: Beyond Politics and Gender." in *Feminism as Critique: On the Politics of Gender.* Minneapolis: University of Minnesota Press, 1987.

Benoist, Jean-Marie. *The Structural Revolution.* London: Weidenfeld and Nicolson, 1978.

Berg, Barbara. *The Remembered Gate: Origins of American Feminism, The Woman and the City, 1800–1860.* Oxford: Oxford University Press, 1978.

Butler, Judith. "Variations on Sex and Gender: Beauvoir, Wittig and Foucault." In *Feminism as Critique: On the Politics of Gender,* 128–42. Minneapolis: University of Minnesota Press, 1987.

Butterfield, Stephen. *Black Autobiography in America.* Amherst: University of Massachusetts Press, 1974.

Carby, Hazel V. "'On the Threshold of Woman's Era': Lynching, Empire, and Sexuality in Black Feminist Theory." In *"Race," Writing, and Difference,* ed. Henry Louis Gates, Jr., 301–16. Chicago: University of Chicago Press, 1986.

Carby, Hazel V. *Reconstructing Black Womanhood: The Emergence of the Afro-American Woman Novelist.* New York: Oxford University Press, 1987.

Clinton, Catherine. *The Plantation Mistress: Woman's World in the Old South.* New York: Pantheon, 1982.

Corngold, Stanley. *The Fate of the Self: German Writers and French Theory.* New York: Columbia University Press, 1986.

Davis, Charles, and Henry Louis Gates, Jr. *The Slave's Narrative.* New York: Oxford University Press, 1985.

Deck, Alice A. "Whose Book Is This?: Authorial Versus Editorial Control of Harriet Brent Jacobs' *Incidents in the Life of a Slave Girl: Written By Herself."* *Women's Studies International Forum,* 10 (1987), 33–40.

De Lauretis, Teresa. *Technologies of Gender: Essays on Theory, Film, and Fiction.* Bloomington: Indiana University Press, 1987.

Deleuze, Gilles, and Felix Guattari. "What Is a Minor Literature?" In *Kafka: Towards a Minor Literature,* trans. Dana Polan, 16–27. Minneapolis: University of Minnesota Press, 1986.

Douglass, Frederick. *My Bondage and My Freedom,* Part I: *Life as a Slave,* Part II: *Life as a Freeman.* New York: Miller, Orton & Mulligan, 1855.

Eagleton, Terry. *Literary Theory: An Introduction.* Minneapolis: University of Minnesota Press, 1983.

Eliot, George. *Essays of George Eliot.* Ed. Thomas Pinney. London: Routledge, 1963.

Flax, Jane. "Postmodernism and Gender Relations in Feminist Theory." *Signs: Journal of Women in Culture and Society,* 12 (Summer 1987), 621–43.

Foster, Frances Smith. "'In Respect to Females . . . ': Difference in the Portrayals of Women by Male and Female Narrators." *Black American Literature Forum,* 15 (Summer 1981), 66–70.

Foster, Francis Smith. *Witnessing Slavery: The Development of the Ante-Bellum Slave Narratives.* Westport, CT: Greenwood Press, 1979.

Fox-Genovese, Elizabeth. "To Write My Self: The Autobiographies of Afro-American Women." In *Feminist Issues in Literary Scholarship,* ed. Shari Benstock, 161–80. Bloomington: Indiana University Press, 1987.

Gallop, Jane. *The Daughter's Seduction: Feminism and Psychoanalysis.* Ithaca: Cornell University Press, 1982.

Gates, Henry Louis, Jr. "Editor's Introduction: Writing 'Race' and the Difference It Makes." In *"Race," Writing, and Difference,* ed. Gates, 1–20. Chicago: University of Chicago Press, 1986.

Gilman, Sander. "Black Bodies, White Bodies: Toward an Iconography of Female Sexuality in Late Nineteenth-Century Art, Medicine, and Literature." In *"Race," Writing, and Difference,* ed. Henry Louis Gates, Jr., 223–61. Ithaca: Cornell University Press, 1986.

Heilbrun, Carolyn G. "Women's Autobiographical Writings: New Forms." *Prose Studies,* 8 (September 1985), 14–28.

hooks, bell. *Feminist Theory: From Margin to Center.* Boston: South End Press, 1984.

Irigaray, Luce. *Speculum de l'autre femme.* Paris: Editions de Minuit, 1974.

Jacobs, Harriet. *Incidents in the Life of a Slave Girl, Written by Herself.* Ed. Lydia Maria Child. New ed. Jean Fagan Yellin. Cambridge: Harvard University Press, 1987.

James, Henry. *The Portrait of a Lady.* New York: W. W. Norton, 1975.

Jardine, Alice. *Gynesis: Configurations of Woman and Modernity.* Ithaca: Cornell University Press, 1985.

Jelinek, Estelle. "The Paradox and Success of Elizabeth Cady Stanton." In *Women's Autobiography: Essays in Criticism,* ed. Estelle Jelinek, 71–92. Bloomington: Indiana University Press, 1980.

Johnson, Barbara. *A World of Difference.* Baltimore: Johns Hopkins University Press, 1987.

Kaplan, Caren. "Deterritorializations: The Rewriting of Home and Exile in Western Feminist Discourse." *Cultural Critique,* 6 (Spring 1987), 187–98.

Kelly, Joan. "Early Feminist Theory and the *Querelle des Femmes,* 1400–1789." *Signs: Journal of Women in Culture and Society,* 8 (Autumn 1982), 4–28.

Lang, Candace D. *Irony/Humor: Critical Paradigms.* Baltimore and London: Johns Hopkins University Press, 1988.

McKay, Nellie Y. "Race, Gender, and Cultural Context in Zora Neale Hurston's *Dust Tracks on a Road.*" In *Life/Lines: Theorizing Women's Autobiography,* ed. Bella Brodzki and Celeste Schenck, 175–88. Ithaca: Cornell University Press, 1988.

Maclean, Ian. *The Renaissance Notion of Woman: A Study in the Fortunes of Scholasticism and Medical Science in European Intellectual Life.* Cambridge: Cambridge University Press, 1980.

Mann, Horace. *A Few Thoughts on the Power and Duties of Woman: Two Lectures.* Syracuse: Hall, Mills, 1853.

Meltzer, Milton, and Patricia G. Holland, eds. *The Collected Correspondence of Lydia Maria Child, 1817–1880.* Amherst: University of Massachusetts Press, 1982.

Miller, J. Hillis. "'Herself against Herself': The Clarification of Clara Middleton." In *The Representation of Women in Fiction: Selected Papers from the English Institute, 1981,* ed. Carolyn G. Heilbrun and Margaret R. Higonnet, 98–123. Baltimore: Johns Hopkins University Press, 1983.

Moi, Toril. *Sexual/Textual Politics: Feminist Literary Theory.* London: Methuen, 1985.

More, Hannah. *The Works of Hannah More.* Vol. 1. New York: Harper and Brothers, 1854.

Nichols, Charles H., Jr. *Many Thousand Gone: The Ex-Slaves' Account of Their Bondage and Freedom.* Leiden, Netherlands: E.J. Brill, 1963.

Niemtzow, Annette. "The Problematic of Self in Autobiography: The Example of the Slave Narrative." In *The Art of the Slave Narrative,* ed. John Sekora and Darwin T. Turner, 96–109. Macomb: Western Illinois University Press, 1982.

Nussbaum, Felicity A. "Eighteenth-Century Women's Autobiographical Commonplaces." In *The Private Self: Theory and Practice of Women's Autobiographical Writings,* ed. Shari Benstock, 147–71. Chapel Hill: University of North Carolina Press, 1988.

Ortner, Sheri B. "Is Female to Male as Nature Is to Culture?" In *Women, Culture, and Society,* ed. Michelle Zimbalist Rosaldo and Louise Lamphere, 67–87. Stanford: Stanford University Press, 1974.

Peterson, Linda H. *Victorian Autobiography: The Tradition of Self-Interpretation.* New Haven and London: Yale University Press, 1986.

Poovey, Mary. *The Proper Lady and the Woman Writer.* Chicago: University of Chicago Press, 1984.

Riley, Denise. *"Am I That Name?": Feminism and the Category of "Women" in History.* Minneapolis: University of Minnesota Press, 1988.

Rousseau, Jean-Jacques. *Les Confessions.* Vol. 1 of Oeuvres complètes. Paris: Pléiade, 1959.

Salvaggio, Ruth. *Enlightened Absence: Neoclassical Configurations of the Feminine.* Urbana: University of Illinois Press, 1988.

Scott, Ann. *The Southern Lady: From Pedestal to Politics, 1830–1930.* Chicago: University of Chicago Press, 1970.

Sekora, John, and Darwin T. Turner, eds. *The Art of Slave Narrative.* Macomb: Northern Illinois University Press, 1982.

Smith, Paul. *Discerning the Subject.* Minneapolis: University of Minnesota Press, 1988.

Smith, Sidonie. *A Poetics of Women's Autobiography: Marginality and the Fictions of Self-Representation.* Bloomington: Indiana University Press, 1987.

Smith, Sidonie. *Where I'm Bound: Patterns of Slavery and Freedom in Black American Autobiography.* Westport: Greenwood Press, 1974.

Spruill, Julia Cherry. *Women's Life and Work in the Southern Colonies*. 1938; rpt. New York: W. W. Norton, 1972.

Stanton, Elizabeth Cady. *Eighty Years and More (1815–1897): Reminiscences of Elizabeth Cady Stanton*. New York: European Publishing, 1898.

Starling, Marion Wilson. *The Slave Narrative: Its Place in History*. Boston: G. K. Hall, 1981.

Stepto, Robert B. *From behind the Veil: A Study of Afro-American Narrative*. Urbana: University of Illinois Press, 1979.

Sukenick, Lynn. "On Women and Fiction." In *The Authority of Experience: Essays in Feminist Criticism,* eds. Edwards, Lee R. and Arlyn Diamond. Amherst: University of Massachusetts Press, 1977.

Wallace, Michele. "Variations on Negation and the Heresy of Black Feminist Creativity." In *Reading Black, Reading Feminist: A Critical Anthology,* ed. Henry Louis Gates, Jr. New York: Meridian, 1990.

Washington, Mary Helen. "Introduction, Meditations on History: The Slave Woman's Voice." In *Invented Lives: Narratives of Black Women, 1860–1960,* ed. Mary Helen Washington, 3–15. New York: Doubleday Anchor Press, 1987.

Welter, Barbara. *Dimity Convictions: The American Woman in the Nineteenth Century*. Columbus: Ohio State University Press, 1976.

Woolf, Virginia. *A Room of One's Own*. New York: Harcourt, Brace & World, 1929.

Yellin, Jean Fagan. *The Intricate Knot: Black Figures in American Literature*. New York: New York University Press, 1972.

Yellin, Jean Fagan. Introduction to Jacobs.

Young, Iris Marion. "Impartiality and the Civil Public: Some Implications of Feminist Critiques of Moral and Political Theory." In Benhabib and Cornell, 57–76.

CHAPTER 5

The Political Is the Personal: Two Autobiographies of Woman Suffragists

ANN D. GORDON

Woman suffragists, like other leaders of women in the nineteenth century, approached the art of autobiography with their public identities well crafted and their public voices tuned closely to a particular pitch of the cultures they sought to influence. In autobiography they might aspire to the definitive variation of their personal story but they did not start afresh. With an acute sense of the historical importance of their work, these leaders knew that they had etched their lives into the history of women and the nation. That record would stand whether or not they retold their story; they would shape its interpretation, fill in its details, but not alter its substance. Because their political goal still eluded women and a political movement still needed its personalities, these leaders created themselves as their followers knew them. To do otherwise would suggest some discomfort with or rejection of their well-known presence, perhaps even some second thoughts about the fight they had waged.

The two best-known autobiographies of suffragists are more particular still. Although they portray women whose social experience, economic fortunes, and personalities differed radically, they are alike in speaking to issues that arose from the leadership of the authors themselves. Frontierswoman Abigail Scott Duniway (1834–1915) grew up in Illinois and Oregon with no formal education. After marriage to a rancher she seemed destined to replicate her mother's life of heavy domestic labor and frequent childbirth. An accident that disabled her husband forced the family into town where Abigail could support them by teaching school, keeping a millinery shop, and, in time, writing, lecturing, and publishing in the cause

111

of woman's rights. For forty years she dominated the woman's rights movement in the Pacific Northwest, never quite breaking away to achieve a national following but indisputably a regional leader. If the written word can be trusted, she had no sense of humor whatsoever, but excelled in direct debate. Of debate she had considerable experience. Alienated from Easterners and at odds with the woman's temperance movement, Duniway's leadership was fraught with acrimony.[1]

At the other end of the continent, Elizabeth Cady Stanton (1815–1902) knew the privileges of wealth and power in childhood. Her father, Daniel Cady, speculated profitably in lands and practiced law. He served one term in the U.S. House of Representatives and was elevated to a judgeship on the New York State Supreme Court. His daughter received one of the best formal educations available to her generation and learned a considerable amount of law from the constant stream of law students who shared the family's household. After marriage to an antislavery activist, Stanton began to use her connections and talents to define a political career, a career that won her national recognition by the time of the Civil War. Witty and playful, she became a popular figure despite her radical social ideas. A thorough scholar of constitutionalism, she had the ear of politicians even when she could not prevail on them to support her cause.[2]

Their autobiographies are strikingly different in content and narrative voice. Duniway, who published *Path Breaking* in 1914, left no doubt that she intended to vindicate her strategies and tactics by concentrating on the political victories that fell to women under her leadership and by attacking her enemies. The text carries the dual burden of autobiography and, as the subtitle indicates, a "History of the Equal Suffrage Movement in the Pacific Coast States."[3] "I have been importuned . . . to write a history . . . ," she began. "These requests invariably call for statement, in autobiographical form, beginning with the personal history of myself . . ." (1). Far less personal than most of her fiction and seldom pausing for introspection, the book rushes past childhood and marriage in order to record her political work. By the book's midpoint Duniway abandons narrative control over the history in favor of publishing a documentary collection that preserves her most significant speeches.

In *Eighty Years and More,* published in 1898, Elizabeth Cady Stanton was freer of the concern about historical documentation that drove Duniway and more inclined to treat the subject of her individuality. She had prepared in the 1880s three volumes of the *History of Woman Suffrage,* which contained her reminiscences of co-workers, her own interpretations of critical moments and moot principles, and a great many of her addresses. The preface to her autobiography tantalizes with the promise of "the story of my private life as the wife of an earnest reformer, as an enthusiastic housekeeper, . . . and as the mother of seven children, [which] may amuse and benefit the reader" (n.p.). Stanton dwelt on her childhood, reconstructing its environments, entertainments, and prevailing values in great detail, and the style of describing settings and sociability carries through her book. Hers is a chatty, often funny, and very personable work, driven by Stanton's zest for life where Duniway's seems driven by indignation.

When Stanton and Duniway wrote their books, neither of them any longer represented the dominant values and experiences within the movement. The goal of voting had widespread support but not for the reasons that these pioneers had advocated. By going back in time through autobiography they could recapture the roots of their movement and highlight its formative events while reasserting the importance of ideals and strategies that they personally championed.

To discover themselves outside of the movement's center near the end of their lives had a familiar feel, evoking the oppositional roles they had played in their younger days. The creation of audiences for themselves and their ideas had been a large part of their political work and the primary source of their incomes. The start of Stanton's public life in 1848 had coincided with the growth of a new female audience in the northern United States, served by novelists, women's magazines, advice books, and encouraged by religious transformations that allowed women's distinct expressions of conversion and faith. By plunging into this literary marketplace with convictions about individualism and political equality Stanton had helped to diversify the ideals under discussion. By the time Duniway entered this marketplace nearly a generation later around 1868, the competition of ideas was intense. Both women had earned their livings by representing — in both symbolic and political senses — a strong tendency within the audience of women.

That tendency, put simply, applied secular republicanism to the problem of women's degradation. What existed in their society as distinctly female reflected not nature and social adaptation to it but outmoded social structures imposed on a nature that rarely in world history had had opportunity to realize its potential. If women indeed had a nature distinct from men it could not be known until females enjoyed the unfettered individualism that inspired the American political system.[4] Thus, the central tendency in the woman's rights movement argued that gender was a product of an unjust society. But most female activism in the antebellum period took an opposing course and justified itself on the strength of gender difference.

Political conflict among women over the significance of gender became more complex after the Civil War. The numbers of women involved in debating the issues increased, and as women embarked in growing numbers on public work—whether philanthropic or economic—the rival ideas had greater social consequences. By the 1880s, many advocates of a female sphere and moral domain arrived at the conclusion that they needed political power and thus entered the movement so far controlled by advocates of political equality. The woman suffrage movement, thus, at the end of the century contained descendants of both tendencies, and the differences in fundamental philosophy emerged in contests over tactics and strategy.

This political framework may seem remote from the texts of autobiographies, but it provides vital clues for reading these works. Duniway and Stanton spent their adult lives in that contest over first principles, law, and tactics. Their commitments to individualism generated political activity, and their power depended in part on the political fortunes of their ideals. When they turned to the task of writing autobiographies they knew very well the history and current condition of those ideals.

Duniway explains that she began her manuscript in 1905–6 (83). Although she omits to explain why she then set the project aside until 1913–14, the pair of dates pinpoint personal and political events that suggest motives. First, surgery in 1903 very nearly killed her and did leave her deaf in one ear. Moreover, by 1905 conflict over Duniway's identity was of public moment. On the one hand, in its centennial Lewis and Clark Exposition, Oregon honored one of its outstanding pioneers and citizens with Abigail Scott Duniway Day. On the other hand, within the same summer, when the National American Woman Suffrage Association (NAWSA) held its annual convention in Portland at Duniway's invitation, the leaders excluded her from the program and planned a takeover of the state association (Moynihan 210–13). The autobiography at one level explained both identities: the person recognized for her longevity and service to the state and the person at war with major segments of the suffrage movement. Perhaps the regularity of state suffrage campaigns thereafter—1906, 1908, 1910, 1912—precluded the private act of autobiography. Perhaps, too, death seemed more remote as she regained some of her health. But in 1912 Oregon women won the vote, and anything Abigail Scott Duniway said about how the movement should proceed gained new credibility. Then, too, confusion about her significance persisted. The governor turned over to her the job of issuing the proclamation declaring equal suffrage, but many state and national suffragists still denounced Duniway and her views (Moynihan 216). When she resumed the autobiography, she wrote not to celebrate a job well done but to improve an ongoing struggle. Women elsewhere in the United States still battled for the right, while in Oregon women used their new power to campaign for prohibition. The completed book spoke directly to her views on why prohibition should not pass and why woman suffragists did violence to their own history and aspirations by favoring it.

There is no evidence to suggest that Stanton began her reminiscences for such proximate and painful reasons as Duniway. She had, however, taken the measure of her co-laborers in the suffrage cause and found them unwilling to follow her into opposition to their religious degradation that would match their resistance to civil degradation. She approached autobiography first by writing short articles for the *Woman's Tribune,* a suffrage newspaper, where they appeared from April 5, 1889, through July 9, 1892.[5] With the series complete or ended in the *Tribune,* Stanton proceeded to supply the same paper with chapters of the "Woman's Bible, Part I," her witty commentaries on the history of women as revealed in the Bible. These articles appeared as a pamphlet in 1895, prompting the NAWSA to disassociate itself from the *Woman's Bible* in order to keep orthodox women in the movement. Still not ready to return to autobiography, Stanton next wrote "Part II" of the Bible project as a series of articles for the *Boston Investigator.* By 1897 Stanton completed the Bible project and revised and extended the autobiography. The simultaneous creation of these two major works defines her political and historical posture toward the suffrage movement. *Eighty Years* would establish that her own route to secularism paralleled the development of a movement for equal rights and more accurately reflected the history of women's liberation than did the emergence of a suffrage movement which wanted to empower its own religious beliefs and cater to ministerial authority.

Individualists make themselves, or so Stanton and Duniway aver in their construction of prepolitical childhoods. Some quality may have set them apart in their youth, but overall they did what women of their generation and social class did. They reacted to forces external to self, whether Calvinism, frontier insecurities, hierarchical family structures, gender differences, or law. A predisposition toward self-reliance, pitted against an environment that would keep children dependent, made a rebel out of Elizabeth Cady. All the Cady children, Stanton explained, were "disposed to assume the responsibility of their own actions." Although material comforts and opportunities abounded, the household ran on fear, fear as the basis for religious faith and fear as the motive for secular respect. In that atmosphere, "nothing but strong self-will and a good share of hope and mirthfulness could save an ordinary child from becoming a mere nullity" (8). She remembered a distinct childhood, governed by rules which served to introduce life in small doses. In four chapters devoted to the years before her marriage, she recreated in equal amounts the sheer joy of learning, daring, dancing, and laughing and dismal impositions like "the theological dogmas" and single-sex education (24, 33–36). Her description of her own parents and childhood may or may not be objective (and there are virtually no sources against which to check her account), but she highlights historical and cultural conflicts that shaped her life, and the lives of women who would endorse her ideas for change.

The account explains how she defined out of childhood what to change in her society. Her mother, Margaret Cady, has a very small role; like all adults in this childhood, she exemplifies a rigid Calvinism and an anti-democratic authority. That she managed a large staff of servants can be inferred from stories about children's activities. Much more than that cannot be learned. The father personifies law and the codification of inequality. He teaches his daughter about law but bucks responsibility for the shape that law has taken. Further, as a father without surviving sons, he gives voice to the worst of patrilineal culture. He believes that daughters offer less satisfaction than sons and have no need for equal preparation as self-reliant adults. As a wealthy patriarch, he can enforce dependency by his control of wealth.[6]

Duniway could state the principal meaning of her childhood concisely and allowed only eight pages to the topic. Childhood had been the time to learn the burdens of womanhood and consequences of dependence. In physical deformities that she attributed to working at jobs too hard for a child's body, she bore the reminders of its burdens through the rest of her life. Duniway focuses more on her mother than her father. Her father had "an adventurous disposition" which translated into financial dreams and westward migration. But her mother was the ultimate victim: an "invalid" who died on the Oregon Trail. This "busy mother," with a "rapidly increasing family of a dozen," intones, "Poor baby! She'll be a woman some day. Poor baby!" (8). Children die, those that live must work, there's no time for school and rarely occasion to play. Duniway prefaced this sketch of misery with a declaration of her adult ideal about human responsibility and self-dependence. Broaching her opposition to prohibition in the book's introduction, she explains that humans share a "natural inheritance of self-government" and can be taught to live "in voluntary obedience to the God-given right of self-control" (xvii). But unlike Stanton she will not trace the roots of this belief to her childhood influences nor make a rebel of the girl. This family serves simply as the perfect foil for a daughter who will recognize sources of female despair and enter the world to change it.

Marriage changes the conditions of their lives but does not in itself break their dependence. Duniway, in particular, finds in marriage yet another external force that determines her reality. She marries herself off in one sentence: "I met my fate in the person of Mr. Ben C. Duniway" (9); then begins her own burdensome wifehood at an age considerably younger than Stanton at marriage. A world explored in detail in her fiction is here only sketched out in a brief chapter—work to feed and house ranch hands without comparable assistance at her own work, butter sales to raise cash, and births. She calls herself "a general pioneer drudge" and refers to "my life of hopeless toil, amid uncongenial surroundings" (10, 29). A new external force, not self-reliance, takes her out of the kitchen. She becomes a breadwinner because of her husband's inability to support the family. Stanton's rebellion begins before marriage in her discovery of the abolitionist cause and selection of Henry B. Stanton for a mate. It is a partnership for which she takes full responsibility. At first the marriage seems to extend the good side of childhood, offering even greater fields of journey and discovery. It takes her four chapters to recount all the intellectual influences, important people, and travels that occupied her time in the first seven years of her marriage. But she too must accept the reality that Henry defines: his vague and unprofitable career, shifting political ideals, retraining as a lawyer, and ill health that drives them from Boston to Seneca Falls.

It is obvious that there are, in these books, two vastly different sectors of American society, separated by income, education, region, and a host of expectations for self in society. And yet they depict young women moving toward similar personal conversions which in turn draw them into the same political movement. Though their conversions are not "moments" in a life, in which by blinding insight or physical triumph they reach salvation, both authors bow to convention with narratives that try to assign a time and place to their change. Duniway would have it that another woman's fate pushed her into action. Joining a friend in search of justice under Oregon's laws of property, she discovers out of her empathy that women can and should state the terms of their own injustice and lobby for change in the law. At home that evening she "sat on the floor beside his couch," while Benjamin "placed his hand on [her] head" and told her that the inequities in women's lives would continue until women won the right to vote (39–40). The scene safely situates the start of her path breaking within a sentimental domestic tradition and assigns it a philanthropic rather than self-interested purpose.

Stanton narrowed in on her response to domesticity as the catalyst for change. Seven years and several babies after her marriage, when the Stantons moved from Boston to Seneca Falls, her new home seemed "comparatively solitary, and the change . . . was somewhat depressing." The novelty of housewifery had worn off. She had fewer urban conveniences, poor roads, no sidewalks, and "poor servants." Henry "was frequently from home," leaving the work of house and children all to be done by "one brain" (145). She solved her problem by calling a woman's rights convention and demanding the vote. She situates her conversion in an ordinary domesticity that links her to a culture of middle-class women but also registers a sharp complaint about her own downward mobility. Problem and remedy seem oddly out of joint.

The conversion consists of the decision to change society and specifically to change law, while the personal consequences of conversion are to become self-reliant and break the hold of immediate circumstances on their identity. But because both women played critical roles in founding a movement, the path to personal conversion serves as allegory for political change too. In Stanton's text this larger history is more evident and also more important owing to her special claim as originator of the demand for suffrage. This account of her young life puts the conflict over religion at the center of her personality by making her childhood resistance to religious dogma the birthplace of her anti-authoritarianism. Her awakening required constant resistance to what religion taught her, beginning with the "depressing influences" of Scotch Presbyterianism which taught her never to "shadow one young soul with any of the superstitions of the Christian religion" (26). A teenage crisis follows, one brought on by an evangelical revival from which "rational ideas based on scientific facts" (44) save her. While reading the Bible in her late teens, she resists the "popular heresy" taught in every one of its books that the "headship of man" is divinely ordained (34).

From questioning religion she learned to question all arbitrary authority. The habit next spread to law. A child's sense of justice brought to her attention the rule of inequitable law, and in a story she began telling her audiences by 1867, she grasped the concepts of law and law books and planned to attack the problem with scissors. Once her father explained the universe of law and role of lawmakers, this precocious child promised to go to Albany and get the laws changed. The resistance penetrates the realm of mothering. At the heart of her chapter "Motherhood," about learning the job with the first of her seven children, is her struggle to break away from the female traditions and male expertise that she finds irrational and unsuccessful. When she succeeds, she explains, she "trusted neither men nor books absolutely after this, either in regard to the heavens above or the earth below . . . " (120). Perhaps too it spread to marital relations. Although she never describes resistance to *her* husband, the chapters concerned with village life in Senaca Falls recount several amusing stories about teaching wives to resist petty tyrannies in household management. If she would not admit at age eighty to straightening out her own husband, she showed she had an intimate knowledge of unequal marriage relations.

But the most significant use Stanton made of the religious theme was to place it explicitly at the center of her history of the origins of equal rights. She told the story of the World's Anti-Slavery Convention of 1840 as a confrontation over clerical authority and biblical interpretation. On the side of reaction, the British delegates reasoned that "women . . . were excluded by Scriptural texts from sharing equal dignity and authority with men," and when women's participation in the meeting came to a vote, "the clerical portion of the convention was most violent in its opposition." Representing progress, George Bradburn championed the women by telling the ministers that if they were right about the Bible, he should "bring together every Bible in the universe and make a grand bonfire of them," while the American women she met espoused "equality of the sexes and . . . did not believe in the popular orthodox religion" (83).

Further fueling her conversion, there were encounters and associations with other rebels who supplied direction to her anti-authoritarian tendency. From her married life in Boston in the early 1840s she selected the religious influence of Theodore Parker and John Greenleaf Whittier for extended comment, linking herself to the traditions of Unitarianism, transcendentalism, the Free Religious Association, and the groups which shared her resistance. She found the will and courage of the reformer at the home of her good friend and cousin, Gerrit Smith. There among abolitionists she discovered alternatives to her family's aristocratic and patriarchal values, an ideal of human liberty in an unfettered environment, and a culture of reform. "The anti-slavery platform," she proclaimed boldly in 1898, in the era of Jim Crow, "was the best school the American people ever had on which to learn republican principles and ethics" (59).

This metaphor for the origins of "her" movement is also a powerful statement about woman's politics by the time she constructed this text of a young life. Every element of this narrative was in contention within the woman suffrage movement itself. Not even the historical connection between abolitionism and woman's rights could be agreed upon, as evidenced when delegates in 1890 asked that antislavery history no longer be mentioned in speeches at the NAWSA conventions.[8]

Duniway's generation on the East Coast would not merit pioneering status, but she came to maturity and her awakening in time to help launch woman's rights on the West Coast. Among western pioneers of woman's rights, she stood out too for having grown up in the region rather than bringing eastern notions in the migrant's baggage. The relationship between an older, eastern movement and an indigenous, western youngster runs as a theme throughout her text. The brevity of Duniway's prepolitical story in part stems from its familiarity to those who knew her work. She had crafted her political and literary personae from the harsh physical reality of frontier womanhood. In fiction, journalism, stage presence, and political manner, she had distilled her mother's life on the Illinois prairie, her own girlhood there, the new settlements of Oregon in which she married, bore her children, and built her political base. When she turned to write *Path Breaking* she could evoke this vast repertoire with small gems of well-hewn phrases. Recollecting her return home after the birth of a sibling, she describes the timing as "after our mother was able, or felt obliged to call herself able, to resume her many cares" (6), and thus simply captures a painful choice in the universe of the overworked wife. With similar passing remarks, she portrays her own frontier physique: "helpless on a bed of illness caused by my own hardships as a pioneer path breaker" (8), "the half-bent farmer's wife" (11). The last domestic details in *Path Breaking,* the last that readers learn about her domestic and economic circumstances, describe her support of her family just before she became a reformer. But preserved in her own misshapen body and physical pain, frontier womanhood gave historical legitimacy to her individuality, long after her back needed to bend over the butter churn and the well.

A detailed account of touring the Pacific Northwest with Susan B. Anthony in 1871 sets up the East/West duality. Anthony survives both the experience and the retelling of it quite well. Duniway enjoys anecdotes that show Anthony's initiation into frontier conditions and thus underscore her eastern origins, while Anthony values local initiative and encourages Duniway to develop the regional movement. Further along in *Path Breaking,* Duniway scatters allusions to the virtue associated with her own time and place, with being a daughter of the frontier, as if disagreements in her life might be explained by the fact that her enemies lacked her cultural roots. Interfering national suffrage leaders are "Eastern invaders" (67). "Eleventh-hour suffragists" crop up repeatedly, ignorant of history and weak in principles (288). Anna Howard Shaw, Duniway's nemesis from the moment of her debut on the suffrage platform, is introduced as "young, inexperienced" and new (202–3).[9] When her story arrives at the stage of her life during which battles with national leaders predominated, the imagery becomes political argument. Easterners fail to understand the West, while Westerners learn "by our many Western defeats, under [Eastern] management, that every locality is its own best interpreter of its own plans of work" (211).

Time and space had defined a body of thought and values which in Duniway's mind produced *the* foundations for a politics of equal rights. Equal rights were born of relentless labor, dependency, economic uncertainty, unequal and inadequate economic opportunities for women, and laws that diminished women's humanity against all reason. They flourished on a frontier where men and women both understood the meaning of equal opportunity.

With conversions complete, the authors move themselves to the center of the story as the principal actors. At that point in the narrative family members become bit players, household work recedes, the social and economic environment of life loses its hold on their identities. In what follows, the private life seems hardly private, lacking intimacy, emotional depth, or dirt, while public life intrudes throughout the narrative. Just when modern readers want to know whether all their personal relationships changed as a consequence of their emergence into selfhood and reform, Duniway and Stanton begin to narrate their political work. The narrative shift mirrors a new identity, new to history as well as to these specific individuals. Empowered by their decision to change an objective order that has defined them within its construction of a female, thereafter they exist primarily in relationship to their role as agents of change. They make, thus, a dual assertion, that female lives are human artifacts subject to change and that the necessary changes result from women's actions. The acts of their own self-creation provide a test case for liberation of the sex.

What Stanton will seek in the last fifty years of her life, she explained in the narrative of youth. From her youthful discoveries, she will teach women to protect the basic principles of American government, to resist orthodoxy and tradition, to develop independent intellectual and scientific traditions, to build family life on a foundation of human dignity and equal rights, and to become self-reliant. Her definition of "personal" no longer connotes domestic or familial life but instead the life of herself while making history. The core of *Eighty Years,* nearly two hundred pages covering 1848 to 1880, describes the busiest years of her leadership. While the chapters parallel a history of suffragism, they dwell on feelings, on the personal side of the work, on the inessentials of travel — lost manuscripts, friendships, bad beds and worse food. They provide a portrait of the reformer. The story is organized into clusters of activity and people which are only loosely placed in a chronology. Susan B. Anthony is introduced in two chapters following the 1848 convention at Seneca Falls, which locates the start of their friendship at the right place, but the chapters exhaust the subject of their half-century collaboration. "Lyceums and Lecturers" places her debut on the commercial lecture platform at its proper point after the 1867 tour of Kansas but then compresses a dozen years of travel and public speaking into its twenty-three pages.

At the point when Stanton recedes from public view due to old age and a preference for writing her ideas rather than speaking them to countless audiences, the narrative shifts again. Time is neatly accounted for by the advent in 1880 of a diary from which she can recreate precise details, and a more sedentary life is reflected in the way that chapters are defined by the places she lived. According to the autobiography itself, on October 18, 1880, Stanton made the decision to keep a diary and began on her sixty-fifth birthday the next month (323–25). Immediately the text reflects her new source in its specificity and triviality. "On November 12, 1880 . . .

it was a bright, sunny day. . . . My thoughts were with my absent children. . . . On November 13 the New York *Tribune* announced. . . . The arrival of Miss Anthony and Mrs. Gage, on November 20 . . ." (325–27). Blocks of time identified by where she was—Toulouse, London, Johnstown, New York—or a major event such as the International Council of Women or the reunion of Troy Seminary graduates divide the text into chapters rather than the themes that shaped her most active years. Here Stanton includes her recreational travels, her reform work in causes other than woman suffragism, and speeches that treat of subjects other than law and constitutionalism. There is something more intimate about these later sections than the more artful constructions of childhood or the historically aware record of campaigning for woman suffrage. This clever crafter of phrase and argument has allowed far more of the detritus of her daily life to fill the space she has allotted to the ongoing agitation of an elderly person.

Religion supplies a narrative thread through all the shifts that Stanton makes, in particular establishing continuity between the formative childhood and the sedentary old age. Anecdotes receive the gloss of religious polemic, as in her visit to the Mormons in 1871 which prompts the statement:

When women understand that governments and religions are human inventions; that Bible, prayerbooks, catechisms, and encyclical letters are all emanations from the brain of man, they will no longer be oppressed by the injunctions that come to them with the divine authority of "Thus Saith the Lord." (285)

Or in explaining why she resided in a convent in Toulouse for a few months in 1883 she pauses to describe High Mass as "a most entertaining spectacular performance" that "belonged to the Dark Ages"; in sum, "the whole performance was hollow and mechanical" (346). By 1878 the account registers the systematic work "to rouse women to a realization of their degraded position in the Church" (383), including among many other avenues the project to issue the *Woman's Bible*. What seems a simple documentary device stemming from elderly pride, to include in this volume the address she wrote for a celebration of her eightieth birthday in the Metropolitan Opera House, carries the challenges further into her present time. In that address to a broad cross-section of organized, middle-class womanhood, she carefully explained why the battle with churches must be fought if women were to end their dependence. Self-reliance required it.

The principles that Duniway endorsed are not gathered for systematic presentation but rather insinuated throughout the political narrative. The principles underlying her opposition to prohibition dominate because of the immediate need to address an audience on the eve of voting whether to amend the state constitution to prohibit liquor. Liquor, she argues in her introduction, exists as one of the elements of the planet like air, fire, and water. Elements are not legislated out of existence. State power can never make man "safe from his own moral delinquency," short of imprisoning everyone. In this fight, she states, the same conflicts are at work as in the battle to secure equal rights: "the two contending elements of force and freedom." One prohibition is of a piece with the other (xvii–xviii).

In the many references to temperance that occur in the book, she carefully defines her abhorrence of intoxication and her knowledge of the damage it wreaks in the lives of men and women. In the highly compressed section on her childhood, she elects to tell of an uncle who "fell into evil ways" when drunk and then met death at the hands of ruffians (4–5). She admits to an early collaboration with the Temperance Alliance, a group committed to moral suasion, not legislation (62). Among the burdens of a mother she always includes the responsibility to raise sons who will not fall victim to drink. Her dispute is with the "temporary expedients" of "the politico-prohibition movement" (62–64). Sensing "fuel for their pulpits," preachers exploited both the cause and women. "Pettifogging politicians saw their opportunity and began to roar" (54). Women, tired of being "servants without wages," enjoyed earning their own money as lecturers for the cause (206). Morally bankrupt, this temperance movement undermined the cause of equal suffrage at three levels: by challenging the ideal of "moral and individual responsibility" which equal suffrage embodied (62); by positing "an arbitrary government over the inalienable rights of men, to which the average voter quite naturally objects" (106), that is, by alienating voters; and by giving rise to a well-financed, political force opposed to woman suffrage in the form of the liquor lobby.

The record of suffrage work after about 1883 becomes in large part a saga of disasters brought on by this powerful and misguided force. Against it Duniway can only utter the plea she made in a speech in the early seventies: "Make women *free!* Give them the power the ballot gives to you, and the control of their own earnings. . . ." The issue will then be settled at home and on the basis of human strength (63).

There are other principles and tactics that Duniway wants to explain. The use of "equal" rather than "woman" suffrage in her title underlines her opposition to a woman-centered movement based on sexual differences. Whole chapters hang together on the thin thread of political assertion. In the chapter called "Starts a Newspaper," she ostensibly recounts her decision to launch the *New Northwest* in 1872. It opens with explanations about how she and her sisters "had had no reason for hating men"; treats two episodes in which the men of her family came to her aid when hostility to woman suffrage took the form of personal attacks on her; makes the dubious claim that her powerful brother, newspaper editor Harvey W.

Scott, was a loving and supportive friend; and then reminisces about businessmen and ministers whose assistance at critical moments made her work possible. This hodge-podge has a theme—the strategical assertion that the "one way by which we may hope to obtain [suffrage] . . . is by and through the affirmative votes of men" (156). It defined her as the antithesis of a newer suffragist who "demand[ed suffrage] as a whip, with which to scourge the real or apparent vices of the present voting classes" (163). Her audiences would recognize an attack on the franchise of moral superiority. The chapter entitled "First Anniversary Meeting," an event of 1872 in Oregon, leaps suddenly to Washington Territory in 1883 because there her tactics succeeded. After explaining why, in Oregon, she did not organize local societies as a basis for popular agitation on the question of suffrage, but before she explains how much criticism her quiet "still hunt" operations warranted over the years, she records how quietly one victory came.

In a sense the whole book works by a similar indirection. Her indignation with fools, her caustic remarks, and insistence on the superiority of her own solutions to troubling problems reveal more of her identity than the selection of details. The intensity of her political recollections as an elderly woman gives the best image of how deeply within the political cause she passed her active years. And the strenuous defense of self measures better than narrative could how deeply troubled she was by the antipathy of her enemies.

In both books, what seems a refusal or inability to construct an identity from the materials of private life may instead be an assertion about identity that would overcome the determining power of gender. Their individualities, indeed their identities, are tied up with how they worked both sides of the divide between politics and family. They portray themselves in new roles, lying between but combining traditional roles of women and men: mothers as lobbyists, wives as political campaigners, housewives as authors, or perhaps more accurately, lobbyists as mothers, and so forth. Duniway goes so far as to merge these outlines explicitly in terms of her three births: a natural one from her mother's womb, a rebirth as wife of Benjamin Duniway and mother to their children, and "my third and latest birth" into the struggle for woman's rights (28). But the best symbol for the middle way that Stanton and Duniway thought they occupied might be the World's Anti-Slavery Convention in 1840, or Stanton's honeymoon. Stanton always, whether writing her life or history, assigned formative experience to this event in the history of woman's rights. She was there not as a delegate but as a bride watching her husband's international debut. By featuring the convention as a major turning point in political history, Stanton assigned to her honeymoon a significance unique in historiography. How much more public can the private become?

Their literary identities made the claim that their new roles were humanly possible and politically desirable to attain. While they contested the debilitating structures grown up around gender differences, Stanton and Duniway had repositioned themselves outside the boundaries of female experience to which they were raised. Further they devoted their lives to destroying spheres both as the means to create a space for their own political work and as the objective for changing laws. The risk of writing about oneself as private, i.e., female, person was that of reinfusing meaning into categories they wanted to shatter. Their own lives had, in real time, continually exhibited new possibilities emergent from nineteenth-century politics and female experience. Thus autobiography should reflect life by insisting that the categories be altered. No preconceived notion of where the line between female selfhood and public discourse might be drawn can capture the dynamic and contested nature of that line in these lives.

Finally there may be miscalculation on their parts. The defining experiences of a woman's movement which required and enabled women to step beyond familial boundaries into public discourse had occurred long before either Stanton or Duniway wrote their books. As elderly, widowed grandmothers with full political careers behind them, they seemed to lose touch with the long-ago struggle to balance conflicting expectations and senses of self. They had made it through the rapids. Memory condensed into pride in their children who grew up amid the confusion. As a personal matter, that, it seemed, was what counted.

But the passage of time had not just dimmed their own recollections or rearranged the importance of life's stages. A period of history had passed. The pioneering work of organizing women's discontent and drawing the connections between personal experience and political power had been done. Whatever sense they had had of the political content in personal life had served its purpose well while they helped to cut the pathway from cookstove to legislative chambers. Two and three generations of women now trod that path, bumping into each other coming and going, tripping over each other's ideas and delusions. Putting their lives out to the service of leadership in 1898 and 1914 called for careful mapping of how this new political mass should move. Like many progressives of their time, they miscalculated the course of change and assumed that the mass of mobilized womanhood had arrived to stay on the political scene. They did not foresee that my generation would want to rediscover the process of awakening an age, that we would have a vital political interest in understanding how private and public lives collide, sometimes to overwhelm and isolate the individual woman and other times to uproot her to be released into collective and political action. Stanton and Duniway died thinking the world had changed.

NOTES

1 An excellent source on Duniway's life, and invaluable aid to my understanding of how her autobiography relates to her life, is Moynihan.

2 For Stanton's life, I have relied principally on my own work as co-editor of the *Papers of Elizabeth Cady Stanton and Susan B. Anthony.* Readers could consult Lutz or Griffith. Griffith's work, however, confounds autobiographical constructions with objective reality.

3 I have used the reprint of Duniway's second edition, issued in 1971, and a reprint of Stanton's *Eighty Years and More: Reminiscences, 1815–1897* of the same date. Citations to these texts appear as page numbers within parentheses.

4 For a discussion of the opposition between two strains of woman's thought in the antebellum era, see DuBois.

5 Manuscripts of most of the *Tribune* articles are within Stanton's papers at the Library of Congress.

6 In an undated typescript called "Reminiscences," probably written about the same time that *Eighty Years* appeared, Stanton compresses events from a decade or more of her early life into a single chain of events and accuses her father of withholding a house in Boston for herself and her husband because she insisted on appearing before the New York State legislature. The reliability of this version is doubtful; every element of the story is erroneously dated; before she ever spoke to the legislature, her father had already given her the house at Seneca Falls. There is no way to know if she is nonetheless closer to the truth about her own dependence or dramatizing the power of paternal wealth over daughters. (E. C. Stanton, "Reminiscences," in the Political Equality Club of Minneapolis Papers, Division of Archives/Manuscripts, Minnesota Historical Society.)

7 Duniway is *less* exceptional among her siblings than Stanton, and thus denies more by avoiding the topic of how her family produced her.

8 See, for example, coverage of the National American Woman Suffrage Association, 22d Annual Convention, in the *Washington Post,* February 19–22, 1890.

9 Duniway died before Anna Howard Shaw laid claim to the imagery of the frontier in her own co-authored biography.

WORKS CITED

DuBois, Ellen C. "Politics and Culture in Women's History: A Symposium." *Feminist Studies,* 6 (Spring 1980), 28–36.

Duniway, Abigail Scott. *Path Breaking: An Autobiographical History of the Equal Suffrage Movement in Pacific Coast States.* Introduction by Eleanor Flexner. 1914; rpt. New York: Schocken Books, 1971.

Griffith, Elisabeth. *In Her Own Right: The Life of Elizabeth Cady Stanton.* New York: Oxford University Press, 1984.

Holland, Patricia, G. and Ann D. Gordon, eds. *Papers of Elizabeth Cady Stanton and Susan B. Anthony.* Microfilm ed. Wilmington, DE: Scholarly Resources Inc., 1990.

Lutz, Alma. *Created Equal: A Biography of Elizabeth Cady Stanton.* New York: John Day, 1940.

Moynihan, Ruth Barnes. *Rebel for Rights: Abigail Scott Duniway.* New Haven: Yale University Press, 1983.

Shaw, Anna Howard, with Elizabeth Jordan. *The Story of a Pioneer.* New York: Harper and Bros., 1915.

Stanton, Elizabeth Cady. *Eighty Years and More: Reminiscences, 1815–1897.* Introduction by Gail Parker. 1898; rpt. New York: Schocken Books, 1971.

CHAPTER 6

Utopia and Anti-Utopia in Twentieth-Century Women's Frontier Autobiographies

LYNN Z. BLOOM

Twentieth-century women autobiographers of the Western frontier invent themselves as new women in a new land, their utopian visions fulfilled, denied, or met partway. In the process, their autobiographies become new chapters of the text of contemporary western American literature ranging in mode from romance to realism, revised to accommodate women's views, voices, and visions.

This study will focus on the works of four representative women autobiographers, all notably well written, arranged on a continuum from the most to the least utopian: Elinore Pruitt Stewart's *Letters of a Woman Homesteader* (1914) and *Letters on an Elk Hunt* (1915); Hilda Rose's *Stump Farm* (1931); Annie Clark Tanner's *A Mormon Mother* (1941); and Annie Pike Greenwood's *We Sagebrush Folks* (1934). All were intended for an external audience remote in geography, culture, or time, rather than primarily for the author or her intimates (compare Davis, Hampsten). All but Tanner's were published, in part or in whole, in the *Atlantic* before being issued as books. All but Rose's work have been reissued within the past fifteen years and are currently in print, testimony of their enduring interest.[1]

These autobiographers use their works to present constructs of frontier societies ranging from utopian to anti-utopian, cast in familiar literary modes, in which they are the central and representative figures. Thereby they perform the simultaneous, interrelated tasks of self-invention and cultural interpretation. They model their autobiographical selves on the heroines of popular fiction and drama, and in the process provide intimate interpretations of women's frontier culture, sometimes separate, sometimes integrated with men's. Their autobiographical selves, like the frontier culture they depict, become the evolving products of "the complex and perpetual negotiation taking place between women's culture and the general culture" (Showalter 261).[2]

Speaking as voices of experience, they address an audience of innocents about the possibilities of life in terra incognita, the Wild West. In their fate, the equation implies, is the fate of all—women in particular—past, present, and future. Stewart, Rose, Tanner, and Greenwood portray themselves as possessing many characteristics needed to succeed on the frontier—as capable, resourceful, hardworking, energetic, vital, as we shall see. But success is not inevitable, even for the determined and the deserving.

THE LITERARY CONTEXT

A published autobiography is the author's ultimate self-representation, a vindication of her choices, values, and way of life. For an author otherwise unknown, this self-construct may be the sole fleshed-out depiction of a life only hinted at by the official records of birth, marriage, childbirth, and death.[3] This is essentially the case with the four authors studied here, whom we know essentially through their autobiographies.[4] In all these works the autobiographers (allowing for editorial emendations) have not only the last word, but essentially the only word, through what they say, what they imply—and where they choose to remain silent. Writing well is the best revenge, the ultimate mode of survival and triumph.

Many nineteenth-century American frontier women recorded their experiences in diaries, letters, oral histories, and autobiographies, but relatively few except for Indian captivity narratives—many dictated to men and used as propaganda for white usurpation of Indian territory—were published until the twentieth century. Although these writings are sufficiently numerous to establish an autobiographical tradition for their twentieth-century successors, most have only recently been made available, either through publication or reissue,[5] or through reprinting or analysis in works by scholars such as Faragher, Jeffrey, Hampsten, Stratton, Schlissel, Riley, Kolodny, Moynihan et al., and Armitage and Jameson. Thus the writers studied here, though thirsting for books amidst the droughts, sandstorms, and blizzards of the frontier climate, had no access to most of the works by either their predecessors or contemporaries, and write in apparent ignorance of these.[6] Even Greenwood, who had large boxes of books shipped for intellectual sustenance to her Idaho farm, erroneously considers her autobiography to be "the first book to be written from the inside by a pioneer farm woman, and, hardest fate of all, a pioneer farm woman of a type never before known—touching elbows with civilization" (319).

Nevertheless, three of the four women, Stewart excepted, were well educated for their time; Greenwood and Tanner, in fact, were educated at Brigham Young Academy (now University) in Provo; Greenwood also attended the University of Utah and the University of Michigan (xiv); Rose and Greenwood were schoolteachers. That these three were voracious readers is evident from the literary references that generously season their autobiographies, as well as from the literary forms their works ultimately take. That Stewart casts her autobiography as a pastoral romance may be due as much to the popular art of the period, or western recruitment propaganda, as to the influence of belles lettres.

Indeed, although living and writing independently of one another, frontier women autobiographers established their own traditions which contradict the prevailing interpretations of frontier women's lives in both high and popular culture during the time in which they were writing. Early twentieth-century male writers of quality literature, such as Ole Rolvaag and Hamlin Garland, present their interpretations of the lives of frontier women with "heartrending lamentations concerning women's work loads, hostility to the frontier, and tendencies toward insanity." These, says historian Glenda Riley, etched an erroneous "picture of a helpless, hopeless, drudge into the minds of generations of American readers" (9).

For example, in *A Son of the Middle Border* Hamlin Garland depicts his mother's situation as horrendous, in part to justify his decision to reject his father's homesteading life—"pioneering madness" (402)—to move east and become a writer. The worse the frontier conditions are, the greater the justification for leaving them. Thus from an Easterner's point of view Garland retrospectively interprets his mother's life as one of incessant, exhausting slavery that caused her to die from a stroke some twenty years after (401–2) the events recounted here:

My own mother had trod a . . . slavish round with never a full day of leisure, with scarcely an hour of escape from the tugging hands of children, and the need of mending and washing clothes. I recalled her as she passed from the churn to the stove, from the stove to the bedchamber, and from the bedchamber back to the kitchen, day after day, year after year, rising at daylight or before, and going to bed only after the evening dishes were washed and the stockings and clothing mended for the night. (366)

Garland portrays his mother throughout *Son of the Middle Border* in the language and imagery reminiscent of the sentimental depictions of Everymother that permeated popular turn-of-the-nineteenth-century literature, as in this anonymous "Tribute to Mother":

Honor dear old mother. Time has scattered the snowy flakes on her brow, plowed deep furrows on her cheek—but is she not beautiful now? The lips are thin and shrunken, but these are the lips that have kissed many a hot tear from childish cheeks. . . . The eye is dim, yet it glows with the soft radiance of holy love which can never fade. . . . Feeble as she is . . . when the world shall despise . . . you, the dear old mother will gather you up in her feeble arms and carry you home. . . . (*Heart Throbs* 117)

Moreover, Garland conveniently ignores the fact that such labor could as readily have occurred in the city as on a pioneer farm, and that his mother, who lived into her sixties, far surpassed the life expectancy of women at the time.[7]

Frontier life for the stereotypical "good women," the romantic heroines of popular fiction and film, usually ended just at the point where it began for many women in real life and in their autobiographies—with marriage. Other fictive alternatives to Garland's dutiful drudges are various women of questionable virtue who parade through popular western novels and films of the period: mail-order brides, dance hall girls, saloon hookers-with-hearts-of-gold, reinforced by the stylized Calamity Janes and Annie Oakleys of Wild West show renown (see Armitage 12).

These stereotypes, real or not, provide a counterpoint to the implicitly counteractive texts of Greenwood, Tanner, Stewart, and Rose, who refuse to "become women writing a man's story . . . removed from the center of power within the culture" they inhabit (see S. Smith 51). The fundamental question is the same in all these autobiographical narratives—will the heroine survive, against greater or lesser odds? But the diverse ways in which the plot and characters are complicated reveal that the literary models these authors use to tell their life stories encourage great latitude of self-characterization. In their works they are their own women, using their own vision and voices to write women's own stories of the West, a context that spans a continuum from utopian to anti-utopian, romance to realism. The utopian vision represents the promise and potential of the West that lured settlers to the frontier; the anti-utopian vision represents, sadly, what many of them found.

ELINORE PRUITT STEWART'S ROMANTIC WEST

Stewart's utopian West fulfills her romantic frontier version of the American Dream. Both of Stewart's volumes, *Letters of a Woman Homesteader* and *Letters on an Elk Hunt,* singly and in combination, create a peaceable kingdom that reinforces the vision of such nineteenth-century western artists as Albert Bierstadt, Carl William Hahn, and Thomas Moran (see Tyler

152–60). These works provide a compelling view of the promised land: "my home among the blue mountains, my healthy, well-formed children, my clean, honest husband, my kind, gentle milk cows, my garden which I make myself" (*Homesteader* 191). This heaven on earth functions as a propagandistic recruitment device, proclaiming with every detail, "Come West, o Women, come West."[8]

Throughout both volumes Stewart romanticizes the context, natural and human. Although one sixty-mile vista has "nothing but sage, sand, and sheep" (*Homesteader* 8), the territory is graced with "snow-capped peaks," "quaking aspen," "dashing, roaring" trout streams where one can "catch plenty for a meal in a few minutes" (19), clear mountain air with "a tang of sage and pine," glorious sunrises and sunsets (18–20); Stewart sees the West "through a golden haze" (10). Her two-room house is made of logs "as straight as a pine can grow," the cracks "snugly filled," the walls perfectly square and smooth," the floors stained walnut and covered with two goatskin rugs (137–40), as snug and cozy as Wilder's little house in the big woods or Mole's underground domain in *The Wind in the Willows*.[9]

The people Stewart sketches resemble the romantic stereotypes of popular fiction and film, almost too good to be true. The cast of characters includes the game warden, "a very capable and conscientious . . . and very genial gentleman" (*Elk Hunt* 85); the forest ranger, a "splendid fellow . . . manly strength and grace showing in every line" whose schoolteacher sweetheart, "a likable little lady," comes from the East to marry him after a long absence (55, 82–89); the "really beautiful" daughters of a "weak-faced, discouraged-looking father" (11) (the only sorry character in *Elk Hunt*), one of whom has scrimped for a dozen years to buy her mother's tombstone (6); the genial Mrs. O'Shaughnessy, who organizes a group of four women (Stewart included) to furnish and refurbish a cabin for a crippled old woman coming to the the the "big, free West" to live with her son just released from wrongful imprisonment. And there is Stewart herself, whose implicit message is, if I, an ordinary "ex-Washlady," can succeed out west, you, dear reader, can also.

The action proceeds briskly, the main narrative line encompassing a series of vignettes, like plums in a pudding, without the threats to the heroine's survival that complicate even romantic fairy tales. Within six weeks of her arrival in Wyoming from a stint in Denver as a "washlady," as she signs her letters to her former employer, Stewart, a thirty-three-year-old Kansas widow with a small daughter, is successfully homesteading her own claim of 240 acres. It does not suit her rhetorical purposes to acknowledge until two-thirds of the way through *Homesteader* (and three and a half years into her Wyoming residence) that she was a mail-order bride who went west for the express purpose of a marriage which also took place six weeks after she got there (187), although she does reveal at the outset that her claim is next to the homestead her new husband had established eleven years earlier (7). Nor does she ever mention the birth—or the death—of their first baby, amidst a raging blizzard during the first year of their marriage (*Elk Hunt* xi). Despite her obvious love for the "gude mon" (225), she is reticent not from embarrassment about the circumstance of her marriage but because the real romance lies not in consummation of a love affair but in establishing a functioning homestead. So Stewart needs to demonstrate first and unmistakably three things: that as a homesteader she is successful through her own efforts; that a woman can do it; and that the American Dream can be fulfilled on the frontier.

The romantic rhetoric of the American Dream equates hard work with success. This is certainly the operative credo of settlers on the western frontier, whether in 1860 or in 1910. Indeed, the frontierswomen of either generation, including all four of the authors studied here, had no choice but to function as the Ideal Mother, as Smith-Rosenberg explains, "expected to be strong, self-reliant, protective, and efficient caretaker" of children and home, cook, seamstress, nurse, physician (199). In addition, frontier women even into the 1930s performed the duties (except for spinning and weaving) that Faragher identifies as common to Midwestern farm women of the 1850s: growing, collecting, and preparing the family food (including planting and cultivating the vegetable garden, milking the cows, tending the chickens, making cheese and butter), washing, ironing, and mending (50–59).[10] Because the nearest support systems—medical, mercantile, religious, even the mail carrier—were miles away Stewart, like other frontier women, also served as a midwife, veterinarian (from chicks to cows), social worker, and nonstop hostess.

Both of Stewart's volumes are bursting with cheerful energy. She begins *Woman Homesteader*: "I have done most of my cooking at night, have milked seven cows every day, and have done all the hay-cutting"—ordinarily a man's job, but men weren't available so she simply "went down to the barn, took out the horses, and went to mowing," using a skill she had learned as a child. "I have [also] found time to put up thirty pints of jelly and the same amount of jam" (17–18). And she concludes, with unabated vigor, "I have tried every kind of work this ranch affords, and I can do any of it. Of course I *am* extra strong, but those who try know that strength and knowledge come with doing. I just love to experiment, to work, and to prove out things, so that ranch life and 'roughing it' just suit me" (282). Hard work, for Stewart, not only gets the job done, but gives the frontierswoman the ability to make the desert bloom; at one with her universe, she can create a harmonious society within it.

This seemingly effortless activity reinforces the thesis of Stewart's *Woman*

Homesteader, that "Homesteading is the solution of all poverty's problems. . . . Whatever is raised is the homesteader's own, and there is no house-rent to pay." "I am very enthusiastic about women homesteading," she says. "It really requires less strength and labor to raise plenty to satisfy a large family than it does to go out to wash." Even her own six-year-old daughter can raise a ton of potatoes with a minimum of effort; picking them up out of the plowed field is but child's play. Cautioning that although "persons afraid of coyotes and work and loneliness had better let ranching alone," "Any woman who can stand her own company, can see the beauty of the sunset, loves growing things, and is willing to put in as much time at careful labor as she does over the washtub, will certainly succeed; will have independence, plenty to eat all the time, and a home of her own in the end" (214–15). The example of Stewart's own life is a paradigm for fulfilling the American Dream on the frontier; her optimistic voice is at one with her romantic message. The conclusion of *Elk Hunt* echoes *A Woman Homesteader*: "I realiz[ed] anew how happy I am, how much I have been spared, and how many of life's blessings are mine" (161). Everything will be all right.

HILDA ROSE'S TRAGICOMIC WILDERNESS

Hilda Rose shares Stewart's utopian vision, but her optimism appears utterly at variance with the plot, setting, and character of *Stump Farm.* As the drama begins, it is 1905 and this eighty-six-pound former Chicago schoolteacher has gone to Montana to cure her TB, married an impoverished homesteader, "Daddy," twenty-eight years her senior, and adopted his goal, to wrest a profitable farm from the resisting, drought-ridden wilderness. In this homegrown Eden she will raise a family and, in opposition to her husband's elitist wishes (as we later learn), create a community where none has existed before, knitting up the raveled lives of a disparate group of hardscrabble settlers into a fabric of cultivated, kindred spirits. Like the other autobiographers, Rose meets Stewart's qualifications for transforming this utopian dream into a reality, for she works long, hard, and with good will.

But the circumstances under which she labors are very different from Stewart's, and were it not for the workings of a double deus ex machina, her efforts would have been love's labor's lost, continually undermined by her husband's incapacities and by the major antagonists, their utterly inhospitable places of settlement. Indeed, the double-edged, double voice in which Rose tells her tale provides a subversive counterpoint to her narrative thrust, and a running, ironic commentary on the circumstances of her life and on "Daddy" himself.

In a series of letters written between 1918 and 1927 because "I have no woman to talk to, so I will write to ease my brain" (30), Rose establishes the parameters of her utopia-in-process, "a ranch, or will be one when we get the stumps out," on a "ledge or bench that hugs up against the mountain range" (3). Here she lives with her sixty-six-year-old husband ("I worship the very ground he walks on"), their four-year-old son, two orphan children, her father (age seventy-six), "partially paralyzed," and her mother (age seventy-four), "too feeble to be up all day" (16–17). Though she says at the outset, "I've never been very strong" (3), Rose gains strength and stature as her tale unfolds, in part as a result of her contrapuntal references to her husband which, though usually loving, invariably depict him as much weaker than she is, "feeble and gray" (13), "he reminded me of old Rip Van Winkle" (17), "so old he doesn't like to go anywhere any more" (7). Indeed, when at seventy he gets "a little slower" every day, he becomes "just a little dearer to me as he depends more on me" (23).

"Daddy" is "broken in health" even when the letters start, "too weak" to try to protect their house from "a solid wall" of approaching forest fire (12–13). In isolation and poverty, her situation exacerbated by several years of drought, Rose has no choice but to do virtually all the work, her husband's along with her own:

> Daddy is more and more feeble, so I have more to do than before; getting wood and water is hardest, and I must do the milking too. . . . I planted and raised a good garden, and potatoes too; dug them and put them in the cellar myself, about one hundred bushels. . . . [I] bought a good hand pump and pumped water on my garden from a spring, so this year I have the cellar full of vegetables. . . . Daddy has been going to make a pump for years, but I saw plainly that I must take the helm and work. (20)

That the letters which comprise *Stump Farm* and Rose's self-assertion begin in the same year is no accident. She can find a voice, an audience in a context far removed from her entourage of powerless dependents.[11] Through a false sense of social delicacy, her husband has proclaimed his wife "so fragile, so nice, so dainty," too good to associate with "anybody who has the least blemish on her reputation." Consequently, he has isolated her from all her female frontier neighbors—women who were divorced, separated, deserted; bigamists; women who used abortion for birth control; mothers of illegitimate children; manual laborers.

But after a dozen years of "minding" her husband, Rose rebels, "glad," she "confesses" to her correspondent, to "see and talk to a bunch of women once more, for it almost drives me wild to be alone" (34). Aided by the University of Montana extension service, she founds and sustains a women's club to help alleviate the misery and distress of the very women her husband would have her shun. In this female community of givers and receivers Rose finds "my life work" and becomes her own person: "As long as I'm true to myself it doesn't matter what other people think about me" (45–50), including her hypocritical husband. She can write her defiance to an audience so far away that her husband will never hear.

Ventilation provides both validation and income; Rose's correspondents begin to publish her letters in the *Atlantic* (v). Her language implies that her husband's mind may be deteriorating along with his body: "He doesn't live [in Montana] any more. His body is here, but his mind is in Canada, where he was born" (23). Nevertheless, Rose uses this money to fulfill her husband's second dream—even more impossible than the first. In misguided search of "a better, milder climate" and cheap land, they move several hundred miles farther north to homestead above Fort Vermilion, Alberta, with a three-month growing season. In transit they survive a train wreck, her husband so exhausted he can't even eat, "just a helpless baby"; her son "almost lost his mind" from the nightly onslaught of voracious mosquitoes. But Rose saves them all single-handed ("It did take grit to go to a strange land"), her romantic stance ("I felt like Robinson Crusoe as I stood on the shore of this mighty river and looked at the swamp that edged it, so dense and luxuriant") tempered by the need even at the moment of arrival to build a fire, cook dinner, feed their "three old horses," make a shelter, and keep away the "singing chorus" of mosquitoes (82–90).

It is impossible to sustain this level of activity. Before winter comes (in September) Rose attempts, virtually single-handed, to build a house, a barn, plant a garden, dig a well, and learn to become a fur trapper—she sets fifty-six traps—an ambition that calls her own sanity into credibility. But the forty-below-zero weather arrives first, while the family is still living in a tent that is impossible to heat. Surely they will perish. But no. Whereas Stewart's calculus expects rewards in direct proportion to effort expended, Rose's tragicomedy, a secular parable, illustrates the blessings of charity, compassion—and good luck. Two dei ex machina arrive, literally from out of the blue, not only to enable the family to triumph over folly and disaster, but to transform a failed utopian dream into an arctic idyll. On Thanksgiving Day a sleighful of good Samaritan woodsmen descend, and in six days build her a "darling House," move her in (even "my dear old piano"), and leave her with a supply of wood (116–20). Then comes a check from the *Atlantic* and assurance that *Stump Farm* will be published. The money will provide a year's supply of groceries and medicine, a means for Rose and her dependents to survive (135). For an improbable plot and an otherworldly cast of characters, a happy though unreal ending.

Rose's contradictory double messages continue to the end, providing interesting complications for what might otherwise seem a naive folie à deux.

Her dearly beloved husband's wishes are to be honored, though because he wears moral blinders they can be undercut. He must be deferred to, though he is incompetent to make decisions or to do any sustained manual work. Therefore, she has no choice but to take charge of everything, for it is she, the frail female, not he, who is the source of strength, and wisdom, and moral superiority. The verbal messages are reinforced by contradictory visual images, of death and of life. Rose's description of their first arctic winter, eight months long, makes readers wonder whether there will be a second: "How we survived is beyond me. The daily work of getting wood, and never a stick ahead, Boy and I under the bright shimmering aurora a mile from the cabin, afraid of the wolves, only our old dog and a 22 rifle at night. Silent, brilliant, and cold" (150). But, fortified by the Bible, Bobby Burns, and *Leaves of Grass* for reading on nights that can reach sixty below zero (169), Rose proceeds with plans to break the thirty acres needed "to prove up on our homestead." A "pig pen, hen house, and barn" of logs (153) will be the foundations of utopia revived, a hard-wrought means of humoring "Daddy" until he dies.

Rose's autobiography unfolds to become an unwitting feminist manifesto, invigorated by her pride in her own judgment, resourcefulness, and capability. Reinforced by her ability to share her vision with the outer world, she creates her own society that while appearing to honor her husband as the center, actually subverts his position, relegating him to the periphery. *Stump Farm* becomes, sub rosa, stump oratory.

ANNIE TANNER'S *A MORMON MOTHER:* PARABLES OF A PATRIARCHAL UTOPIA, FATALLY FLAWED

Frontier autobiographies of Mormon women designated for a secular audience invariably focus on polygamy rather than on other aspects of the frontier, and they make a case against it through the example of their own lives.[12] Tanner, a deeply religious woman, presents *A Mormon Mother* as a series of parables calculated to teach moral lessons about the patriarchal institution of Mormon polygamy. Mormonism, personified by the author's husband, has promised heaven on earth in the form of a self-sustaining, closed society in which industry, reinforced by piety, will make the desert bloom. This patriarchy concentrates on its own survival, in the process oppressing and suppressing a host of innocent, benign victims — its own women and children. Through purporting to explain what she actually condemns, Tanner's *A Mormon Mother* anticipates Atwood's anti-utopian *The Handmaid's Tale* in substance and message, and has become a classic among critical Mormon and ex-Mormon women.[13]

Deeply religious, profoundly devoted to home, marriage, and children,

Tanner presents the parables of her life to gentile (i.e., non-Mormon) readers, though her ostensible audience is her Mormon granddaughters. In her mature dignity she is beyond a redress of grievances. She writes instead to express measured, often covert outrage at the injustice and humiliation of the triply patriarchical institutions of marriage, church, and state, which conspired to deprive her and her female peers of property, family, and social standing. In 1890 the Mormon church paid the price of statehood for Utah Territory by repudiating polygamy. As a consequence Tanner became a wife doubly outlawed by church and state, mother of eight doubly illegitimate children.

Tanner makes explicit what she demonstrates throughout the book: "I am sure that women would never have accepted polygamy had it not been for their religion. No woman ever consented to its practice without a great sacrifice on her part" (132) because it undermines the "security and confidence . . . requirements for happiness" that monogamy makes possible (272). She repeatedly alternates between negative reflections on "this obscure and lonely life" (136) and assertions that "I was happily married"—qualified by the oxymoronic "so far as happiness goes in a polygamous marriage" (152).

Tanner's rhetorical task is complicated by her paradoxical devotion to this very church. Thus like Rose, Tanner speaks deliberately in a double voice. Her overt voice is integrative, reinforcing the values and behavior of her husband and of the frontier culture. Her covert voice, like Rose's, is contradictory, subversive—and necessary to maintain her dignity, sanity, and sense of self. Sotto voce these women indict the frontier culture's relentless exploitation of women. Their contrapuntal voices give them distance, independence, control over the otherwise debilitating, dehumanizing circumstances of their lives; their subversive commentary can turn potential tragedy into triumph by transforming their personae from victims of circumstance and incompetent or callous husbands into independent, self-assertive women who take charge of their own lives and assume the responsibility for them. The dominant female voices and personae of these texts diminish and mute the male characters they displace. The farther removed the reality of their culture is from the utopian ideal, the louder these voices become.

Tanner frames her narrative with visual and verbal portraits in the first two and last two chapters that are at great variance with the body of the text they embrace. They show the author in a state of grace, fully integrated with her society before and after the twenty-five-year period of marriage, ostracism, and exile on which the text focuses. Tanner's opening chapters, "Girlhood Homes" and "Young Womanhood," create a peaceable, bourgeois kingdom that expresses a fulfillment of Mormon ideals:

a climate of piety, industry, prosperity, order, harmony—and hierarchy—among the first two families of her father's plural marriage in Farmington, Utah, in the 1870s. The first and second wives and their numerous children lived in "cordial . . . companionship" (2) across the street from one another in sumptuous, well-shaded brick houses. Annie, the eldest daughter of the second (and therefore subordinate) wife, was as a child well dressed, well fed, petted, adored. Only in retrospect does her childish trust in plural marriage become an ironic commentary on her own: "My father at that time seemed to me so successful in its practice that I firmly believed it was truly of Divine origin, and, in my simple faith, I believed it would last forever" (6). The cover portrait shows an attractive young woman, curly hair piled high above a white ruff and silk collar.

But by the third chapter she has met the man who will be responsible for her expulsion from the Garden of Eden; in the fourth chapter she presents her wedding day in 1883 as an emblem of her entire marriage. At nineteen she became the second wife of Joseph Tanner, her professor at Brigham Young Academy, selected by his childless first wife to bear his children. After a brief courtship ("he came to see me a few times in the fall" [64]), the wedding ceremony, with the first Mrs. Tanner—the only woman with legal standing in a Mormon plural marriage—as a full participant, is performed at Mormon headquarters in Salt Lake City. The trio then departs by train, in total silence. While Joseph and his first wife continue on to their home in Ogden, the new bride gets off in the dark at her parents' home in rural Farmington, a context of security and happiness she is never to experience in her own marriage. Painfully "conscious of the obscurity" of her wedding night, while eating her wedding supper of leftover bread and milk, Tanner volunteers to her silent family, "The experience wasn't half bad." To which her father, an opponent of the marriage that would make her a second wife, replies, "You haven't half begun yet" (66–67).

Tanner can count on her readers to make the invidious comparison, as she does, between the conventions of ideal public weddings, "elaborate festivals" incorporating banquets, wedding gowns, the acknowledgment and support of family and friends, and their absence in her case. "'What a contrast,' I said to myself. 'No one will ever congratulate *me*'" (66)—and no one ever does. Although she says, "I was sure I had taken the right step," she has already described—with irony clear to her readers—a destabilized situation that signals the beginning of what will only get worse: her second-class, outlaw status, marked by ostracism, isolation, estrangement from a husband who regarded marriage as an economic relationship, with a plethora of wives and children serving him as overlord. His utopia, her exile. That Tanner tries to invest the polygamous transaction with ardent love and a monogamous orientation is to doom her to repeated disappointment.

Two weeks later Joseph initiates the pattern of uncertainty that characterizes the twenty-five years of their nominal marriage, until he totally abandons his wife. He breaks his first appointment with her: "I was so disappointed that . . . the very angels wept" (67). After Tanner becomes a mother, her husband has "his liberty," but his wife, like other plural wives, is obliged to live underground: "One never knew how long one would stay at a place, nor with whom they would stay, nor where they would go next. . . . It was a move in the dark" (101)—the darkness heralded by the dying of the light on her wedding eve. For six years she hides out, giving birth to her second child "on the floor" (127), with no midwife, husband, or companion in attendance. When Joseph goes east, to study at Harvard, Annie follows—against his will. In order not to "jeopardize his reputation there," he insists "that my home must be in the slums," a "filthy place" not fit for the MIT students she takes in as roomers—so he allows her to move (135). Not until she stages a three-day hunger strike does he deign to come to dinner on alternate Sundays, leaving "a five dollar greenback in a little leather box on the mantle"—as one might pay a prostitute —for the week's groceries and clothing for the next expected baby (136–37). Again Tanner can depend on her readers' sense of social equity to compare her subterranean life, her childbirth and existence in isolation, with what is fitting, proper, and public. Her very description of these practices becomes an indictment of them.

Although nominally expressing respect for her husband, who provides no emotional sustenance and only token economic support for his family, Tanner's repetition of the church's teaching, that "man is superior to woman and that he should be obeyed," becomes progressively more ironic. Joseph, like Brutus, is an honorable man. With irony, she holds his misjudgment responsible for the death of one of their twin daughters: "it was his right to command [the change to an incompetent doctor]; it was my duty to obey." But, another ironic refrain, her husband "never dwelt on unpleasant experiences," then or, for example, when he invested all of his wife's comfortable inheritance—and lost every penny, without apology or remorse: "he did have a wonderful mental capacity" to ignore responsibility (169–72). Worthy of respect, Joseph, a distinguished educator, is also deserving of defiance for trying to impress his children into hard labor on his Canadian wheat farm (269) instead of sending them to college.

As a consequence of a series of such experiences, Tanner emerges quickly from her sheltered youth to become a figure of increasing strength, dignity, and independence "that women in monogamy never know" (269), born of the necessity to support eight children as a single parent. The prevailing voice in A Mormon Mother is the subversive, contrapuntal voice. It expresses not a shred of self-pity, but pride in the author's progressive self-reliance, in her ability to educate her children and to maintain a good home for them even if it meant working as a nurse, a domestic, running a boarding house — and denying herself a winter coat for years rather than "going into debt" (253). Through her efforts, not her husband's, the seven children who survived to adulthood have fulfilled her ideals, becoming eminently successful "by the highest standards," as prosperous business executives, professors, lawyers, all Mormons. Tanner, finding inspiration in Job's "grand" story, is rewarded, too, with twenty-eight grandchildren, seven great-grandchildren, a paid-up home in Salt Lake (after her Farmington home burned to the ground) and the consciousness of her new status, "the contrast in being a 'Nobody' when a professor's plural wife, and a 'Somebody' as a professor's mother" (321). Her utopian dream is fulfilled not in a place, but tightly bound in a web of relationships that can now be publicly acknowledged.

In the beginning is the end; the frontispiece of *A Mormon Mother* promises an auspicious conclusion. Tanner stands, erect, gracious, and gray-haired, again wearing a simple black gown trimmed in lace, this time complemented with a necklace and bracelet. She holds a large book, its title stamped in gold, perhaps *The Book of Mormon*. Her concluding chapters reinforce the photograph's aura of bourgeois solidity, with scarcely a hint of the poverty, humiliation, and hardscrabble frontier life she endured as a lower-caste, outlaw second wife.[14] Indeed, they reinforce both her philosophy of life and her concept of autobiography. "We shape ourselves," she takes as her motto, *"The tissue of the life to be / We weave with colors all our own,"* and demonstrates in the end as in the beginning how her "personal responsibility in shaping my life" (336) has resulted in prosperity, travel, a thriving, successful family, and restored social status. Though Tanner remains a devout Mormon, she is the author of her own destiny and the autobiography that demonstrates her power, authority, and reintegration into the upper-middle-class society from which she had been exiled during her marriage. As Tanner grows to fit the final image in the frame she has constructed her dominance pushes her husband out of the picture.

ANNIE PIKE GREENWOOD'S ANTI-UTOPIA

As established in the opening chapter of *We Sagebrush Folks,* the Greenwoods went west with the same hopes, in the same optimistic spirit, at the same time, and almost to the same place as Elinore Pruitt Stewart. Yet Greenwood's universe is the antithesis of Stewart's, an irony of great expectations, for *We Sagebrush Folks* anatomizes an anti-utopia, a naturalistic inversion of the American dream. Over and over, this intermittently bitter, cautionary tale demonstrates that determination, enterprise, back-breaking work from sunup to midnight, good will, and a cheerful spirit cannot create utopia even in an irrigated desert and cannot save the frontier farm family from total loss and despair.

Greenwood knows there are other, better ways to live. At the outset of *We Sagebrush Folks* she establishes a cultural frame of reference for her fifteen years of life on a farm near Hazelton, Idaho, "the last frontier of the United States" (vii). A doctor's daughter, she grew up in Provo, Utah, in a "luxurious" "twenty-room mansion." A portrait of "The Bride," a stunning Edwardian ingenue on whose upswept hair perches a spectacularly plumed Napoleonic tricorn, reinforces this initial impression of elegance and culture (3–8), and resonates throughout the rest of the text. Her first six years of marriage to Charley (whom she sometimes calls "The Baron," with ironic reference to both his German ancestry and their debt-ridden Idaho "estate") promise to replicate this upper-bourgeois life.

But when Charley decides to "give up a perfectly good salary from the million-dollar sugar-factory in Garden City, Kansas, to go to a perfectly unknown, sight unseen, undeveloped wilderness farm in Idaho" (6), their citified Eden is supplanted by an ambiguous triple vision: the husband's expectation of the frontier as promised land, his wife's determination to fulfill his American Dream, and her retrospective knowledge as she writes, that their efforts are doomed to failure through forces in a deterministic universe beyond their control.

Her Promethean destiny is clear at the outset, embedded in the cosmic impossibility of her task: "I was to live on land untrod by the foot of white woman in all history! I was going to make my home where there had never been a civilized home before! I was to be a living link between the last frontier and civilization! I was a pioneer!" (14). The civilization Greenwood left behind remains the normative society whose values of sanitation, nutrition, and culture she labored for fifteen years to replicate on the frontier (see Riley chaps. 5–8), working nonstop at two full-time jobs, farm wife and one-room schoolteacher, and in addition organizing a Sunday school, directing plays and concerts—and writing for publication. With luck, she would get "a precious, precious hour after nine to sit at my old typewriter and write the tiredness out of my aching back and my cracked-heeled, burning feet" (33).

Yet Greenwood's frame mocks the inadequacies of her innocent and partial vision, before frontier life opened her eyes to the true grit and moral superiority of farm women to their city cousins. The ironic tone of her first reference to farm women is directed not at her subject but at her dainty, childhood self. When she thought as a child she regarded with "cold revulsion" the "grotesque" farm women who came to town, "their bunching muscles and great, awkward frame of large and knobby bones" in contrast to her own "quick brain and little hands and feet" (3–4).

However, she learns quickly. Another ironic cinematic scene captures her arrival in Idaho, alighting at a whistle stop in "a Paris model" hat, wool suit "from Best and Company, New York," and "very beautiful little shoes, evidence of one of the foolish passions of my life" (12). There she is met by Charley in a farm wagon, no longer "Baron Karl" after several months on the frontier, but a "red-leather-necked farmer . . . a stranger to me" (9). That the sagebrush country and its values will prevail is signaled not only by her mocking sketch of herself in inappropriate city clothes, but by the frontispiece which, in stark contrast to the best-dress portraits of Tanner and many other frontier autobiographers,[15] is a photograph of "miles of sagebrush, stretching to the Minidoka mountains," as far as the eye can see. Cracked, dry earth dominates the foreground of this statement, literal and metaphoric, that there is no evidence that human effort has made a particle of difference in this landscape or ever will.

Greenwood's Idaho exists in ambivalent contrast to Stewart's Wyoming. Prophetically, her entrance to the promised land is at Milner, Idaho, a whistle stop that existed during construction of the dam that was to "slake the thirst of the fertile volcanic-ash desert" and make farming possible. Dam completed, Milner is "breathing its last gasp" (9). The foreground, littered with the detritus of hard human labor, contradicts the breathtaking natural background. Greenwood and her husband pass the construction debris, a wrecked steam shovel, "piles of twisted wire," "huge piles of empty tin cans," rusted, "with ends gaping in ragged edges," intermingled with the "bleached skeletons" of "slaughtered animals," the vision a "prophetic menace" (13–14) that the beauty of the natural setting can only partly counteract.

Nevertheless, although many narratives by women writers dwell on and in interiors, Greenwood's heart and soul are outdoors in all seasons. The physical setting resembles Stewart's utopian context, with "the changing beauty of the vast cloud-filled skies, the purple and gold sunsets, the blue and white mountains," and "our own lovely, undulating farm, with its ivory wheat-fields, its green beet-fields, its purple-blooming alfalfa" (170–71). No human construction can match nature, despite reiterated evidence that nature is indifferent to its human inhabitants.

Greenwood's single glimpse of indoors is the paragraph that interprets the family's diminished status after a decade in the West through the metaphor of their floor coverings: "Gone now is the velvet carpet, followed by the grass rug, and now the covering is a linoleum" that could be considered a rug only by a woman "gone crazy and half blind." "Bedroom rug worn out, and gone. . . . Almost everything gone now. Painted bare floors" (157). The only surviving relics of "more prosperous days" are Greenwood's books and her typewriter, iconic, ironic reminders that despite her incessant, hard labor on the farm and at school, she is really "a born writer" (32). She doesn't belong in her ugly farmhouse with its "glowering, sullen face" (16) and its daily invasion of bedbugs, wood ticks, flies, pack rats, "mice with donkey ears and hairy tails" (44), and flies, slaughtered daily in summer by the "dustpanfuls" (178). When possible, she even writes outdoors in the orchard (168). No wonder the house scowls.

Unlike Stewart's population of cinematic dear hearts and gentle people (fittingly transported into a movie, *Heartland*), Greenwood's West is inhabited by a mixture of the good, the bad, the beautiful, and the ugly, fleshed out in ways that humanize and undercut the stereotypes of popular films and literature. In particular, she apotheosizes the "patient, hardworking," "self-sacrificing, self-immolating, pioneer farm women," "the *backbone* of the earth," without whose efforts "the world must perish. For no man would go on farming alone, or even working as the farm woman does" (317–19). Women like Mrs. Bancroft, "who milks twelve cows night and morning, besides raising a large garden, caring for over a hundred fowls, doing all her own housework, and sewing, washing, ironing, cooking for a family of six" (258), are as fit for Stewart's utopia as for Greenwood's antithetical version of the west.

Greenwood presents a society that is at times collaborative, as when a herd of threshers works its way, locust-like, not only through the fields but through the noon meal of a fifteen pound roast, three quarts of coleslaw, potatoes, chocolate cake, and "lots of pie, and all kinds of pie" (174). The same society can be confrontive: "many a farmer kills his neighbor with a spade each watering season, when the two meet at a head-gate" where one is stealing the other's irrigation water (186). The society of the energetic, capable, and attractive, including both Greenwood and her husband, is subverted by a society of the shiftless ("'When Bill Sellers's wife married Bill, she didn't ixpect nothin', 'n she got it!'" [155]) and the slovenly (lusty Blanche, who proclaims, "'I'll wrastle yuh, 'n' I kin lick yuh,'" and who never washed the dishes or used the outhouse [69–73]).

Greenwood's view of children is largely anti-utopian; she uses them as examples of lives as blighted by poverty as their parents'. Greenwood teaches in her one-room school pupils whose "childish hands [are] scoured raw by the constant handling of dirty, rough potatoes, . . . backs, bent painfully. . . . 'ithout no supper, till 'leven o'clock at night,'" they explain, counteracting the image of Stewart's daughter gaily harvesting her ton of tubers (78–79). Poverty has denied them toothbrushes as it has made their parents toothless after thirty. Poverty has left these families, "so isolated from the world," devoid of culture, but eager to enjoy the games, dramatic readings, and classical records that Greenwood's school provides, with considerable effort and ingenuity on her part: "It takes deep hearts to love deep music" (98–102). Poverty leads to child abuse, incest, and murder, says Greenwood, citing the case of fifteen-year-old Reffie, who to defend his sister from their incestuous father, shot the old man — and was acquitted in a "very brief trial" (290). A compensation of poverty, one of very few, is its exposure of Greenwood and her four beloved children to the outdoors at all seasons. Heaven for her would be a place smelling of "white clover and new-mown hay, where laughing women like me can go and be with the little children" (272).

Whatever their capability of character, nearly all the sagebrush folks bear the indelible marks of poverty and "that terrible forced labor, too much to do, too little time to do it in, and no rest" (116). As the substratum of Greenwood's negative social vision, poverty and the ruinous government farm policies that exacerbate it signal throughout *We Sagebrush Folks* the ultimate fate of these farmers. The villains, though offstage, are the congressmen, government officials, bankers, grain dealers, merchant middlemen who make and enforce these policies (see 80–83 and passim), forcing the farmers off the land. The farmers have to sell their crops "below the cost of production," their farms "painfully extracted from them by means of the Federal Land bank" (189). Farming, says Charley, "is the greatest get-poor-quick scheme on earth" (153); his wife adds, "The only plenty we had was mortgages" (161).

Two cases in point illustrate the consequences of the hard life in Greenwood's bleak view of this hard land. Sally Howe represents an extreme negative example in this book studded with cautionary tales; the Greenwoods themselves are the norm. Mrs. Howe, mother of five, is the victim of a husband who "had thrown up his good job and put their savings into sagebrush land, persuaded by speculators to that madness." In Illinois, though frail, she "had been able to get along," buttressed by the material comforts of "good furniture," books, and music. When she arrived in Idaho to live in a tar-paper shack, "cold in winter, broiling in summer," she was "beautiful, with dark eyes, and a great rope of chestnut hair . . . immaculate and dainty." But poverty debased them all; living without hope only "to eat and sleep" made them "lower than the farm animals," and Mr. Howe became a wife beater. To escape, she took to her bed and, plagued by bedsores, illness, and bedbugs, "almost totally lost her mind." Rescued by a trio (including Greenwood) from the Ladies Fancywork Improvement Club, she spent her last years in a sanitarium, "clean, well-fed, but she yearned not at all for the tar-paper shack, her five children, or her husband" (118–22).

The Greenwoods, in contrast, exemplify all the virtues. Charley, handsome, witty, cultured, with "beautiful manners" and unbounded vigor (187), is a loving father and such a devoted husband that on the rare occasions when his wife is ill he washes and irons her bed linens, bathes her, prepares tempting food, and reads to her (400–401). Both are movers and shapers of the community; Charley, a "good mixer" (187) and natural leader, serves two terms as a state legislator. Both labor seventeen-hour days to make the American Dream a reality, Greenwood's small teaching salary being plowed back into the ever-hungry land. Yet farm life subverts, aborts itself. As the "parade of debts, mortgages," increases with "nothing ahead but more debts, more mortgages," Charley begins to drown "in frightful despair." Finally, deeply in debt "with no prospect of paying" after fifteen years on the ranch, they can survive no longer, and leave (269–70). If such able, committed people as the Greenwoods fail, no one can succeed; in the Greenwoods' fall, fall all. Utopia, as this naturalistic interpretation demonstrates, is dead.

Yet the autobiographer concludes her narrative not with an image of defeat but in an angry sermon against the nemesis of the Sagebrush Folks, the federal farm policy:

We farm folks in the sagebrush were drafted [during World War I] to shed our life's blood just as surely as were the soldiers on the field of battle. When you steal a man's labor, you steal his life. The Government saw to it that the farmer could have no profit on the foodstuffs he raised, but did nothing about lowering the cost of the things the farmer had to buy and the labor he had to hire. (467)

Greenwood loves the land she cannot live on: "If the actual value of farm products had been paid while the Baron and I were on the farm, we would still be there. I loved it then; I love it now; but I am not sorry to be gone" (480). The last photographs are of "The road out and away"—through towering canyon cuts and more sagebrush—and of Greenwood's four handsome adult children, none in a farm setting. Greenwood's frame circumscribes the antithesis of utopia.

NEW WOMEN IN A NEW LAND

To construct the self is the ultimate act of autobiographical integration. The literary characters of these autobiographers have a number of features in common, which emerge clearly through their interpretations of utopias and anti-utopias. No matter what the context, these women present themselves as the antithesis of the hopeless, worn-out drudges that populate men's writings about frontier women. In different voices, double or subversive voices at times, they demonstrate the independence, energy, capability, and resilience required to lead autonomous (Rose, Tanner) or symbiotic (Stewart, Greenwood) lives. They take especial pride in their ability to "make excellent, clean, properly fed homes" (Greenwood 317), rear healthy and accomplished children, perform public service and good works. They take especial pleasure in friendships with other women — the rare creatures befriended by Rose, nurtured by Stewart and Greenwood; the only society available to Tanner's underground. Even when external forces — the climate, the church, national politics, male society — are beyond their control, they can control their writing.

For these frontier women autobiographers interpret and shape their lives and their culture in works that create a new tradition even while modifying conspicuous features of common literary forms — romance, tragicomedy, parable, and realistic fiction. Writing an autobiography for external, unknown readers becomes a powerful way of reshaping their lives, of turning tragedy or trauma into ex post facto triumph. The more arduous the life, the more satisfying the survival — if not of the fittest frontierswomen, certainly of the most articulate autobiographers. In gaining control of their past through reinventing it in their works, these autobiographers also exercise control over their future; they will be known by the constructs that become their autobiographical works and lives (see Geertz, passim). As characters in their own works, then, they fulfill their destiny, utopian, anti-utopian, or in between.

NOTES

1 This study excludes unpublished literature, particularly letters singly or in collections, diaries, and fragmentary autobiographical sketches, because these introduce too many diverse elements that would dissipate its focus. For instance, Davis identifies two functions of women's frontier diaries that are directly contrary to the functions of the published autobiographies: they "substitute for personal contact with women friends or relatives," reducing "the impact of the author's isolation"; and they help "the author preserve her mental equilibrium" as she copes with "feelings of fear and estrangement in the chaos of early trail and settlement days" (8, 10). In works intended for publication these functions are subordinate, if they exist at all.

This study also excludes vanity press autobiographies, such as the pseudonymous Angela Sagsam's *I Was a Country Girl* (1947). Often inartistic, these do not demonstrate the authorial control over the text that exists in trade and university press publications, and unintentionally subvert their self-presentations.

2 Lerner's observation concerning women's culture in general is particularly rele-

vant to frontier women's autobiographies: "It is important to understand that 'women's culture' is not and should not be seen as a subculture. . . . Women live their social existence within the general culture and, whenever they are confined by patriarchical restraint or segregation into separateness (which always has subordination as its purpose) they transform this restraint into complementarity (asserting the importance of woman's function, even its 'superiority') and redefine it. Thus, women live in a duality—as members of the general culture and as partakers of women's culture" (52).

3 As Laurel Thatcher Ulrich notes in *A Midwife's Tale,* her historical and biographical amplification of *The Life of Martha Ballard, Based on Her Diary, 1785–1812:* "without the diary [Ballard's] biography would be little more than a succession of dates. Her birth in 1735. Her marriage to Ephraim Ballard in 1754. The births of their nine children in 1756, 1758, 1761, 1763, 1765, 1767, 1769, 1772, and 1779, and the deaths of three of them in 1769. Her own death in 1812." Indeed, the local paper's single-sentence obituary said only: "Died in Augusta, Mrs. Martha, consort of Mr. Ephraim Ballard, aged 77 years." "Without the diary," explains Ulrich, "we would know nothing of her life after the last of her children was born, nothing of the 816 deliveries she performed between 1785 and 1812. We would not even be certain she had been a midwife" (5).

4 Elizabeth Fuller Ferris has provided a brief biographical sketch of Elinore Pruitt Stewart in the preface to *Letters on an Elk Hunt* (v–xiii), but we are interested in this information only because of our interest in Stewart's autobiographical writings.

5 To take as an example the publications of one press that specializes in western literature, in the past decade the University of Nebraska Press has published or reissued forty volumes of American pioneer women's autobiographical works, compared to three that it had in print before 1970—a 1200 percent increase (see Bloom).

6 It could be argued that because Tanner was a devout Mormon, she would of necessity be familiar with the daily diaries that Mormons are obliged to keep in fulfilling their religious obligations. Although she never acknowledges such an influence, throughout *A Mormon Mother* she quotes extensively from her own diary.

7 The year of Mrs. Garland's birth is uncertain. Because she was married in 1856 and bore her first child in 1859, she must have been born before 1840. Consequently, she would have been at least sixty when she died in 1900, perhaps older. The life expectancy for Massachusetts women born in 1850 was 40.5 years; the average age of American women dying in 1900 was 49.0. By even the most conservative of estimates Mrs. Garland exceeded the life expectancy of women of her time by between 20 and 33 percent—hardly the sign of an exhausted constitution.

8 Stewart's frame of reference, choice of examples, and primary addressee ("Mrs. Coney") are all oriented toward women. Moreover, she assumes that other women can make autonomous choices about whether to move west and how to live, as she did, and that they are capable of acting on them.

9   She mentions that it abuts her husband's (*Homesteader* 77), but the language of her description, seventy pages later (137–42), makes it appear to be free-standing. For instance, it is "my house" (137), not "our house," occupied by Stewart and her young daughter but not her husband, if readers are to believe the prevailing singular pronoun. N. C. Wyeth's illustration reinforces the impression of a freestanding ranch house in the mountains.

10 All the autobiographers studied here, possessing seemingly inexhaustible energy and stamina, came of age in an era when middle- and upper-class women, at the onset of puberty, were expected to suffer from "increased bodily weakness . . . biologically rooted timidity and modesty, and the 'illness' of menstruation" (Smith-Rosenberg 186). Hysterical or neurasthenic women "took to their beds because of pain, paralysis, or general weakness"; some, such as Alice James, a career invalid, "remained there for years" (Smith-Rosenberg 202).

　　Prolonged illness is not an option for these frontier women; although occasionally confined to bed by childbirth, back problems, or the virulent flu in the epidemic of 1919, as Greenwood says: "When I go down, I go down dead, and the faintest complaint is a serious signal. And when I come up, I come up bounding. No lingering convalescence for me." She explains why: "There are too many interesting things to do, and see, and smell, and hear, and taste, and feel. . . . Suddenly one day I insisted on being wrapped in blankets and propped up before the typewriter. I cannot stop writing. Then I must read. . . . The next day I would try to dance. The third day I would be tottering about my work, on the job again" (400).

11 Rose dotes on this correspondence because it provides communication, "friends who will be glad to see me when I go back to the world for a visit or to stay," and because her correspondents send magazines, "something to read" during the long winters, "or go crazy." Rose's epistolary outlet is a way of escaping being beaten down by the frontier to resemble the "overworked farmers' wives, with weather-wrung and sorrow-beaten faces, drooping mouths, and a sad look" (6–7). Indeed, the frontispiece photograph depicts a sprightly, smiling woman in a white middy dress and kerchief, one elbow leaning on a washtub. Her diminutive size makes her look more like a young girl than a seasoned frontierswoman of thirty-eight. In appearance she could be the granddaughter of the slight, slumping, gray-bearded subject of "My Most Precious Picture — Mr. Rose during the last winter on the stump farm" (photograph facing 82).

12 For another notable example, see Fanny Stenhouse, *"Tell It All": The Story of a Life's Experience in Mormonism: An Autobiography*. That it has an introduction by Harriet Beecher Stowe is a clue to the work's significance as a document of social protest.

　　It should also be noted that the frontier autobiographies of Mormon men designated for a secular audience invariably focus on missionary work at home and abroad, or on being persecuted by the gentile (i.e., non-Mormon) community. The authors take polygamous marriages for granted, and spend little time on them. Characteristic works are *The Orson Pratt Journals* and *The Life and Times of Joseph Fish, Mormon Pioneer*.

13 Conversation with Patricia Gardiner, Joyce Kinkaid, Jan Roush, and Christine
    Hult at Utah State University, Logan, Utah, August 7, 1987.
14 Indeed, the frontispiece photographs of many frontier autobiographies depict
    the subjects in their best clothes, thereby undercutting the emphasis on where
    they lived and what they lived for. Whether this is because photographs were
    so rare that people dressed up to have them taken on special occasions, or
    because the autobiographers or their editors deliberately selected the most
    bourgeois representations to lend stature to their workaday subjects, is un-
    clear. Other typical examples of "best dress" frontispiece photographs appear
    in Christiana Holmes Tillson's *A Woman's Story of Pioneer Illinois,* Rebecca
    and Edward Burlend's *A True Picture of Emigration,* and Mary Ann Hafen's
    Recollections of a Handcart Pioneer of 1860.
15 Greenwood's formal portrait appears near the end of the book, sadder, wiser,
    the delicacy of youth gone despite the stylish short bob, sleeveless silky dress
    with a shimmering artificial flower on the shoulder, and three strands of crys-
    tal beads. Captioned "After fifteen years of it," the *it* says it all.

WORKS CITED

Armitage, Susan, and Elizabeth Jameson, eds. *The Women's West.* Norman: Uni-
    versity of Oklahoma Press, 1987.
Bloom, Lynn Z. "Auto/Bio/History: Modern Midwifery." *Prose Studies* 14 (Sep-
    tember 1991), 12–24.
Burlend, Rebecca, and Edward Burlend. *A True Picture of Emigration.* Ed. Milo M.
    Quaife. 1968; rpt. Lincoln: University of Nebraska Press, 1987.
Davis, Gayle R. "Women's Frontier Diaries: Writing for Good Reason." *Women's
    Studies,* 14 (1987), 5–14.
Faragher, John Mack. *Women and Men on the Overland Trail.* New Haven: Yale
    University Press, 1979.
Fish, Joseph. *The Life and Times of Joseph Fish, Mormon Pioneer.* Ed. John H.
    Krenkel. Danville, IL: Interstate, 1970.
Garland, Hamlin. *A Son of the Middle Border.* 1917; rpt. Lincoln: University of
    Nebraska Press, 1979.
Geertz, Clifford. *Works and Lives: The Anthropologist as Author.* Stanford: Stan-
    ford University Press, 1988.
Greenwood, Annie Pike. *We Sagebrush Folks.* New York: Appleton, 1934. Rpt.
    Boise: University of Idaho Press, 1988. [Quotations are from 1st ed.]
Hafen, Mary Ann. *Recollections of a Handcart Pioneer of 1860: A Woman's Life on
    the Mormon Frontier.* 1938; rpt. Lincoln: University of Nebraska Press, 1983.
Hampsten, Elizabeth. *Read This Only to Yourself: The Private Writings of Mid-
    western Women, 1880–1910.* Bloomington: Indiana University Press, 1982.
Heart Throbs, in Prose and Verse, Dear to the American People. Ed. Joe Mitchell
    Chapple. Boston: Chapple, 1905.

Jeffrey, Julie Roy. *Frontier Women: The Trans-Mississippi West.* New York: Hill and Wang, 1979.

Kolodny, Annette. *The Land before Her: Fantasy and Experience of the American Frontiers, 1630–1860.* Chapel Hill: University of North Carolina Press, 1984.

Lerner, Gerda. *The Majority Finds Its Past: Placing Women in History.* New York: Oxford University Press, 1979.

Moynihan, Ruth B., Susan Armitage, and Christine Fischer Dichamp, eds. *So Much to Be Done: Women Settlers on the Mining and Ranching Frontier.* Lincoln: University of Nebraska Press, 1990.

Pratt, Orson. *The Orson Pratt Journals.* Comp. Elden J. Watson. Salt Lake City: E. J. Watson, 1975.

Riley, Glenda. *The Female Frontier: A Comparative View of Women on the Prairie and the Plains.* Lawrence: University Press of Kansas, 1988.

Rose, Hilda. *The Stump Farm: A Chronicle of Pioneering.* Boston: Little Brown, 1931.

Sagsam, Angela [Sarah Muirhead]. *I Was a Country Girl.* Philadelphia: Dorrance, 1947.

Schlissel, Lillian. *Women's Diaries of the Westward Journey.* New York: Schocken, 1982.

Showalter, Elaine. "Feminist Criticism in the Wilderness." In *Feminist Criticism: Essays on Women, Literature, Theory,* ed. Elaine Showalter, 243–70. New York: Pantheon, 1985.

Smith, Sidonie. *A Poetics of Women's Autobiography: Marginality and the Fictions of Self-Representation.* Bloomington: Indiana University Press, 1987.

Smith-Rosenberg, Carroll. *Disorderly Conduct: Visions of Gender in Victorian America.* New York: Knopf, 1985.

Stenhouse, Fanny. *"Tell It All": The Story of a Life's Experience in Mormonism: An Autobiography.* Ed. Harriet Beecher Stowe. Hartford: Worthington, 1874. Rpt. as *The Tyranny of Mormonism or An Englishwoman in Utah.* New York: Praeger, 1971.

Stewart, Elinore Pruitt. *Letters of a Woman Homesteader.* 1914; rpt. Boston: Houghton Mifflin, 1982.

Stewart, Elinore Pruitt. *Letters on an Elk Hunt.* 1915; rpt. Lincoln: University of Nebraska Press, 1979.

Stratton, Joanna L. *Pioneer Women: Voices from the Kansas Frontier.* New York: Simon and Schuster, 1981.

Tanner, Annie Clark. *A Mormon Mother.* Salt Lake City: University of Utah Library, 1983.

Tillson, Christiana Holmes. *A Woman's Story of Pioneer Illinois.* Ed. Milo M. Quaife. Chicago: Donnelly, 1919.

Tyler, Ron. *Visions of America: Pioneer Artists in a New Land.* New York: Thames and Hudson, 1983.

Ulrich, Laurel Thatcher. *A Midwife's Tale: The Life of Martha Ballard, Based on Her Diary, 1785–1812.* New York: Knopf, 1990.

CHAPTER 7

Gertrude Stein and the Lesbian Lie

CATHARINE R. STIMPSON

Gertrude Stein began to write seriously around 1903. A decade later, she had a reputation, especially but not exclusively in avant-garde circles. As that reputation expanded to ever larger publics, it divided against itself. In a repetitive binary opposition, two "Steins" competed for attention in an arena that Stein herself could at best partially control. One "Stein" was the "Good Stein," whom the public liked. In 1933, it made a best-seller of her *jeu d'esprit*, *The Autobiography of Alice B. Toklas*. After passing through the market, *The Autobiography* went on to please a second set of cultural gatekeepers: doyens of the syllabi, denizens of the college curriculum. If Stein appears in the United States classroom, *The Autobiography* or *Three Lives* usually represents her.

The second "Stein" was the "Bad Stein," whom the public hated and ridiculed. The Bad Stein was guilty of a double transgression: first, and more blatantly, she subverted generic and linguistic codes; next, and more slyly, she subverted sexual codes. Both her word and flesh violated normalities. Since the 1970s, a mélange of audiences has inverted Stein's reputations. The Old Good Stein is the New Bad Stein. She is too obedient to convention. The Old Bad Stein is the New Good Stein. Her transgressions are exemplary deeds.[1]

The Autobiography of Alice B. Toklas and a companion text, *Everybody's Autobiography*,[2] mingle the two, pre-1970 Steins. So doing, they undercut, sometimes incisively, sometimes impotently, the binary opposition that her reputation embodies. Skillfully, the Old Bad Stein, the transgressive Stein, is cajoling a potential reader more decorous than she into accepting a story about the Old Good Stein. Indeed, that story will establish the Old Good Stein. In a complex act of deception, confession, and assertion, a misunderstood, under-published author is giving the public what she calculates it can take. Her gift demands that she handle a subgenre we insufficiently understand: the lesbian lie. This lie insists that no lesbians lie abed here. To imagine erotics is to fall victim to cognitive errotics. The author respects, indeed shares, a reader's sense of decorum. At its finest, such decorum construes all sexuality as private and then begs private things to stay private. At its worst, such decorum is repression's etiquette. Stein's lie, then, is at once manipulative and courteous. The author delicately refuses to stir her readers up too much. Proper manners prevail. So, less fortunately for post-Stonewall sensibilities, will ignorance.[3] Not surprisingly, the tact that renders sexuality invisible also renders money invisible. *The Autobiography* is genteel about Stein's income. The circulation of her desire and that of her dollars/francs are each veiled.

An effect of Stein's lesbian lie is to permit us to regard the Old Good Stein as if she were both a "character" in the colloquial sense of "What a character!" and a literary character in an autobiographical gesture. This is an ironic turn for a cultural analyst who believed that the mass media now spew out personalities (the Duchess of Windsor, for example) in such profusion that these manufactured personalities have driven the character (Gwendolyn Harleth, for example) from fiction's dreamy stage. Indeed, *Everybody's Autobiography* shrewdly meditates on the distinctions among having a sense of personal identity, no matter how momentarily, creating a literary identity, and being a mass media personality. As character and literary character, Stein is a jolly, bluff, discreet celebrity who plays with crowds of famous men: Picasso, Matisse, Hemingway. Each of these attributes—jolliness, bluffness, discretion, fame, the company of men—is vital to her appeal. She has her anxious moments, but they test, rather than damage, the bulkhead of her cheer. Moreover, this character exists within a readable narrative. Such readability attracts two audiences that perhaps would agree only about the readable: a heterosexual audience generally suspicious of transgression, and a homosexual audience that longs to celebrate sexual, but not literary, differences.

In brief, Stein's lesbian lie pins up an accessible star, a brilliant amalgam of democratic openness, spirited realism, and enchantment. Her modulation of subversion into entertainment both follows and refines a homosexual method of seeking acceptance in modern heterosexual culture.[4] *La Cage aux Folles* is a commercially triumphant example. Camp is a complex, wickedly self-conscious extreme. Because this modulation of subversion into entertainment is often for profit, for financial as well as psychological and physical security, it is part of the *packaging* of homosexuality. Stein's estranged brother Leo hated *The Autobiography*. "God, what a liar she is," he grumped.[5] Leo was wounded because he thought his sister was being untruthful about him and perhaps vengeful as well. In his narcissism, he was dully sharpening a real point: *The Autobiography* does lie. What packaging does not? What packaging cannot? If only through omission?

In the package of *The Autobiography of Alice B. Toklas,* a woman is apparently putting down the story of a feminine life as if it were a sparkling wine. She seems to be artless and spontaneous. She is also a lady, "gently bred." Neither striving career woman, nor raving anarchist, she behaves properly in drawing rooms. (Elsewhere, Stein gives us drawing and quartering rooms.) Born in San Francisco, Alice has cared dutifully for her father and brother after her mother's death. Combining responsibility with delight, she plays the piano. She reads Henry James. She says lightly: ". . . I myself have had no liking for violence and have always enjoyed the pleasures of needlework and gardening. I am fond of paintings, furniture, tapestry, houses and flowers and even vegetables and fruit-trees" (4).

Modern narratives of femininity demand some revolt, no matter how gently bred or in-bred. In 1907, bored, restless, Alice goes abroad. Nature itself seems to endorse her quest, for the catastrophe of the San Francisco earthquake helps her. It has brought back some traveling members of a local family, the Steins. They tell her about Europe and inspire her to go. In Paris, Alice meets their relative, the great Stein, a stoutish woman with a strong laugh and temper. In a much-repeated line, Alice declares:

"I may say that only three times in my life have I met a genius and each time a bell within me rang and I was not mistaken." (5)

The Autobiography has a number of techniques with which to stress Stein's genius: the sheer steadiness of Toklas' admiration; anecdotes about people of talent and the other two people of genius (Whitehead and Picasso) who respect Stein; Stein's own self-esteem. Underwriting her doubts, overwriting her pride, *The Autobiography* extols her as the most creative literary figure of the twentieth century. Firmly, Toklas announces:

"The young often when they have learnt all they can learn accuse her of an inordinate pride. She says yes of course. She realizes that in english literature in her time she is the only way. She has always known it and now she says it." (77) The focus on Stein's genius is as crucial to the packaging of lesbianism as it was to the Stein/Toklas "marriage." As Stein's genius justifies Toklas' devotion, so it defuses the erotic threat of that marriage. For the genius is a spectacular exception, not a rule. Genius watchers need not fear that the habits of the genius will become a common part of daily life. Moreover, because the genius transcends ordinary intellectual and artistic categories, she or he can rationalize an escape from ordinary social and moral judgments.[6]

Simultaneously, as Stein is using the sign of "genius" to reassure her readers, she is using the sign of "art," which genius produces, to deflect her reader's attention from sexuality itself. This maneuver is weirdly crystallized in *Everybody's Autobiography.* Stein and Toklas are at Bryn Mawr

College where Stein is to lecture. They are given "Miss Thomas' old room in the Deanery" (184). Stein refuses to precede the substantive "room" with "bed" or "living" or any other qualifier, an act of self-protective vagueness. Miss Thomas, of course, is M. Carey Thomas, whose legendary rule of Bryn Mawr had ended fourteen years earlier in 1922. The Deanery had been her residence. Around 1904–5, Stein had written a novella, *Fernhurst,* rooted in a Bryn Mawr scandal. Fernhurst is a women's college. Its dean, Miss Thornton, based on Thomas, is about to lose her special friend, Miss Bruce, to a married man, Philip Redfern. Yet, with tenacity and subtle skill, Miss Thornton banishes Redfern and regains "all property rights" to Miss Bruce. Now, over three decades later, Stein looks around Miss Thomas' room and notices that "it was as it was." It has the same photographs of "capital works of art." Then, a little meanly, Stein moves from art to gossip about art lovers: "Clive Bell used to be funny when he objected that Roger Fry and Mrs. Bell always went to see capital works of art" (184). Her gossip alludes to sexuality, the adulterous love affair between Roger Fry and Vanessa Bell. She is reminding her readers that heterosexuals can sin, too.

Unlike Oscar Wilde, Stein does not valorize the sign of "art" over "life"; the sign of "the lie" over "truth"; the sign of "artifice" over "nature." Often indulging herself in sweet pastoral, Stein prefers the green hills of her summer home, where she wrote *The Autobiography,* to green carnations. She experiments with the rhetoric of spontaneity, be it of the fragment, the paragraph, or the narrative tale. Wilde's dramatic structures and aphorisms are contributions to the rhetoric of control. Unlike Wilde, Stein never went to prison. She was far too careful. Like Wilde, Stein must ask how to write about the erotically and socially unprintable. Their theories of art and artists substitute for more explicit representations of the forbidden. Like chaff in modern weapons systems, shot out to deflect an incoming missile from its intended target, these texts distract a potentially hostile gaze from the zone of vulnerability.

In *The Autobiography,* by about 1910, Toklas and Stein have set up their home and salon together. They go out. They travel. They have lots of visitors: artists, writers, journalists, socialites. Toklas, as ostensible narrator and real homemaker, works to *familiarize* their mutual setting. It seems comfortable, close, cozy. Stein's domestication of the different is a sophisticated prophecy of *People* magazine and its vulgar television cousin, "Life Styles of the Rich and Famous." Stein/Toklas also enjoy surrogate family members. They include the five-year-old son of their janitor, who leaps rapturously into Stein's arms when he sees a luscious Matisse, and American "doughboys" in France during World War I. For them, the couple provides the nurturing services of an exotic Welcome Wagon and warmly eccentric spinster aunts.

As Toklas chats and remembers, Stein is constructing a four-act comedy. Stein is the heroine of Act 1, her life before meeting Toklas. Act 1 ends with that staple of the women's plot: marriage, Stein to Toklas. Act 2, which lasts from 1907 to 1914, is the period of youthful innocence. Everyone is young, talented, and poor. They have fun. They think their radical thoughts and do their avant-garde work. Act 3, the period of World War I, is the season of sorrow. Stein's characters grow up, but maturity extracts a terrible price, which the death of Apollinaire symbolizes. Grieving for him, Toklas' voice is bleak, quiet, elegaic. However, *The Autobiography* is a comedy. Act 4 begins with peace. The cannons are carried away. Act 4 ends with the writing of *The Autobiography* itself. The young, the talented, and the poor are the middle-aged, the talented, and the no longer poor. (At his death, Picasso would leave an estate worth at least $200,000,000. In 1989, one of his paintings, *Pierrette's Wedding,* would bring $51.3 million at an art auction.) Stein is now "Stein." A younger generation seeks admission to the salon.[7] It is a credential to be there.

Like a Hollywood movie during the Depression of the 1930s, *The Autobiography* is a fable about going from rags to riches, not from riches to rags or rags to rags. It offers a fantasy about some people who became financial successes through their commitment to the arts, to the imagination, to fantasy itself. The comic structure of *The Autobiography,* like Stein's ostensible self-confidence, makes it a buoyant text. That charm is disarming. Smile, and the world smiles with you. Weep, and you weep alone. The representation of success is even more lavish in *Everybody's Autobiography.* A best-selling author, Stein is making money. She "counts." She is a significant person with cash to think about. Her lecture tour of America is a triumph. On the boat to America, a prosperous throat doctor asks her to autograph his copy of *The Autobiography.* Both she and Toklas do so. Small wonder that the last paragraph of *Everybody's* repeats a verb of pleasure and happiness, "I like," five times.

This charm is a refreshing contrast to two other texts that famously codify sexual ideology between 1918 and 1939. The first is *A Farewell to Arms,* which Hemingway, the lost and betraying son of *The Autobiography,* published in 1929. Set in World War I, the novel announces that heterosexual lovers may achieve a physical unity that has metaphysical strength, heroic grandeur, and mystical consolation. Hideously, they need that consolation. For the world will kill the very good and the very gentle and the very brave impartially. It will shatter strength, grandeur, and consolation into bloody parts. Catherine Barkley will die giving birth. The baby itself will be stillborn. These double deaths—the mother's hemorrhages (an awful "Hem") and the infant's suffocation—show a culture bleeding to death and strangling new life. Having said farewell to the arms of Mars, Frederick Henry must say farewell to the arms of Venus.

If *A Farewell to Arms* consolidates the myth of romantic, tragic hetero-sexuality, the second text, *The Well of Loneliness,* consolidates that of romantic, tragic homosexuality. Published in 1928, immediately found le-gally obscene, *The Well* is a self-conscious polemic against homophobia. However, homosexuality is as doom-laden for homosexuals, as much an urn full of ashes, as love is for Hemingway's heterosexuals. Homosexual underworlds are demonic, sordid, gloomy, ill.

When Stein does hint at a darker lesbian, she, who disdains repetition, returns to a pungent but opaque figure: a Madame Caesar, who wears trousers, the sign of the butch.[8] In *Everybody's Autobiography,* Madame Caesar seems to be "with" Madame Steiner, but she meets an "English-woman" in a tuberculosis sanitorium. The Englishwoman comes. Madame Steiner goes away. The Englishwoman returns. Then she is dead, with two bullets in her head and her Basque cap on the rock beside her. Officially, the death is a suicide. Then, the wife of an electrician moves in with Madame Caesar. Yet, Stein sends this story up. It becomes a fairy tale, a sample of black humor, and a grammatical exercise. Describing her visit with Bernard Faÿ to Madame Caesar, after the discovery of the English-woman's body, Stein writes: "I weep I cry I glorify but all that has nothing to do with that. / He weeps he cries he glorifies" (82).

The end of *The Autobiography,* Stein's glorification of life with Toklas, her gambol/gamble, her ludic romp, is much annotated.[9] In the last para-graphs, a reader learns that the narrator is not Toklas, but Stein. Teleo-logical certainties and narrative conventions waver. The book's title has been illusory. The "real" autobiographer is Stein. She says nearly all of the last words to Toklas:

"You know what I am going to do. I am going to write it for you. I am going to write it as simply as Defoe did the autobiography of Robinson Crusoe. And she has and this is it." (252)

This joke about authorship has at least three consequences, two episte-mological. First, the ending demonstrates Stein's theory about the impos-sibility of autobiography if autobiography swears that it is the narrative of a unified self, a core subject; that the narrator and the subject of the narration are the same person; that the narrator's memory has been a reli-able guide to his/her past; and that the person who writes about the past is at bottom the person of the past.[10] Later, Stein would shrug. "That is really the trouble with an autobiography you do not of course you do not really believe yourself why should you, you know so well so very well that it is not yourself . . ." (*EA* 68). Next, the ending turns *The Autobiography* into a cautionary tale about the ease with which "fact" can slip into "fic-tion," "fiction" into "fact." The very slipperiness of these devilish categories helps to justify Stein's doubts about autobiography. So read, *The Auto-biography* anticipates a prominent category of postmodern art that Linda

Hutcheon has named "historiographic metafiction." Such a text "inscribes and then subverts its mimetic engagement with the world. It does not reject it . . . nor does it merely accept it. . . . But it does irrevocably change any simple notions of realism or reference, by confronting the discourse of art with the discourse of history."[11]

A third result is to reveal a contradiction in Stein's packaging of lesbianism. On the one hand, the coda is a tribute to the lesbian couple. Its unity is at once regressive and a leap beyond individuation and its perils. The twinned voices of the women are intertwined. The paragraph of their being merges the sentences of their voices. Indeed, the couple represents a merger-and-acquisitions policy based on feeling rather than on corporate worth. Unified, Stein/Toklas assert their rights to love as they please and work as they wish. Without relying on foundational principles or master narratives, for lesbianism lacks both in any plausible form, they assert the value of their loving, working presence in the world, their capacities for breath and brain. Their story, no matter what they leave out, is the proof of their worth.[12] On the other hand, the coda maintains heterosexual roles. The husband, male-identified woman, has actually done the work of writing. The wife, the lady, merely speaks. Stein further placates her readers through surprising (but not shocking) them and then giving them something to do. Getting to play "Author, author, who's got the author," her readers swing their attention away from the lesbian couple and onto the game the couple is offering them, rather as if the coda were a party treat or tea cake.

The coda of *The Autobiography* recapitulates mixed messages about sexuality that Stein has tapped out throughout the text. First, the social calendar of Stein/Toklas seems to be largely heterosexual. Heterosexuals need not be monogamous. Ironically, the lesbian couple upholds the principles of monogamy. Hardly Rotarians, the friends of Stein/Toklas live out of wedlock, commit adultery, break hearts, flirt, tease. They practice the conventions of wild Western romanticism. However, they are heterosexual, even dogmatically so. Their spokesman is another genius, Picasso. He finds sexual ambiguity upsetting. He says of certain Americans: ". . . ils sont pas des hommes, ils sont pas des femmes, ils sont des américains . . ." (49). He does, however, approve of one American woman, a Bryn Mawr graduate, the wife of an artist. She is both beautiful and dumb: ". . . having once fallen on her head (she) had a strange vacant expression" (49–50).

Next, Stein mentions the names of lesbians and gay men: Natalie Barney, Marsden Hartley, Stein and Toklas.[13] However, she strips these names of their sexuality. Like words themselves, the names are fleshless. Lovers become, at best, friends. *The Autobiography* prospectively half answers Ed Cohen's witty question, "What if someone wrote a novel about homosexuality and no body came?" (805). The pictures of Stein and Toklas together are as tasteful as a middle-class Baedeker. Take, for example, a passage about Stein, Toklas, and the weather:

"Gertrude Stein adored heat and sunshine although she always says that Paris winter is an ideal climate. In those days it was always at noon that she preferred to walk. I, who have and had no fondness for a summer sun, often accompanied her. Sometimes later in Spain I sat under a tree and wept but she in the sun was indefatigable. She could even lie in the sun and look straight up into a summer noon sun, she said it rested her eyes and head." (55)

In Stein's straitlaced, middle-class reticence is a double rejection of textual alternatives available to her. The first is of the romantic excesses of Natalie Barney and Renée Vivien, inseparable from her disdain for modern explorations of dreams, the irrational, and the "primitive." Stein looks straight at the sun, not into "the night." The next is of the intelligent, elegant sensuousness of Colette. In 1932, *Ces Plaisirs* evoked some of the figures that *The Autobiography* was to treat a year later. Yet, Colette gazes at the velvet of the peach, the curve of a breast, the linens of the bed of Lady Eleanor Butler and Miss Sarah Ponsonby, and then, the stone of their tomb.

However, Stein leaves a paper trail about homosexual realities. Spatially, she sets *The Autobiography* in the houses that Stein/Toklas inhabited, emotionally, in their marriage. The narrative voices are theirs. A lesbian world, the water in which the fish of anecdotes swim, is so fluidly embracing that it seems both invisible and natural. Moreover, Stein refers obliquely to her more openly erotic work, to "Ada" or to her "lost" novel, *Q.E.D.*. Two sorts of readers can pick up the pieces of this trail. Some, personal friends, already know the score. Others, like me, are trying to learn the score. All of us are engaged in conspiracies. The friends, engaged in a conspiracy of silence, will not tell how much they know. The strangers, engaged in an alternative conspiracy of revelation, insist on telling how much we have learned. Our revisionary impulse is to amplify Stein's whispers into hearty speech.

Everybody's Autobiography rambles on with an equivalent mixture of messages. However, if Toklas seems to write up *The Autobiography*, Stein writes her down in *Everybody's*. To be sure, Toklas is always there. She is Stein's companion, interpreter, housekeeper, secretary. They eat oysters and pies together. They drive around Chicago in a police car together. They are inseparable, except when Stein steps up alone to a podium. However, Stein casually and quickly dismisses Alice as the author of *The Autobiography*. So doing, she erases Alice as the gaze, the eye, that fixes Stein's identity, Stein's "I." Stein now thinks about other, less singular stabilizing gazes:

her audience, her little dog, and her own. Her regard for her mirror image as "genius" is now overweening. Being straightforward about her Jewishness, she now has two names on her genius list for the twentieth century: Gertrude Stein and Albert (Ein)stein. One is female and literary; the other male and "philosophic" (21). Both are Jews.

Playfully, *The Autobiography* might seem to foreshadow postmodern theories of the death of the author, but, in another contradiction, it at once defends and defeats them. Toklas can be Stein, but only if Stein dictates that. So doing, *The Autobiography* balances an unstable subject, i.e., a Stein who can seem to be Toklas for nearly an entire book, against a stable self, a Stein who can reassert her Steinishness at will. Less ambiguously, *Everybody's Autobiography* asserts the authority of the self, especially that of the genius/author. Together, the texts exemplify Nancy K. Miller's theory that feminist critics can read women authors in ways that rewrite subjectivity without erasing it. Similarly, African-American critics can read African-American authors, postcolonial critics postcolonial authors. Miller warns us against foreclosing on the properties of authorship, and, I would add, against foreclosing on the properties of agency by using authorship as a synecdoche for agency. She states, "The postmodernist decision that the Author is Dead and the subject along with him does not . . . necessarily hold for women, and prematurely forecloses the question of agency for them. Because women have not had the same historical relation of identity to origin, institution, production that men have had, they have not, I think, (collectively) felt burdened by *too much* Self, Ego, Cogito, etc. Because the female subject has juridically been excluded from the polis, hence decentered, 'disoriginated,' deinstitutionalized, etc., her relation to integrity and textuality, desire and authority, displays structurally important differences from that universal position" (106).

As Stein packages the female lesbian subject, she also dramatizes the creation of the modern art and literature that developed simultaneously with modern sexual identities. Her lesbianism is acceptable because she either evades it or stylizes it as a joke about authorship. In a reversal, she renders modernism acceptable through turning art into life. Presenting the movers and shakers of modernism as "real people," she parcels out cultural history as anecdote and story. This technique is a prophecy of television's dominant method of conveying ideas through having a figure embody them. Watch modern physics become Einstein and Oppenheimer. Aiding Stein in her minibiographies is the myth of Bohemia, a narrative about artists that had become a well-understood formula well before 1933. Indeed, *The Autobiography* has a revealing scene. In 1907, Toklas meets Stein at an avant-garde art show in Paris. Just before Stein touches Toklas on the shoulder, she marvels, "it was indeed the vie de Bohème just as one had seen it in the opera . . ." (18). "Bohemia" is a space in which people have permission to be different, to be wild and crazy kids. A modern version of the rituals of misrule and of the rites of inversion, Bohemia sanctions a preference for art over commerce; feeling over reason; style over conformity; experiment over tradition.

Perhaps most crucially, both autobiographies pull back from Stein's upsetting challenge to representational codes and generic conventions. Telling her comic stories, Stein writes *of* modern art. Despite some shrewd narrative tricks, she does not write modern art itself.[14] She is a guide, not a practitioner. She is teacher, mentor, docent, not a disquieting savage on a fling. The fourth paragraph of *Everybody's* is about a Miss Hennessy's wooden umbrella. Miss Hennessy is eccentric, but Stein's prose is not. The umbrella is "carved out of wood and looks exactly like a real one even to the little button and the rubber string that holds it together" (3). In contrast, the eighth paragraph of *Tender Buttons* is also "about" Mildred's umbrella, but the prose is a riot, "A cause and no curve, a cause and loud enough, a cause and extra a loud clash and an extra wagon . . " (*Writings and Lectures* 164).

In deliberate retreat, Stein's autobiographies cultivate a lively, but plain and simple, style. Stein even has Toklas say that she is always "literal." *Everybody's Autobiography* obviously revises James's *The American Scene,* an earlier account of a famous expatriate's return to the landscape of origins. Far more subtle an observer of American democracy, far more sensitive to injustice, James writes much more deeply and more densely than Stein. However, her plainness and simplicity are masterstrokes in covering up and covering over her lesbianism. For her immediacies and limpidities promise that her language is a transparent window onto reality, even onto the reality that fact and fiction can blur into each other. She is direct. She tells her friends the truth, even about the trickiness of truth. In return, she takes no chaff, no guff. How could she be such a packager? How could she lie? Deliberately, egregiously, meanly deceive?

However, a gap does exist between style's apparent promise of full disclosure and the actuality of partial disclosures. Because of that gap, the texts are not literal but ironic. Yet, the same gap makes the autobiographies mimetic. For they dramatize an actuality, the homosexual dissimulation of which Colette speaks so cleverly and respectfully. Dissimulation is a tax that homosexuals pay in order to go on being members of a society that would abhor their honesty. When Stein put her hand on Toklas' shoulder, lesbians in Paris could not wear men's clothing unless the prefect of police said they could. Stein's public silence makes much more sense when we admit the power of the legal and social codes that governed her. She efficiently chose her method of strategic dissimulation: write as if you wrote

about everything and everybody. Her lie was to write as if she were incapable of lying. If she did lie, if she pretended that Alice B. Toklas wrote
a book, she would reveal the trick at the end and call it a playful fiction.
The creator of this Alice would show the rabbits of a literary magic trick
moving from hutch to hat. If we practice pragmatics, we must note her
pragmatism.

Stein's survival mechanisms, her repressions, exact their price. A passage
in *Tender Buttons,* which puns on what the body and the voice can do,
wryly comments on such an expense:

> South, south which is a wind is not rain, does silence choke or does it not.
> Lying in a conundrum, lying so makes the springs restless, lying so is a reduc-
> tion, not lying so is arrangeable. (200–201)

Stein's most public autobiographies lack a measure of the pleasure of many
of her more radical texts. *Everybody's Autobiography* is often dogged in
its descriptions of fun. Neither text has the intricate lyricism and sophisticated engagement with the naive of "A Sonatina Followed By Another."
Here, Stein retains traditional marital roles (Stein as husband, Toklas as
wife), but transforms the foul into the fowls of a joyous, homey bestiary.

> And a credit to me she is sleepily a credit to me and what do I credit her with
> I credit her with a kiss.
> 1. Always sweet.
> 2. Always right.
> 3. Always welcome.
> 4. Always wife.
> 5. Always blessed.
> 6. Always a successful druggist of the second class and we know what that means.
> Who credits her with all this a husband with a kiss and what is he to be always
> more lovingly his missus' help and hero. And when is he heroic, well we know when.
> Win on a foul pretty as an owl pretty as an owl win on a fowl. And the fowl
> is me and she is pretty as an owl. Battling Siki and Capridinks is pretty and winks,
> winks of sleep and winks of love. Capridinks. Capridinks is my love and my Coney.
> (*Bee Time Vine* 32)

Moreover, Stein's public evasions of her sexual marginality and otherness
help to distort her perceptions of other marginalized groups. Her comments on American blacks, for example, can be genial. They are also pa-
tronizing, inept, and foolish. She anesthetizes black history.

I am passing a judgment, at once sympathetic and truculent, on Stein's
passing. The ambivalence of my judgment is related to larger, unresolved
problems in feminist theory to which I can only point now. One problem
is the shape of a feminist response to the lesbian lie. So far, the most influential voices have denounced the lie while exculpating the liar. In both

her poem "Cartographies of Silence" and her essay "Women and Honor: Some Notes on Lying," Adrienne Rich writes eloquently of the destructive consequences of the lie, for lesbians and for all women: amnesia, "the silence of the unconscious"; madness; the erasure of trust among women (187 and elsewhere). Yet, the lesbian lie ("No lesbians here") has also been a source of a courageous, jaunty, often outrageous style. The Old Bad Stein, fibbing a little about the Old Good Stein, did dash off *The Autobiography*. The liars, when they speak together, as Stein and Toklas do in Stein's more radical texts, can create a ritualistic theater. This theater's purpose is to strengthen the community of liars, to remind them that the lie is a lie, and to give the liars enough rest and relaxation to go on to further feats of linguistic inventiveness. *Their* purpose is to deceive a public that is both vigilant and unwary as it patrols the borders of permissible speech and behavior. This theatrical tongue is more apt to be spoken than written. A feature of Stein's more radical texts is their interrogation of the diglottism of conversation and conversation on the page.

Rich's argument rests on our ability to draw, finally, reliable distinctions between true and false, between language in the service of truth and language in the service of fraud. Yet feminist postmodernism questions this ability. Some of us might interpret the phrase "the lie of language" in other ways. We might ask about the lie of language in the sense of the position of language, in ways that wash away the binary distinction between "true" and "false" itself. Feminist postmodernism might then give a lesbian lie two connotations. First, it is performance that both precedes and follows a lesbian's perception of her powerlessness because of the well-muscled stigma against lesbianism. She believes that only if she merges the false ("I am not a lesbian") with the true ("I am a lesbian") can she live as a lesbian. Next, the lesbian lying might also be a parable about the inexorably secretive powers of language. Like language, the lesbian lies. Neither vicious nor exploitative, she still knows more than she overtly lets on or out. Is the Old Bad Stein inventing the Old Good Stein a paranoid story about language in operation? If so, how paranoid should we be?

NOTES

I read earlier versions of this paper at Brown University, Skidmore College, Harvard Feminist Literary Theory Seminar, and Columbia University. A version also forms one section of "Are the Differences Spreading? Feminist Criticism and Postmodernism," *English Studies in Canada*, 15/4 (December 1989), 364–82. I am grateful to Margo Culley for her patience, support, and suggestions.

1   I discuss Stein's reputations more fully in "Humanism and its Freaks."

2   In part because it deals with fewer celebrities, in part because it deals with
    a less celebrated setting (Stein's American lecture tour rather than Bohemian
    Paris), in part because it is more intellectually tiring, *EA* has lacked the popu-
    larity of *ABT*.

3   Carolyn G. Heilbrun (79) recalls her first readings of *ABT*. She and her mother
    interpreted Stein as an image of freedom. She adds, "We did not, of course,
    recognize them as lesbians; I'm not sure I even knew the word." When her
    husband suggested Stein/Toklas might be a lesbian couple, Heilbrun "snorted"
    in disbelief.

4   Leibowitz calls *ABT* a "cagy performance" (219).

5   "Supplement: Testimony Against Gertrude Stein by Henri Matisse, Tristan
    Tzara, Maria Jolas, Georges Braque, Eugene Jolas, Andre Salmon" also ac-
    cuses Stein of being a liar, a poseur, and a fool.

6   Winston (243) suggests that the use of Toklas' voice permits the representa-
    tion of Stein as genius to be more assured and confident than it is in *EA*. Win-
    ston is exploring a problem in Stein criticism beyond the immediate scope of
    this essay: the relationship of the very experimental, difficult *Stanzas in Medi-
    tation* to *ABT* as autobiographical texts.

7   Seigal calls this period the Americanization of the French avant-garde. Unfor-
    tunately, I find no Stein in Seigal.

8   Several critics have noted that "Caesar" was also a pet name for Stein in her
    marriage with Toklas.

9   Schmitz (203–26) reads Stein's double narrative with great flair and plausibility.

10 Stanton (18) correctly names *ABT* an open rejection of the autobiographical
    pact of "identity between a real person, the subject, and the object of enuncia-
    tion." The text then cuts against strongly felt feminist notions of a female iden-
    tity that an author can present and valorize.

11 Hutcheon (25). Although Timothy Dow Adams lacks Hutcheon's postmod-
    ernism, he praises Stein as the inventor of the "mock-autobiography," an influ-
    ential subgenre that dances on the border between fiction and nonfiction.

12 Several of the most compelling feminist theories of autobiography explore
    women's explorations of a divided self. Martin (82) claims that contemporary
    lesbian autobiography opposes "self-evidently homogeneous conceptions of
    identity." Brilliantly, Lionnet examines the multiple self in postcolonial and
    African-American autobiographies by women. Because of Stein's narrative de-
    vices, *ABT* illustrates such theories. At the same time, her tributes to the les-
    bian couple uphold the possibilities of psychological unity and integration.

13 Three recent explorations of the lesbian subworlds that Stein erases are
    Benstock; Blankley; Jay.

14 Although I stress this point, I recognize the modernity of *ABT*. Breslin (149–62)
    shows how formidably Stein interrogates the formal problems of autobiography.
    Among recent feminist critics of autobiography, Sidonie Smith (175) notes how
    Stein invests herself with another's voice. Friedman (54–55) outlines the ad-
    vantages Stein gains through the fluidity of the writing "I." Merrill reads these

permeable ego boundaries through Lacanian psychoanalysis. Brodzki and Schenck (9) locate the modern in *ABT*'s relational quality, process of defamiliarization, and drama of a self "in pieces, fragments, refractions."

WORKS CITED

Adams, Timothy Dow. "'She Will Be Me When This You See': Gertrude Stein's Mock-Autobiography of Alice B. Toklas." *Publications of the Arkansas Philological Association,* 6/1 (1980), 1–18.

Benstock, Shari. *Women of the Left Bank, Paris, 1900–1940.* Austin: University of Texas Press, 1986.

Blankley, Elyse. "Return to Mytilène: Reneé Vivien and the City of Women." In *Women Writers and the City: Essays in Feminist Criticism,* ed. Susan Merrill Squier, 45–67. Knoxville: University of Tennessee Press, 1984.

Breslin, James E. "Gertrude Stein and the Problems of Autobiography." In *Women's Autobiography: Essays in Criticism,* ed. Estelle C. Jelinek, 149–62. Bloomington: Indiana University Press, 1980.

Brodzki, Bella, and Celeste Schenck, eds. *Life/Lines: Theorizing Women's Autobiography.* Ithaca: Cornell University Press, 1988.

Cohen, Ed. "Writing Gone Wilde: Homoerotic Desire in the Closet of Representation." *PMLA,* 102/5 (October 1987), 801–13.

Friedman, Susan Stanford. "Women's Autobiographical Selves: Theory and Practice." In *The Private Self: Theory and Practice of Women's Autobiographical Writings,* ed. Shari Benstock, 34–62. Chapel Hill and London: University of North Carolina Press, 1988.

Hall, Radclyffe. *The Well of Loneliness.* With a commentary by Havelock Ellis. New York: Covici Friede, [1928].

Heilbrun, Carolyn G. *Writing a Woman's Life.* New York and London: W. W. Norton and Co., 1988.

Hemingway, Ernest. *A Farewell to Arms.* With an Introduction by Ford Madox Ford. New York: Modern Library, [1932].

Hutcheon, Linda. "Beginning to Theorize Postmodernism." *Textual Practice* 1/1 (Spring 1987), 10–31.

Jay, Karla. *The Amazon and the Page.* Bloomington: Indiana University Press, 1987.

Leibowitz, Herbert. *Fabricating Lives: Explorations in American Autobiography.* New York: Alfred A. Knopf, 1989.

Lionnet, Françoise. *Autobiographical Voices: Race, Gender, Self-Portraiture.* Ithaca: Cornell University Press, 1989.

Martin, Biddy. "Lesbian Identity and Autobiographical Differences." In Brodzki and Schenck, 77–103.

Merrill, Cynthia. "Mirrored Image: Gertrude Stein and Autobiography." *Pacific Coast Philology,* 20/1–2 (November 1985), 11–17.

Miller, Nancy. *Subject to Change: Reading Feminist Writing*. New York: Columbia University Press, 1988.

Rich, Adrienne. *On Lies, Secrets, and Silence: Selected Prose, 1966–1978*. New York: W. W. Norton, 1979.

Schmitz, Neil. *Of Huck and Alice: Humorous Writing in American Literature*. Minneapolis: University of Minnesota Press, 1983.

Seigal, Jerrold. *Bohemian Paris: Culture, Politics, and the Boundaries of Bourgeois Life, 1830–1930*. New York: Viking, 1986.

Smith, Sidonie. *A Poetics of Women's Autobiography: Marginality and the Fictions of Self-Representation*. Bloomington and Indianapolis: Indiana University Press, 1987.

Stanton, Domna C. "Autogynography: Is the Subject Different?" *The Female Autograph*, 3–20. New York Literary Forum, 1984.

Stein, Gertrude. *The Autobiography of Alice B. Toklas (ABT)*. New York: Random House, [1933]. Vintage Book edition, 1960.

Stein, Gertrude. *Bee Time Vine and Other Pieces, 1913–1927*. New Haven: Yale University Press, 1953.

Stein, Gertrude. *Everybody's Autobiography (EA)*. New York: Random House, 1937. Vintage Book edition, 1973.

Stein, Gertrude. *Writings and Lectures, 1909–1945*. Ed. Patricia Meyerowitz. Baltimore: Penguin, 1971.

Stimpson, Catharine. "Humanism and Its Freaks," *boundary 2*, 12/3–13/1 (Spring/Fall 1984), 301–19.

"Supplement: Testimony Against Gertrude Stein by Henri Matisse, Tristan Tzara, Maria Jolas, Georges Braque, Eugene Jolas, André Salmon." *transition*, no. 23 (July 1935).

Winston, Elizabeth. "Gertrude Stein's Mediating Stanzas." *Biography: An Interdisciplinary Quarterly*, 9/3 (Summer 1986).

CHAPTER 8

Orphanhood and "Photo"-Portraiture in Mary McCarthy's Memories of a Catholic Girlhood

JANIS GREVE

In the first chapter of *On Photography,* Susan Sontag describes an important interrelation between the camera and family life. "Cameras go with family life," she states, and continues,

> Through photographs, each family constructs a portrait chronicle of itself—a portable kit of images that bear witness to its connectedness. It hardly matters what activities are photographed as long as photographs get taken and are cherished. Photography becomes a rite of family life just when, in the industrializing countries of Europe and America, the very institution of the family starts undergoing radical surgery. As that claustrophobic unit, the nuclear family, was being carved out of a much larger family aggregate, photography came along to memorialize, to restate symbolically, the imperiled continuity and vanishing extendedness of family life. Those ghostly traces, photographs, supply the token presence of the dispersed relatives. A family's photograph album is generally about the extended family—and, often, is all that remains of it. (8–9)

Given photography's vital role in laying claim to a family history, one can easily see how the camera would have a weighty significance as the auto-biographical tool for an orphan; the search for family moves, in this case, much closer to home, and the burden of familial "proof" becomes more immediate. *Memories of a Catholic Girlhood,* Mary McCarthy's chronicle of her life from early orphanhood to young womanhood, reveals photography as a lurking preoccupation in her autobiographical act. Real photographs of family members, references to photography, and a satiric verbal portraiture which aims to create "likenesses" of her life's authority figures, all lend credence to Sontag's claim that photography becomes a "defense

167

against anxiety" for individuals who feel themselves robbed of a past. By examining some of the intricate problems of orphanhood and selfhood which McCarthy exposes throughout the chapters of *Memories,* one gains a better understanding of photography's significance in this autobiography. The interwoven themes of memory, language, and class reveal a persistent fear of self-obliteration which begins with the event of McCarthy's orphanhood. Autobiography is the obvious counter to this negative drift; it is the life-opting and -ensuring mechanism of the adult. Photography, then, as a part of this life impulse, details the more subtle motives of the autobiography, and exposes a central and troubling conflict for McCarthy as she rewrites and attempts to "set right" her life.

In her preface "To the Reader" McCarthy details the complex unreliability of memory as the source of "fact" in the autobiographical pursuit. Emotional and mental cross-currents such as the desire to remember something a particular way, or remembering something incorrectly, cloud memory's clarity. Also, memories are sometimes acquired secondhand, as when one learns of a past event from someone else, which renders the "memory" not a memory at all, since it is not rooted in firsthand experience. McCarthy has a particular reason to be preoccupied with memory as a truth source: she equates the untimely loss of her parents at age six with a tragic theft of epistemological truth. As the biological originators of her life, they alone can offer the "correct" versions of her history. Hence, her memory is forever foundationless, having been orphaned along with herself, and she must always seek corroboration of her memories as if to fortify them with a makeshift "truth." Having to rely on memory, then, is an insecure process at best, which McCarthy reveals when she calls remembering a "reduction" (6)—the very act casting her back to her imperiled childhood self, her own life figuratively without a future because it has been "cut short" by the deaths of her parents.

So closely aligned for McCarthy are her orphanhood and the emotional fabric of her memory that she seems to see them as one, describing them in similar terms. When she and her brothers awaken from their illnesses to discover their newly orphaned state, they perceive that they have a "diminished importance" (36) to the adults around them. We even see Mary become the very embodiment of memory, when she describes the "special" treatment she got from her Grandmother McCarthy, following her parents' deaths: "I was six—old enough to 'remember' and this entitled me, in the family's eyes, to greater consideration, as if this memory of mine were a lawyer who represented me in court" (38). Similarly, Mary describes her memory of her former life in Seattle as very likely the key to Uncle Myers' remarkable cruelty toward her:

Anything that smacked to him of affectation or being "stuck up" was subject to the harshest reprisals from him, and I, being the oldest, and the one who remembered my parents and the old life best, was the chief sinner. . . . (62)

As the oldest of the children and the one best able to remember, Mary is a threat to her guardians and a danger to herself, because of what her memory can "claim"—making her either inconveniently emotional or capable of drawing unfavorable comparisons—and consequently her orphanhood becomes an even greater burden to them. Gayle Whittier explains McCarthy's rejection of memory as a valid *kind* of experience, and her understanding of her parents as essential "fact-bearers," as the result of an exclusion from cyclic nature:

The loss of one's parents loosens this bond with nature and unsettles the embryonic personality; McCarthy significantly locates the origin of the lies which pervade her childhood in the death of her parents, her human link with both nature and historical time. . . . (43–44)

Detached from nature, which commemorates itself, McCarthy turns to documentation as her form of truth. (51)

The writing of her life through remembering is for McCarthy a shaky enterprise, but, as I will show later, this very uncertainty provides her the opportunity to become her own documenting source, and effectively "parent" herself.

Language is another crucial determinant in the problems of orphanhood and memory. Part and parcel of being an orphan, McCarthy tells us, is having one's past interpreted by others; because of the absence of the "verifying" parents, the past—particularly that time including the living parents—presents itself as a ready text-to-be-read by any eager interpreter. One feels keenly the tension generated in the preface, between Uncle Harry and the narrating McCarthy, in the dispute over whether Roy McCarthy was a drunkard or a hapless, impractical romantic. Although the narrator finally rejects Uncle Harry's version of her father, his "sobering" interpretation lingers on, which is precisely what it is meant to. McCarthy shows her relatives hard at work in bracketing her past with explanations that clearly oppose, or at least injure, the narrator's sense of things: the children were brought up foolishly spoiled, the marriage of her parents must have been a mistake, her Grandmother Preston's beautiful black hair must have been dyed instead of natural. McCarthy even describes these "readings" of her life as infiltrating and changing her own memory of how things were: "Like all children we wished to conform, and the notion that our former ways had been somehow ridiculous and unsuitable made the memory of them falter a little, like a child's recitation to strangers" (37).

The implied parallel here between memory and speaking is one of many illustrations in *Memories* of a life that is linguistically contested by others, as well as by the narrating voice. The life "recited" by the children is intruded upon by others' verbal reformulations of that life, both sides contending for "ownership" of it through language. Mary perceives that just as her guardians seem to possess her, they also aspire to own her earlier life through what they say about it; she feels language to be a particularly sensitive register of what for a long time is a losing battle in demarcating her own life and identity. In many ways, the first few chapters of *Memories* is an argument of possession artistically orchestrated by McCarthy, who understands that part of "inhabiting" one's life is speaking it—that is, the way a human being interprets her world through language is the way she makes it uniquely her own. Because of the powerlessness her new status of orphan brings, Mary finds the adults of her world usurping her memories through their own authoritative word appropriations of them. She objects to her grandmother's begrudging framings of her mother as something like a "pretty secretary with whom he [her father] wantonly absconded" (29), and to the humiliation of being made to pray for their parents at night by her guardians Myers and Margaret:

It embarrassed us to be reminded of our parents by these persons who had superseded them and who seemed to evoke their wraiths in an almost proprietary manner, as though death, the great leveler, had brought them into their province. (39)

McCarthy also describes in detail the strange manner in which her grandmother nostalgically recalls the death day, as if she had successfully stage-managed a romantic death scene:

. . . for the fact that, as she phrased it, "they died in separate rooms" had for her a significance both romantic and self-congratulatory. . . . (44)

She goes on to recount her grandmother's occasionally letting her and her brothers into the darkened death rooms as a special mortuary treat:

My parents had, it seemed, by dying on her premises, become in a lively sense her property, and she dispensed them to us now, little by little, with a genuine sense of bounty. . . . (45)

McCarthy adds: "these memories doled out by our grandmother became our secret treasures." A remembered life that is rightfully hers is confiscated by others, and "doled" back, as if a gift.

One sees in Grandma Lizzie's interpretive stories a struggle between her words and Mary's word memories. Myers and Margaret are less articulate, but simply by commanding the children to pray for their parents' souls, project a "proprietary" manner that makes the children feel that their inherited claim to their parents' "memory" is seriously jeopardized. Also, the suggestion that their parents' souls should *require* prayer supersedes their far more idealizing notion of their parents, making the memory "falter." As orphans, the McCarthy children are not only without rights but essentially without language. The condition of orphanhood is too unfamiliar, and its implications are too somberly uncertain, for their parent-nurtured language to contain. Add to this quandary their unique orphan's position of being both pitiable because of their poverty, and worthy of respect because of the wealth and reknown of their grandfather. The few times Mary and her brother Kevin break out of their word-denying prison — Mary by seeking the aid of a friend's mother who feeds the half-starving Mary breakfast, and Kevin by running away to an orphanage and getting the attention of a worker—they find themselves unable to change things by putting words to the pathetic reality of their life. McCarthy's autobiography, then, is a devoting of language to those endured cruelties and paradoxes; it puts language in the orphan's mouth, and because of its nature as a "final say," strives to wrest power away from the previously nondisputable words of her early life's authority figures.

This notion of her life as a text "opened up" by orphanhood, its ownership debated among the control-oriented words of her relatives and herself, also implies class conflict. A Bakhtinian view of words as "living utterances" can help explain the disputatious aspect of language in McCarthy's text. According to Bakhtin, every word—both spoken and written—is shaped by social and historical forces, and is "living" because it is always changing in dialogue, as the result of these forces at work. Language is "stratified" by varied social forces, and because of this

there are no "neutral" words and forms—words and forms that can belong to "no one"; language has been completely taken over, shot through with intentions and accents . . . all words have the "taste" of a profession, a genre, a tendency, a party, a particular work, a particular person, a generation, an age group, the day and hour. (293)

Bakhtin continues to elucidate the "tension" that embodies a word when it is used in dialogic exchange:

As a living, socio-ideological concrete thing, as heteroglot opinion, language, for the individual consciousness, lies on the border between self and other. The word in language is half someone else's. It becomes "one's own" only when the speaker populates it with his own intention, his own accent, when he appropriates the word, adapting it to his own semantic and expressive intention. (293)

Because of the socially charged nature of words, the child Mary finds herself in particular conflict with Uncle Myers. Although we are not given a dialogue between them, McCarthy lets us know that the source of Myers' fury toward her, and of her sometimes-arrogance toward him, often lies in language. He cannot bear it when she talks "stuck-up," and she, detesting his crude manners and knowing him to be uneducated, uses words that show off her privileged background; language is fertile ground for their social differences to come head-to-head. Thus, the struggle for ownership of her past/"memory" is intensified by a perception of class difference. As a young girl in a strange environment, Mary doesn't know how to make words "her own," and watches resignedly as others ruthlessly appropriate her past with words that are especially alien because of their social "other"-ness.

It is often difficult to ascertain in *Memories* whether all of McCarthy's class comments are under her artistic control, or if some of them slip by her, unincluded in any authorial plan. As in the case of Grandma Lizzie, whose "vulgarity" seems to be the unacknowledged source for much of her satire, the Catholic laywomen in the preface appear to be the subtle targets of class bias as well. Here McCarthy reviews her Catholic correspondence on her published memories, drawing a distinction between the priests and nuns, who are surprisingly generous toward her unorthodox religious opinions, and the Catholic laywomen, who are greatly angered by them. Notes McCarthy on the latter group's letters: "They are frequently full of misspellings, though the writers claim to be educated; and they are all, without exception, menacing" (22). Although McCarthy makes this comparison to point up two kinds of Catholicism, one can't help but suspect that what she perceives as "menacing" is as much the social "inferiority" of these women as their exclusionary and smug Catholicism. Numerous critics have been bothered by what they detect as elitist attitudes in McCarthy's *fiction*. Dawn Trouard defends the author on that point, however, explaining that "McCarthy lives in all of her major characters . . . her snide remarks point to flaws, but the flaws are tempered by the author's own identification with the characters" (100). Trouard sees McCarthy's literary snobbism as "a dilemma rooted in [her] own life concerning peer group standards . . . [a] disparity between her past and present, herself and others, made her painfully aware of a double standard that kept her an outsider in her own family" (101). McCarthy's fragile sense of identity results either from "a lack of confidence in her value system or from dread commitment to one class . . ." (103).

I believe also that McCarthy's references to class differences, and her clear but precarious identification with the "elite," can be explained in terms of the circumstances of her early life. Various clues embedded in her autobiography's early chapters, and the ways in which these hints later play out, reveal that for Mary, aspiration toward the highest social goal is a mechanism of survival; it is a matter about which she has no choice. Because of the starkly contrasting experiences of her mother and father's loving indulgence, and Myers and Margaret's emotionally paltry guardianship, Mary begins to see the activity of living as divided into two basic impulses: as "forward" movement, which is life-ensuring and equivalent to "beauty," and as regressive movement, which is self-denying and ultimately implies the total loss of self. What results is a crude philosophy which defines life as social advancement, and death as social stasis which *feels* like regression to a helpless, infantile state. This manner of viewing life begins with her childhood association of her luxurious life, and of her attentive parents, with "beauty" and privilege. Writes McCarthy of her mother's conversion to Catholicism: "She was proud and happy to be a convert, and her attitude made us feel that it was a special treat to be a Catholic, the crowning treat and privilege" (13). Mary's early experiences of physically beautiful parents, a comfortable home, loving if not spoiling care, and the "specialness" of her religion form her expectations of life, which are of course bitterly disappointed by the reality of life with her aunt and uncle. What McCarthy recalls quite vividly about this major transition in her life is an "aesthetic shock" she experienced:

even if my guardians had been nice, I should probably not have liked them because they were so unpleasant to look at and their grammar and accents were so lacking in correctness. I had been rudely set down in a place where beauty had no value at all. (17)

Aunt Margaret's managing of her household like a military regiment, in combination with Myers' tyranny, forever distort the meaning of the word "equality" for Mary. Because of the way she feels "reduced" as the result of Aunt Margaret's steamrolling expediency—in which all of the children are treated as equals, but acknowledging any differences or individuality among them is adamantly out of the question—and of the way Myers humiliates her, Mary equates the notion of social equality with self-negation. In describing her popularity at St. Stephens School, McCarthy writes:

There was no idea of equality in the parochial school, and such an idea would have been abhorrent to me, if it had existed; equality, a sort of brutal cutting down to size, was what I was treated to at home. Equality was a species of unfairness which the good sisters of St. Joseph would not have tolerated. (19)

Mary thrives in competitive environments because in them there is ample opportunity to distinguish herself, to move "up." Because of the very serious suggestions tied to them, the ideas of "specialness" and "equality" become polarized for Mary, acquiring the meaning of a dire "life" and "death" ultimatum.

Since the democratic principle signifies for Mary a loss of privacy and selfhood, even a common classroom experience like explicating a Byron poem becomes a weighty "social" issue, and shakes her sense of who she is:

I had read the poem before, alone in my grandfather's library; indeed, I knew it by heart, and I rather resented the infringement on my private rights in it, the democratization of the poem which was about to take place. (94)

Here the reading and absorbing of a poem become embued with an intense, but fragile, feeling of rightful ownership. McCarthy lets us know that it is by no means easy to seek constant recognition at "whatever price," while in a "cold, empty gambler's mood" (110–11). The desire for distinction is so fierce that it ironically places her in an insider/outsider double door, as Trouard describes. This double bind is perhaps best expressed in Mary's secret naming. At the Ladies of the Sacred Heart, her endeavor to be "in" on the jokes of Elinor and Mary has the eventual result of making her the *butt* of the joke: she finds herself nicknamed "C.Y.E." and hasn't a clue as to its meaning, while *everyone else* knows. The lesson learned is that a desire to be conspicuous — being associated with the "in" group — can make one conspicuous in ways over which one has no control. Later, at the Annie Wright Seminary, McCarthy provides another example of how a relentless drive to excel can be complicated business. Here, in recounting her role as Catiline in the play *Marcus Tullius,* she writes:

It was senior year and I was a big shot: the very oddities that had made me an object of wonder in my first years had, with time's passing, won me fame and envy. And yet this victory did not satisfy me, for it had come about too naturally, in accordance with orderly processes — one senior class and its leaders graduated and the next came up in succession, like a roller towel being pulled. So it happens in real life, but there is something irritating in its slow unfurling of the generations, each with its own roster of poets and politicians gradually moving into the ascendancy, by sheer virtue of staying power; the question of value is begged. (145)

In aspiring to outperform others, Mary must even outdo the natural world of time. It is simply not good enough to reach an ascendancy through the "aid" of time, because, after all, others are being distinguished along with you, and the validity of such superiority is necessarily "begged."

The process of memory, others' interpreting her "open," unverified life, and the possibility of social equality are all reductive for McCarthy because of what she perceives as their threateningly regressive paths. Because unconsciousness, or death, is promised at the end, McCarthy "reverses" this fated direction in her autobiographical act by assuming a hypercon-sciousness, or heightened state of authorial awareness. Her texts and after-texts are the opposite of unconsciousness, as they allow her to "take con-trol" and be self-aware on several linguistic planes. McCarthy's aftertexts also serve the important function of "creating" memory. Since the real an-chors of memory are gone, the organizational structure of memoir-text and aftertext composes the very fundamental and primary relationship she has felt herself missing. The aftertexts—with their varied activities of correct-ing, interrogating, embellishing, and bridging—have in common the one chief task of referring *back* to the preceding written memory. In that back-ward-looking glance, the linguistic memory becomes infused with author-ity—Mary gets to quote *herself*—and fills the gap of the missing parents. The memoir-texts become both the primal Ur-text, and her text, to which McCarthy can always refer in an authorial gesture that forges an episte-mological base, "secures" memory, and supplies self-parenting.

Given the serious problems of self-definition for an orphan, which McCarthy so clearly delineates, photography, as a form of "filling gaps," has a special allure. The pseudo-family album in the middle of her text attests to her desire to "prove" her past. McCarthy, as we have seen, has reasons to feel as though her life has been somehow "unreal." If memories can never be relied upon unless "verified," the reality of the past is con-tinually questioned. The photographs, then, tell us that her experience of having had parents, brothers, grandparents, and relatives is real. One feels McCarthy's distress when she tells us that she has no picture of Uncle Myers; for a man who was almost evil incarnate, it is vital to demonstrate his flesh-and-blood existence. Particularly for him, but also for other people in the photos, the quality of this-ness—the fact of their living, material presence—is extremely important, and no other expressive mode can provide it in so pure a form as photography. Along these lines, Roland Barthes describes a photograph as a "weightless, transparent envelope" which

always leads the corpus I need back to the body I see; it is the absolute Particular, the sovereign Contingency. . . . Show your photographs to someone—he will im-mediately show you his: "Look, this is my brother, this is me as a child," etc; the Photograph is never anything but an antiphon of "Look," "See," "Here it is"; it points a finger at a certain vis-à-vis, and cannot escape this pure deictic language. (4–5)

Barthes also notes the photograph's close relation to death. Because of the "funereal immobility" (6) it projects, its subject is a "spectacle" which evokes "that rather terrible thing which is there in every photograph: the return of the dead" (9). Accordingly, Barthes explains, the photograph contains a Life/Death paradigm. While photographs are proof of someone's corporeal life, in gazing at them we inevitably confront the face of death: "however 'lifelike' we strive to make it (and this frenzy to be lifelike can only be our mythic denial of an apprehension of death), photography is a kind of primitive theatre, a kind of Tableau Vivant, a figuration of the motionless and made up face beneath which we see the dead"(31–32).

Thus, McCarthy's display of family photographs embodies several conflicting intentions. In the case of Aunt Margaret, and perhaps also the grandparents McCarthy, one can perceive McCarthy enjoying the "death face" of these photographs: the evidence of their bodily existence is proof of their mortality, and by extension, signifies the historical death of a previous and painful way of life. For this reason, Uncle Myers' lack of photographic "proof" is especially troubling for Mary—his escape from the death grip of the photographic frame makes it seem as if he hadn't died at all, but lingers on, as maliciously and mysteriously as ever. On the other hand, McCarthy obviously does not mean to exult in the death containment of her parents' photographs, but the "ghostly traces" of these pictures are especially palpable: for the viewer, and doubtless for McCarthy also, the image presence of her parents in these photographs immediately calls to mind their absence throughout Mary's life due to their early deaths. McCarthy's intention to "prove" her parents' lives and lovingly preserve them in a photographic display clashes with her unannounced but detectable aim to limit, inhibit, and imaginatively "kill" her enemies in photographic containment. Insofar as McCarthy herself selected and arranged the photographs for *Memories*—thereby placing her own critical and volitional "frame" around that of the photographers'—she participates in a symbolic killing of these persons, a motive we shall see more clearly in her written portraits. Given the silence of photography, then, one senses an important predicament for McCarthy in this photographic compilation: how can she separate the idealizing and fond framing of her parents from the aggressively retributive framing of her more injurious family members?

McCarthy's family album contains the combatting impulses to protect and destroy not simply particular family members and past times, but the connotations or "stories" of the photographs as well. McCarthy's verbal treatment of the photographs dating from the Minnesota period of her life reveals an understanding of photography as speaking only the "pure deictic language" that Barthes describes. The photograph of the four smiling McCarthy children surrounding a pony on a sunny day is a case in point: as McCarthy explains in her aftertext to "A Tin Butterfly," the happy scene is a fake, its cheeriness the product of an itinerant photographer who had a horse for a prop. Similarly, the cozily serene photograph of Grandma Lizzie knitting in her sun parlor, and the snapshots of Mary on her First

Communion and dressed as a flower for a school play, we come to find out also tell "lies." The sun parlor scene is darkened by our knowledge of Grandma Lizzie's parsimonious and "sun"-less disposition, and Mary calls our attention to the girlhood photos to make sure we don't misread them: the smile on her face and her body posture signify discontent and oppression rather than the pleasure of an important event. In short, these photographs demonstrate nothing besides the simple bodily and historical existence of the persons whose images they capture; they say only "look" and "here it is," and the stories they might suggest are not reliable. However, McCarthy applies little or none of this critical sophistication to the photographs of her mother and father in the days of their courtship and early family life, and her deconstructive silence fuels the impression that these, by contrast, do *not* contain the possibility of falsifying frames, and *can* speak for themselves. These opposing intentions and assertions involved in McCarthy's photo display show us, among other things, that the "proof positive" offered by actual photographs to the orphan who aspires to re-create a past is severely limited: they may help populate her past, but certainly do not supply memory, and cannot even reliably, and without uncertainty, fortify what is so shakily remembered.

The satiric verbal portraits of members of the McCarthy clan, and the guardians Myers and Margaret, aspire to be a kind of photography in themselves, and complicate McCarthy's position as an autobiographer who wants to both criticize and protect the past she is seeking to establish. In the midst of McCarthy's portrait of her Grandmother McCarthy, she interrupts herself to say:

Luckily I am writing a memoir and not a work of fiction, and therefore I do not have to account for my grandmother's unpleasing character and look for the Oedipal fixation or the traumatic experience which would give her that clinical authenticity that is nowadays so desirable in portraiture. (33)

In this passage we can begin to see how McCarthy's verbal portraiture is like photography in some of its apparent motives and effects. Sontag explains that much of photography is essentially an "act of non-intervention," of ignoring one's responsibility to fellow human beings. She writes:

While people are out there killing themselves or other real people, the photographer stays behind his or her camera, creating a tiny element of another world: the image-world that outlasts us all. (11)

Photojournalism has particularly serious connotations in terms of human responsibility:

The person who intervenes cannot record, the person who is recording cannot intervene. . . . Although the camera is an observation station, the act of photography is more than passive observing. Like sexual voyeurism, it is a way of at least tacitly, often explicitly, encouraging whatever is going to happen to keep on happening. (12)

Although McCarthy can by no means be accused of "passive observing" in her portraits of Grandma Lizzie, Myers, and Margaret, her passage on "not having to account" for the character of her grandmother calls up issues of responsibility similar to those of photography. Writing a memoir becomes a special excuse for not having to look for sources, explanations, motives—in short, for not having to treat characters humanely. The act entitles her to "frame" the objects of her satire, the frame beginning precisely where the purposes of her satire end—that is, allowing her to close off, or ignore, a possibly vast body of "clinical authenticity" which would lead to a more sympathetic rendering of these subjects. Because McCarthy's satires are propelled chiefly by a desire for revenge, the subjects of her portraits become objects. As she states in the aftertext to "Yonder Peasant," the chapter is "not really concerned with individuals" but instead holds its subjects up as "specimens of unfeeling behavior"(49), just as "A Tin Butterfly" will isolate and anatomize Myers and Margaret.

McCarthy's portraits of those who she feels have done her grievous wrong involve "exposing" them in exchange for the ways she feels they had exposed her as a child. McCarthy morally balances this public "shaming" of her early authority figures with a portrayal of herself and her brothers as orphan "spectacles." As soon as the children awaken to the news of their parents' deaths, they become aware of the pathetic "image" they present to others, and consequently begin to see themselves in this new way. What results is a pained self-consciousness which McCarthy describes at a family gathering: "we appeared so dismal, ill-clad, and unhealthy, in contrast to our rosy, exquisite cousins"(30). The McCarthy children discover themselves frequently the center of attention, but as freaks or curiosities, not particularly as human beings. Again, of the evening prayer time, McCarthy writes: "Our evening prayers were lengthened to include one for our parents' souls, and we were thought to make a pretty picture, all four of us in our pajamas with feet in them, kneeling in a neat line" (37).

Under the guidance of Myers, and as a part of this newly diminished status which renders them a societal spectacle, the children are consigned to become stare-ers themselves—or essentially outsiders—who must be content to gape as the rest of the world parades by. As Mary gets older, the self-consciousness of orphanhood develops into a double consciousness, which we see at the climax of her staged loss of faith at The Ladies of the Sacred Heart: "I seemed to have divided into two people, one slyly watching, the other anxious and aghast at the turn the interview was taking"

(122). Mary's familiarity with being a spectacle-unto-herself, combined with her yearning for social distinction, leads her to the stage and her ambition to become an actress. At the same time, these aspects of herself imperil her, creating the constant risk of being taken for a clown, and becoming a "spectacle" in the worst sense of the word.

The critical lens of McCarthy's verbal portraiture, then, involves a gesture both of getting even and of attempting to restore through rewriting the power and selfhood she has felt herself tragically without. Her portraiture is photographic in its seeking to infinitely "arrest" certain figures of her life in an imagery that "frames" them, indeed, much in the way a criminal is framed and arrested by police. Writes Sontag of these powerful and dangerous aspects of the photograph:

Photographs furnish evidence. Something we hear about, but doubt, seems proven when we're shown a photograph of it. In one version of its utility, the camera record incriminates. . . . In another version of its utility, the camera record justifies. A photograph passes for incontrovertible proof that a given thing happened. The picture may distort; but there is always a presumption that something exists, or did exist, which is like what's in the picture. (5)

In the photograph, McCarthy can't prove Aunt Margaret's unbelievably wrongheaded treatment of her, but in her portraiture she certainly can try. Her exposés of Margaret and Myers offer evidence, incriminate, and justify her incriminations all at once. As we have seen, the furnishing of evidence is particularly important to McCarthy, and she vividly portrays a crisis of "fact" which begins immediately after the deaths of her parents. Mysteries abound: people behave inexplicably in a variety of ways, and the wickedness of Myers, a man with no family or known history, becomes the darkest formulation of mystery; he is fact's cruel opposite. "A Tin Butterfly" is all about this nightmarish absence of evidence, as it traces the search for the missing butterfly until it appears under the tablecloth at Mary's seat, and she is falsely accused and beaten.

However, in the course of her portrait-filled autobiography, McCarthy hints that she begins to see a connection between the falsifying and exploitative framing to which she has drawn our attention in the photo album, and herself as author/autobiographer. The tone of the self-interrogating aftertexts which follow each written memory is largely confessional, as McCarthy frequently and apologetically refers to the "framing" hand of the author which rendered "truth" into "fiction." We begin to see that a vital autobiographical problem for McCarthy is keeping the manipulations involved in her own authorial framings separate from, and on a higher moral plane than, the contriving photographer's hand which arranged the children in a false pose, and the dishonest "framing" intentions of Myers and Margaret, who then sent the photo out to the West Coast grandparents as proof of the children's well-being. The brutally funny verbal portraits of Myers and Margaret—which aim to "contain" the tyrannical power of these old guardians, as well as disclaim them as family, in spite of Margaret's blood connection—ironically align McCarthy with these persons in what must be for her a vexing manner because of the "criminal" implications.

"Ask Me No Questions," the final chapter of *Memories,* which focuses on McCarthy's paternal Grandmother Preston, dramatizes a correlative peril to this autobiographer dilemma: if McCarthy aligns herself with those she critically casts off, she also cannot identify herself with those whom she wishes to embrace—a botching of intention and effect aided by the text's photographic modes. In contrast to the apparent ease and absence of scruples with which she lays bare her aunt and uncle, she has difficulty beginning the "likeness" of her Grandmother Preston. Her sense of doing her grandmother wrong by writing about her is so intense that she guiltily images meeting up with her in Limbo, where the old woman waits for her on "some stairhead with folded arms and cold cream on her face" (198). In this chapter, when McCarthy and her grandmother are looking through family photos, the latter first accuses her granddaughter of writing bad things about her, and then reveals that she is angry at her for writing about her husband. Continues McCarthy:

But why, precisely, she was angry, I could not find out from her. Certainly I had not said anything that she could call "bad" about Grandpa. It occurred to me that she was jealous because she had not been included in these writings. . . . When she accused me of putting her in, did she really mean she felt left out? (197)

What McCarthy reveals in her musings is a powerful tension that troubles her as an autobiographer. The implicit questions she poses are these: Is it possible to give a likeness of this grandmother whom she wants to protect without exposing her, and metaphorically killing her, as she does with her old guardians—but this time with unintentional "killing" detail"? Where precisely does destructive portraiture end, and familial including begin? This is McCarthy's precarious position. As a portrait maker who is rewriting her life—that is, writing "over" the other authorities' texts about herself, and establishing her own memory—she also toes an ambiguous line in claiming those whom she seeks to destroy, and destroying those whom she seeks to embrace. The many references to closed doors in the chapter show McCarthy continually butting against obstacles in her attempts to get "inside"—to know, understand, love, and claim—her grandmother. We see McCarthy in the awkward fix of a critic who wants to stop being a critic, who wants to get inside the frame of her camera's eye, and magically merge with its subject-object. But it is precisely this which points up McCarthy's problem: in spite of the inherent critical angle of her predominating photographic mode, it is also extremely important for her to keep some of her life's subjects subjects — to "let them be," to preserve and cherish them, albeit in a profoundly fragile memory. But, if she recognizes these two strands of her autobiographic and photographic operations, she seems unable to acknowledge them, a silence which suggests that an intriguing confusion plagues this symbolic "killing" and "saving": she is, in fact, uncertain of whom she destroys and whom she preserves.

A more explicitly psychoanalytic view of this ambivalence unearths a compelling connection between McCarthy's photographic portraiture and her book's fundamental construct of text-and-aftertext. Bella Brodzki asserts in "Mothers, Displacement, and Language in the Autobiographies of Nathalie Sarraute and Christa Wolf" that the figure of the mother— whether living or dead — is pivotal in these authors' sense of "struggle with the complicitous (and not always revolutionary) relationship between displacement [of self] and language" (245). She continues:

Still powerful and now inaccessible (literally or figuratively) she is the pre-text for the daughter's autobiographical project. Indeed, these autobiographical narratives are generated out of a compelling need to enter into discourse with the absent or distant mother. As the child's first significant Other, the mother engenders subjectivity through language: she is the primary source of speech and love. And part of the maternal legacy is the conflation of the two. . . . Classically, the autobiographical project symbolizes the search for origins, for women a search for maternal origins and the elusive part of the self that is coextensive with the birth of language. (245–46)

If we view McCarthy's autobiography as a pursuit of maternal origins through the voicing of her life's early and abiding trauma, the *performative* aspects of text-and-aftertext invest the autobiography with a keen psychological drama. When seen for what it *does* rather than what it says, each published memory demonstrates a decisive and aggressive act — a stepping, or striking out, in which McCarthy asserts herself as the legitimate author of her life, rightfully equipped with her own opinions and fictions of her life's events. The aftertexts, in this light, then enact a curious retraction: each symbolically "backs off" as it corrects, questions, and infuses with doubt the previously unambivalent "declaration."

Melanie Klein's theories of the paranoid-schizoid and depressive positions in an infant's developing ego formation and object-relations provide one way to articulate this vacillating dynamic in *Memories*. In her *Introduction to the Work of Melanie Klein,* Hanna Segal summarizes the important elements of these psychological stages. To contend with "the anxiety

stirred up by the inborn polarity of instincts—the immediate conflict between the life instinct and death instinct"(25), the paranoid-schizoid position in an infant's psyche allows him to imaginatively divide the mother

into two parts, the ideal breast and the persecutory one. The phantasy of the ideal
object merges with, and is confirmed by, gratifying experiences of love and feeding
by the real external mother, while the phantasy of persecution [death instinct] similarly merges with real experiences of deprivation and pain, which are attributed
by the infant to the persecutory objects. (26)

As the developmental advance of this stage, Klein's "depressive" position
is described by Segal as follows:

When the infant recognizes his mother, it means that now he perceives her as a
whole object. He begins to see that his good and bad experiences do not proceed
from a good and bad breast, or mother, but from the same mother who is the
source of good and bad alike. . . . As these processes of integration proceed, the
infant realizes more and more that it is the same person—himself—who loves and
hates the same person—his mother. (68, 69)

Like the paranoid-schizoid position, the depressive stage generates its own
related anxieties which "spring from ambivalence, and the child's main anxiety is that his own destructive impulses have destroyed or will destroy, the
object that he totally depends on"(69). In response to such fears, the infant
experiences a

mourning and pining for the good object felt as lost and destroyed, and guilt, a
characteristic depressive experience which arises from the sense that he has lost
the good object through his own destructiveness. (70)

McCarthy's text reveals aspects of both developmental periods. Her strict
bifurcation of her biological parents and stepparents into "superlatively
good and beautiful" and "unbelievably mean and ugly" descriptive categories shows just how deeply she wishes us—and, more importantly, herself—to keep these two sets of parents separate. Lest the qualities of one
set merge or become confused with the qualities of another, she confines
these parents in fairy-tale stereotypes. Thus, we might view this act as a
"paranoic" splitting of the mother figure—keeping the biological mother
permanently pristine and blameless, unsullied by the (infant-interpreted)
arbitrary cruelty of which Aunt Margaret becomes the projection. At the
same time, a "depressive" mood is detectable in the dialogue between text
and aftertext. If, in the memory text, McCarthy implicitly but rigorously
aims to keep the object of her idealizing love intact, the aftertext, in its
anxious sorting and separating (fact from fiction, fact from fact, desire from
truth) reveals her suspicions that she has not, with certainty, accomplished
this—that perhaps her simultaneous verbal "performances" of punishing

the bad parents in both their literal and their symbolic forms have met the wrong target, and tragically "destroyed" the mother she loves. The aftertexts, then, bespeak a fretful and reparative endeavor to straighten things out; they struggle to ensure that powerful satiric denouncements "affect" the proper and deserving objects. Thus, the infantile fantasies revealed in McCarthy's text-and-aftertext dialectic through a Kleinian reading closely parallel the "including" and "excluding," "keeping" and "killing," dualisms—and the troubling uncertainties that these produce—which characterize the autobiography.

McCarthy's aftertexts, however, are complexly multilayered in their effects. As mentioned earlier, they create "memory" by casting a deferring glance back to the written memoir, and embuing it with the "authority" of the absent parents. But her sense of the power of her own language— indeed, of her absolute omniscience in the textual authoring of her life— matches the infant's and young child's belief in her own magical omnipotence: the superstitious belief that powerful feelings can of themselves *act* upon things in the external world. As McCarthy's handling of her Grandmother Preston suggests, there is the sense that scrutiny itself, tainted with the barbed observations of Myers, Margaret, and others, will irreparably harm her grandmother's very important "living" memory. Similarly, although her autobiography seeks to reestablish ties with the lost mother and thereby reinforce her own selfhood, the very use of language—the "mother tongue"—fragments the figure of the mother called forth and embodied in the text, and simultaneously evokes the disintegration of McCarthy's own ego.

As a means to rectify some of the ways in which she herself becomes vulnerably "exposed," an important dimension of McCarthy's aftertexts allows her to perform gestures of self-protection and defense with, again, a "framing" hand. By placing a critical frame around the preceding text, McCarthy suggests that only *she* can legitimately scrutinize her life-text, and by "containing" it with her own afterthoughts she anticipates the queries of other critics—either living friends and relatives, and/or internalized censors—and beats them to the punch. This critical encapsulation also constrains, with an adult hand, the ways in which McCarthy "becomes" a child in her risk-laden process of remembering through writing. However, it is this photographic propensity to views things from a critical, empowering distance that finally makes McCarthy ill at ease with the nuances of her autobiographical project.

Gordon O. Taylor writes that McCarthy's oft-described "'reduction' to personal recall" is also the "narrative circumstance she recurrently seeks, an intensification more than an impoverishment of self" (80). While this is decidedly true, the details of this final chapter suggest that maybe an unfortunate by-product of that "intensification"—fostered by photographic maneuvers of recovering a past and gaining control—is a feeling of being "glutted." Mary's identification with her grandmother's "cannibalistic" nature, as well as her teenage infatuation with her Catiline role, shows that she recognizes a devouring part of herself. Of her old Catiline crush, the narrating McCarthy writes: "Little as it meant to me then, I cannot get it out of my mind today that Catiline, in his brilliant costume, was a murderer, who slew his own brother-in-law and tortured a man to death" (161). In the "brilliant costume" of her triumphant authorship, McCarthy seems to recall the thought of her own figurative slayings, aware of her own involvement in the sort of complicity Sontag describes. Having frozen the shame of family members into eternity in order to "free" herself, she cannot escape the knowledge that she shares in their murderousness.

WORKS CITED

Bakhtin, M. M. *The Dialogic Imagination*. Ed. Michael Holquist. Trans. Caryl Emerson and Michael Holquist. Austin: University of Texas Press, 1981.

Barthes, Roland. *Camera Lucida*. Trans. Richard Howard. New York: Hill and Wang, 1981.

Brodzki, Bella. "Mothers, Displacement, and Language in the Autobiographies of Nathalie Sarraute and Christa Wolf." In *Life/Lines; Theorizing Women's Autobiography*, ed. Brodzki and Schenck, 243–59. Ithaca: Cornell University Press, 1988.

McCarthy, Mary. *Memories of a Catholic Girlhood*. 1947; rpt. New York: Harcourt Brace Jovanovich, 1981.

Segal, Hanna. *Introduction to the Work of Melanie Klein*. London: Hogarth Press for the Institute of Psycho-Analysis, 1973.

Sontag, Susan. *On Photography*. New York: Farrar, Straus, and Giroux, 1977.

Taylor, Gordon O. "The Word for Mirror: Mary McCarthy." In *Chapters of Experience: Studies in Twentieth-Century American Autobiography*, 79–100. New York: St. Martin's Press, 1983.

Trouard, Dawn. "Mary McCarthy's Dilemma: The Double Bind of Satiric Elitism." *Perspectives on Contemporary Literature*, 7(Spring 1981), 98–109.

Whittier, Gayle. "Nature as Birthright and Birthloss: Mary McCarthy and Colette." *Perspectives on Contemporary Literature*, 5(Spring 1979), 42–54.

CHAPTER 9

Dorothy Day and Women's Spiritual Autobiography

MARY G. MASON

Dorothy Day was a visionary and a prophet, belonging to the radical tradition of American women's social and spiritual witness. Daniel Berrigan, S.J., her friend and fellow antiwar activist, wrote in March 1981, a few months after her death in November 1980, that "her place in the history of the century would seem already secure" (vii). Others have attested to the importance of her role in American social and religious history. Mel Piehl, author of *Breaking Bread: The Catholic Worker and the Origin of Catholic Radicalism in America,* attributes to her the "invention" of American Catholic radicalism — the joining of radical social action to conservative Catholic religiosity. Robert Ellsberg, in his introduction to *By Little and By Little,* a collection of her writings, calls her a lay apostle, comparing her travels throughout the United States to the "missionary wanderings" of Saint Paul "spreading the 'Good News'" (xxxvi). Like her other admirers and disciples, such as Robert Coles and James Forest, Ellsberg pays tribute to the tremendous impact she had on his life as an exemplar of a life of consistency where being and action were one.

Dorothy Day's autobiographical writings reflect this coherent vision and untiring commitment. However, they also reflect an inconsistent self-perception about her identity as a woman. While the story of the development of her spiritual journey (which includes her development as a radical and social activist) shows a logical progression toward a vocation which is consistently radical, the story of her journey through womanhood is more of a debate, ending in a victory for conservatism in all issues relating to womanhood. This double perspective, as we might call this disharmony in Dorothy Day's life story, does, in fact, place her life writing squarely in the tradition of women's autobiographical writing as distinguished from the representative male tradition.

185

There is a growing body of critical material that argues that women have developed a separate tradition in the autobiographical genre, one in which "singularity" of selfhood, which is characteristic of the dominant male tradition, is replaced by a selfhood that is "mediated", as Bella Brodzki and Celeste Schenck have described it (1). In *A Poetics of Women's Autobiography* Sidonie Smith has explained this different mode of autobiographical inscription as the result of the interaction of women's marginality with the self-authorization that comes in writing their life stories. As a result, the genre, she argues, is characterized by a "double voice." I have written elsewhere that women's unique perspective is a consciousness of alterity that forces or enables them to recognize an autonomous "other" in their own creation of selfhood. Susan Stanford Friedman points out, in "Women's Autobiographical Selves: Theory and Practice," that this alterity can involve an interdependence with a community as well as with personal relationships, and she further argues that the double perspective of this mode is also characteristic of autobiographies from other marginalized groups. [1] To those who argue that women have not been able to *acknowledge* a singular self—Patricia Spacks argues, for instance, that in *The Long Loneliness* Dorothy Day has a strong sense of self but "struggles constantly to lose it" (130)—Friedman points out that we must not try to place women's "presence" in the context of male selfhood. "Their signs," she writes, "remain marginal or even untranslatable when they are placed in a context in which individuation is defined as the separation of the self from all others" (56). But, she argues, when placed in the proper context, women's sense of collective identity is a source of strength and transformation and creates a "new consciousness."

In her autobiographical writings Dorothy Day shares with other women the dual consciousness that comes from the paradox of creating a self, on the one hand, and merging the self, on the other hand. Her spiritual autobiography illustrates how women are characteristically empowered by their assertion of spiritual leadership but at the same time especially marginalized by their position as women in this most patriarchal form of self-writing. In the spirit of a "feminist undertaking," as Carolyn Heilbrun would call it, to add to our knowledge of "how women's lives have been contrived" (20), my inquiry will examine Dorothy Day's four autobiographical works —*The Eleventh Virgin* (1924), her autobiographical novel; *From Union Square to Rome* (1938), her conversion narrative; *The Long Loneliness* (1952), her official autobiography; and her posthumous spiritual journal, "All Is Grace"[2] —to illustrate how these writings fit into the tradition of women's spiritual autobiography, particularly as represented by the American conversion narrative, and how they illustrate the unique perspective of women's autobiographical writing.

Before we look at Dorothy Day's autobiographical texts, we shall look at the context of her life story, for although the autobiographer shapes her materials and to an extent creates herself, she also exists in a time and place. As Brodzki and Schenck note, a feminist undertaking should resist the postmodernist banishment of self into textuality and "provide the emotional satisfaction historically missing for the female reader, that assurance and consolation that she does indeed exist in the world which a femininity defined in purely textual terms cannot provide" (14).

Although most of Dorothy Day's autobiographical writing can be loosely classified as spiritual autobiography and more specifically as "conversion narratives," her life stories make it clear that she was formed intellectually and psychologically by political ideology in the American radical tradition. This ideology gave Day her lifelong commitment to social justice — whether in support of labor organizing in the Depression, or of the civil rights movement in the sixties, or of farm workers in the seventies, or of pacifism throughout her life. Radical social commitment was her first religion, and her saints were the Haymarket martyrs. As Mel Piehl notes, "She saw herself clearly as an American radical activist in the tradition that stretched back through Greenwich Village to the IWW, Debs, and the nineteenth century" (*Breaking Bread* 22).

As a young journalist in New York City in the first decades of the twentieth century, Dorothy Day worked for the socialist newspaper the *New York Call* and later for the *Masses,* and in Chicago for the communist paper, the *Liberator.* She was friends with the group of young New York radicals that included Max Gold, Floyd Dell (who was managing editor of the *Masses*) and Max Eastman, the "new intellectuals" of the socialist movement.[3] In *From Union Square to Rome,* she is very explicit about her relationship to radical political movements in the United States:

I was part of the Communist movement in this country, in as much as I was a reporter, a writer. I was a member of the Socialist Party, later a member of the International Workers of the World, a member of many Communist affiliate organizations, but I was never a "signed up" member of the Communist party. (146)

As a writer and activist Dorothy Day belongs in an autobiographical tradition of American women socialists and radicals who witnessed their activism in writing, including Frances Willard, Charlotte Perkins Gilman, Elizabeth Gurley Flynn, and Emma Goldman. In her autobiographical writings Dorothy Day mentions both Goldman, whom she never met, and Gurley Flynn, the labor organizer and secretary of the Communist Party of the United States, for whom she had a lifelong admiration. In 1964, she was asked to speak in New York at a memorial service for Flynn, and although she was unable to attend, she sent a message to be read aloud.

In it she speaks of her feeling of sisterhood with Gurley Flynn, a sister-hood that she characterized as part of a spiritual community. "She was," she writes, "also my sister in this deep sense of the word" (*By Little and By Little* 145–46). She recalls that as an eighteen-year-old reporter, she first met Gurley Flynn when the latter was lecturing at some workers' hall in Brooklyn and that she met her again years later on Christmas Eve in 1957. Day and Ammon Hennacy, a Catholic Worker pacifist and anarchist, had gone to Flynn's apartment just off Second Avenue after making their yearly pilgrimage to the Women's House of Detention in Greenwich Vil-lage to sing Christmas carols. Day notes that the night before writing her tribute in November 1964, she had a dream recalling that visit to Gurley Flynn on Christmas Eve:

In my dream I was there again with Ammon and Gurley Flynn, experiencing again her warmth, her equanimity, her humor and above all, the *purpose* of her life—her aim to help bring about the kind of society where each would work according to his ability and receive according to his needs, truly one of the noblest possible aims in life. (145)

The description of Gurley Flynn's purpose in life describes Dorothy Day's vocation as well. She never rejected the basic ideals of communism as it represented a radical notion of community and a redistribution of mate-rial goods. Commenting on Flynn's membership in the IWW (the Interna-tional Workers of the World), an organization which, Day notes, was "fought as bitterly as the Communists are today," she writes, "In fact, it seems to me that anything that threatens money or property, anything that aims at a more equitable distribution of this world's goods, has always been called communism. I like the word myself; it makes me think of the communism of the religious orders" (145).

Although Dorothy Day would find few radical women to identify with in the American Catholic tradition, she did have a mentor in "Mother Jones" (Mary Harris), the union organizer and activist who traveled across the United States, organizing strikes, going to jail, and outwitting the local officials and employees until she was into her nineties. Dorothy Day men-tioned Jones in a letter written to her friend Nina Polcyn in 1976, when Day was suffering from ill health and was forced to restrict her own traveling:

Right now I'm in a feeble state. Too conscious of my 79 years! But Mother Jones, the great labor organizer, tramped the country from Colorado to West Virginia at a great age! (*All Is Grace* 192)

She asks her friend to pray for her so that she can get her strength back and continue her work in the spirit of her predecessor.

Day would have learned much about class struggle from Mother Jones's

Autobiography (published in 1925), a life narrative which reveals some of the same intensity and single-mindedness of Day's commitment to helping the working class. Mother Jones calls it "my class" and shows her dedication to fighting for her people across national and racial boundaries:

> I know no East or West, North nor South when it comes to my class fighting the battle for justice. It is my fortune to live to see the industrial chain broken from every workingman's child in America, and if then there is one black child in Africa in bondage, there shall I go. (Jones 100)

Dorothy Day would also be sympathetic—especially in her later writing —to Mother Jones's position on working women's issues, particularly on their role as homemakers. In her autobiography, Jones is scornful of women's careers, because, she notes, most of them were in factories where they were exploited. She writes, "If men earned enough money, it would not be necessary for women to neglect their homes and their little ones to add to the family's income" (238). Day takes a similar position in the sixties when she argues for adequate wages for men so that working women can stay home and care for their families.

Dorothy Day is associated with another tradition of social reformers — the generation of women at the turn of the century who, like the earlier Moral Crusader feminists, were social activists. Many of these women turned to the needs of the urban poor. Foremost among them, Jane Addams (1860–1935), whose two volumes of autobiography describe her pioneer settlement house work at Hull House in Chicago, shared Dorothy Day's commitment to helping the working class and also shared her passionate commitment to pacifism. However, the differences between the two reformers also underline the uniqueness of Day's contribution and the difficulty of placing her in feminist social movements. Apart from her pacifism, developed later in her life, Addams did not belong to a radical tradition. As Alice Rossi notes in *The Feminist Papers,* "She ruffled no feathers, since her views carried no threat to the basic institutional structured society" (603). In addition, Addams' religious concerns were not as primary as those of Dorothy Day and the Catholic Worker movement. Mel Piehl notes in his essay "The Catholic Worker and the American Religious Tradition" that Addams in her later writing "tended to downplay the intensity of her religious concern," and, he continues, "because of this decline of direct religious commitment, as well as its still somewhat paternalistic attitudes toward those it served, the settlement house movement was never really a model for the Catholic Worker" (263).

Because Dorothy Day was intellectually formed in a socialist tradition and not a religious tradition, she is hard to place in the religious history of American women. Furthermore, she grew up outside of institutional religion in a family which had few religious connections. She was, in a sense, self-created in her early spiritual life before her conversion to Catholicism. In her autobiography, she tells us about her childhood religious experiences and about a stage during which she read religious works, such as the Bible, the lives of early Christian saints, *The Imitation of Christ*, the sermons of John Wesley, and, later, *The Confessions of Saint Augustine*. She also describes her alienation from religion in her adolescence and young adulthood when she developed a social conscience and turned to the intellectual sources of socialism. It was probably to Day's advantage that she did not inherit a strong institutional religious connection. Her sense of self-creation made her more bold in taking a leadership role when she did embrace a religious institution. In their introductory essays to *Women and Religion in America*, Rosemary Radford Ruether and Rosemary Skinner Keller seem to suggest that historically, when women take leadership roles in religious institutions, they find that initially they gain autonomy and influence but that eventually they are relegated to a secondary, supporting role in the institution. Even in the nineteenth-century religious revivalist movements when church women began to take important roles in the public sphere and "social reform became a religious calling" (Ruether and Keller 1:xii), women were still confined in their work by definitions of "feminine roles." When Dorothy Day joined Peter Maurin to start the Catholic Worker movement, she was not aware of the limitations on institutional roles for women although she was to learn about them later on.

When Dorothy Day began to develop a religious framework in the Catholic church, it was primarily from the European intellectual Catholic tradition, and not surprisingly from male mentors. Peter Maurin instructed her in personalism, the movement started by Emmanuel Mounier, and introduced her to other French Catholic writers, such as Leon Bloy, Jacques Maritain (who visited the Catholic Worker in New York), and the poet Charles Péguy. She also read French Catholic novelists, such as François Mauriac and Georges Bernanos. William Miller places Day's spirituality in a prophetic, antihistory tradition, citing three major formative influences: the novels of Dostoyevsky, the religious philosophy of Nikolay Berdyayev, and the spiritual writings of Simone Weil (Day, *All Is Grace* 28–38). After 1940 (when she began retreats), Day found spiritual advisors in America but their sources were also French, particularly in the teachings of the French Canadian Jesuit Father Onesimus Lacouture, who represented an ascetic, slightly Jansenist Catholicism.

Despite her heavily male-centered spiritual formation, Day also was influenced by some strong female models from the Catholic tradition, whom she admired for the way they managed to make their daily lives consistent with their vocations. She frequently refers to Saint Teresa of Avila, Saint Thérèse of Lisieux (about whom she wrote a book),[4] Julian of Norwich, the English medieval anchoress, and Catherine of Siena. In *The Long Loneliness,* she quotes from another strong spiritual leader, Mary Ward, an English Renaissance nun, who was imprisoned as a heretic for her "dangerously novel ideas." A member of one of the persecuted Catholic families in England in the seventeenth century, she went to Europe and tried to create a community of women who lived outside of the cloister but who followed the rule of Saint Ignatius.[5] In the American tradition, Dorothy Day read the writings of Rose Hawthorne (Mother Mary Alphonsa Lathrop), inspired by her work in New York City with the indigent poor who were victims of cancer.[6]

Daniel Berrigan insists that Day was "American to the marrow." In fact, in her spiritual autobiography Day can be connected to the deepest roots of the *expression* of American culture and spirituality through her use of the tradition of the conversion narrative, a form of the spiritual autobiography that has Puritan roots and is part of our literature up through the outburst of conversion narratives in the "Second Awakening" of the early nineteenth century. The narratives, written as often by women as by men, provided a tradition in which women's spirituality was nurtured and formed.

Daniel Shea in his *Spiritual Autobiography in Early America* identifies two main streams of influence in American literary history that developed from seventeenth- and eighteenth-century conversion narratives: the conservative self-scrutiny of the Puritan conversion narrative and the more radical "illuminist" autobiography represented by the Quaker tradition. Both traditions, he argues, are characterized by the importance of community which gives the autobiography focus and substance.

In her spiritual autobiography Dorothy Day reflects both of these traditions in her concern to establish and validate ties with the community which she addresses, but she is closer in spirit to the "illuminist" tradition because of the prophetic strain in the work and also because of the radical spiritual and social message. This radical message or witness often makes Day an outsider in the larger society in which she lives. Carol Edkins, in her essay on the spiritual autobiographies of eighteenth-century Puritan and Quaker women in America, points out that Quaker women often found themselves in "social isolation and conflict" because they were preaching and witnessing views that were heretical to those outside of their calling (50).[7]

From the nineteenth century, another tradition of radical witnessing by women relates closely to Day's spiritual autobiographies. This is the tradition of pilgrimage (Day used "pilgrimage" in the title of two of her works), which includes the stories of itinerant women preachers who often traveled to carry their message and witness their conversions. For instance, the autobiographies of Jarena Lee (b. 1783), Zilpha Elaw (b. 1790), and Julia Foote (b. 1823), three African-American women in the Evangelical tradition, tell the story of leaving domestic lives—homes, husbands, and children—to carry out their vocation of itinerant preaching and missionary work, sometimes traveling abroad and sometimes through slave states where they were single black women in a white racist society. William Andrews, who edited their autobiographies in his collection *Sisters of the Spirit*, describes their vocation as a radical challenge to the patriarchal church, which strongly opposed their leadership, and he characterizes their relationship to their own society as nonconformist. "They lived," he writes, "experimental lives, exploring the possibilities of a deliberately chosen marginal identity that morally and spiritually engaged the world without being socially engulfed by it" (12). Dorothy Day also chose a marginal identity so she could carry out her radical witness. She, too, was a spiritual leader and challenged the religious establishment, though not, as we shall see, on grounds of gender.

Although Dorothy Day reflects the radical pilgrimage tradition in her spiritual and political witness, she also reflects in her autobiographies a more introspective witness of conversion, relating her to the Puritan tradition of self-scrutiny. Daniel Shea describes spiritual autobiographies as developing "by psychological and moral changes which the autobiographer comes to discern in his past experience" (xxviii). This psychological emphasis suggests that conversion is a discovery of a new identity, "a rebirth." Day's personal story is partly a search for identity, particularly her identity as a woman. Her narratives are distinctly *gendered*. Two recent studies of conversion narratives, which have focused on gender in their analysis, come to rather different conclusions about the function of gender in this particular religious experience. Susan Juster and Barbara Epstein both studied conversion narratives by men and women in the Evangelical movement of the early nineteenth century. Epstein concludes that women's conversion narratives show a strong pattern of gender conformity, "with an ultimate submission to God confirming their adherence to the female role" (87). Unlike Epstein, Juster makes a case that the narratives do not show marked sexual polarization and suggest "an androgynous model of conversion experience" (56). A case for androgyny cannot be made for Dorothy Day's conversion narratives. Her stories are inscribed as a woman's experience although they reveal a strong ambivalence about women's roles.

Three out of the four autobiographical writings of Dorothy Day fit loosely into the mode of the conversion narrative. The autobiographical novel, *The Eleventh Virgin*, which is primarily about her identity as a woman, uses the conversion "model" when, at the end of the novel, there is an unexpected conversion—not a religious one—from one ideology of womanhood to another; from the credo of independence and bohemiansim to the ideology of domesticity, prophesying the transformation of the "emancipated woman" of the twenties to the icon of domestic motherhood of the thirties. The spiritual journey in this autobiographical novel is only a subtext to the narrative of womanhood. *From Union Square to Rome* is Dorothy Day's official conversion story, written to explain her defection from communism to Catholicism. In it she traces the spiritual, psychological, and moral changes leading to her conversion. The narrative of "rebirth" is framed by introductory and concluding chapters addressed specifically to her brother, a communist, to whom she explains the abandonment of her political cause for a religious commitment. She emphasizes the continuity and compatibility between the two ideologies. In the main part of the narrative, however, where she traces the steps of her spiritual growth to the climax of her conversion, we are surprised to find the religious experience almost eclipsed by her description of the birth of her daughter, which becomes the central focus of the narrative and which is a celebration of natural motherhood. Although the story of her identity as a woman is not the main narrative here, it is a very important subtext. In *The Long Loneliness,* subtitled "an autobiography," Dorothy Day repeats her conversion story in the first half of the narrative, but it is now a more conventional religious conversion because the birth of her daughter is put into the context of her own "rebirth" in the Catholic church. The second half of the autobiography is the story of the vocation she found in the Catholic Worker movement with her co-founder, Peter Maurin, who now shares the narrator's life story. In a way more typical of women's life narratives, Day expresses a clear alterity in her identification with her mentor and with her community. This narrative also reveals clearly the disharmony between the "woman's narrative" and the story of the radical activist and spiritual leader. A strong theme of renunciation is introduced in the second half of the narrative and an increasing reference to a new identity—that of a solitary and a celibate.

"All Is Grace"—a spiritual journal which is selected, edited from unpublished materials, and published posthumously by her biographer, William Miller—continues the theme of solitude and renunciation. It is not a conversion narrative but a series of meditations put together by Miller. Nevertheless, it is relevant to her two other spiritual autobiographies because it reexamines the basis of her spiritual conversion. Specifically, it looks back over her life with the Catholic Worker movement and witnesses her second spiritual awakening experienced almost twenty years after joining the Catholic church. In her fifties, she took a year's leave of absence from her duties with the movement to go on a retreat in order to renew her spiritual life. In these meditations, her vision of her spiritual and political mission is still consistently radical, but the source of her conflicting attitudes toward her role as a woman is clearer.

Dorothy Day uses the conversion narrative to focus and refocus two threads in her life story. One is the discovery of her identity as a woman and of how her vocation will fit into her life; the other is her witness of a commitment to radical social and spiritual activism. The two threads constitute two voices—one private and personal and the other one a public voice—the two different perspectives or the double consciousness of women's autobiography.

Her life narrative starts with her only published novel, *The Eleventh Virgin*, written in 1920 (published in 1924), during her brief marriage to Barkeley Tobey, a forty-two-year-old literary promoter (the marriage lasted barely a year). In their wedding trip abroad, Dorothy Day found her husband incompatible, and she spent some time alone, several months on the isle of Capri, where she apparently wrote her novel. In her early twenties at the time, Day still identified with the "Greenwich village set," a group of young socialists, artists and writers, including Eugene O'Neill, with whom she had spent much time. The novel is something of a *Künstler-roman* (she was reading Joyce's *A Portrait of the Artist*), tracing her artistic development as well as her education as a young radical; however, it is primarily an exploration of and debate (from the point of view of her heroine, June) about the issues of womanhood, particularly the issue of female independence, including sexual emancipation versus the "imperative" of domesticity and motherhood.[8] The conversion, at the end of the novel, which comes as a surprise to the reader, occurs after June has gone into nursing in a search for "usefulness" during World War I. She meets a fascinating newspaperman—Dick Wemys, a determined bachelor (in real life, Lionel Moise)—and falls in love and has an affair, which ends after her desperate attempt to keep her lover by having an abortion when she finds herself pregnant. He leaves her anyway, with Baudelairean farewell notes, and the story ends with a monologue in which June renounces the "emancipated" woman and resolves to have the security and comfort of traditional marriage and motherhood. She tells all this to her sister: "I know what I want. It's Dick and marriage and babies! And I'll have them yet. Wait and see" (*The Eleventh Virgin* 312).

The Eleventh Virgin is the most "woman-centered" narrative that Dorothy Day wrote. In none of her other autobiographical writings do we get such a full picture of the role of other women in her life.[9] For instance, she gives us an affectionate portrait of her own mother in the thinly veiled characterization of "Mother Grace." She is portrayed as a mother who was not only "exceptionally dainty" and feminine but also a friend who could discuss issues of sexuality, romance, the relative roles of promiscuity in men and women, or the conflicts between careers and motherhood. As a young college student, June says of her mother, "You recognize me as an individual," and she continues with a critique of motherhood:

Most mothers refuse to recognize their children as individuals with minds and aims of their own. Usually the instinct of motherhood is merely a desire to perpetuate themselves or their husbands. (91)

At the end of the novel, she seems to abandon this critical appraisal of motherhood. Other women are important in her life as well: her sister Adele (Della), her college friend, Regina (Rayna Simons Prohme), and Billy Burton (Peggy Baird) with whom she debates the pros and cons of women's chastity before marriage. In addition, her descriptions of assignments as a young reporter working for a socialist newspaper reflect her deep interest in women's issues even more than political issues. The newspaper stories she mentions include her coverage of a settlement house for unwed mothers, the trial of "Edith Burns," an advocate of birth control, and the suffragist march in Washington where she and her friend Billy are jailed.

The narrative of her jail experience with the suffragists foreshadows the heroine's renunciation of feminist views and also picks up the theme of a search for a spiritual vocation. On the train in which the demonstrators are being transported after they have been moved from place to place, June presses her face against the train window and watches "the blue twilight pierced with the bare black shapes of many scrawny trees" (198). The beauty and somberness of the night scene make her almost forget the particular circumstances for which she is going to jail. She later confides her feelings to her friend Billy:

"Somehow," June told her when they reached the little country station which was their destination, "life and struggle seem very tawdry in the twilight. This bleak countryside makes me feel that I should struggle for my soul instead of my political rights. . . . I feel peculiarly small and lonely tonight." (198)

Loneliness — a recurring theme throughout Day's autobiographical writing, relating closely to her spiritual experiences, appears initially in *The Eleventh Virgin* as a keen sense of human isolation and desolation. In her reporter days in New York she almost revels in this isolation. For instance, she moves, at one point, to a particularly abandoned, almost cell-like room on the Lower East Side, which, she says, appeals to her for "the completeness of its desolation." In *From Union Square to Rome*, Day interprets this stage of her life, with its attraction to extremes, as "the Baudelairean downward path to salvation," a state of despair that propelled her into conversion. Like the heroes in the novels of writers of the French Decadent

movement—such as, J.-K. Huysmans, whom Day was reading along with
Swinburne and Baudelaire—her heroine is intent on experiencing all of
life, from the idealistic to the nihilistic. She is absorbed with the freedom
to choose her own life-style. By the end of the novel, June is disillusioned
with this freedom. She confides to her sister, Dell:

Women are more interested in men than in ideas. . . . I thought that I was a free
emancipated young woman and I found out that I wasn't at all really. . . . it looks
to me that this freedom is just a modernity gown, a new trapping that we women
affect to capture the man we want. (312)

She has found that her free choices have been controlled by her drive
"to capture" a man, and she is devastated to learn that she has not freely
chosen her own destiny. Unlike the male heroes of the fin de siècle decadent novels, Day's heroine in her novel despairs because of the tyranny of
biological determinism not because of the tyranny of dissipation and spiritual ennui. Her story is distinctly a woman's story. In *From Union Square
to Rome* Day changes her view of this part of her life and sees it as a stage
of nihilism in her journey toward a religious conversion.

Dorothy Day disliked her first novel, and when in 1975 she presented
William Miller with one of the few copies left, she asked him, "What should
I do about this?" She continued, "It's all true" (Miller xiii). The autobiographical nature of the novel was no doubt the reason that she could not
simply get rid of it or ignore it. She was too committed to using the story
of her life as a cautionary tale for others.

In *From Union Square to Rome* (1938), Dorothy Day reverses the narrative pattern of *The Eleventh Virgin*. The story of her womanhood becomes the subtext to her religious conversion, but it is still a dominant
theme. Unlike the autobiographical novel, the conversion narrative was not
written all in a piece but rather put together from previously published
pieces.[10] Since writing her novel in the twenties, Dorothy Day had tried
different life-styles. She did not get "Dick and marriage" (she followed Lionel
Moise to Chicago but the relationship did not work out), but she did continue her life as a writer and a radical, and she established a common-law
marriage with Forster Batterham, a biologist and fervent naturalist. They
lived in a cottage on Staten Island bought from the proceeds of the sale
of the movie rights to Day's novel (she had a brief sojourn in Hollywood
as a script writer), and it was here that her daughter, Tamara Teresa, was
born in March 1927. Dorothy Day's conversion to Catholicism followed
soon after when she was baptized on December 28.

In her introductory apologia to her brother, explaining her conversion
to Catholicism, she emphasizes the continuity of her political and spiritual life. She speaks of the mystic's love of God and compares this love to

the bonds between radical workers: "Often there is a mystical element in the love of a radical worker for his brother, for his fellow worker" (11). Or again, she compares the workers' solidarity to the unity of the Mystical Body of Christ. She concludes, "We are all members or potential members of the Mystical Body of Christ." She still believes, she insists, in revolution. In one of her concluding chapters, she writes, "I still believe the social order must be changed, that it is not right for property to be concentrated in the hands of the few" (145). She argues, however, that the revolution, which is "inevitable," can be "a Christian revolution of our own, without the use of force" (145).

In contrast to *The Eleventh Virgin*, this life story emphasizes the stages of growth of a political and spiritual consciousness, particularly the latter. She tells her brother, "I will try to trace for you the steps by which I came to accept the faith that I believe was always in my heart." Her narrative of these stages includes her early contacts with religious neighbors and friends as a child, her period in the Episcopal church, her rejection of religion as a teenager and throughout her two years of college and her bohemian New York experience when she became identified with the poor and oppressed. She also recounts a climactic jail experience while she was living in Chicago—the second jail experience in her life. She was arrested in a police raid on a boardinghouse frequented by members of the IWW where she was visiting a young woman who was ill. After very callous treatment by the police, she was placed in solitary confinement and experienced a feeling of complete abandonment. She explains that she was saved from despair by reading the Psalms, particularly Psalm 129 ("Out of the depths I cry to Thee"), where her identification with the psalmist's despair was a turning point in her spiritual life.

Some of the material about her childhood, adolescence, and young adulthood is repeated from her earlier novel, but in her conversion narrative she looks more critically at her life as a reporter and a radical. She wonders, for instance, why she always "built up a case" in her stories for socialist causes without capturing the heroic or joyous moments of the poor and oppressed people whom she depicted. The freedom that she desired in *The Eleventh Virgin* is now described as a kind of arrogant frame of mind: "I was seventeen, completely alone in the world, divorced from family, from all society, even from God. I felt a sense of reckless arrogance and with this recklessness, I felt a sense of danger and rejoiced in it" (45). Her only reference to the period of her love affair, abortion, and marriage is a brief mention of *The Eleventh Virgin:* "I wrote a book, a very bad book," she says and mentions that the sale of the movie rights enabled her to buy the beach cottage on Staten Island.

After tracing her spiritual growth, her narrative in two chapters, "Peace" (chapter 11) and "New Life" (chapter 12), takes on a completely different tone. A new voice is introduced. A new text. This section, we are told by the author, was compiled from notes and journals that she wrote at the time of the events themselves. It tells the story of her life as a writer at her beach house on Staten Island (she was living with Forster Batterham at the time) and the climactic story of the birth of her daughter in March. Chapter 12 ends with a brief account of her daughter's baptism in July 1927, and finally her own baptism. Here it seems as if the recognition of the religious conversion gives way to a celebration of nature—her own natural motherhood (outside of the institution of marriage) and her life at the beach lived in harmony with the natural order—which in itself is a kind of spirituality for the author.

The references to sin and guilt and self-accusations of "the deliberate choosing of evil" are gone. The desolate loneliness gives way to the treasured solitude of "my life as a sybaritic anchorite." The days, before her daughter is born, are spent between writing and visiting with the local fisherman—the hermit "Smiddy"—or the international community of Russian, Belgian, and Italian families who live in the neighboring cottages. Above all she enjoys the beauty and contentment of walking alone on the beach:

I wander every afternoon up and down the beach for miles, collecting mussels, garlanded in seaweed, torn loose from the piers,—pockets full of jingle shells which look as though they are made of mother of pearl and gun metal. When the tide goes out these little cups of shells are left along the beach, each holding a few drops of water which serve to glorify both the shape and the coloring of the shell. (113–14)

Reference to her spiritual life is one of fragility, symbolized by a small wax statue of the Virgin Mary made in Czechoslovakia and given to her by her friend Peggy Baird. The statue, though fragile, is an emblem of the traditional church (and traditional role of women) that she will soon embrace. Her description shows her attraction to the simple, almost primitive quality of the statue:

There is a garland of roses around her head to which is attached a golden halo which resembles a watch spring pulled out. She stands on a bright blue ball the same color as her cape and around the ball is entwined a snake, bright green with a pink and yellow apple in it red mouth. And the blue ball stands on grass which is like green noodles, garlanded with little rosebuds. It is very sweet but it is very fragile, already cracked down the back of the cape. (118)

In this description, Day emphasizes the naive yet fragile concept of the Virgin. She does not note the stark symbolism of Mary as the instrument of atonement for the evil done by the first woman "Eve" (evoked by the serpent with the apple in his mouth), who was responsible—in medieval theology—for the Fall of mankind in the Garden of Eden. She seems unaware of the misogyny of this particular representation of Mary, but the emblem foreshadows the institutional ideology of womanhood which will later conflict with her own experience as a woman.

The actual account of the birth of her daughter is short but should be read along with an article (which she refers to in this chapter) that she wrote for the socialist paper the *New Masses,* about her experience of childbirth. The article has the same direct and intimate voice as the two chapters about her idyllic life on Staten Island. She wrote it, she says, to share her joy with all women "no matter what their grief at poverty, unemployment, and class war." The account is a detailed, thoroughly woman-identified picture of the process of childbirth in a public clinic, which she attended for prenatal care and for the delivery. It is told with simplicity and humor, recreating the atmosphere and sketching in the people she saw there, particularly the women who were sharing the same experience of pregnancy and childbirth. She does not hestitate to draw a picture of the rather indifferent and blasé treatment of the patients by the doctors and nurses, and she shares her good-humored way of revenging herself on one particularly obnoxious group who were ignoring her increasingly difficult labor pains:

They [the doctors and nurses] disposed themselves on the other two beds, but my nurse sat on the foot of mine, pulling the entire bed askew with her weight. This spoiled my sleeping during the five-minute intervals. . . . mindful of my grievance against her. . . . I took advantage of the beginning of the next pain to kick her soundly in the behind. She got up with a jerk and obligingly took a seat on the next bed. (*By Little and By Little* 30)

The account in the *New Masses* is as free of platitudes and sentimentality as the description of her Staten Island life. However, in the course of narrating this part of her life in her conversion narrative, the other voice reappears—the voice of the sinner and convert. Commenting on the experience of childbirth, Day takes on a hortatory tone:

A woman does not want to be alone at such a time. Even the most hardened, the most irreverent is awed by the stupendous fact of creation. No matter how cynically or casually the worldly may treat the birth of a child, it remains spiritually and physically a tremendous event. God pity the woman who does not feel the fear, the awe, and the joy of bringing a child into the world. (127)

The last line of this quotation edges into a different attitude toward childbirth and reflects an increasingly didactic treatment of motherhood. In contrast to this attitude, Day's description of her life with her newborn is free of all self-conscious assigning of women's roles, even of the presence of a husband. Although we know, in fact, that Forster Batterham was returning to the cottage every weekend and that he was a loving father, much of her account is written as if he did not exist. The aloneness which in the above passage she says that women fear at such a time, she herself seemed to embrace. She describes her daily routine with the infant during the week:

Supper always was early and the baby comfortably tucked away before it was dark. Then, tired with all the activities that so rejoiced and filled my days, I sat in the dusk in a stupor of contentment. (131)

Of course, Batterham *was* significant in her life, and she soon realizes she will have to choose between him and religion. "It is impossible to talk to him about religion or faith," she writes; "A wall immediately separates us." An anarchist and a scientist, Batterham could not accept her conversion or the baptism of their child. The narration of Day's struggle over the decision to join the church is brief but poignant. She writes, "I did not want to give up human love when it was dearest and tenderest." When she does make the decision to be baptized in December of that year, she notes that it happened with no dramatic sense of rebirth: "I had no sense of peace, no joy, no conviction even that what I was doing was right" (141).

In the closing chapters of the book, she summarizes for her brother her final explanation of her conversion as a choice between two alternatives — faith or nihilism — reemphasizing that she was converted from a state of despair and decadence. She concludes, "I will choose Him and hold fast to Him. *For who else is there?* Would you have me choose Nothingness?" (173). This assertion is strangely at odds with the picture of her contented and fulfilled life in her ocean cottage before and after the birth of her child.

The reception of *From Union Square to Rome* was lukewarm. In the *Catholic World,* (January 1939) the reviewer wrote, "Large in size for its rather niggardly measure of self-revelation, the book is also uneven and highly emotional." It is not surprising that the reviewer would find the book hard to identify as a traditional conversion narrative. First of all, it does not renounce a whole way of life for a "rebirth." The author does not give up her past commitment to the ideals of communism and anarchism. Rather she fuses the two ideologies. Second, the tone of the book is disunified. There are two voices in it: the public voice of the convert and sinner and the personal voice of the young woman recording and affirming the joys of her experience of unmarried love and of single parenthood, regardless of the social consequences. As in many women's autobiographies, these two voices or perspectives remain separate in most of her narratives. In her second conversion narrative, *The Long Loneliness,* the slight disharmony in the personal voice of *From Union Square to Rome* will become more pronounced, and the theme of renunciation, introduced here in the touching reminiscence of her decision to separate from her lover, will become a dominant theme. Finally, the autobiographical subject will gradually become merged with others—her mentor, Peter Maurin, and the Catholic Worker community.

The Long Loneliness (1952) is subtitled "an autobiography" but Dorothy Day still insisted in a later comment on her book, recorded by Jim Forest in his biography, that she was not writing a complete revelation of her life. Rather she placed it clearly in the context of a conversion narrative: "It [the book] is really a selection of periods of my life searching for God and not at all a story giving the whole truth. . . . I feel, to put it simply, that it is not the whole truth about me" (213). Part of this missing truth is undoubtedly the story of her life and consciousness as a woman. In the autobiography this consciousness is submerged in the story of her community, the Catholic Worker.

The autobiography is divided into four parts: "Searching," "Natural Happiness," "Love Is the Measure," and a short "Postscript." The first two parts repeat (in some cases verbatim) most of the "steps toward grace" in *From Union Square to Rome*. This section ends with her meeting with Peter Maurin in New York in 1933, on her return from a hunger march of the unemployed in Washington. She writes, "And when I returned to New York, I found Peter Maurin—Peter the French peasant, whose spirit and ideas will dominate the rest of my life" (166). The second part of her book contains her new material: the story of the consequences of her conversion, her alliance with Peter Maurin, and the story of the Catholic Worker movement as it had developed up until the early 1950s when she was recording most of this material in her autobiography.

Dorothy Day treats the appearance of Peter Maurin in her life as a divine intervention. She calls him her "master" and refers to herself as his disciple. Although biographers and commentators have pointed out that she was anything but a "follower" in her role as editor and leader of the Catholic Worker movement, Maurin becomes, nevertheless, the dominant image in the second half of the story. He is given two separate chapters, one at the beginning of part 3, "Peasant of the Pavements," and the other at the end of the book in a chapter on his death, in which she details his last years and commemorates him as a saint. She opens the chapter, "Precious in the sight of the Lord is the death of saints, and the details of such a death are precious" (273).

As she presents it, Maurin was the answer to a prayer that she had made in her novena in the national shrine at Catholic University in Washington when she sought to find a way to bring to her new religious life the social and political commitments she had so optimistically predicted that she could fuse with her spiritual life. Through Maurin she did find the way to fulfill that commitment. Their meeting resulted in the creation of the *Catholic Worker* newspaper—first distributed on May 1, 1933, at a communist rally in Union Square—and subsequently, in the opening of the soup kitchen, the development of Catholic Worker houses of hospitality throughout the country, and the implementation of Maurin's ideas of agrarian Christian communities and of round table discussions that characterized the intellectual "teaching" component of the movement.

The chapters that follow her introduction of Maurin detail and explain the day-to-day life of her community, such as the houses they settled in, the people who worked with them, including a series of young men and women who came to do a period of "service" and the group of seamen whose strike they supported during the formation of the National Maritime Union. She portrays a number of important figures in her own life, such as the French Canadian priest Father Pacifique Roy and Father John J. Hugo, both of whom were central in the development of her own spirituality. In these chapters she also describes her travels and work with labor unions and with all those who were trying to serve the interests of the working class.

Brotherhood and community, so important in *From Union Square to Rome,* are here equally strong in her spiritual life. Day now takes on the role of teacher and explains the implications of the Catholic Worker positions, particularly of their stand on pacifism. She writes, "There were a great many who seemed to agree with us who did not realize for years the Catholic Worker implicated them; if they believed the things we wrote, they would be bound, sooner or later, to make decisions personally and to act on them" (264). As in her first conversion story, Day addresses a community, but in *The Long Loneliness* she has replaced the political community with the spiritual community of the Catholic Worker movement, which includes her readers.

In the second half of the narrative, the author's identity is not only shared with Maurin; it becomes more and more merged with her community. Even the narrative point of view changes, illustrating what Susan Stanford Friedman calls "fluid ego boundaries." The point of view in the first two sections ("Searching" and "Natural Happiness") is the "I" of first person singular. In the second half of the book it shifts to the collective "we" of the first person plural. Finally, in the "Postscript," the collective we becomes part of a dramatized scene in which the community recollects their common experience and shares a communal meal. It begins, "We were just sitting there talking when Peter Maurin came in" (285). The narrator speaks of the casual, spontaneous character of their collective experience:

We were just sitting there talking and people moved in on us. Let those who can take it, take it. Some people moved out and that made room for more. And somehow the walls expanded.

We were just sitting there talking and someone said, "Let's all go live on a farm."

It was as casual as all that, I often think. It just came about. It just happened. (285)

While the scene is on one level a family gathering, sharing a communal meal, it is also a metaphor for the larger spiritual community of which they are a part—the mystical body of Christ. The meal represents communion. She writes, "Heaven is a banquet and life is a banquet, too, even with a crust, where there is companionship" (285).

In the middle of this final scene in which she has become part of the collective consciousness of the group and of the larger community of the church, Dorothy Day suddenly injects a personal and individual identity in one short paragraph:

I found myself, a barren woman, the joyful mother of children. It is not easy always to be joyful, to keep in mind the duty of delight. (285)

Suddenly the story of Dorothy Day, the troubled young woman of the twenties, the aspiring writer, the energetic journalist, the dedicated radical, the passionate lover, and the proud unwed mother is reconfigured at the very end of the narrative of the collective experience. Flashed before us in one sentence is the "I" of this spiritual autobiography, which has been submerged in the whole second part of the narrative. We are forced to review the narrative and to find this individual identity again.

When we focus on the woman's text in *The Long Loneliness* and compare it with the story in *From Union Square to Rome,* we find that several important changes have occurred in the narrator's attitude toward herself as a woman. First of all, there is a different attitude toward sexuality; second, there is an increased sense of self-blame; and third, there is a clearer division of gender roles—at the same time, there is more ambivalence about how the narrator fits into these roles.

In *From Union Square to Rome,* we found a disjunction between the voice of the "redeemed" bohemian and that of the unapologetic natural woman and mother, but in *The Long Loneliness* Day clearly puts this personal story—of her relationship with Batterham and her unwed motherhood—in the context of life before conversion. The title of the chapter, "Natural Happiness," suggests a state of natural innocence where the "sinner" is unaware of the moral imperatives of the church. Her sexual promiscuity is presented as part of an unconverted state which can be forgiven through baptism. Furthermore, in this version motherhood clearly becomes an agent of conversion; whereas in *From Union Square to Rome* the agent of conversion was her "downward path" of dissolution and despair.

In this account Day still does not refer to her affair with Moise, her abortion, or her marriage, but we know she was always bothered by this era of her life as her comments to Miller about *The Eleventh Virgin* suggest. In his memoir of Dorothy Day (much of which was taken from taped conversations in the 1970s), Robert Coles comments on her censuring attitude toward her sexual emancipation in this period of her life and later toward the young people around the Catholic Worker who were part of "the sexual revolution" of the sixties. He found himself "estranged" from her on this issue:

> She may have had reason to berate herself for her earlier life. . . . Yet she hadn't been just "floundering," as she put it, nor "sinning," either. Like so many young activists she was trying to be true to herself and to her ideals and to learn more about what the word *love* means. (38)[11]

He tried to explain this "context" to her, arguing that the sexual revolution wasn't all that bad—"that it has its positive side," but, he continued, "she would have none of my modernist apologies" (390).

In *The Long Loneliness,* written before the sixties, Day shows her puritanism in different ways. For instance, in recalling life-styles in the New York radical group, she comments on Emma Goldman and her notorious number of sexual alliances referred to in her autobiography, *Living My Life:* "I was revolted by such promiscuity and even when her book came out would not read it because I was offended in my sex" (60). At other times, she turns the censoring attitude on herself. Changes made in the text of *The Long Loneliness* when she describes her jail episode in Chicago illustrate her increased sense of guilt about her careless moral lifestyle. The episode, describing her arrest and her treatment by the police as if she were a prostitute, was humiliating (most of the other people in the house escaped). In *From Union Square to Rome* her tone is matter-of-fact about the circumstances. She does not blame herself, and, in fact, she is angry at the authorities and at their misinterpretation of her presence in the boardinghouse:

> I felt at first a peculiar sense of disgust and shame at the position I was in, shame because I had been treated as a criminal and made to feel exactly as though I were guilty of the charge on which I had been arrested. (102)

In the second version of this episode in *The Long Loneliness,* the anger gets shifted from the authorities who arrested her to herself. She feels "a victim of my own imprudence, of my carelessness of convention." Not only does she blame herself for not being aware of the imprudence of staying in such a boardinghouse at night, but she also concludes that the experience left her with "a deep feeling of self-contempt":

I do not think that ever again, no matter of what I am accused, can I suffer more than I did then of shame and regret, and self-contempt. (101)

Along with this change in her attitude toward her sexual identity and an increased sense of guilt and self-contempt, the author, in her second conversion narrative, adopts a more explicit definition of the roles of men and women, separating women into the private, domestic, nurturing sphere. For instance, in her autobiography she writes about her nursing training as appropriate and satisfying to a woman: "We were given nursing to do, straight nursing, which delights woman's heart" (88). Such a sentiment was not characteristic of her two other autobiographical descriptions of this choice of vocation. In *The Long Loneliness* women's roles are more narrowly defined not only as private and domestic but also as "natural" (biological) to women. Furthermore these roles are now shown as conflicting with public roles. Again, focusing on her culpability, the author blames herself for wanting both men's and women's roles and emphasizes that this attitude is selfish:

I wanted the privileges of the woman and the work of the man, without following the work of the woman. I wanted to go on picket lines, to go to jail, to write, to influence others and to make my mark on the world. How much ambition and how much self-seeking there was in all that! (60)

Ambition and public leadership are here made incompatible with "the work of women." Echoing June's despairing conclusion in *The Eleventh Virgin,* that women are biologically determined to be more interested in relationships (men) than ideas, she continues her self-analysis by concluding that she is not a good "revolutionary" and, indeed, that all women are, by nature, not good revolutionaries. "Men who are revolutionaries," she writes, ". . . do not dally on the side as women do, complicating the issue by an emphasis on the personal" (60). She goes on to elaborate on the limitations of women in their commitment to an idea:

I am quite ready to concede now that men are the single minded, the pure of heart, in these movements. Women by their very nature are more materialistic, thinking of the home, the children, and all things needful to them, especially love. (60)

Here the personal and the public clash. Women are limited by their commitment to the personal — home and children. Reflecting on her own decision to give up the personal (husband and home) for her public vocation, she acknowledges the pain it caused:

That conflict was in me. A woman does not feel whole without a man. And for a woman who had known the joys of marriage, it was years before I awakened without that longing for a face pressed against my breast, an arm about my shoulder. (236)

At times, Day also seems to apologize for her choice of a public vocation. She emphasizes that she *has* experienced the joys of marriage and, above all, that she should not be considered a "single" woman. Responding to a letter from a priest who remarked that if she were a "woman of family," her articles about community in the Catholic Worker newspaper would have more validity, she angrily "validates" her womanhood by claiming the traditional roles:

But I *am* a woman of family. I have had husband and home life—I have a daughter and she presents problems to me right now. How can I let anyone put over on me the idea that I am a single person? I am a mother and the mother of a large family at that [she includes her extended family of grandchildren]. (236)

On the other hand, although she insists on her authority to speak as a woman on matters of motherhood and family, she also insists on the necessity of her renunciation of these and other personal roles and on the pain of having to do it repeatedly. She says, "No matter how many times I gave up mother, father, husband, daughter for His sake, I had to do it over again."

In an essay published in *Commonweal* in 1943, we get a further insight into her renunciation of her role as a mother. She recalls that at the birth of her daughter she felt inadequate as a mother and decided to "turn her over" to Mary, "The Blessed Mother":

You, I told the Blessed Mother, will have to be her mother. Under the best of circumstances I'm a failure as a homemaker. I'm untidy, inconsistent, undisciplined, temperamental, and I have to pray every day for final perseverance. (*By Little and By Little* 161)

This negative evaluation of herself as a mother is in sharp contrast to her description of herself in *From Union Square to Rome* where she seemed at ease, confident, and competent to care for her child.

What we see in her second conversion narrative is that she has been refashioning her image of womanhood to fit the traditional image (particularly the Catholic version) of what a woman and mother should be. As June O'Connor notes in "Dorothy Day and Gender Identity," Day's view of women "conforms to a conventional patriarchal outlook wherein women are accepted as naturally and instinctively different from men and inferior to them" (8). At the same time, this model of womanhood—of a woman who is dependent and confined to domestic concerns—does not represent her life. Jim Forest, one of her greatest admirers, and at one time an editor of the *Catholic Worker* newspaper, notes affectionately in his biography of her that Dorothy Day was known around the Catholic Worker as "the abbot." In fact, we shall see that Day increasingly creates a public image of herself as a specially chosen spiritual leader which contrasts with her traditional image of womanhood. Her growing awareness of herself as a person who must renounce the comforts of the personal world of women is brought home in a startling comparison that she makes about her special calling and the sacrifices it has demanded of her:

It was a price I had paid. I was Abraham who had sacrificed Isaac. And yet I had Isaac. I had Tamar. (236)

Her image of herself here as a spiritual leader from the Old Testament male patriarchy is the most contradictory that she could have chosen to complement her portrait earlier in the chapter of woman as "less singleminded," "less pure of heart," "more materialistic." The ambivalence is startling.

To return to the "Postcript." The last image we have of the autobiographical "I" is of "the barren woman" of Psalm 113, to whom God has given the joys of motherhood. We are reminded that in this, Day's second conversion narrative, the agent of conversion was the gift of motherhood. By returning at the end of the narrative to the image of the barren woman, the author of *The Long Loneliness* ties the biological knot begun in *The Eleventh Virgin* where the heroine gave up her vocation as a writer to embrace her female destiny—that of mother and wife. Woman's creativity as artist or as spiritual leader seems to be indissolubly linked to reproductive functions. In *The Eleventh Virgin* this view of womanhood at the end of the novel was in contradiction to the freedom that the heroine explored in her roles throughout the rest of the story. In *The Long Loneliness* the assignment of traditional roles to women (linked to their biological identity) is more pervasive; even so, the identification with the converted "barren woman" is contradicted by the earlier identification with the spirituality of the patriarchal leader Abraham. These two contradictory images suggest the tension in the gender identity in Dorothy Day's personal narratives.

The "Postscript" ends on the recurring theme of loneliness, which also entitles the book. She concludes, "We have all known the long loneliness and we have learned that the only solution is love and that love comes with community." The theme of loneliness is the unifying thread that ties together the two narrative voices in *The Long Loneliness*—the narrative of the spiritual leader and radical witness, and the narrative of the "barren woman" and woman of community. The theme operates on two levels: on the one hand, Day emphasizes that loneliness is a condition particular to women. Earlier in the narrative, when writing of her brief stay in Hollywood as a film writer, she suggested that women's loneliness is a sign of social dependence:

I was lonely, deadly lonely. And I was to find out then, as I found out so many times, over and over again, that women especially are social beings, who are not content with just husband and family, but must have a community, a group, an exchange with others. (158)

Here Day goes beyond *The Eleventh Virgin*'s despairing acknowledgment of the need to fulfill a biological role of wife and mother to women's need of social context and community. Furthermore, she adds to another comment earlier in the story that women are failures as revolutionaries an implication that women are inferior spiritually:

Young and old, even in the busiest years of our lives, we women especially are victims of the long loneliness. Men may go away and become desert Fathers, but there are no desert mothers. Even the anchoresses led rather sociable lives, with book binding and spiritual counseling, even if they did have to stay in one place. (158)

In this passage women are "victims" and thus cannot live the more heroic spiritual life of "desert Fathers." The suggestion that women's biological identity and social needs create a limitation to their spiritual life occurs again in "All Is Grace" where in a description of her extended retreat in 1943, she writes, "I came to the conclusion during those months that such a hermit's life for a woman was impossible" (106).

On the other hand, Day also uses the theme of loneliness in her spiritual autobiography in a more universal way. The final reference in "Postscript"— "we have all known the long loneliness"—takes in the whole community that she is addressing in her story and refers to the human condition of spiritual isolation. In choosing her title, "The Long Loneliness," from a quotation of Mary Ward, Day also seems to be referring to a universal spiritual condition:

I think, dear child, the trouble and the long loneliness you hear me speak of is not far from me, which whensoever it is, happy success will follow.

However, when we look at the context of this quotation, we see that Day is speaking more personally, identifying with the isolation of the spiritual leader who suffers for her devotion to her vocation. The quotation is taken from a letter to Ward's friend and compatriot Winifred Wigmore. She is telling her friend about the premonition she has had of "dark days" ahead, foreshadowing her imprisonment for heresy. The letter continues:

You are the first I have uttered this so plainly to. Pray for me and for the work. It grieves me I cannot have you also with me to help bear a part, but a part you will and shall bear howsoever. (Chambers 138)

When Day quoted from this letter, she apparently deleted this section and quoted instead the words of confidence and resignation with which Mary Ward concludes: "The pain is great, but very endurable, because He who lays on the burden also carries it." Like Mary Ward, Dorothy Day feels the isolation of her special vocation, but she also shares Ward's belief that this loneliness is an assurance of being one of God's chosen leaders.

In conversations with Robert Coles about what she meant by her use of the concept of loneliness, Dorothy Day refers to loneliness as a "spiritual hunger." Coles summarizes his understanding of her use of the word, giving it a nongendered universality: "Her loneliness, then, was existential, her restlessness the impatience and hunger of the voyager whose destination is far off" (64). The "long loneliness" in Day's autobiography expresses, on the one hand, the human quest for spiritual life, including the special isolation of the spiritual leader; on the other hand, it expresses the particular loneliness of women, who hunger for community and relationships.

The period after she published *The Long Loneliness* in 1952 until she gave Miller her notes and the manuscript "All Is Grace" in 1975 was a particularly active time in Dorothy Day's life. She wrote hundreds of columns for the *Catholic Worker,* published four books, traveled extensively throughout the United States, visiting Catholic Worker houses of hospitality and farms and giving speeches wherever she was invited. She also traveled outside the country—to Cuba and to Mexico, to Poland and Russia. She was particularly active in the pacifist movement (she started Pax Christi), the civil rights movement, the anti-Vietnam protests as well as in labor movements. The last time she was arrested was in 1973 in the picket line with Cesar Chavez and his United Farm Workers.

Her last spiritual autobiography, "All Is Grace" is not one unified and authored text. It was put together by her biographer, William Miller, from her entries in the manuscript "All Is Grace" about her retreats and also from other notes taken from the papers Day turned over to Miller. In his introduction, Miller says that Dorothy Day "fretted" about this intended book for years, starting from her spiritual "awakening" during her retreats in the 1940s. On June 27, 1967, her journal entry speaks of her attempts to record her experience: "Trying to write. 2 pages, no more and I awake wondering how I can possibly get that book done. Then I . . . remember my promise . . . to write about the retreat, and must toil on." She continued to add to her manuscript until she gave it to Miller.

The record of her life in "All Is Grace" reveals the same consistent witness to her original social and political vision. She writes, "The social order which depends on profits, which does not consider men's needs as to living space, food, is a bad social order and we must work 'to make that kind of society where it is easier for men to be good'" (137). Her journal concentrates on her own spiritual journey and on her search for sanctity (Miller calls this the "true work of her life"), but it also exhorts her society as a prophet and spiritual leader. She condemns, for instance, modern society for the Holocaust: "The modern states which built up a Hitler [by the terms of the Versailles treaty], which did not depopulate concentration camps and gas chambers by giving asylum are monstrosities" (145).

The references to her personal conversion experiences in these entries are to her spiritual "awakening" during her retreats after 1940. Like her other conversions, the experience reflected here is gendered. She is very conscious of her spiritual journey *as a woman*. The entries collected under the title "Faith and Senses" reflect her concern about the nature of a woman's body as an "earthen vessel," emphasizing the material, sensory nature of women: however antithetically, she also refers to a woman's body as "that temple of the Holy Ghost," suggesting as she had in *The Long Loneliness* (the barren woman) that a woman's sexuality needs to be transformed by grace. Reflecting on the choices she might have made in her life, she describes them in terms of her sexuality. She contemplates what her body might have been like if she had chosen "the vocation" of wife and mother:

I would have given myself to my husband and children, and then my flesh, well used, would droop and my breasts sag but my eyes and lips would rejoice and love and laugh with happiness. (72)

Then she wonders what would have happened had she remained a "single woman, a virgin," here referring to the fact that she was *not* single and that she had a common-law marriage with Batterham. She speculates, "Would I have willingly cast myself into the arms of God or have longed for earthly love, and then have let it pass me by?" Finally, she concludes that she has not fulfilled either of those vocations—wife and mother or celibate nun—but rather God has *chosen* her for a third vocation, neither wife nor virgin but God's lover (in the traditional imagery of the mystics):

But God has chosen me and "blessed are those who have not seen but believed" in this love, this terrible overwhelming cruelly demanding love of the living God. (72)

The three options open to women are clearly outlined here: wife and mother, celibate nun, converted sinner and chosen lover of God (whose vocation would require celibacy).[12] In his memoirs of Dorothy Day, Robert Coles admits that he wanted to ask Day why she felt that she had to embrace celibacy after her conversion, particularly as she had acknowledged both in her autobiography and in their conversations what a conflict it was for her to leave her common-law marriage. Coles writes, "Why, then, did she determine upon celibacy as a necessary aspect of her conversion, her new Catholic life?" Then he continues, "Such questions raced across my mind, but her expression made me swallow them whole" (54). He notices that Day conveyed—by her expression—her unwillingness to discuss the question further.

Dorothy Day seems to answer Coles's question—or at least explain her choice—in her summary of the teaching of one of her spiritual mentors, René Voillaume, on the relationship of the sensual and the spiritual. The passage counsels that we must not expect unity between the body and the spirit in this life; on the contrary, we must rise above the conflict and "the psychological plane" to find the spiritual life:

Sensual . . . love blinds the spirit which is striving to love God. We will not find any unity of life around us . . . unless we free ourselves from dependence on the world, from our sensitive nature raising ourselves above the psychological plane. . . . Those who wish to realize unity on a psychological plane of their life cannot attempt it without the risk of destroying the supernatural elan of their deepest life. (73)

Clearly Day is accepting here a condition of psychological disharmony and the notion that there is a fundamental duality between the material and the spiritual—between the body and the spirit. To live a truly spiritual life, one must give up sensuality and turn away from the body and the material world. Thus, in answer to Coles's question—why celibacy was a necessary condition of conversion—Day would suggest here that she must be celibate to carry out her vocation, particularly because she is a woman. She has defined woman in terms of the body ("the earthern vessel") and the material ("women by their very nature are more materialistic") and thus, according to traditional dualism, women's closer relationship to the body makes the achievement of spiritual life especially difficult. Although recent feminist critics have sought—with some credibility—to point out ways in which Dorothy Day embraced many feminist ideals, particularly in the interconnection of social injustices on the basis of race and class and culture,[13] Day's perception of women's nature and women's roles, as she understood them in traditional Christian teaching, separates her from the current generation of Catholic women theologians, such as Elisabeth Schussler

Fiorenza and Rosemary Ruether, who have challenged the church's view of women's nature and the "absolute heirarchal dualism," as Carol Christ has called it, that supports this view.[14]

Despite her separation from current feminist theology, Dorothy Day's spiritual autobiography reveals moments that transcend the tensions and conflicts of her self-identity and which express a harmony with the material world, not a rejection of it. Carol Christ would describe them as moments "when we are aware that we are part of a community, a history, or the natural world, which is larger than ourselves yet still subject to change" (xiv). Day frequently uses images of the sea to express this harmony. In "All Is Grace," referring to her conversion, she writes, "I was 'born again by the word of the Spirit' contemplating the beauty of the sea and the shore, wind and waves, the tide" (62). And in a passage from *On Pilgrimage,* a collection of writings from the period of her life that she recorded in "All Is Grace," she describes one of those unifying moments, a day of solitary enjoyment at the farm on Staten Island:

"In the beginning God created heaven and earth." Looking out over the bay, the gulls, "the paths in the sea," the tiny ripples stirring a patch of water here and there, the reflections of clouds on the surface—how beautiful it all is.

Alone all day. A sudden storm in the night. Vast dark clouds and a glaring lightning flash with thunder. Reading *Dr. Zhivago* a second time. (*By Little and By Little* 357)

These visionary moments are rare in Dorothy Day's autobiographical writings. Her vocation immersed her in a world of institutions, causes, conflicts and personal tensions, but her spiritual journals show that the "work of her life" included a search for this harmony and transcendence.

Dorothy Day's "conversion narratives" reveal the public spiritual leader and social activist and radical. They also reveal the private woman who struggled to make her identity consistent with her vocation. Her conversions, which are never quite what you expect them to be, reveal the paradox of women's experience, particularly as it is expressed in spiritual autobiography. June O'Connor explains the paradox of Day's identity as a woman in terms of "rhetoric" and "reality," suggesting that the reality is the Dorothy Day who shares many of the current feminist values and that the "rhetoric" is the traditionalist, who accepts woman's dependent and limited role. However, the autobiographical writings of Dorothy Day reveal—as many women's life stories reveal—that the reality of her identity *is* a paradox. Women often live with contradictions and the consciousness of a double identity, and their autobiographies tell this story. Day's spiritual autobiography belongs in this tradition. It also belongs to the American tradition of the conversion narrative, in which the authors use their own experience to define spiritual truths. As Patricia Caldwell notes in her study of the Puritan conversion narrative, the authors take "something real in their experience . . . not something from a dream or from a book . . . but from the text of their own lives" and define a new "imaginative framework" (186). Dorothy Day's conversion narratives add something unique—"a new imaginative framework"—to the tradition of women's spiritual autobiography, and they also share a commonality with that tradition.

NOTES

1 Nellie Y. McKay pursues the subject of minority autobiographies' identities with a community.
2 William Miller edited her journal and other unpublished materials in *All Is Grace: The Spirituality of Dorothy Day.*
3 In *Women and American Socialism, 1870–1920,* Mari Jo Buhle discusses this new generation of young socialists who joined the ranks of the party in 1910. She characterizes them as challenging the narrowness of the old guard membership with new, more culturally based ideas. She writes, "For a time in the 1910s artist and audience gave a socialist magazine like the *Masses* an unprecedented vogue. Never before had the upper reaches of American culture—its painting, fiction, poetry, criticism—felt so keenly the influence of individuals spiritually socialistic" (259).
4 Day admired both of the Teresas, but she shifted her interest to Thérèse of Lisieux after her retreats in the 1940s.
5 In 1882–85, a biography of Mary Ward was written by Mary Catharine Elizabeth Chambers of the Institute of the Blessed Virgin: *The Life of Mary Ward 1585–1645.*
6 Rose Hawthorne, the daughter of Nathaniel Hawthorne, converted to Catholicism in 1891. She started her work in New York City with cancer patients in 1896, and in 1900 she started the Dominican Congregation of St. Rose of Lima. In *House of Hospitality,* Dorothy Day credits Rose Hawthorne with influencing her in her determination to find a way to continue her social activism after her conversion to Catholicism. Day writes, "If I had not been reading the lives of the saints, canonized and yet uncanonized, St. John of Bosco and Rose Hawthorne, for instance—I probably would have listened, but continued to write rather than act" (xvii).
7 In his introduction to Dorothy Day's *On Pilgrimage: The Sixties,* Stanley Vishnewski writes of the isolation and opposition Dorothy Day and her community experienced: "When the Catholic Worker was launched during the Great Depression, it was much alone in its advocacy for social reform. . . . The CW

has had the satisfaction of seeing many of its policies, often pioneered in loneliness and disgrace, become an accepted part of Catholic life" (8).

8   Mari Jo Buhle refers to this debate in her chapter "Sexual Emancipation." The
new generation of socialists, she explains, "placed the ideal of a sexually emancipated woman at the center of their cultural aesthetic" (262). They argued
their views in the *New York Call,* the *Masses,* and the *Liberator* (all papers
for which Dorothy Day worked). However, a backlash occurred, Buhle explains, and the debate on woman's economic independence versus motherhood began.

9   Janet James, late professor of history at Boston College, noted in conversation
that many major transformations in Dorothy Day's life occurred in connection with another woman—Rayna Simons in college, Peggy Baird in Day's
participation in a Washington suffrage march, for instance.

10   As Carol Hurd Green, co-editor of *Notable American Women,* pointed out
in conversation, the piecing together of materials is characteristic of most of
Day's works, attesting to her training and vocation as a journalist.

11   In her book about the sixties, *On Pilgrimage: The Sixties,* Dorothy Day comments on the sexual revolution and on her attitude toward chastity: "I can
only write what I truly believe, and that is that outside of marriage, and to
some extent inside of marriage, there must be a fine regard for chastity and
purity, and some emphasis on their necessity" (239)

12   In her book *In Memory of Her: A Feminist Theological Reconstruction of
Christian Origins,* Elisabeth Schussler Fiorenza discusses the powerful biblical imagery that has dominated the Roman Catholic view of women. The images are very parallel to Dorothy Day's images of her options as a woman:
"The Roman Catholic variation of these alternative biblical images [Eden home
and Exodus] is the image of Martha, as lay woman, serving Jesus and the
family in the home, and that of Mary, as nun-woman, leaving the world of
family and sexuality and serving Jesus in 'religious life' and patriarchally defined ecclesiastical orders. The dichotomy evoked by the images of Exodus
and Eden becomes structurally expressed in a dichotomy of lifestyles: virgin-
mother, religious-lay, spiritual-biological" (348).

13   In her study of gender identity, June O'Connor argues that Day shares many
contemporary feminist values: "A prominent theme in contemporary feminist
ethics is recognition of the connections among a wide range of social injustices:
discrimination on the basis of gender, color, culture, age, sexuality, and some
would add, species. Day shared this point of view" (14). Sally Cuneen in
"Dorothy Day: The Storyteller as Human Model" also argues that Day shared
many feminist values but concedes that her "timing was out of step with that
of many women" (293) and that Dorothy Day and the women's movement
"passed each other by" (292).

14   In *Diving Deep and Surfacing: Women Writers on Spiritual Quest,* Carol Christ
rejects this dualism, which, she argues, is based on the notion that there is
"a world beyond this world which is unchanging and infinite and therefore
superior to this world of finitude and change" (xiv). She believes, on the other

hand, that finitude and limitation are "rooted in the structure of our lives" (xiv). In *Sexism and God-Talk: Toward a Feminist Theology,* Rosemary Radford Ruether argues for a new feminist theology where "The God/ess who is primal Matrix, the ground of being-new being, is neither stifling immanence nor rootless transcendence. Spirit and matter are not dichotomized but are the inside and outside of the same thing" (85).

WORKS CITED

Andrews, William L., ed. *Sisters of the Spirit: Three Black Women's Autobiographies of the Nineteenth Century.* Bloomington: University of Indiana Press, 1986.

Berrigan, Daniel. Introduction to *The Long Loneliness* by Dorothy Day. New York: Harper & Row, 1952.

Brodzki, Bella, and Celeste Schenck. Introduction to *Life/Lines: Theorizing Women's Autobiography* 1–15. Ithaca: Cornell University Press, 1988.

Buhle, Mari Jo. *Women and American Socialism, 1870–1920.* Urbana: University of Illinois Press, 1981.

Caldwell, Patricia. *The Puritan Conversion Narrative: The Beginnings of American Expression.* Cambridge University Press, 1983.

Chambers, Mary Catharine Elizabeth (The Institute of the Blessed Virgin). *The Life of Mary Ward (1585–1645).* Ed. Henry James Coleridge, Society of Jesus. Vol. 2. London: Burns and Oates, 1885.

Christ, Carol P. *Diving Deep and Surfacing: Women Writers on Spiritual Quest.* Boston: Beacon Press, 1986.

Coles, Robert. *Dorothy Day: A Radical Devotion.* Reading, MA: Addison-Wesley, 1987.

Cuneen, Sally. "Dorothy Day: The Storyteller as Human Model." *Cross Currents,* 24/3 (Fall 1984), 283–93.

Day, Dorothy. *All Is Grace: The Spirituality of Dorothy Day.* Ed. William D. Miller. Garden City: Doubleday, 1987.

Day, Dorothy. *By Little and By Little: The Selected Writings of Dorothy Day.* Ed. and introd. Robert Ellsberg. New York: Alfred A. Knopf, 1984.

Day, Dorothy. *The Eleventh Virgin.* New York: Albert & Charles Boni, 1924.

Day, Dorothy. *From Union Square to Rome.* Silver Spring, MD: Preservation of the Faith Press, 1940.

Day, Dorothy. *House of Hospitality.* New York: Sheed and Ward, 1939.

Day, Dorothy. *Loaves and Fishes.* New York: Harper & Row, 1963.

Day, Dorothy. *The Long Loneliness: An Autobiography.* Introduction by Daniel Berrigan. Reprint, New York: Harper & Row, 1981.

Day, Dorothy. *On Pilgrimage: The Sixties.* Introduction by Stanley Vishnewski. New York: Curtis Books, 1972.

Edkins, Carol. "Quest for Community: Spiritual Autobiographies of Eighteenth-

Century Quaker and Puritan Women in America." In *Women's Autobiography: Essays in Criticism,* ed. Estelle C. Jelinek, 39–52. Bloomington: Indiana University Press, 1980.

Epstein, Barbara Leslie. *The Politics of Domesticity: Women, Evangelism, and Temperance in Nineteenth-Century America.* Middletown, CT: Wesleyan University Press, 1981.

Fiorenza, Elisabeth Schussler. *In Memory of Her: Feminist Theological Reconstruction of Christian Origins.* New York: Crossroad, 1983.

Forest, Jim. *Love Is the Measure. A Biography of Dorothy Day.* New York: Paulist Press, 1986.

Friedman, Susan Stanford. "Women's Autobiographical Selves: Theory and Practice." *The Private Self: Theory and Practice of Women's Autobiographical Writings,* ed. Shari Benstock, 34–62. Chapel Hill: University of North Carolina Press, 1988.

Heilbrun, Carolyn G. *Writing a Woman's Life.* New York: W. W. Norton, 1988.

Jones, Mother. *Autobiography of Mother Jones.* Ed. Mary Field Parton, Chicago: Charles H. Kerr, 1925. Rpt. Arno Press, 1969.

Juster, Susan. "'In a Different Voice': Male and Female Narratives of Religious Conversion in Post-Revolutionary America." *American Quarterly,* 41/1 (March 1989), 34–62.

McKay, Nellie Y. "Race, Gender and Cultural Context in Zora Neale Hurston's Dust Tracks on a Road." In *Life/Lines: Theorizing Women's Autobiography,* ed. Bella Brodzki and Celeste Schenck, 175–89. Ithaca: Cornell University Press, 1988.

Mason, Mary G. "The Other Voice: Autobiographies of Women Writers." In *Autobiography: Essays Theoretical and Critical,* ed. James Olney, 207–35. Princeton: Princeton University Press, 1980.

Miller, William. *Dorothy Day: A Biography.* San Francisco: Harper & Row, 1982.

O'Connor, June. "Dorothy Day and Gender Identity: The Rhetoric and the Reality." *Horizons,* 15/1 (Spring 1988), 8–20.

Piehl, Mel. *Breaking Bread: The Catholic Worker and the Origin of Catholic Radicalism in America.* Philadelphia: Temple University Press, 1982.

Piehl, Mel. "The Catholic Worker and American Religious Tradition." *Cross Currents,* 24/3 (Fall 1984), 259–69.

Rossi, Alice S., ed. *The Feminist Papers: From Adams to de Beauvoir.* New York: Bantam Books, 1974.

Ruether, Rosemary Radford. *Sexism and God-Talk: Toward a Feminist Theology.* Boston: Beacon Press, 1983.

Ruether, Rosemary Radford, and Rosemary Skinner Keller, eds. *Women and Religion in America: The Nineteenth Century.* Vol. 1. San Francisco: Harper and Row, 1981.

Ruether, Rosemary Radford, and Rosemary Skinner Keller, eds. *Women and Religion in America: 1900–1968.* Vol. 3. San Francisco: Harper and Row, 1986.

Shea, Daniel B. *Spiritual Autobiography in Early America.* Madison: University of Wisconsin Press, 1988.

Smith, Sidonie. *A Poetics of Women's Autobiography: Marginality and the Fictions of Self-Representation.* Bloomington: Indiana University Press, 1987.
Spacks, Patricia Meyer. "Selves in Hiding." In *Women's Autobiography: Essays in Criticism,* ed. Estelle C. Jelinek, 112–32. Bloomington: Indiana University Press, 1980.

CHAPTER 10

Choosing Sides, Choosing Lives: Women's Autobiographies of the Civil Rights Movement

ARLYN DIAMOND

The women's autobiographies brought together for this essay are as various in form as the personalities and backgrounds of the women who wrote them. What unites them most obviously is a historical moment, the 1960s, and their passionate engagement in the struggle for a radical transformation of American society. The selection I have made is idiosyncratic. It is also circumscribed by what was written and what was published. Thus in its own formation this essay replicates the intersection of the personal and the political, the personal and the social, the personal and the historical which is its subtext, just as the reading of it must replicate this intersection. As producers and consumers of our own and others' memories we are all shaped by our experiences of domination and resistance as we have lived them in our society. This is a hard and necessary lesson for Americans, seduced as we all have been by the pervasive rhetoric of individualism. As feminist scholars I believe we ought constantly to be learning and teaching it, as I have tried to do here. Any individual's past is also history; the world we experience separately is also social. Our conscious interventions in its activities are our politics as well as our scholarship. The narratives introduced here say much about these crucial truths.

Perhaps coincidentally, the six life stories described below are those of bright students, sufficiently pretty, with remarkable drive, energy, and self-discipline. As girls they appeared to have at least some of the conventional attributes for conventional success. But, since success would also have meant docilely entering a world in which inequality was woven into the social fabric, they chose to enact their commitments to justice in unconventional lives and in narratives which represent not only different origins but also different aims and different rhetorical strategies. Compelling as separate life writings, together they generate an intricate web of connections and antagonisms which demand a socially conscious reading, and undo the mystifications of a dehistoricized subjectivity. I have quoted them extensively, in part as a way of encouraging readers to go back to the originals, and in part to give a fair account of the ways in which their differences are consciously produced in their texts. Difference is their theme, their way of knowing themselves and others, the problem they never solve, the reality we inherit.

VIRGINIA FOSTER DURR, *OUTSIDE THE MAGIC CIRCLE*

In a series of witty interviews which demonstrate a lifelong practice of the anecdote as an art form, Durr chronicles her transformation from an aspiring southern belle in the 1920s, with the requisite Confederate ancestors and old family plantation, to a unique position as interpreter and representative of modern southern history. Her devotion to economic and racial justice was nurtured in New Deal Washington. Although her support for civil rights and other progressive causes alienated her from family and friends in postwar Alabama, she and her husband, the lawyer Clifford Durr, had a privileged if exhausting role in the struggles of the sixties, as part of a small but influential group of white activists.

ELINOR LANGER, "NOTES FOR NEXT TIME: A MEMOIR OF THE 1960s"

Langer's brief memoir is simultaneously introspective and abstract. Rather than offering Durr's detailed account of specific historical events or personal milestones, she provides a deliberately hesitant analysis of the successes and failures of what was loosely known as "The Movement" from the perspective of a white Northerner with an elite education and a history of professional success. In explicating her own personal and political frustration she seeks a deeper understanding of a group of idealists who never lived up to their revolutionary ambitions, unable to "invent tactics that corresponded in a convincing way to what it was that we did understand" about the evils of racism and poverty and imperialism.

ANGELA DAVIS, *AN AUTOBIOGRAPHY*

Like Durr, Angela Davis grew up in Alabama, but in a crucially different time and neighborhood. Durr's earliest memories are of Edenic visits to a family plantation. "I was brought up, you see, on the romantic tradition of the benevolent slave system" (5). Davis remembers growing up on Dynamite Hill, so called because of the regular bombings of black homes by resentful whites. In the 1960s she achieved notoriety because of her role in black and student uprisings in California. For the media and the right wing she personified the simultaneous threats of black and communist revolution, philosophy graduate student turned gun-toting terrorist. Her autobiography uses the dramatic events of her trial for complicity in murder as a springboard for an analysis of race and class in America.

SALLY BELFRAGE, *FREEDOM SUMMER*

Belfrage's account of her experiences as a SNCC volunteer in Mississippi in 1964 tells us almost nothing about her as an individual, except what can be inferred from her polished prose. She is white, educated, traveled, and a blonde Californian. Her narrative transparency allows her to achieve an evocative portrait of what it felt like to experience the Movement, and Mississippi racism, as a sympathetic outsider.

ANNE MOODY, *COMING OF AGE IN MISSISSIPPI*

Coming of Age is, in contrast, an insider's account. Moody's may be the most traditional autobiography in form, describing what it means to grow up a bright and rebellious girl in a culture where poverty and despair are assumed to be the natural conditions of black life. She is more angry, pessimistic, and self-revealing than the other writers, using an apparently naive artfulness to suggest the weight of racism in the dehumanizing events of ordinary Mississippi lives.

MARY KING, *FREEDOM SONG: A PERSONAL STORY OF THE 1960S CIVIL RIGHTS MOVEMENT*

King's extensive, detailed, and yet reserved description of her years in SNCC and of the family background which led to her involvement is also a carefully researched history of SNCC and the civil rights movement. As one of the few whites to serve on the SNCC staff, she was both leader and outsider in the southern struggle, a position her narrative in part is meant to help her finally come to terms with.

The titles suggest the range of approach and intent in these stories, and also the multiplicity and variety of styles available to even the most politically committed of writers. Ironically, given Davis' discomfort with her role as celebrity, she is the only one whose name alone is sufficient to identify her book. Moody's title, with its reference to Margaret Mead's classic text, signals an interest in portraying a culture as well as a life. Her Mississippi, like Belfrage's, is as primitive a society as any considered a proper object for study by Western anthropologists. King's subtitle frames her life in the historical moment. Langer's tentative "Notes" suggests an ongoing task, just as the subtitle points, like King's, away from self toward history, "next time." All are about a position, "outside," and a vision, "freedom," which despite any doubts they continue to affirm.

These autobiographical narratives, like the lives they depict, inhabit the uneasy realm where the personal and social merge into and confront each other. Having chosen to work for change in an unsatisfactory world, the writers step "outside the magic circle" of social acceptance, the space assigned to them by family and society. In so doing they begin to question the dominant values and beliefs about individual merit, and the naturalness of the assigned categories of race, class, and gender which define the circle. Inevitably they begin to question their own uniqueness in light of what they begin to learn about society. Their initial resistance to its most blatant hypocrisies compels it to reveal its power more fully, in their own lives as well as the lives of others. The comfortable divisions between "public" and "private" which American culture everywhere reinforces no longer work for them, as what they do and who they are become entangled.

The motto which the women's movement early adopted, The Personal Is Political, acknowledges the gap between the two even in denying it. How to give a truthful representation of the tangle of desire, event, action, memory, will, law, while affirming the value of her original vision of a transformed America, remains a problem for each writer, and they offer eloquent justifications for very different solutions:

I was not anxious to write this book. Writing an autobiography at my age seemed presumptuous. Moreover, I felt that to write about my life, what I did, what I thought and what happened to me would require a posture of difference, an assumption that I was unlike other women — other black women — and therefore needed to explain myself. I felt that such a book might end up obscuring the most essential fact: the forces that have made my life what it is are the very same forces that have shaped and misshaped the lives of millions of my people. . . . I was reluctant to write this book because concentration on my personal history might detract from the movement which brought my case to the people in the first place. I was also unwilling to render my life as a personal "adventure"— as though there were a "real" person separate and apart from the political person. (Davis, "Preface" ix, x)

Most of what I have written here is personal. When I began writing, I distrusted abstraction and felt unable to make sense of anyone's experience but my own.

Only autobiography seemed "true." More recently, I have been able to see how autobiography may also mislead, and not just in the simple senses of omission and individuality. Political autobiography, especially, emphasizes aspects of personality formed by culture. . . . It is apt to attribute to "the times" things that come from the chronological age of the writer at the time being recalled, or at the time of writing. I do not know how to cure possible distortions in this essay except by stating them: sociology is not the whole truth of a person, and political autobiography is not all of life. (Langer 50)

This is a personal account. Mine is not a definitive history of the civil rights movement, something that I believe no participant in the struggle writing out of memory and experience could produce. Furthermore, I am a white woman writing about my experiences working in a mostly black, largely male-led organization. While this is one person's story, inasmuch as I have attempted to present my experiences in an accurate and clear historical framework, it is also a partial history. (King 24)

There are familiar ways to think about the diversity of these voices. One, probably more popular in a culture addicted to *People* and a constant stream of intimate revelations—addictions, affairs, binges and purges—is to identify with (and exaggerate) Langer's distrust of sociological abstractions, and to suspect Davis of a dishonest Stalinist puritanism. The concept of "truthfulness" is central to the way we generally discuss autobiography, unreflectingly equating truth with the acknowledgment of suppressed desires or unacceptable behaviors. In this we are the heirs of *Tristram Shandy* and Freud and Lytton Strachey.

Another, more academic way to think of the differences is to think of them as lying in the realm of representation. Granted the final impossibility for reader or writer of a fully known or articulated self, we can treat each work as a unique rhetorical production, and abandon the (futile) attempt to decide who is telling more or better truths. Such an approach would allow us to see how each author situates herself in her unique circumstances, how she defines her unique self. Taken together, these texts would offer a sense of the variety of women's experiences, of possibilities, an appreciation of heterogeneity in style that frees us of the necessity to choose or judge. But, as contemporary theorists of autobiography point out,

the duplicitous and complicitous relationship of "life" and "art" in autobiographical modes is precisely the point. To elide it in the name of eliminating the "facile assumption of referentiality" is dangerously to ignore the crucial referentiality of class, race and sexual orientation; it is to beg serious political questions. (Brodzki and Schenk, "Introduction" 12–13).

Shari Benstock, in her introduction to *The Private Self: Theory and Practice of Woman's Autobiographical Writings,* speaks of

the expected "subjects" of women's autobiography: women situated within conflicting and mutually constricting roles (wife, mother, daughter, sister, lover); women
placed in societies that make rigid distinctions between "man's world" and "women's
domain," between the public sector and the domestic; black women writing under
the power of the dominant white culture; middle-class women seeking freedom
from bourgeois definitions of women's intellectual and imaginative abilities; public women defying patriarchal definitions to open new avenues of professional and
personal experiences for women; women who find through autobiographical writing
a means to survive childbirth, illness, the deaths of spouses and children, loss of
cultural identity and personal regard, fear of failure, aging, death, loss of beauty
and physical strength. (5)

Her multiplication of examples is a self-conscious strategy to encompass diversity by unrolling an infinite series of texts. Others suggest the
inadequacy of a normative concept of the autobiographical self by looking
at so-called marginal women—nonwhite, lesbian, revolutionary. Their conclusions are remarkably similar.

Rather, these intensely lived testimonial narratives are strikingly impersonal. They
are written neither for individual growth nor for glory but are offered through the
scribe to a broad public as one part of a general strategy to win political ground.
(Doris Sommer, in Brodzki and Schenck 109, speaking of Latin American women
activists)

Scholars . . . have demonstrated that for those outside the dominant group, identification with community is pervasive for the unalienated self in life and writing.
(Nellie McKay, in Brodzki and Schenck 175, writing on Zora Neale Hurston)

This autobiographical writing has specific purposes in the (not always synchronous)
histories of the community and of the individuals who write or read them; it aims
to give lesbian identity a coherence and legitimacy that can make both individual
and social action possible. (Biddy Martin, in Brodski and Schenck 83, writing on
lesbian identity)

As the special cases accumulate, unless we choose to divide the world
into pure individuals who are part of the dominant culture and who write
purely individualistic autobiographies, and outsiders who are different and
write differently, we must begin to suspect that there can be no such thing
as a purely personal autobiography, no matter what the intent of the writer.
If blacks or communists or lesbians et al. are forced to define themselves
"in opposition to, rather than as an articulation of condition" (Elizabeth
Fox-Genovese, in Benstock 64), then "normal" people are forced to define

themselves in relation to those conditions in which they too participate, by an act of denial.

You can't imagine the contradictions in my life, the total contradictions . . . at the same time that I was surrounded by lovely, decent black people, I would go to see *Birth of a Nation* and believe that the Klan was noble and wonderful. (Durr 44)

To read autobiography is to understand that it is embedded in the realm of the social, for whites, heterosexuals, the well-off, the physically able, anyone within the magic circle, since privilege is as real as the oppression which enables it. It may be that for us what is most powerfully repressed is not the Freudian unconscious but what might be termed the Marxist conscious, the acknowledgment of the determining role of social life.

These complex relationships between history and self reveal themselves in the different ways in which the murder of Emmet Till, meant to inscribe in blood permanent boundaries between black and white, male and female, becomes part of individual psyches.

While I was aware that an irrational and disgraceful racial injustice was woven into the fabric of our society and had distorted and reduced the lives and possibilities of our black citizens, I had no real knowledge of the history and evolution of this reality. . . . Like many of my generation, my first graphic confrontation with this social evil came from an incident in Mississippi in September 1955 that, concerning as it did someone who was also a teenager, had a powerful and traumatic effect. A fourteen-year-old black youth named Emmett Till had come from Chicago to visit his relatives near the little town of Money, Mississippi, in the Delta. Three white men grabbed him from a private home and dumped him in the Tallahatchie River, a crude heavy weight tied to his neck with barbed wire. . . . Following this event I spoke to my social studies class at New York City's special High School of Music and Art, using *Life* magazine's article about the murder as my source. My voice broke as I told the class, most of whom were, like me, fifteen years of age, that he was only one year younger. This was my first speech about an issue of justice. . . . (King 250–54)

The progression from knowledge to feeling to action she describes is not simply a matter of individual conscience. In order to understand the genesis of her politics as she recalls it, we would also need to understand why the media chose to make possible a "graphic confrontation" like this, after suppressing or distorting the racism of the South. We would need to talk about who owns newspapers, the cold war, and a whole series of other issues invisible to King in her classroom. One of the difficulties in discussing autobiography is how to incorporate such issues without appearing to erase the unique subject in the process. Here, however, our task is made easier because the writers themselves are taught to make the connections by their political work.

Although as King and others came to see, racism was pervasive in American life, initially her awareness of her possible connection to a black male teenager was dependent on the transmission of images from what appeared to be a very distant world. As media liaison for SNCC King was actively involved in trying to recreate in others the revulsion which brought her to the movement. For Anne Moody, however, Till's murder becomes a means to prevent the move from feeling to action.

I was now working for one of the meanest white women in town, and a week before school started Emmet Till was killed. . . . [Mrs. Burke told me] "See, that boy was just fourteen too. It's a shame he had to die so soon. . . ." I went home shaking like a leaf on a tree. For the first time out of all her trying, Mrs. Burke had made me feel like rotten garbage. Many time she had tried to instill fear within me and subdue me and had given up. But when she talked about Emmet Till there was something in her voice that sent chills and fear all over me.

Before Emmet Till's murder, I had known the fear of hunger, hell, and the Devil. But now there was a new fear known to me—the fear of being killed just because I was black. (103–7)

Drawn together by horror and rejection, King and Moody are simultaneously separated by their comparative distance from Till, and their assigned roles as witnesses to his murder. The myth of the autonomous individual which characterizes the dominant American discourse on the self erases these brutal intrusions of history in the construction of personal being. It also erases the distinctions of race and gender which determine how Till's death will be incorporated, as social revelation or direct threat, speech or silence. The facts about life in Mississippi that must be taught in the Ohio orientation for Freedom Summer volunteers are what Moody and Davis learn experientially as black children in the South.

No one was willing to believe that the event [the disappearance of Goodman, Chaney, and Schwerner] involved more than a disappearance. It was hard to believe even that. Somehow it seemed only a climactic object lesson, part of the morning's lecture, an anecdote to give life to the words of Bob Moses. To think of it in other terms was to be forced to identify with the three, to be prepared, irrevocably, to give one's life. (Belfrage 12)

Emphasis on the individual focuses our attention on courage as a personal attribute, one of the most striking in these narratives, and away from the conditions of state-supported terrorism which made that courage necessary. Belfrage and King meticulously and extensively document local, state, and federal complicity in the daily harassment of blacks and civil rights workers. The others simply include it in descriptions of their ordinary activities. Till, Goodman, Chaney, Schwerner, Liuzzo, Evans—as the martyrs and victims are recalled in each text, we begin to understand that

Moody's graphic account of her breakdown is not a description of personal pathology but the logical consequence of resistance, something common and terrible. Deprived of sleep, of food, of space, shot at, Moody and her fellow workers pay a huge price for their courage. In her case, it is hard not to feel that we as readers also pay the price, since despite her remarkable talents as a writer she has produced little beyond this one work. Only in the movies can people come back unscathed from trauma. Who these women are now is inseparable from what has happened to them. It is a lesson Belfrage first observes and then lives.

When I first arrived I often wondered about the people who had been working here for years—why they sometimes walked around like zombies, never ate or slept, and fell off into some great depth in the middle of a sentence, so that you'd have to wait for them to come back from hell or the middle distance; and how it was that though they had the sense to be here and to run an intricate, methodical campaign, they failed to see that such a sacrifice of themselves was a loss to the very effort they were making. There are incipient nervous breakdowns all over Greenwood. One of the best left yesterday. He'd been wandering around in a trance, deteriorating every day, and had forgotten by now what he ought to be doing about it—some synaptic connection in him had worn out in his year here, and the only choice was sink or flee. I haven't had time enough for the full array of symptoms to immobilize me completely—I still tell myself to go to bed, though am far too tangled up to do it, while the negative feedback operating on the veterans has tired them out too disastrously for them even to know how tired they are any more. It has something to do with fear. Fear can't become a habit. But there is something extra every minute from having that minute dangerous, and if you can't convert the extra into something you have nowhere to put it. You can't assimilate it; you can't subtract from it (since the tension is necessary, the fear reasonable); so that leaves addition: aggravate it, bite on the sore, collide with it head on, and in that way at least stay awake on nerves when you might otherwise fall into a walking sleep. (195–96)

The systematic operations of social power are not always violent. Sometimes social limits are drawn in benign forms, in triumphs and affirmations. The ways in which episodes in one life are replayed in another are not just critically gratifying—they remind us of shared cultures. Women learn to see themselves through images of femininity which appear to cross the lines of class and race, and which are deeply rooted in utopian dreams of community. There are rewards for acquiescing in injustice, as well as costs for resisting.

The memory of the Confederacy was still very much alive. Lots of Confederate reunions were held in Birmingham, all the nice girls from the age of about twelve to twenty would serve as pages. . . . Then we would ride in the parade and the politicians would make speeches about pure white Southern womanhood—and

I believed it. I was pure white Southern womanhood and Southern men had died for me and the Confederate flag was flying just to save me. I got to thinking I was pretty hot stuff, to have the war fought for me. (Durr 44–45)

As soon as I was seated [as the Negro Homecoming Queen], the floats started lining up behind the band. A few minutes later we were slowly moving toward town. As we turned the corner into Main Street, it looked like just about every Negro and white in Centreville had turned out for the parade. . . . When the band reached the center of Main Street, they stopped marching and began playing. . . . "Dixie" seemed to have made everyone happy, Negroes and whites. . . . It seemed like the whole town was singing now. As they sang I sat up there on that float and had the strangest feeling. Somehow I had chills all over my body and I was overcome by a sudden fear. The faces of the whites had written on them some strange yearning. The Negroes looked sad. . . . The feeling that the song conveyed stayed with me all evening, and I was cold. I shivered throughout the rest of the parade. That night, when I was crowned Homecoming Queen during half time of the football game, I felt even colder. (Moody 90–92)

Inevitably, as the ironies and contradictions of the American dream accumulate, resonating in different and yet connected ways in life after life, it becomes impossible to maintain the conventional focus on autobiography as a record of one individual's achievements and/or psychic-sexual-intellectual growth. The writers draw our attention away from themselves with elements like extended character sketches of people they encounter, or socio-economic southern history, or journalistic accounts of crimes and trials. Formally, the consequence is a text which often seems to have more in common with a collage than with a self-portrait. Belfrage, for example, doesn't use "I" until she has established the context in which her experiences, and by implications those of others, each with his or her possible story, take place. To intervene in history is knowingly to situate one's life within it, so that these autobiographies are concerned with factual and analytic accuracy.

Because they have cut themselves loose from traditional reverences, and because each remains in some way an outsider, the overlapping canvases they give us have unfamiliar perspectives. Women like Fannie Lou Hamer and Ella Baker fill the foreground. Baker, for example, is credited with a major theoretical and strategic role in the development of radical student activism, and of women leaders. Martin Luther King, in contrast, is a peripheral figure, "De Lawd," a media star and spokesperson for a relatively conservative male religious establishment. Images of female friendships abound: Mary King and Casey Hayden staying up all night to read *The Second Sex;* Anne Moody and her friends in jail, making cards out of toilet paper, teaching each other dance steps, taunting the guards; Clifford Durr complaining that the ladies from the Women's International League for Peace and Freedom would "talk all night long and then leave him to wash the dishes" (Durr 227).

The popular rewritings of the past, from *Birth of a Nation* through *Gone With the Wind* to *Mississippi Burning,* can be and have been confuted by moving personal testimonies. The Grimké sisters and Frederick Douglass and Harriet Jacobs are eloquent progenitors of these eyewitness accounts. As feminists we need to be particularly aware of our heritage of women leaders, women who chose to be active in struggles for justice, women working with others unlike them. Taylor Branch's magisterial *Parting the Waters,* thanks to its elegance and comfortable liberalism, will undoubtedly become the standard history of the civil rights movement. Unfortunately it essentially marginalizes women, making them footnotes to the activities of what even he acknowledges is a patriarchal religious leadership. Some feminist histories, with their emphasis on sexism in the New Left and other student movements, diminish women's crucial roles within them. As a result our version of progressive politics tends to oppose feminists to others, thus reifying (admittedly real) splits and turning our attention away from (too often tenuous) connections. I hope that my presentation of these testimonies reminds us of the connections, and of why we need to keep struggling to make them.

Eleanor Langer speaks for all six narrators when she says:

American radicals have never been able to reach each other across the decades very well. Each radical movement has risen and fallen in an historical moment gone before it has begun to be understood. Its leaders, its troops, its perception of issues, its solutions appear either sentimentally valorous, or else archaic, to its successors. But any movement for a different social order in America will not be the work of one generation alone. We have to mend discontinuities in the radical impulse if we can, head off generational misunderstandings, stand before others neither as false heroes nor as fallen idols. For this reason, it seems useful to try to begin to tell our story. (50)

"Our story," however, is not one of bloodless nobility. Each one memorializes a moment of passionate intensity of the sort usually associated with what is supposed to represent the apogee of a woman's life—falling in love. Langer, interviewing a leader of the Berkeley Free Speech Movement, is shown a newspaper clipping of some student radicals: "They were sitting in some basement, in shirtsleeves, their faces intelligent and intense. I wanted them to become my friends" (60). King's description of her first sight of SNCC headquarters, like her first sight of Casey Hayden, has this same vivid and concrete quality, as does Davis' memory of her first Black Youth Conference, when she "walked around calling everyone sister and brother;

smiling, elated, high on love" (158). What captures them all is a vision of a "beloved community," a radically egalitarian, unalienated world in which differences are dissolved and their best selves freed. As Davis says, "We felt we had the energy of stallions and the confidence of eagles as we rushed into the neighborhoods of L.A.—on the streets, in houses, campuses, offices—driving, walking, meeting, greeting. We experienced the heights of brotherhood and sisterhood doing something openly, freely and above ground about our own people" (170).

Sorrowfully, the vision could not hold. There were reasons for its failure. Externally and internally it was vulnerable to the complex entanglements of gender and race, what Durr calls "the dreadful sexual cesspool."

These men who claimed to be Southern gentlemen would get up and make vile speeches about white women of the South and how they were protecting them. Every black man wanted to rape a white woman and every white woman apparently wanted to be raped. (Durr 175)

Ironically, the same obsession fueled frenetic affairs between young white women volunteers and black males trying to defy a taboo they could not escape. The affairs drove a wedge between black and white women, and were used to impugn the motives of civil rights workers, while those who most vehemently enforced the public codes were, as everyone notes, pathologically denying the real situation—the pervasive exploitation of black women by white men. When Moody comes back from New Orleans

I looked so good that it became somewhat of a problem. Whenever I was in town white men would stare me into the ground. . . . [Mama] warned me that I must never be caught in town after dark alone and if I was ever approached by white men again, I should walk right past them like I was deaf and blind. (162)

Even between people of goodwill, ostensible allies, the "cesspool" twists human relationships. Mr. Amos won't sit at the same table with Sally Belfrage, even though she is living in his house. His teenage son is afraid to meet her eyes. Ellie Langer notes her distance from the movement when "Stokely Carmichael called me 'ma'am' in my own house" (59). King, in her typically dispassionate style, recounts a painful story—black male friends from SNCC are visiting King and Casey Hayden at their apartment. When armed men burst in, the friends, famous for their bravery in other circumstances, flee in instinctive terror at being caught with white women (301–3).

White or black, they were never allowed to forget that they were women. Each of them writes from a position that we would identify as feminist, whether or not the writer does so—and most do. As Belfrage notes, "One of the puzzles of the movement was the way it seemed to attract more women than men" (76). These women are still not celebrated in the way that male leaders were and are, but their presence, the generosity and courage and tenacity of Ella Baker and Virginia Durr and Fannie Lou Hamer and Mrs. Amos and all the other "movement mamas" gave birth to modern feminism, and their role in the human and civil rights struggle has yet to be written.

Davis joins the communist party because "I was tired of ephemeral ad-hoc groups that fell apart when faced with the slightest difficulty; tired of men who measured their sexual height by women's intellectual genuflec-tion" (187). As she writes to George Jackson, "For the Black female, the solution [to nationalist charges that there is a matriarchal conspiracy to rob black men of their manhood] is not to become less aggressive, not to lay down the gun, but to learn how to set the sights correctly" (373). For her, as for the others, human liberation and women's liberation are inex-tricably linked. When King, who has the most extensive analysis of sexism within the movement, talks about the genesis of the famous memos on the subject she and Casey Hayden wrote, "SNCC Position Paper, Novem-ber 1964" and "A Kind of Memo . . . To A Number Of Other Women In The Peace And Freedom Movements," she puts them in the context of the civil rights struggle (chapter 12). She wrote her memo not because women had no status within SNCC, but because they did have status.

I was convinced I was making a lifelong commitment based on the ideals of popu-lar democracy and self-determination. But slowly, and perhaps inevitably, self-determination was coming to mean not only politics but also literally self. For both Casey and me, this translated into our growing conviction that we had an obliga-tion to find ways to communicate our deepening sense of political definition, which included the political definition of ourselves as women. (442–43)

These commitments are never repudiated. Langer says,

Friends find my account of the movement "bitter," and though I see what they must be seeing in it, bitterness is not my verdict. The opposite. I have a great sense of pride in having been part of it. . . . It was painful and sometimes terrible to be involved. But it was where I wanted to be. . . . If I regret anything it is that I was not clearheaded enough for most of my time in the movement to have helped make it stronger or to prolong or reinforce its impact. (82)

Even Moody, the one most ambivalent about the possibilities of change, never repudiates her hopes.

Autobiography can never really explain to us or even to the authors themselves why these women chose to see, to resist, to act, although they and we seek for clues in their lives. It can show what strengths and tradi-tions nourished them, what prevented them from achieving their vision. As readers we inevitably agree or disagree with certain ways of seeing, or ideological positions or personal choices, and that, I would argue, is the point. In taking up these autobiographies separately or together, we are engaged in our own making-of-history, immersing ourselves in what Doris Sommer calls "the medium of resistance and counter-discourse" (Brodzki and Schenck 111). We are compelled to take politics as seriously as these six women did, and in what seems to be a diminished and reactionary world, we are encouraged by recollecting the possibilities of heroic engagement for women. We are reminded of how much organizational hard work goes into even the most spiritual of campaigns for a better world. The nuts and bolts of politics may not be what we look to autobiography for, but these are instructive texts for women working for change. They are even more instructive about the ways in which compromises with racism or sexism or red-baiting (and, we would now add, heterosexism) undermine the integrity and effectiveness of coalitions for good causes. The tension between the dream of community as experienced by Durr and Moody and Langer and Davis and Belfrage and King, and the messy, painful, improvised ways in which the realities of race and class and gender were also experienced remains with us still. In the end, of course, the value of autobiography or memoir for us is not the suppression of the subject in the realm of the social, or in abstract lessons, but in the fascinating interplay between the political and personal which forms our lives as feminists, too.

WORKS CITED

Belfrage, Sally. *Freedom Summer.* New York: Viking, 1965.

Benstock, Shari, ed. *The Private Self: Theory and Practice of Women's Autobiographical Writings.* Chapel Hill: University of North Carolina Press, 1988.

Brodzki, Bella, and Celeste Schenck, eds. *Life/Lines: Theorizing Women's Autobiography.* Ithaca: Cornell University Press, 1988.

Davis, Angela. *An Autobiography.* New York: Random House, 1974.

Durr, Virginia Foster. *Outside the Magic Circle.* Ed. Hollinger F. Barnard. Tuscaloosa: University of Alabama Press, 1985.

King, Mary. *Freedom Song: A Personal Story of the 1960s Civil Rights Movement.* New York: Morrow, 1987.

Langer, Elinor. "Notes for Next Time: A Memoir of the 1960s." *Working Papers,* 1/3 (Fall 1973), 48–83.

Moody, Anne. *Coming of Age in Mississippi.* New York: Dial, 1968.

CHAPTER 11

No Laughing Matter:
The WASPs Climb Down

NANCY WALKER

I

In 1977, at the height of the contemporary women's movement and amid increasing consciousness of the multiplicity of women's racial and ethnic experiences in America, Margaret Halsey published her autobiography, *No Laughing Matter: The Autobiography of a WASP.* The first part of the title is derived from Halsey's early success as a writer of satire: her 1938 book *With Malice Toward Some* pokes fun at the foibles of the British, and it was an overwhelming best-seller in America. By the time she wrote her autobiography, however, Halsey had endured a series of personal and professional ordeals that she attributes in large part to her upbringing as a white Anglo-Saxon Protestant, taught to feel superior to those with different backgrounds. Although Halsey's social and political attitudes underwent dramatic changes while she was still a young woman, and she spent most of her life espousing liberal causes such as racial equality and political ethics, she never overcame either her sense of superiority or her sense of guilt at being part of the WASP establishment. *No Laughing Matter* thus differs sharply from both traditional white male autobiographies and also from the autobiographies of women whose marginality in American culture is the focal point of their stories. At the same time, Halsey's autobiography—both its statements and its silences—provides a paradigm of female WASP experience in the twentieth century, serves as a cautionary tale about the limitations of American liberalism, and reveals the limits of the female autobiographical text in presenting the reality of "self."

At the time that *No Laughing Matter* was published, Margaret Halsey was living in England, far from the scene of her childhood in Yonkers, New York, where she was born in 1910. Like her countryman Benjamin

Franklin nearly two hundred years earlier, Halsey apparently found the trans-Atlantic distance valuable in assessing a life that had been intimately involved with changes in American culture. Also like Franklin, Halsey views herself as a rational, enlightened person with the capacity to effect change — improvement — in the values and habits of those around her. But whereas Franklin offers his *Autobiography* (1791) to his male descendants as describing a life worthy of emulation — "my Posterity may like to know, as they may find some of them suitable to their own situations, and therefore worthy of imitation" — Halsey highlights her mistakes and failures as representative on a personal level of the mistakes and failures of American social and political culture in the mid-to-late twentieth century.

In fact, the reason Halsey announces for writing her autobiography has less to do with constructing a version of her own life than with challenging WASP superiority: "The cutting down to size of the WASPs being a matter of historical necessity, it seemed as if an examination of WASP conditioning and WASP consciousness (as far as the latter goes) might be of interest and significance" (12). Thus, in contrast to Franklin, Halsey sees herself not as an exemplar of progress, but rather as an exemplar of a decline in superiority and hegemony that mirrors that of WASP culture: "in an odd way my tiny personal history has seemed to parallel the recent history of my country" (14). Robert F. Sayre has proposed that "American autobiographers have generally connected their own lives to the national life or to national ideas" (149), and this is true in a fundamental way of *No Laughing Matter,* whose author's overwhelming concern with public issues allowed her to conceal from herself her personal failures. Yet even though the autobiography is to a great extent the confession of those failures, Halsey does not confront the issues of gender that caused her isolation and frustration, and which tease beneath the surface of the text.

The success of *With Malice Toward Some* in 1938 brought Halsey the kind of money and celebrity undreamed of in her middle-class Yonkers childhood, where respectability rather than fame was the chief value in life, but it also confirmed in Halsey the sense of her own superiority that had been inculcated by her parents. As she writes, "One very happy part of my childhood was the comfortable awareness that there were people in the world who were not as good as I" (23); and having a best-selling book at the age of twenty-eight merely solidified her sense of self-importance:

Success does not implant bad characteristics in people. It merely steps up the growth rate of the bad characteristics they already had. I grew up in a household of four people who shared a dominating pattern of self-concern. When in my late twenties I suddenly revealed what looked like a considerable money-earning potential, that concern was echoed from the outside by almost everybody I came in contact with.

... My conscious objective ... was to be thought of as modest and unspoiled, but by "unspoiled" I meant always being courteous to waiters. (108)

By this time married to Henry Simon, brother of one of the founders of the Simon and Schuster publishing company, Halsey demonstrated her self-concern by having affairs with two men to whom she played Lady Bountiful, buying an airplane for one and paying for the psychoanalysis of the other. Her marriage ended soon thereafter.

What should have been the turning point in Halsey's life—similar to Franklin's discovery of Deism—was the awakening of her liberal political consciousness in the early 1940s. Shortly after the Japanese bombed Pearl Harbor in 1941, she began working as a volunteer at the Stage Door Canteen in New York. Having been earlier attuned to the concepts of liberal politics by some of her college professors and by a brief period spent working for Max Eastman, editor of the *Masses,* Halsey was appalled by the racism and anti-Semitism of many of the volunteers at the Canteen, which was one of the few in the country open to all servicemen regardless of racial or ethnic background. The germ of Halsey's second book, *Some of My Best Friends Are Soldiers* (1944), was overhearing a member of the canteen board of directors say, "As soon as I have time, I'm going to clean up this place and get rid of the Jews" (112). *Some of My Best Friends,* written in the form of a series of letters to a brother in the service, is a plea for ethnic and racial tolerance that has a witty if somewhat condescending tone; one section of the book, "A Memo to Junior Hostesses," was widely reprinted in books on American social problems during the 1940s, and the book was praised by opinion makers such as Eleanor Roosevelt and Walter Winchell.

The tone of moral superiority in *Some of My Best Friends,* while common in the writing of the newly converted, reflects Halsey's own sense of her importance as a crusader. As she acknowledges in her autobiography, "I thought I had written a Deathless Message which would eventually take its place in people's minds and hearts a little below the Gettysburg Address" (118). She found herself outraged that this second book did not have the resounding success of the first, and that it did not instantly change public attitudes about blacks and Jews:

I had always had a consuming need to get people to agree with me, and if they stubbornly adhered to what I considered their dangerously wrong opinions, I seethed with rage and despair. (119)

Halsey's political and social sensibilities had been almost entirely reversed from her parents' smug racism, but her sense of self-importance remained that of the WASP; what she terms "the Sealed Mind of the Halseys" had merely closed on another set of truths, without any change in her conviction of righteousness.

A similar pattern of conviction, moral outrage, and ultimate despair attended the remainder of Halsey's career as a social critic, from the 1940s through the 1960s. In *Color Blind* (1946) she again attacked racism; middle-class consumerism and complacency are the target of *The Folks at Home* (1952); and in *The Pseudo-Ethic* (1963) she pointed to the decline in public ethics that permitted the Alger Hiss-Whittaker Chambers debacle and the McCarthy era. In each case, she began with zeal to analyze what she believed were dominant flaws in American culture, and ended by being angry and hurt when she could see little effect of her work. One reason why Halsey's social criticism failed to produce the widespread changes in attitude for which she wished is that such books are seldom effective in galvanizing public opinion in America; we are far more apt to be shaken out of complacency by a war, a decline in the stock market, or the election (or assassination) of a popular president. But equally important is the fact that each time Halsey took up a cause, she was at least a decade in advance of widespread liberal sympathy for it. It was not until the civil rights movement of the 1950s and 1960s, for example, that the white American public became much concerned about racial prejudice and segregation; consumerism has only recently, with the media image of the "Yuppie," been generally seen as a social problem rather than the rewards of the "good life"; and it was not until Watergate that many Americans became convinced that their elected officials had been operating for decades on a different set of ethical principles from the one advocated publicly.

Thus, while Halsey's various critiques of American social problems were both probing and prescient, they failed to have the impact or achieve for her the stature that she desired. In fact, the only book Halsey wrote that came close to having the wide readership of *With Malice Toward Some* was her only other foray into humor. *This Demi-Paradise: A Westchester Diary*, published in 1960, is similar in many ways to other accounts of suburban domesticity of the period, such as Jean Kerr's *Please Don't Eat the Daisies* and Shirley Jackson's *Life among the Savages*. Even in *This Demi-Paradise*, Halsey's social consciousness is strikingly evident—one of the themes of the book is the far-reaching effect of Senator Joseph McCarthy's communist witch-hunts of the 1950s—but the book is essentially in the genre of postwar domestic humor, detailing a housewife's daily rounds with the PTA, Girl Scout cookies, shopping, cooking, and raising a daughter. And although such works characteristically embody a good deal of protest against the trivialization of women's lives in the middle-class, mid-century suburbs, they are nonetheless amusing accounts of relatively affluent people living relatively comfortable lives.

Yet the actual life that Halsey details in *No Laughing Matter* is starkly at variance with the cozy domesticity she describes in *This Demi-Paradise*. Frustrated by her apparent powerlessness in the public arena, at home with her husband and daughter Halsey became, as she describes herself, a "personal imperialist" and a "one-woman multinational" (14). After her marriage to Henry Simon ended, she married, in 1944, Joseph Bloch, a man eight years her junior who shortly thereafter was sent overseas by the army. Joseph's absence confronted Halsey with both her helplessness and her tendency to use other people:

Suddenly I had no one on whom to rely for the instant encouragement, praise and reassurance without which I seemed unable to function. As the poet says, I fell upon the thorns of life, I bled. I had always been spaciously ignorant of practical matters. I did not know how to return things to department stores, how to read a contract, whom to call when things broke down or how to put new batteries in a flashlight. And I hugged my ignorance. Tacitly, I blackmailed people into doing things for me by a highly conspicuous display of helplessness. (117)

Shortly thereafter, Halsey began an eleven-year bout with an ultimate helplessness to which women are especially susceptible: agoraphobia, the paralyzing fear of public places. Her first attack occurred the day after Franklin Roosevelt's death, as though the sudden absence of the national father figure had caused her sense of personal helplessness to coalesce into a numbing anxiety that kept her from leaving her own house. At the same time, she became heavily dependent on alcohol, an addiction that was made easier by the fact that Halsey had, as she describes it, "a tolerance for liquor that Bacchus himself might have envied and did not know the meaning of the word 'hangover'" (120). When Joseph returned from overseas in 1946, he found himself with a wife who, to the outside world, appeared to be a fearless social critic, but at home threw a tantrum when he bought her the wrong color belt, and drank herself to sleep every night.

Despite these problems, Margaret and Joseph adopted an infant girl— named Celia and called "Cora" in *This Demi-Paradise*—in 1948, and settled into an apparently tranquil life, with "family jokes, coziness, trust and even a pair of Siamese cats" (146). In 1950, they moved to the house in Westchester County, New York, that is the setting of *This Demi-Paradise,* and Halsey, like so many suburban women, settled into a domestic routine: "I made curtains and bedspreads, painted the kitchen and bathroom, planted bulbs, mowed the lawn and had people to dinner" (156). Yet the problems of the world outside this cozy domestic scene occupied the major part of Halsey's energy during the postwar years, and the failure of her articles and books to bring the nation to a kind of moral attention increased both her anger and her dependence. *The Folks at Home,* published years before a countercultural attack on American materialism became a reality, "dropped like a plummet into an abyss of silence" (166). When her books that emerged from true moral conviction were virtually ignored by the press, Halsey felt redoubled despair and outrage. In her autobiography, she reflects upon this circumstance in her characteristically self-mocking tone:

Confronted with such a rejection, what was the happy Protestant—the self-appointed guide to the Good, the True, and the Beautiful—going to do next? That was the problem. (167)

Halsey's feelings of failure and moral outrage intensified her agoraphobia to the point that she sometimes found it difficult to leave her bedroom in the morning, and her increased dependence on Scotch led to furious arguments with Joseph in which, she reports, "I ranged like a tigress over the vast landscape of my grievances" (171). Desperation ultimately drove her into the last of several experiences with psychoanalysis—this time with a woman therapist whose empathy with Halsey's phobic terror helped her to begin a long, slow process of recovery.

Just as Halsey began to shed her irrational fears, however, she became subject to some quite rational ones. Joseph McCarthy's investigations of communist activities were, for the majority of Americans, remote if chilling, but in 1954, after Halsey gave a speech on civil liberties sponsored by the League of Women Voters, the local newspaper launched a campaign to discredit her by associating her with allegedly communist groups. Although the furor over Halsey's supposed communist sympathies eventually died down, it had the one permanent effect of creating a rift between Margaret Halsey and her sister, Mary, that was never bridged. Having never shared Margaret's liberal social and political views, Mary became angry and perhaps frightened by the notion that her sister might be tainted by communist associations, and the sisters ceased communicating altogether at that point. A similarly irrevocable split between Halsey and her mother occurred two years later, not long after her father's death. The two women had always had an uneasy relationship, and Halsey reports that after an acrimonious exchange of letters, they had no further communication. In 1977, when *No Laughing Matter* was published, Halsey's mother was still living, in her nineties, but they had not seen or spoken to one another for more than twenty years.

With the exception of her husband and daughter, about whom she wrote in *This Demi-Paradise,* family matters continued to become increasingly secondary to national affairs in Halsey's life. Despite the failure of *The Folks at Home,* she had continued to write articles for liberal publications such as the *New Republic* and the *Progressive;* the focus of her reforming zeal in the late 1950s was the lack of ethical behavior among politicians

and other public figures. Halsey saw—beginning with the trial of Alger
Hiss in 1948, and intensifying through the McCarthy era and the early
presidency of Richard Nixon—the inexorable growth of what she termed
"the institutionalized lie," which would be the subject of her next book,
The Pseudo-Ethic, published in 1963. With her usual prescience, Halsey
posited what Watergate and the war in Vietnam would later confirm: that
Americans seemed willing to tolerate a less rigid standard of ethics for their
elected officials than that which they taught their children. *The Pseudo-
Ethic* turns, as do Halsey's other books of social criticism, on the premise
that conformity, competition, and the quest for wealth have contributed
to a sense of moral complacency that allows injustice, hypocrisy, and materialism to run rampant through American society.

Once again, Halsey's perceptions and warnings had far less impact than
she believed they deserved, but her disappointment was this time over-
shadowed by the ending of her marriage to Joseph and the discovery that
their daughter, Celia, had an apparently inoperable brain tumor. The two
events happened simultaneously, shortly after the family had moved from
New York to the Midwest. While Halsey fought Joseph's plans for divorce,
Celia slowly recovered and returned to art school in London, where Halsey eventually joined her, and where she lived when she wrote her autobiography. Having finally conquered her dependence on alcohol, Margaret
Halsey decided to take stock of her own life from the perspective of her
mid-sixties, and produced an autobiography that is at once a personal confession, a defense of sociopolitical liberalism, and a paradoxical chronicle
of a woman who, despite her efforts, never quite comes to terms with herself as a woman.

II

Margaret Halsey's *No Laughing Matter* is in many ways an anomaly in
American autobiography—and especially in American women's autobiography. Unlike such authors as Benjamin Franklin and Henry Adams, she
does not take pride in being a member of the dominant WASP culture;
indeed, she repudiates her heritage, feeling that what she terms the "Martin Luther-Cotton Mather syndrome" has been responsible for many of
America's social and political problems. Also, unlike many autobiographies
by women, Halsey's does not focus primarily on the personal, relational
aspects of life, but instead explores the interrelationship between national
events and values and the course of an individual life. As a woman, Halsey
does not present herself as isolated from the dominant culture, except insofar as the majority of Americans have not shared her liberal views. The

problems she describes come not from powerlessness, but instead from an excess of power, particularly in the domestic arena. Nor does she feel, as do many women who write from the cultural margins, cut off from the language of dominant discourse: the many allusions and quotations throughout *No Laughing Matter* testify to Halsey's sense of connection to the traditions of Western culture.

That Halsey views herself as a member of a group that no longer deserves its dominant position in American culture is clear from the first paragraph of her autobiography:

We have heard a great deal from Jewish writers about what it means to come from a Jewish background, but so far not much has been written about growing up WASP. For the ethnic minorities in the United States, the problem is to climb up; but for the WASPs—who were once, but are no longer, the dominant group in the culture —the problem is to climb down. (11)

By "dominant group," Halsey means not numerical force, but privilege and power; and she feels the WASPs must "climb down" because they have failed in their leadership role, not because they are being pushed aside by other groups. The issue for her is moral and ethical responsibility rather than a balance of power. The democratic experiment that Franklin regarded with so much optimism—and in which he was so potent a force, both politically and socially—has in Halsey's view failed in the twentieth century. The Judeo-Christian ethic of selflessness and service to which Franklin adhered—if somewhat self-importantly—has been overtaken by what she terms the "robber barons": business and military organizations whose overriding concern is the gross national product instead of public service and social responsibility. It is partly to analyze the process by which this has happened that Halsey writes her autobiography: "Whatever happens to the WASPs, they have deserved it; but it might be a mere matter of common sense to sift out of their streaky legacy whatever it contains of proven usefulness" (15).

By choosing to write of her own life as a means of investigating the downfall of WASP dominance, Halsey connects the private and the public, the personal and the national, in ways that are unusual in women's autobiography. In the autobiographical tradition, men have tended to concentrate on their lives in the public arena, often paying scant attention to their lives as husbands, fathers, and members of intimate social groupings. Conscious of having made some mark on the world—as authors, politicians, military leaders, or businessmen—male autobiographers commonly address their progress toward this goal, whether as insiders such as Franklin or outsiders such as Malcolm X. Wives, lovers, and children typically receive little attention in such autobiographies; these are public testimonials rather than private revelations. The focus of women's autobiographies is often quite the reverse, as Estelle Jelinek has pointed out:

Women's autobiographies rarely mirror the establishment history of their times. They emphasize to a much lesser extent the public aspects of their lives, the affairs of the world, or even their careers, and concentrate instead on their personal lives — domestic details, family difficulties, close friends, and expecially people who influenced them. (7–8)

Even women whose professional contributions and careers have been significant have tended to emphasize the personal, relational aspects of their lives rather than the development of their professional lives. Jelinek notes, for example, that neither Edith Wharton, in *A Backward Glance* (1934), nor Ellen Glasgow, in *The Woman Within* (1954), describes writing the novels for which she is known; and Margaret Mead, in *Blackberry Winter* (1972), skips over the twenty years during which she was professionally most active, choosing to focus on the raising of children as her central theme. There are, of course, a number of exceptions to Jelinek's generalization — among them, Jane Addams, Ida B. Wells, and Gertrude Stein, all of whom concentrate on their public roles rather than their personal lives. What sets Halsey's *No Laughing Matter* apart is its projection of an unresolved and largely unacknowledged tension between the two.

There may be many reasons for the frequent difference in focus in male and female autobiography, especially before the late twentieth century. One obvious reason is that the domestic and relational aspects of life have traditionally occupied a far greater role in most women's lives than in the lives of men, despite similar professional attainments. Another is that the achievement of professional status has for women frequently been attended by the struggle to balance public and private lives, so that the autobiography may be a record of that struggle or an attempt to assess its impact on the woman's professional activities. A case in point is *The Living of Charlotte Perkins Gilman* (1935), which focuses on the psychological and emotional obstacles that Gilman had to confront and overcome in order to work for social reform. Halsey's autobiography reverses this pattern by arguing for the primacy of her professional activities and analyzing the negative effects of this commitment on her personal relationships. Yet another reason may be that women writing in any genre have commonly written to and for other women, just as men have for men (Benjamin Franklin, after all, assumed he was a role model for his male, not his female, descendants), and sharing private experience addresses more directly the commonalities of women's lives than does the detailing of public success or failure. It is this last point that Jane Marcus makes in "The Private Selves of Public Women," using the Greek term *themis* to refer to the sense of community:

> The idea of themis as a structure of communal ritual that shapes the individual life to that of the community might be seen as the spirit of women's autobiographical discourse. The structure that insists on the reader's response and sets the writer in conversation with her own community is "common" and "mediocre" culture. Despite what men do in parliaments and on battlefields, it is the women writing their autobiographies, invincible in their "mediocrity," who make civilization. (141)

Halsey's *No Laughing Matter* differs markedly from the typical woman's autobiography in this respect: her career as a writer, and the national events and changes in values that inspired that career, are at least as important as her private life. Indeed, the two are presented as inseparable. Halsey quotes George Eliot, writing in *Felix Holt* that "there is no private life that is not determined by a wider public life" (151), and her own life, as presented in her autobiography, seems a perfect example. Not only does she announce as her purpose the analysis of a WASP upbringing as a key to failures in American values; the autobiography ends, not with the resolution of her personal and family problems, but with a further analysis of contemporary sociopolitical ills and an exhortation to her readers to maintain their integrity in the face of them. Toward the end of the last chapter, Halsey addresses the interrelationship between the private and public parts of her life:

> Does it all add up to anything? Was there any point or meaning to those many years of being the kind of wife and mother who scorns cake mixes—while at the same time struggling, as a writer, to make a point about political morality that was being expressed a little before its time? I can only say that the two seemingly disparate aspects of my life actually reinforced each other, all along the way. The comforts of intimacy and domesticity assuaged some of the loneliness of writing. (243)

In this, her "summing up" statement, Halsey posits the personal, domestic part of her life as a refuge from the isolation of her work.

Yet in light of the autobiography as a whole, such a statement seems disingenuous, for it was, as she repeatedly tells us, in her domestic relations that she was a selfish tyrant, while both her husbands adopted the nurturing, supportive—indeed wifelike—role. With Henry she was spoiled and unfaithful, and upon Joseph she inflicted egocentric tirades—one of which, against his mother, she later identifies as the crack that would widen to a gulf between them. What emerges in *No Laughing Matter* is the portrait of a woman unable to come to terms with the split between her public and private lives, coming of age in a period in which suburban domesticity—including the scorning of cake mixes—was touted as the ideal of

female fulfillment, and yet feeling compelled to adopt the public role of
writer and social critic, the frustrations of which she took out on her family in a vicious circle. One conversation with Joseph appears to the reader—
though not, apparently, to Halsey—to crystalize the syndrome. Coming
home from work one day when she was emerging from her agoraphobia,
Joseph remarked, "I've spent years holding your hand and giving you emotional support, and it suddenly came to me that you don't need it the way
you used to." He continued:

It came to me in a flash, just the other side of Scarsdale. If I don't accommodate
to your increased independence, you'll have to revert to dependence again, to preserve the marriage. Or else you'll eventually go off and find someone else to be
married to. (178–79)

Halsey reports this as a pleasant, even flattering statement, proof that "after
twelve years of marriage, one is being looked at with an eye unglazed by
habit" (179), but for the reader it underscores a pattern of co-dependence
in which Halsey's need for reassurance and Joseph's understanding and
strength were held in delicate—and dangerous—balance.

Yet as both her autobiography and her works of social criticism attest,
Halsey felt sincere conviction about the public issues she addressed. Her
experience on the Race Relations Committee of the Stage Door Canteen
during World War II convinced her that even though "the climate of the
times was so unenlightened that the Red Cross even segregated the blood
plasma" (124), public education about racism was both possible and necessary, and so she wrote *Color Blind,* addressing the fundamental absur-
dity of racial prejudice. "With the publication of *Color Blind,*" Halsey notes,
"I had completed a seemingly eccentric trajectory from entertainer to
reformer" (131). And a reformer she remained, although with less and less
success. *Color Blind* reached a great many people—among other things,
copies were ordered in great numbers by the NAACP—but her subsequent
books were far less successful, a fact that disturbed her because of both
the depth of her sociopolitical convictions and what the woman who once
interpreted her Rorschach test called her "towering egocentricity" (134).
The sense of righteousness that Halsey attributes to her WASP childhood
both impelled her fury at injustice and ignorance, and made her unable
to accept anything less than unqualified acceptance. Regarding the writing
of *Some of My Best Friends Are Soldiers,* which anticipated the theme of
Color Blind, Halsey describes the anxiety that many writers must feel, but
which for her was all-absorbing:

After you have put into a book what you have to put into it—have lived with the
prospect of exposing yourself in ways you do not even know of to uncaring strangers,
have forced the balky mind to take fences it does not want to take, . . . and have

brought your stomach back ten thousand times from that nadir to which it sinks when you contemplate your inadequacy—after you have done all that for a period of months or years, how can the result *not* be one of the world's great masterpieces? And what anguish when it is treated as something immeasurably lower! (118)

Halsey's burning desire to effect social reforms thus occupies a central position in her autobiography, overshadowing the personal, relational aspects of her life. Indeed, in contrast to the typical woman's autobiography, *No Laughing Matter* is a record more of personal isolation than of connectedness. Despite more than twenty years of marriage to Joseph Bloch and despite her obvious delight in her adopted daughter, Halsey's major reaction to these two central people in her life is a combination of guilt and anger. One senses that an important impetus for the writing of her autobiography was to atone for her treatment of her husband and her daughter. In spite of some scenes of domestic harmony similar to those in *This Demi-Paradise,* Halsey recalls primarily her tantrums and her late-night solitude with a bottle of Scotch. Only after Celia was an adult did she tell her mother how much the drinking had bothered her, and also acknowledged that she had always felt her mother to be somewhat distant and cold. "The coldness my daughter felt came from my self-concern— the primacy I automatically gave to my own concerns" (241). The most striking instance of this primacy occurred when Halsey turned her attention to her dissolving marriage while Celia—then nineteen—was recovering from brain surgery. What Halsey calls "the most shameful blot on my escutcheon" is the fact that she devoted all her emotional energy to fighting Joseph's desire for a divorce while Celia faced what at the time seemed certain death:

I took good care of her physical requirements, but she did not have my real attention. Blinded by egotistic fury at Joseph's astonishing rejection of me, I ministered to her wants punctiliously but mechanically, and the worst thing of all was that I even had fleeting seconds of being grateful for her illness, because if it came to the crunch vis-à-vis divorce, it really did put all the cards in my hands. (213)

By the end of her autobiography, Halsey and her daughter have reached an accommodation with each other, but Halsey warns against a "fairy-tale ending": "The essence of life is problem-solving; and my daughter and I will certainly continue, separately or together, to have problems" (243).

Except for her relationship with her daughter, Halsey does not seem to have had close relationships with any women. After she has finished describing her childhood, she does not mention her sister, Mary, except to tell of their permanent estrangement after 1954 because of differing social views and Halsey's alleged communist connections. Halsey's mother, to whom she refers as either the "Lady Prioress" or by her given name, Annie, is presented consistently as a cold woman with whom, especially after Halsey's father's death, she had a distant, painful relationship. After their parting of ways in 1956, Halsey says merely, "She is over ninety, and I have heard indirectly that she is in an old ladies' home, but where I do not know" (190). Such abrupt dismissal stands in sharp contrast to the mother-daughter identification or the search for meaning in the mother's life so common in women's autobiographies. Rather, it seems that Halsey identified primarily with men who served as father figures: her own father, Reinhold; President Roosevelt, whose death seemed to trigger her agoraphobia; and her two long-suffering husbands. Indeed, she remarks that her first psychoanalyst "talked Oedipus until the cows came home" (140). And it is striking that this woman who normally foresaw social movements at least a decade in advance seems to have paid little attention to the widespread discontent of women during the 1950s and 1960s. Only once does Halsey mention the women's movement, and she does so rather dismissively. Rationalizing her pursuit of social reforms despite its disruption of Celia's childhood, Halsey says, "I was aware that an embattled mother is not the ideal maternal type. Or, at least, was not so considered back in the days before we had Women's Lib" (178).

Indeed, despite the fact that Halsey repeatedly confesses her sins as a wife and mother, both the tone and the narrative of *No Laughing Matter* distance her from the intimacies of female experience. Sidonie Smith, in *A Poetics of Women's Autobiography*, has argued that women autobiographers have been acutely conscious that their lives will be judged by male eyes and standards:

Attuned to the ways women have been dressed up for public exposure, attuned also to the price women pay for public self-disclosure, the autobiographer reveals in her speaking posture and narrative structure her understanding of the possible readings she will receive from a public that has the power of her reputation in their hands. (49)

Having spent much of her adult life dependent upon the approbation of primarily male reviewers and policymakers, Halsey seems conscious throughout her autobiography of the public that will judge her. Even in her "confessional" statements she adopts a remote, ironic tone that serves to distance her from the personal force of the confession. Writing about her alcohol-inspired tirades to Joseph, for example, she claims for herself a depth of guilty candor greater than that found in most autobiographies:

Every self-respecting autobiography—and this one is no exception—has intermittent, fully orchestrated crescendos about How I Suffered! But the corollary—How I Made Others Suffer (no exclamation point)—is usually rendered in the softest of pianissimos. (171)

The tone of such passages is removed, coolly intellectual, rather than intimate, so that Halsey remains the public figure writing for a sophisticated audience rather than revealing a self in the throes of self-discovery.

Smith also points out that the female autobiographer is perforce adopting a male role in accepting the ideology of individual authority and force, claiming "the authority to write about herself in the fit of her life to stories of the representative man" (52). At the same time, Smith asserts, "she silences that part of herself that identifies her as a daughter of her mother" (53). This pattern infuses *No Laughing Matter* on the levels of both style and narrative. Halsey's detached analysis of her upbringing and subsequent relationships with her parents—epitomized in her references to them as Annie and Reinhold—is more sociological than personal, consonant with her purposes of demonstrating almost clinically the effects of a WASP upbringing. Even more telling is Halsey's allegiance to her father and her quite literal casting off of her mother and sister. The lack of warmth between Halsey and her mother, a pattern later repeated in Halsey's relationship with her own daughter, removes her further from a female-identified context.

Yet Margaret Halsey may unwittingly reveal more about the lives of middle-class WASP women in this century than do writers who more consciously explore their commonalities with other women. In what she says as well as what she does not say, and in the tone and style of *No Laughing Matter,* Halsey suggests some important truths of women's experience. To be a best-selling author in 1938 meant—far more than it does fifty years later—that most of one's peers were men; few women writers enjoyed that kind of success, even with books that were written for a popular audience. Also, raised in a patriarchal household—in which her father waited at the top of the stairs with a nightstick for her to return from dates—Halsey might well have sought the support and approbation of men rather than women, viewing them as the authority figures they in fact were. Equally understandable is Halsey's eagerness to excel as a housewife after she and Joseph moved to Westchester County. With women's magazines and advertisers adjuring women to perfect the nests where postwar healing and what was termed "normalcy" were to occur, Halsey, like so many other women, felt enormous pressure to succeed domestically. She recalls her perfectionism as a housekeeper, and her realization that she worked hard as a homemaker not to make life more comfortable for the family, but in response to the demands of what she terms the "Invisible Critic":

This Invisible Critic inhabited a corner of the room, up near the ceiling, and I unconsciously expected, whenever I had completed a task, to hear a loud, clear voice saying from the corner of the ceiling, "Margaret Halsey, that's the best goddamned mayonnaise that any woman has ever made." Of course, no such voice ever made itself heard, but I never gave up hope, and what chronic, unassuageable tension that unrecognized hope generated! (141)

The "unassuageable tension" to which Halsey refers is what Betty Friedan described as "the problem that has no name" in *The Feminine Mystique,* published in 1963. The fact that Halsey recognized that other suburban women shared her discontent is indicated when she quotes one of her neighbors as saying, "I'm lonely, and there aren't enough letters in the local paper saying that I'm a good mother" (163). But rather than identifying this discontent as specifically a women's problem, as did Friedan, Halsey turned her attention to national politics, publishing *The Pseudo-Ethic* in the same year as *The Feminine Mystique,* addressing problems originating in the "man's world" in which she wanted success, and in which the critics were quite visible.

Halsey's deference to and concurrent resentment of male authority are amply demonstrated in her reactions to criticism of her work and in her relationships with her husbands. Even the "Invisible Critic" who judged her homemaking skills seems somehow to have a male voice, and her rages at Joseph are emblematic of her anger at an establishment that failed to see her as the moral visionary that she felt herself to be. Alcoholism and agoraphobia also represent dependence and fear; they are the two "hidden" diseases women have suffered as a result of isolation and powerlessness. Although Halsey does not make this connection overtly, she does suggest that it was no accident that her agoraphobia began immediately after Franklin Roosevelt's death, and she ties her long nights with the Scotch bottle directly to her anxiety about her work, both professional and domestic.

A pervasive theme in *No Laughing Matter* is the difficulty of freeing oneself from the effects of childhood socialization. Halsey frequently uses the images of "claws" and "talons" to describe her parents' influence. As part of her effort to overcome agoraphobia, she kept a diary, "always with the purpose of bending back, a sixty-fourth of an inch at a time, the talons my parents had buried in me when I was a child" (141). The legacies of egotism and perfectionism proved difficult to reject, however, and when her daughter, as an adult, accused her of being a cold and distant parent, she realized that this had been her major criticism of her own mother—that she has repeated the parental pattern rather than reversed it. Indeed, insofar as the autobiography is an attempt to come to an understanding of the influences of her early life on her later behavior, Halsey is very much in the tradition of female autobiography. Estelle Jelinek posits that, typically, male autobiographers view "their childhoods as idylls of innocence and redemption and . . . their lives as heroic," whereas women tend to use autobiography to sort out the meanings of their lives:

What their life stories reveal is a self-consciousness and a need to sift through their lives for explanation and understanding. The autobiographical intention is often powered by the motive to convince readers of their self-worth, to clarify, to affirm, and to authenticate their self-image. (15)

The image that Halsey seems to want to affirm in *No Laughing Matter* is that of the penitent, the sinner who has confessed her guilt—guilt not only for being a WASP, but also for the feelings of personal superiority she derived from that heritage. It is in this sense that the book is a "confession." Stephen Spender has written of the confession that "no one confesses to meanness, cowardice, vanity, pettiness; or at least not unless he is assured that his crime, instead of excluding him from humanity, brings him back into the moral fold" (121). It is Halsey's dilemma that she wants to be taken "into the moral fold" at the same time that she indicts the entire WASP tradition that she represents.

III

Just a year before Margaret Halsey's *No Laughing Matter* was published, Maxine Hong Kingston published her autobiography, *The Woman Warrior: Memoirs of a Girlhood among Ghosts*. As a first-generation Chinese-American woman, Kingston is in most ways the obverse of Halsey. Instead of being a member of the dominant ethnic group, she belongs to a group that, as Halsey puts it, is trying to "climb up" in American society, a task made difficult by vast differences in language and cultural heritage. Whereas Halsey's is an insider's view of the damaging effects of WASP values, Kingston's is the outsider's awareness of exclusion. In contrast to Halsey's attempted rejection of the values of her upbringing—and her actual rejection of her mother—Kingston imaginatively explores her ancestors' lives, and focuses especially on her mother's past and present selves as a means of understanding herself. The silences that Kingston describes are those imposed by language and cultural barriers, gender, and family secrets; whereas Halsey, outspoken even in childhood, is silent in her omissions. Both Halsey and Kingston use humor as a narrative technique, but Halsey's style is determinedly intellectual and distanced, while Kingston's is frequently lyrical and impassioned. Although both narratives have as a central focus the experience of being female in twentieth-century America, Halsey's approach to this circumstance is oblique and ironic while Kingston's is direct and emotive. A brief counterpointing of these two very different autobiographies will further illuminate Halsey's immersion in WASP culture and her ultimate inability to repudiate it.

The "ghosts" of Kingston's subtitle are both her distant Chinese ancestors and those around her who are not Chinese-American: Japanese, blacks, and WASPs. Their ghostliness derives from the fact that in some real ways they are insubstantial. The ancestors, such as her disgraced aunt in China,

Kingston will never know, and so must recreate imaginatively in order to construct her own heritage; those other Americans who surround her are alien and potentially threatening, and so must be denied actual substance. In contrast to the solid, even desperate respectability of Halsey's childhood surroundings, the environment in which Kingston grew up was ambiguous: neither fully Chinese nor fully American, it required imagination rather than reason for the discovery of a self in context. Therefore *The Woman Warrior* is composed of fantasies and dreams rather than chronological narrative; its five sections range over time and space as Kingston attempts to integrate her family history with her personal history in order to locate herself. Unlike Halsey, who knows quite well the origins and meanings of her family's values, Kingston must reconcile her family's life in China with their partially Americanized life in California, living among the ghosts of both past and present.

Especially problematic for both writers is their relationship with their mothers, though for vastly different reasons. For Halsey, Annie—the "ersatz Lady Prioress"—represents the repressive puritanism of those who cling to a sense of WASP superiority: "My mother wanted everybody to think that our household was one of unimpeachable dignity, where all human passion was completely under control" (19). One of her ways of trying to maintain this facade was to close the windows during family arguments so that the neighbors could not hear. Naturally in such a household, Halsey and her sister were told nothing about sexuality, and it was not until she began college that she found (in the Skidmore library) a pamphlet explaining sexual intercourse. Despite her mother's coldness, Halsey spent years defending her and blaming her father for the atmosphere of the household because of his frequent rages. Only with the assistance of her second husband, Joseph, did she begin to see her father as a person of sincere moral conviction as opposed to her mother's selfish hypocrisy. Yet one of the silences of *No Laughing Matter* is Halsey's failure to explore the relationship between her own cool behavior toward her daughter and her tendency toward moral outrage and her parents' tenacious grip on WASP respectability. Instead of trying to understand the significance of the relationship with her mother, Halsey merely reports its conclusion when she was in her forties.

Silence of a very different kind opens *The Woman Warrior*, as Kingston's mother warns, "You must not tell anyone what I am about to tell you," before divulging the story of her illicitly pregnant aunt drowning herself in the family well (3). But rather than being repressive, the story liberates Kingston's imagination, so that she recreates the life of her aunt in China as a way of mediating between East and West. Even more liberating is her mother's "talk-story" of Fa Mu Lan, which allows Kingston to imagine herself as the "woman warrior" of the title rather than a worthless female. Constantly trying to reconcile female heroism and power with her immigrant family's denigration of girls—a common family saying is, "Better to feed geese than girls"—Kingston must also deal with her mother's former life as a doctor in China and her current life as a subdued, dutiful wife. The mother's name—Brave Orchid—and her heroism in China are at odds with the cowed immigrant woman, and a central issue in The Woman Warrior is Kingston's struggle to discover what being a Chinese-American woman means for her own identity. At the end of the "White Tigers" section of the book, Kingston acknowledges that the only solution has been to remove herself from her family:

I live now where there are Chinese and Japanese, but no emigrants from my own village looking at me as if I had failed them. . . . When I visit the family now, I wrap my American successes around me like a private shawl; I am worthy of eating the food. From afar I can believe my family loves me fundamentally. . . . I refuse to shy my way anymore through our Chinatown, which tasks me with the old sayings and the stories. (62)

Yet despite her decision to become Americanized, Kingston works constantly toward understanding and integrating her mother's Chinese heritage, and she finally accomplishes this in the final section of The Woman Warrior, "A Song for a Barbarian Reed Pipe," when she completes a story of her grandmother that her mother has begun: "The beginning is hers, the ending, mine" (240).

Kingston consciously and deliberately carries on her Chinese cultural heritage; Halsey attempts, but fails, to break with her WASP background. Although she rejected intellectually her parents' narrow, conservative views, she spent much of her life espousing more liberal values with a similar intolerance and sense of superiority. In her personal relationships she repeated the pattern of her parents, all the while congratulating herself on her freedom from them. The "Invisible Critic" hovered over not just her housework, but every facet of her life, leaving her with a residue of guilt about her imperfections, and one senses that an important motive for writing her autobiography was to confess that guilt. Toward the end of No Laughing Matter Halsey comments on the writing of autobiography:

It would seem as if nothing could be easier to write than autobiography. You just sit down and tell what happened, starting at the beginning and proceeding to the end. In reality, however, one is balanced on a knife edge all the time between being cursory and/or evasive on the one hand or long-windedly self-important on the other. (222)

There is too much apparent candor in No Laughing Matter for Halsey to be accused of evasion, and the very sin that she confesses most often is self-importance. As a child, she describes herself as "smug and pious" (34); as a young woman, "Most Self-Absorbed Girl on the Eastern Seaboard" (73); at the time Joseph left her, she notes that she had always felt herself to be "too special and privileged a person to have to share in the common human experience of forlornness" (223).

The dominant impression with which *No Laughing Matter* leaves the reader is an intense solitude and isolation, and in a curious way this may be what makes the autobiography so essentially American, and links it to Franklin's *Autobiography* after all. One of the central traditions of WASP culture since the eighteenth century is a belief in human perfectibility, which is an essentially lonely enterprise. Franklin reports a modest success, quite proudly; Halsey—perhaps unwittingly—exposes the dangers inherent in the very concept. Wendy Lesser, distinguishing between English and American autobiographies, points to the fact that "the American's audience is either so vast as to be impersonal, or else nonexistent":

Whereas the English autobiographer is present in our living room, quietly conversing with us in normal tones, the American is either up in the pulpit shouting at us or secluded in his study, reluctantly permitting us to look over his shoulder. We are not an important presence in his work; *he* is the occasion for the conversation, and we are mere accidental recipients. (26)

Margaret Halsey spends much of her time in the pulpit, speaking from a position of moral dominance that renders her isolated. *No Laughing Matter,* like Halsey's other books, anticipated trends in social thought by recognizing the need for a radical critique of the dominant culture and its ideologies—with the striking exception of that culture's construction of women. Unlike Kingston, who sees herself as belonging to a long if sometimes uncomfortable Chinese tradition, Halsey represents the dilemma of the once-dominant, who, in "climbing down," may find they have nowhere to go.

WORKS CITED

Halsey, Margaret. *With Malice Toward Some.* New York: Simon and Schuster, 1938.

Halsey, Margaret. *Some of My Best Friends Are Soldiers.* New York: Simon and Schuster, 1944.

Halsey, Margaret. *Color Blind: A White Woman Looks at the Negro.* New York: Simon and Schuster, 1946. 2d ed. with an epilogue by the author and introd. by Whitney M. Young, Jr. New York: Mcgraw-Hill, [1965].

Halsey, Margaret. *The Folks at Home.* New York: Simon and Schuster, 1952.

Halsey, Margaret. *The Pseudo-Ethic: A Speculation on American Politics and Morals.* New York: Simon and Schuster, 1963.

Halsey, Margaret. *No Laughing Matter: The Autobiography of a WASP.* Philadelphia: Lippincott, 1977.

Jelinek, Estelle C. Introduction to *Women's Autobiography: Essays in Criticism.* Bloomington: Indiana University Press, 1980.

Kingston, Maxine Hong. *The Woman Warrior: Memoirs of a Girlhood among Ghosts.* 1976; New York: Vintage, 1977.

Lesser, Wendy. "Autobiography and the 'I' of the Beholder." *New York Times Book Review,* November 27, 1988.

Marcus, Jane. "The Private Selves of Public Women." In *The Private Self: Theory and Practice of Women's Autobiographical Writings,* ed. Shari Benstock, 114–46. Chapel Hill: University of North Carolina Press, 1988.

Sayre, Robert F. "Autobiography and the Making of America." In *Autobiography: Essays Theoretical and Critical,* ed. James Olney, 146–68. Princeton: Princeton University Press, 1980.

Smith, Sidonie. *A Poetics of Women's Autobiography: Marginality and the Fictions of Self-Representation.* Bloomington: Indiana University Press, 1987.

Spender, Stephen. "Confessions and Autobiography." In *Autobiography: Essays Theoretical and Critical,* ed. James Olney, 115–22. Princeton: Princeton University Press, 1980.

CHAPTER 12

The Tradition of Chinese American Women's Life Stories: Thematics of Race and Gender in Jade Snow Wong's Fifth Chinese Daughter *and* Maxine Hong Kingston's The Woman Warrior

SHIRLEY GEOK-LIN LIM

My essay attempts to recover the tradition of "lifestory" behind Chinese American women's writing, and to read these works in the light of ideas raised in feminist critical theory. The latter project is made more urgent because of a history of male misreadings which have deliberately excoriated the divided consciousnesses in these texts. In 1974, the Asian American editors of *Aiiieeeee!* abandoned the "objective," aesthetic approach and insisted on a politically charged interpretation of Asian American literature. In the introduction to their influential anthology, these editors, all male, criticize Chinese American women writers such as Jade Snow Wong for reinforcing "the stereotypically unmanly nature of Chinese Americans (xxxi)" and, more seriously, for subscribing to the psychological notion of divided or dual identities (xxiv–xxv).[1] Throughout their critical introduction, Frank Chin, Jeffery Paul Chan, Lawson Fusao Inada, and Shawn Wong address the writer (except where speaking of specific women writers) as male. In their final page they list Asian American writers canonized in death or still active in struggle; they name thirteen writers, all male.

They base their poetics of Asian American writing on a unitary construction of male identity:

Language is the medium of culture and the people's sensibility, including the style of manhood. . . . On the simplest level, a man in any culture speaks for himself. Without a language of his own, he is no longer a man. The concept of the dual personality deprives the Chinese-American and the Japanese-American of the means to develop their own terms. (xlviii)

To argue a theory of language on a single concept of "manhood"—as if "manhood" were a hard and certain construction by which all writing is measured—is, to my mind, to willfully misread all writing, especially women's writing. Redressing the imbalance, a feminist reading would include women writers and privilege interpretation of ambiguities and fluid boundaries in writing and in the subject constituted in the writing.

To the *Aiiieeeee!* critics, "the subject matter of minority literature is social history. . . . There is no reference, no standard of measurement, no criterion to evaluate these [Asian American] works" (xxxv). Their narrowly sociological approach denies the possibility of locating Asian American texts in a system of language/cultural achievements, even the possibility of reading these texts in a particular Asian American literary tradition. Their highest praise is reserved for John Okada's novel *No-No Boy,* which they isolate from any other textual productions, under the claim that "Okada's novel invented Japanese-American fiction full-blown, was self-begotten, arrogantly inventing its own criteria" (xxxv).

My essay, on the other hand, will attempt to sketch a tradition of Chinese American women's lifestories, which extends back to the early twentieth century and includes Maxine Hong Kingston's *The Woman Warrior.*[2] Our recognition of these Chinese American women's texts, particularly in the light of an established tradition, cannot simply be contained in reading them as sociohistorical documents. In taking a body of communal stories (the Chinatown family, legends, myths, and talk-stories) and rewriting these old narratives into new texts, books such as *The Woman Warrior* challenge us to read them as "over-written" texts in which the written language figures as significantly as, if not more than, the subject matter. Especially with *The Woman Warrior,* the blurring of boundaries between fact and fiction, history and myth, personal story and public document, poetry and prose, casts doubt rightfully on attempts to present it as accurate Chinese American social history.[3] Kingston uses the term "talk-stories" frequently in her book to refer to the oral tradition of narratives which she transforms into written text. The term itself is a common idiom drawn from Cantonese to signify any kind of oral tale, whether personal, familial, communal, or historical.[4] Of course, in a larger context, these women's autobiographies form part of that fundamental American literary subgenre, the immigrant and ethnic autobiography. As Holte notes, "the American question is a question of self, and the autobiography is a central part of the

American literary tradition" (25). Chiefly, this essay will attempt to read Jade Snow Wong's *Fifth Chinese Daughter* and Kingston's *The Woman Warrior* in the tradition of Chinese American women's lifestories.

The tradition of Chinese American women writing lifestories is "short and partial" (Virginia Woolf's words in another broader context of women's writing), but it is nonetheless certain and existent. In the totality of writing, both prose and poetry, produced by Chinese American women, lifestories and autobiographies are present in number and in emphasis.[5] The presence of these texts is even more remarkable in the face of the linguistic and sociopolitical restraints historically placed on Chinese American women for most of whom English was a foreign language and whose numbers were exceedingly small. While the first Asians to come to America in large numbers were Chinese who worked in the California gold fields and on the Central Railroad in the 1850s and 1860s, they came without their women, and the Chinese Exclusion Act of 1882 made it even more difficult for the women to come. It was not until the exclusion laws were repealed in 1943 that Chinese wives and their children entered the United States in any number. Moreover, a series of laws passed between 1878 and 1922 prohibited intermarriage between Asians and whites and denied citizenship to Chinese and Japanese. This legislation kept Chinese American women as well as men socially in the underclass, a position in which writing and publishing were not generally available cultural productions. The early autobiographies written in English were by Chinese women who had immigrated to the United States, and reflected the relative and absolute privileged positions of these first-generation Chinese American women authors who had received sufficient education to achieve a command of the language and whose lives were supposed by mainstream publishing houses to hold a high interest for their chiefly white American audience.[6]

An example of "autobiography" produced under these circumstances is Anna Chennault's *A Thousand Springs*. Chennault's book contains one chapter on her life in China before she met the charismatic American general who organized the air resistance against both the Japanese and the communist forces in China in the 1930s and 1940s. Chennault's organization of her materials clearly shows a privileging of the American general over her self. Her self-portrait is dimmed by the presence of the white male whose adventures and exploits are foregrounded, so that the book becomes actually a biography of a white male under the guise of an interracial love story.

This autobiographical side step, in deference to subjects believed more significant than and overshadowing the autobiographer's life, is still evident today, as in the recent publication of Cynthia Chou's book, *My Life in the United States*. Chou's lifestory is, in effect, a series of essays on cross-cultural intersections between Americans and Chinese. It presents to the uninformed reader the conventional insider's knowledge of her ethnic culture with the added humoristic theme of the outsider/rube assimilating into the national culture. Structurally, it follows the classic paradigm of the immigrant story, looking back to the values of the Old World while sifting through the New World's myriad bewildering experiences. What makes it both charming and offensive are the many anecdotes offered as testimony to the ignorant and admiring immigrant's assimilation in her adopted culture; for example, Chou's initial rapture with and hoarding of toilet paper or her enthusiasm for automat dining. The accounts of her naive fascination with American technological culture are humorous precisely because they play up to the assumed superiority of this technology in the childish or primitive mind of the immigrant. A disturbing question deepens as the volume predictably progresses through Chou's gradual assimilation and success in the United States. What kinds of larger cultural attitudes and ideologies does this autobiography support and why would it be published when so much more serious Asian American writing is being produced?

Chou's autobiography should be read as yet another of the many volumes written and published by parties who wish to present an uncritical and much varnished global portrayal of twentieth-century American superiority. Chou's new chauvinism is naively and charmingly explicit, but it is chauvinism nonetheless: "I sensed that the idea of the British English being superior and the American expression being inferior is certainly out-of-date. . . . Although there has never been such an activity like 'a culture contest' in international affairs, there is an inclination and consequences of such a culture contest among all nations. . . . No doubt, the most influential culture at the time would be the winner. China was the winner in the past and the United States is the winner in the present world" (112–13). Chou adds, "Utopia can be built only by natural elements. It seems to me that Americanization is the chief element among the natural elements. Of course, Americanization is not involved in the foreign policy of the United States. If it was, it would become the so-called 'American Imperialism.' I have not found that the foreign policy of the United States involves Americanization" (113). With such statements, a reader may well question if Chou's Chinese American volume was published as "autobiography" or as American propaganda.

Judy Yung's *Chinese Women of America: A Pictorial History* forms a useful corrective to Chou's pseudo-lifestory. Although not an autobiography, the 135 images of Chinese American women collected in this history, from 1834 to the 1980s, provide an essential visual and documentary dimension to the literature. More than the portrait gallery of exceptional

Chinese American professional women, the photos and accompanying stories of Chinese American pioneer women, prostitutes, and nightclub performers in Wyoming, Idaho, California, and Alaska (17–29) remind us that Chinese American women share a common gender and class history with other American women.

The best-known of Chinese American women's lifestories, Maxine Hong Kingston's *The Woman Warrior: Memoirs of a Chinese-American Girlhood among Ghosts,* has had many serious antecedents. Kingston's portrayals of nourishing/constricting family ties, conflicts between Chinese customs and American culture, and differences in ways of talking, thinking, and experiencing between the immigrant Chinese and Americans are unlike Chou's cultural caricatures, and echo well-worked materials in many texts. Jade Snow Wong covered similar cultural materials in *Fifth Chinese Daughter* and *No Chinese Stranger;* Virginia Lee in her novel *The House That Tai Ming Built* attempted something of the same. Many novels, such as Diana Chang's *The Frontiers of Love* and Amy Tan's *The Joy Luck Club,* are also partly autobiographical.

In the tradition of Chinese American lifestories, *Fifth Chinese Daughter* would be considered the mother text to *Woman Warrior.* In fact, in a recent interview with Angeles Carabi, when she was asked about her literary tradition, Kingston replied, "I am not sure that I got help from a former generation of Chinese-American writers except for Jade Snow Wong: actually her book was the only available one" (11). Yet, on first appearance, *Fifth Chinese Daughter* seems to be the antithesis of Kingston's book.[7] Wong explains in an author's note that her use of the third person is a racial and ideological choice: "Even written in English, an 'I' book by a Chinese would seem outrageously immodest to anyone raised in the spirit of Chinese propriety" (vii). Significantly, Wong's second book, *No Chinese Stranger,* is written in two parts; in part 1, "To the Great Person of Father," the author again addresses herself in the third person. Part 1 ends with the literal and figurative death of the patriarch: "At thirty-six, she could no longer turn to him as head of their clan, a source of wise counsel, philosophical strength, a handy Chinese reference" (149). Part 2, consequently, is titled "First Person Singular," when, after the father's death, the narrator/author is able finally to take on her full subjectivity, and speak (write) in (as) the first person. In *The Woman Warrior,* the narrator first-person is foregrounded, and the voices of female rebellion, impatience, anger, and assertiveness produce the figures of female outlaws, warriors, shamans, and storytellers. The ideological choice of speaking as a Chinese or as an American is also reflected in the authors' choices of pen names. Jade Snow Wong chose an Anglicized translation of her Chinese name, while Maxine Hong, married to an Anglo-American, adopted her Anglo husband's name. *Fifth Chinese*

Daughter would appear therefore to be a Chinese text, where Kingston's flamboyant use of the first person would make *The Woman Warrior* an American text.

Both books, however, treat the knotted theme of race, made even more difficult by the threat of male, legalistic power and shame over female sexuality. In the first chapter of *Fifth Chinese Daughter,* the putative Chinese narrator shows the gap between "Chinese" life and reality: "life was a constant puzzle. No one ever troubled to explain. Only through punishment did she learn that what was proper was right and what was improper was wrong" (3). This "constant puzzle," the struggle between Chinese silence and "propriety" and the daughter's desire to understand and to be free of patriarchal law, is also the knot in Kingston's memoirs: "Even the good things are unspeakable, so how could I ask about deformities? . . . Never explaining. How can the Chinese keep any traditions at all? . . . You figure out what you got hit for and don't do it again if you figured correctly" (185). Kingston, unlike Wong, goes further in decoding this mystery of cultural silence:

I don't see how they kept up a continuous culture for five thousand years. Maybe they didn't; maybe everyone makes it up as they go along. If we had to depend on being told, we'd have no religion, no babies, no menstruation (sex, of course, unspeakable), no death. (185)

What allows Kingston the latitude in furthering her critique of Chinese American silence and law is her positioning of the narrator. A first-person narrator who is able to move through all the personal pronouns (I, they, everyone, we) permits no distance between herself and her cultural materials, no matter how puzzling and alien. Alice Jardine in her book *Gynesis* points to this complex question of the speaking subject, now that "Lacanian psychoanalysis and Nietzschean and neo-Heideggerian philosophies in France have torn this concept apart" (58). "First, the 'I' and the 'we' have been utterly confused; the 'I' is several, psychoanalysis has shown; and, further, one of the major ruses of Western metaphysics' violence has been the appropriation of a 'we' by an imperialistic if imaginary 'I' (a whole individual with an interior and exterior, etc.)" (54). In *The Woman Warrior,* plural and shifting pronouns create a constant stream of narrator's "subjectivities" in which everything is transformed, "digested" by an omnivorous and multiple subject.

Wong, on the other hand, separates the author/narrator from the daughter/subject, so that the book's "constant puzzle" is presented at a distance, as an object. A relentless linearity parallels the chronological life of the "protoganist's" twenty-four years. The racial puzzles are framed, constrained, and contained in narrative chronology, and admission of rebellion is more often repressed than expressed. The conclusion to chapter 2 demonstrates Wong's muting of consciousness of racial splitting: "she was now conscious that 'foreign' American ways were not only generally and vaguely different from their Chinese ways, but that they were specifically different, and the specific differences would involve a choice of action" (21). Ironically, the passage treats "specificity," the "specific differences," in the most general terms. The objective author/narrator, describing the (auto)-biographical subject, represses the very subjectivity of the subject, objectifies it into a distant third-person protagonist. Thus, the new "consciousness" of specific splittings, so crucial to the story of Jade Snow's early life, is muted and distanced in Wong's memoir; the reader is merely informed, "the comparison made her uncomfortable" (21). "Specific differences" are elided into a "comparison"; the "new consciousness" of race difference becomes only an "un-comfort."

Yet it is this very "un-comfort" that forms the motive behind the narrative. It is most displayed in the relation between father and daughter. Wong narrates at many points the quarrel between a patriarchal Confucian system and an American "unfilial theory" (128). "'Oh, Mama!' Jade Snow retorted. 'This is America, not China. . . . Both of you should understand that I am growing up to be a woman in a society greatly different from the one you knew in China. . . . You must give me the freedom to find some answers for myself'" (129). To the daughter's American ethos of individual freedom the father poses the irreducible reality of race and origin: "Your skin is yellow. Your features are forever Chinese. . . . Do not try to force foreign ideas into my home" (130). The division between father and daughter falls along a crack between Chinese and American, oppression and freedom, patriarchy and female autonomy, home and outside, past and present. Wong's choice of an objective narrator and objectification of subjectivity in a third-person protagonist make it easier to read her book as a simple chronology built on two polarities, the second subverting and eventually defeating the first. And at some level this is an accurate reading of the author's structuring of elements.[8]

Fifth Chinese Daughter is a book about daughters and fathers. The patriarchal Confucian ethos (Chinese propriety) which led to Wong's choice of the narrative third person rules the text in indelible ways beyond the surface of progressive polarities. "But while the open rebellion gave Jade Snow a measure of freedom she had not had before, and an outer show of assurance, she was deeply troubled within. . . . No matter how critical she was of [her parents], she could not discard all they stood for and accept as a substitute the philosphy of the foreigners" (130). The daughter's rebellion would extend only to the point where the father is compelled to accept her "value," an acceptance which already subverts a major Confucian tenet, that women are unworthy of respect. Through her successes and prizes, the daughter is an individual example of the exceptional Asian woman, an example made possible only through living in American society; and her achievements finally wring from the patriarch a concession on the rights of women.

Paradoxically, the daughter's rebellion results from and in her desire to win the father's approval. The narrator is careful to qualify each point where the daughter struggles and succeeds in vanquishing her father, indicating the tremendous ambivalence surrounding the struggle. For example, when she graduates from Mills College, the narrator tells the reader, "in her moment of triumph, she could find no sense of conquest or superiority. . . . she could feel no resentment against . . . Daddy, who wanted so much to record a picture of her" (181). Authorial anxiety is evident in the attempt to conceal and negate feelings of superiority and resentment. Indeed the daughter would be forgiven a sense of conquest over her father at this point, a father who consistently refused to support her education and who belittled her abilities at every point, who rejected her when she would not accept his definition of her as valueless. But the language works to conceal the daughter's desire to vanquish the father and to prove her superiority here (as it does throughout the book), pointing to an extreme ambiguity and anxiety rising from the vacillation between two contradictory cultural poles. The narrator's choice of position — "for her there had to be a middle way" (131) — can be sustained only by such acknowledged denials and unacknowledged ambiguities and silences.

Where *Fifth Chinese Daughter* is linear and chronological, *The Woman Warrior* is nonlinear, nonchronological, dealing with multiple time planes (personal, family and social history, myth) which flow in unstructured circularities.[9] *Fifth Chinese Daughter* maps the daughter's story in binary oppositions; *The Woman Warrior* inscribes a female subject which is itself multiply conflictual. In the passage from *The Woman Warrior* previously cited, the first-person point of view shifts from "I" to "they" (the Chinese), then to "everyone/they" (the not-I) before concluding as "we" (I/the Chinese/everyone). These shifts in point of view underlie the instability of authorial and narrator identity and tell the hidden story, of ambivalent, ambiguous, multiple presences in a text of multicultures and amicultures.[10]

It is precisely silences, ambiguities, and anxieties such as these that the first-person narrator acknowledges in *Woman Warrior*. Like its predecessor, *The Woman Warrior* is a daughterly text, bypassing the father's position, and inscribing in its place a woman's text. It concerns chiefly stories about daughters and mothers, about recovering lost matrilineal genealogies. Kingston's book opens with the mother's words, words which request female silence, express female shame, describe a patriarchal world of punitive law against female outlaws and outcasts, and paradoxically instruct the listening daughter on the presence of the lost or invisible female ancestor. "You must not tell anyone," my mother said, "what I am about to tell you. In China your father had a sister who killed herself" (3). This aunt of unlawful sexuality and shameful suicide is the negative model the mother holds up in order to compel her daughter into compliance with patriarchal constraints on female psychosexual behavior: "Don't let your father know I told you. He denies her. Now that you've started to menstruate, what happened to her could happen to you. Don't humiliate us. You wouldn't like to be forgotten as if you had never been born" (5). Still, the mother's legalistic injunctions are themselves illicit; she is herself breaking the rule of silence and keeping alive the memory of someone "forgotten" as if she had never been born, the fate of women in a patrilineal society. The narrator's role in maintaining this outlawed memory, continuing the mother's defiance against the paternal injunction on silence, is also deeply ironic. For, in writing the mother's story, she is both subordinate to and repudiating the mother's request for silence.

The narrator is aware of the mother's ambiguous position as an enforcer of the patrilineal family's rules. "Whenever she had to warn us about life, my mother told stories that ran like this one, a story to grow up on. She tested our strength to establish realities. . . . Those of us in the first American generations have had to figure out how the invisible world the emigrants built around our childhoods fit in solid America" (5). The warning story is also a story "to grow up on"; seeming to enforce female compliance and obedience, it actually "tested strength." Telling of "forgotten as if . . . never born" ghosts, it in fact establishes realities. This opening talk-story contains all the paradoxical elements of the maternal discourse which overflows in the book. The "mother who marked your growing with stories" constructs and subverts the oppressive realities which are peculiar to this particular girlhood.

Kingston ties the maternal discourse, powerfully unsettling in its instabilities of message, hypnotic in its relish for earthy details, to the Chinese emigrant culture.

The emigrants confused the gods by diverting their curses, misleading them with crooked streets and false names. They must try to confuse their offspring as well, who, I suppose, threaten them in similar ways—always trying to get things straight, always trying to name the unspeakable. The Chinese I know hide their names; sojourners take new names when their lives change and guard their real names with silence (5).

Chinese sojourners in America, like Chinese women in a patriarchal system, use deception, invisibility, and silence to protect themselves. "Their real names," the reality of their cultural selves, are hidden and muted, and they take "new" and "false" names in order to confuse and divert the powerful gods. To Chinese sojourners, their children, first-generation Americans, are also powerful gods to whom they cannot reveal their true cultural beings, their "real names."

What marks Kingston's memoirs as literary is the way in which "naming" or language figures in her work to deconstruct and deny any single reality of Chinese American female identity. What marks it as feminist is its persistent constructions and reproductions of female identity, the continuous namings of female presences, characters, heroines, and figures. No Name Woman is the first of these figures (and behind No Name Woman the storyteller/mother), a victim valorized by the narrator as hero. In this first narrative act, the narrator's self-conscious "writing" is presented as a rescue of the ancestor from the punishment of silence. No Name Woman's name is itself an oxymoron. She has no name, but the narrator in naming her No Name Woman has given her a name. No Name Woman's identity is that of lack, her presence inscribed in her absence. No Name Woman is a figure for woman as that which is displaced by man and from man, a gap in the his-storical memory. But the act of writing is itself not unambiguous; the rescue into memory through writing is after all a testimony to No Name Woman's sins, and the opening chapter closes on the instability of the writer's position in the feminist project of reclaiming a matrilineal genealogy: "My aunt haunts me—her ghost drawn to me because now, after fifty years of neglect, I alone devote pages of paper to her. . . . I do not think she always means me well. I am telling on her" (16).

The ambivalence of relationship between writer and ancestor echoes the ambivalences between narrator/daughter and mother. The maternal discourse informs the daughter, producing such strong female figures as the swordswoman, Fa Mu Lan: "When we Chinese girls listened to the adults talking-story, we learned that we failed if we grew up to be but wives or slaves. We could be heroines, swordswomen" (19). Or the figure of the shaman, the mother as midwife and healer. But it also deforms the daughter: "My mother has given me pictures to dream—nightmare babies that recur, shrinking again and again to fit in my palm" (86). The discourse is disturbingly female, of "nightmare babies," and it is also racial: "To make my waking life American-normal, I turn on the lights before anything untoward makes an appearance. I push the deformed into my dreams, which are in Chinese, the language of impossible stories" (87). Race and gender intersect in the daughter's response to her Chinese mother's talk-stories, as do form and deformity, language and dream, American and Chinese. Chinese is "the language of impossible stories," impossible because the dreams are nightmares, because the language is Chinese in an "American-normal" life, and because the reality of that dream-Chinese language is denied (as No Name Woman was denied) in the American-normal waking life. The mother's talk-stories are in Chinese (Cantonese), and the narrator, head stuffed "like the suitcases which they jampack with homemade underwear," is engaged in the project of disburdening herself of them. As with No Name Woman, the narrator is "telling" on her mother who "does not always mean me well."

The narrator's self-consciousness about her writing (storytelling) is a consistent thread in the book which she picks up in various metaphors. One figure is that of the forbidden stitch, that knot of embroidery so fine that in sewing it thousands of embroiderers reputedly lost their sight. The narrator claims: "There was one knot so complicated that it blinded the knotmaker. Finally an emperor outlawed this cruel knot, and the nobles could not order it anymore. If I had lived in China, I would have been an outlaw knotmaker" (163). The knot is what the narrator makes, a figure so tightly and complexly interwoven that its making leads to blindness. The metaphor of the knot covers the making of the mother/daughter relationship in the text, a figure so tightly and complexly tied that the greatest skill will be needed to unknot it. In China the knots were made into buttons, frogs (fasteners), and bellpulls, figures of joining, tying, connection, and sound. The metaphor of the knot leads to the story of the mother cutting the daughter's tongue. The image is of silencing, but it is actually the frenum the mother cuts "so that you would not be tongue-tied" (164). The mother cuts the knot so the daughter can speak, in a figure which paradoxically conveys both silencing and speech; the daughter's desire is to be a knotmaker, a figure for art and affiliation. The daughter's empowerment by maternal action and discourse is expressed in these series of figures, together with the powerful ambivalences of response that these figures produce: "Sometimes I felt very proud that my mother committed such a powerful act upon me. At other times I was terrified. . . . 'Did it hurt me? Did I cry and bleed?'" (164). The mother is informing and deforming power; the reinscribing of maternal talk-stories, of oral into written speech, is the daughter's act of appropriating the power of the maternal discourse for herself.

The book closes with the story of Ts'ai Yen, a Chinese poetess captured by barbarians for twelve years, whose "children did not speak Chinese" but who "imitated her with senseless sing-song words and laughed" (208). Finally moved by the beauty of the barbarians' flute music, she sang "a song so high and clear, it matched the flutes" (209). In this tale of racial reconciliation and harmony through the power of art, the two languages of Chinese and barbarian coexist: "Her words seemed to be Chinese, but the barbarians understood their sadness and anger. Sometimes they thought they could catch barbarian phrases about forever wandering" (209). The figure of Ts'ai Yen's song is the closing figure of a Chinese-American art that is a possible dream. Of this figure the narrator tells us, "Here is a story my mother told me, not when I was young, but recently, when I told her I also am a story-talker. The beginning is hers, the ending, mine" (206).

The narrator locates her memoirs, her memories, specifically in a Cantonese mother's talk-stories; she seeks her authority from this specified maternal and racial origin, and her materials and traditions from this maternal/racial well. "I also am a story-talker," the narrator finally claims, emerging from the well in which No Name Woman was drowned. The beginning of the book, of the story, the drowned and forgotten woman, the captured poetess, was the mother's story. The ending of the book, when the narrator steps up finally before the mother to claim authorship, when Ts'ai Yen returns to China with her songs, one of which still is sung by Chinese "to their own instruments" and which "translates well," belongs to the daughter. *The Woman Warrior* is finally the daughter's story, orally given by the mother and written, completed, by the daughter.

Between *Fifth Chinese Daughter* and *The Woman Warrior* is a breathtaking leap in female consciousness. The fifth Chinese daughter, struggling in her schooling in the father's strict patriarchy, escapes and does not escape his narrow definitions. The third-person separation of autobiographical subject from narrative point of view subtly reinforces this "distancing" or "muting" of female subjectivity. The narrative never escapes the logocentrism of chronological documentation. It is a life presented as always controlled by the demands of narrative "history" with its emphasis on apparent "objectivity," "facticity," "chronological ordering," "the third-person point of view." *The Woman Warrior,* however, is an "over-writing" of given Chinese-American stories. In this attempt to "over-write," all stories are equal, whether from history, myth, legend, family lore, or individual invention. The first person dominates, and in overflowing female terms. Thus the book is replete with nouns and pronouns referring strictly to female gender: mother, aunt, she, girl babies, etc. More significantly, the presence of mother, aunts, and daughter places it in a woman-gendered tradition, whereas the constructing/constraining pole of the normative and Confucianist patriarchy locates *Fifth Chinese Daughter* in a male-constituted society. The daughter in Wong's autobiography defines herself against and through negotiations with the other gender; she is above all the patriarch's daughter. On the other hand, the presence of the daughter's discourse in *The Woman Warrior* is a "talking-back-to" the mother culture, which is also the racial culture. The appropriation of the mother's talk-stories, the conversion of oral to writerly tradition, is both the American daughter's reclamation of her Chinese mother's story (history) and her vanquishing of it, swallowing of it into her American presence (present). Logocentricism is repeatedly shattered; in its place are what appear to be fragments, of stories, ideas, thoughts, images, asides, which circle around and accumulate to form the expression of the idea of Chinese American female subjectivity.

The Woman Warrior, therefore, unlike *Fifth Chinese Daughter*, has not an autobiographical story to tell but a racial and gendered consciousness to intimate and create. It shares with another contemporary Asian American woman's text, *Obasan*, in interrogating identities and reconstituting in their place an emergent daughterly subject, just as *Fifth Chinese Daughter* shares with Sone's *Nisei Daughter* an earlier generation's submergent subjectivities and eventual submission to patriarchal discourse.[11] The differences between the two books are arguably differences of generational thematics; read together, *Fifth Chinese Daughter* and *The Woman Warrior* deepen each other's cultural constructions of Chinese American daughters, moving from any kind of single or singly divided consciousness to an expression of multiple subjectivities, the consequence of American daughters resignifying their Asian origins.

NOTES

1   The masculinist theory of literature offered in the introduction to *Aiiieeeee!* is given a pseudo-sociological rationale in the argument that "The subject matter of minority literature is social history" and that "There is no reference, no standard of measure, no criterion (to evaluate these works)" (xxxv). Oddly enough, although *Fifth Chinese Daughter* is clearly a nonfiction autobiography containing many passages of ethnographic descriptions, the *Aiiieeeee!* editors reject it for, among other things, not fitting their "sociological" constraints; that is, for its portrayal of the psychological underpinnings of the conflict between Chinese father and Chinese American daughter.

2   As Amy Ling points out, "For most of the reading public, the award-winning writer, Maxine Hong Kingston, apparently sprang full-bloom from the empyrean, for most people would be hard put to name another Chinamerican woman writer. And yet women of Chinese ethnicity have been producing and publishing books in this country for nearly a century" (29).

3   See Elizabeth J. Ordóñez, "Narrative Texts by Ethnic Women," for a succinct description of "the mixing of genre and discourse" in *The Woman Warrior* and relation of stylistics to thematics of "the dynamic and dialectical experience of being Chinese in America" (20).

4 See Maxine Hong Kingston's foreword to *Talk story* in which she notes the pattern for Hawaiian playwrights to "work more and more with pidgin. Paradoxically, the older works are written in an English closer to the mainland's 'Standard' English. . . . We are still experimenting with how to render pidgin—the language used at home, the language of childhood and the sub-conscious, the language used in emotion—with writing, figuring out its spellings and phonics" (6). Kingston's style in *The Woman Warrior* exhibits her experimenting with infusing the syntactic traces of "pidgin" or Cantonese-influenced English in written prose.

5 See the bibliography in Lim, Tsutakawa, and Donnelly, specifically 278–79.

6 See, for example, Winnifred Eaton, *Me, A Book of Remembrance;* Hui-lan Koo (Madam Wellington Koo) As told to Mary Wan Rensselaer Tahyer, *Hui-lan Koo;* and Tan Yun (Adet Lin), *Our Family.*

7 These two texts have been paired as thematically oppositional by Patricia Lin Blinde in "The Icicle in the Desert," while in their response Loh and Paulson argue for their similarities in "effectively render[ing] the divided consciousness of dual-heritage" (59).

8 Loh and Paulson, for example, argue that the use of the third person allows Wong to treat herself "as the object of a process of education" (54) and that the autobiography shows "the division of Wong's life and how she questions and rejects the Chinese conventions which no longer apply in the context of the duality of experience she faces."

9 French feminist critics such as Hélène Cixous and Luce Irigaray argue that women's writing is radically different from patriarchal logocentricism; a female language is "open, nonlinear, unfinished, fluid, exploded, fragmented, polysemic, attempting to speak the body; i.e., the unconscious, involving silence, incorporating the simultaneity of life as opposed to or clearly different from pre-conceived, oriented, masterly or 'didactic' languages" (Makward 96). While many Anglo-American feminist critics such as Nina Baym (from whose brilliant counterargument the above citation was taken) disagree with this essentialist position, the passage above is an appropriate description of prose style in *The Woman Warrior.*

10 Leslie W. Rabine, among other critics, has insightfully discussed these multiple shifts in Kingston's work. She points out that "like the feminine writing of Cixous and Irigaray, Kingston's writing violates the law of opposition, making gender dichotomies proliferate into unresolvable gender differences" (474). *The Woman Warrior* has attracted a great deal of commentary from both Asian American and white critics. Sidonie Smith reads *The Woman Warrior* as "an autobiography about autobiographical storytelling" (150), while Sau-ling Wong reads the book as a thematic development of the tension between Chinese immigrant acceptance of necessity and the human impulse toward extravagance. A summary of the critical essays on the book can be found in Lim, *Approaches to Teaching* The Woman Warrior.

11 See Shirley Geok-lin Lim, "Japanese-American Women's Life Stories," for a discussion of the mother-daughter thematics in Sone's and Kogawa's books.

WORKS CITED

Aiiieeeee! An Anthology of Asian-American Writers. Ed. Frank Chin, Jeffery Paul Chan, Lawson Fusao Inada, and Shawn Hsu Wong. Washington, D.C.: Howard University Press, 1974.

Baym, Nina. "The Madwoman and her Languages." In Benstock 45–61.

Benstock, Shari, ed. *Feminist Issues in Literary Scholarship.* Bloomington and Indianapolis: Indiana University Press, 1987.

Blinde, Patricia Lin. "The Icicle in the Desert: Perspectives and Form in the Works of Two Chinese-American Women Writers." *MELUS* 6/3 (Fall 1979), 51–71.

Carabi, Angeles. Interview with Maxine Hong Kingston. *Belles Lettres* (Winter 1989), 10–11.

Chang, Diana. *The Frontiers of Love.* New York: Random House, 1956.

Chennault, Anna. *The Education of Anna.* New York: Times Books, 1980.

Chennault, Anna. *A Thousand Springs: The Biography of a Marriage.* New York: Paul S. Eriksson, 1962.

Chou, Cynthia L. *My Life in the United States.* North Quincy, MA: Christopher Publishing House, 1970.

Eaton, Winnifred. *Me, A Book of Remembrance.* New York: Century, 1915.

Holte, James Craig. "The Representative Voice: Autobiography and the Ethnic Experience." *MELUS,* 9/2 (Summer 1982), 25–46.

Jardine, Alice A. *Gynesis: Configurations of Woman and Modernity.* Ithaca and London: Cornell University Press, 1985.

Jardine, Alice, and Hester Eisenstein, eds. *The Future of Difference.* Boston: G. K. Hall, 1980.

Kingston, Maxine Hong. Foreword to *Talk story: An Anthology of Hawaii's Local Writers.* Ed. Eric Chock et al. Honolulu: Petronium Press/Talk Story, 1978.

Kingston, Maxine Hong. *The Woman Warrior.* New York: Knopf, 1976.

Kogawa, Joy. *Obasan.* Boston: Godine, 1982.

Koo, Hui-lan [Madam Wellington Koo]. As told to Mary Wan Rensselaer Tahyer. *Hui-lan Koo.* New York: Dial, 1943.

Lee, Virginia. *The House That Tai-Ming Built.* New York: Macmillan, 1963.

Lim, Shirley Geok-lin. *Approaches to Teaching* The Woman Warrior. N.Y.: Modern Language Association Press, 1991.

Lim, Shirley Geok-lin. "Japanese-American Women's Life Stories: Maternality in Monica Sone's *Nisei Daughter* and Joy Kogawa's *Obasan." Feminist Studies,* 16/2 (Summer 1990), 289–312.

Lim, Shirley Geok-lin; Mayumi Tsutakawa; and Margarita Donnelly, eds. *The Forbidden Stitch: An Anthology of Asian American Women's Writing.* Corvallis, OR: Calyx, 1989.

Ling, Amy. "A Rumble in the Silence: *Crossings* by Chuang Hua." *MELUS* 9/3 (1982), 29–37.

Loh, Kathleen Swee Yin, and Kristoffer F. Paulson. "The Divided Voice of Chinese-American Narration: Jade Snow Wong's *Fifth Chinese Daughter." MELUS,* 9/1 (Spring 1982), 53–59.

Makward, Christiane. "To Be or Not to Be . . . a Feminist Speaker." In Jardine and Eisenstein.

Okada, John. *No-No Boy*. Rutland, VT: Charles E. Tuttle, 1957.

Ordóñez, Elizabeth J. "Narrative Texts by Ethnic Women: Rereading the Past, Reshaping the Future." *MELUS*, 9/3 (Winter 1982), 19–28.

Rabine, Leslie. "No Lost Paradise: Social Gender and Symbolic Gender in the Writings of Maxine Hong Kingston." *Signs*, 12/3 (1987), 471–92.

Smith, Sidonie. *A Poetics of Women's Autobiography: Marginality and the Fictions of Self-Representation*. Bloomington: Indiana University Press, 1987.

Sone, Monica. *Nisei Daughter*. 1953; Seattle: University of Washington Press, 1979.

Tan, Amy. *The Joy Luck Club*. New York: Putnam, 1989.

Tan, Yun [Adet Lin and Anor Lin]. *Our Family*. New York: John Day, 1939.

Wong, Jade Snow. *Fifth Chinese Daughter*. New York: Harper, 1950; Seattle: University of Washington Press, 1989.

Wong, Jade Snow. *No Chinese Stranger*. New York: Harper and Row, 1975.

Wong, Sau-ling. "Necessity and Extravagence in Maxine Hong Kingston's *The Woman Warrior*: Art and the Ethnic Experience." *MELUS*, 15/1 (1988), 3–26.

Woolf, Virginia, *A Room of One's Own and Three Guineas*. London: Chatto and Windus, 1984.

Yung, Judy. *Chinese Women of America: A Pictorial History*. Seattle: University of Washington Press, 1986.

CHAPTER 13

Indian Women's Personal Narrative: Voices Past and Present

KATHLEEN MULLEN SANDS

American Indian women are essential to America's record of historical development. Where would America be without Pocahontas' timely rescue of John Smith? What would have become of the Lewis and Clark expedition without the loyal guidance of Sacagawea? Yet from the beginning of colonization, Native American women have been accorded recognition only as symbols of a primitive nobility which contributed to the progress of the American enterprise. And even that symbology is ambivalent; the reverse of the Indian "princess" is the "squaw," an object of sexual abuse and debasement. Thus the powerful image of the "princess" is neutralized by the powerless image of the native woman as "object of scornful convenience" (Green 713).

In the American mind, the Indian woman in relation to Indian men is insignificant—a breeder of "papooses," gatherer of berries and roots, and curer of buffalo hides. Reduced to menial tasks, she remains humble and mute. In relationship to colonizing males she is either primitive sexual object or dusky virgin "royalty"—an abstraction to be manipulated for political or physical motives—easily abandoned because she has no distinct personal identity. Her existence, as portrayed consistently through American history and popular culture, is defined exclusively in relationship to her usefulness to males. As Cherokee critic Rayna Green comments:

It is time that the Princess herself is rescued and the squaw relieved of her obligatory service. The Native American woman, like all women, needs definition that stands apart from that of males, red or white. Certainly, the Native woman needs to be defined as Indian, in Indian terms. (714)

The princess/squaw stereotypes, however comforting they may be to the American sensibility, allow the American Indian woman not only to be marginalized by race and sex, but, perhaps more than any other minority group in America, to be perversely distorted.[1] By examining the lives of real Indian women, historical and contemporary, some appreciation for the substance and range of American Indian women's lives may be achieved, and the absurdly elevating and demeaning images traditionally attached to them may begin to lose their power.

American Indian women have had force and voice within their own tribes. Traditionally Indian women have been repositories of knowledge to be passed down from generation to generation, and they have also been the keepers of spiritual ideals and tribal values. As one contemporary Navajo woman points out, in the American stereotype "the Indian woman is totally a cardboard figure, a shadow of the man. In reality the women are the lifeline of their people" (Bataille 5). Frequently they have been powerful forces in the leadership of their tribes in roles as curers, warriors, and as respected counselors. As Sioux spokesman Vine Deloria, Sr., points out, "men did not hold office without the approval of the mature women of the tribe, and if they did not fulfill their responsibilities adequately, they were not likely to be given roles of power again" (Bataille and Sands 18). One Indian woman sums up this balance of roles by saying:

There was a very fine line, a fine bond between a man and a woman and their responsibility as members of a tribe. . . . every single tribe believed that both sides had to equally join together in balance or there would be no life. You have to have a man and a woman and with that there is unity and balance and harmony in the world. (Bataille 6)

Native American women, then, have traditionally been and still are central to tribal well-being. At the center of kinship systems in matrilineal societies, tribal women may control substantial amounts of property. Tribal societies consider menstruating women extremely powerful, and mature women are held in high esteem for their wisdom and knowledge. It is no wonder, then, that many Indian women reject the notion of women's liberation, finding within their own societies suitable outlets for their needs and ambitions without rupturing the fabric of their traditional communities. However, it must be recognized that power does not constitute dominance within Indian tribes, and tribal roles and behavior for both men and women are carefully defined and regulated by such means as ceremonial obligations and community gossip; so while Native American women have been misperceived by Euro-Americans and do, in fact, have considerable influence within their tribes, limitations, rooted firmly in tradition, do govern their behavior.

Though the impact of Indian women on mainstream culture has been largely a product of misinformation, stereotyping, and political convenience,

Indian women have, over the past century and a half, been frequent and eloquent spokespersons for their tribes and activists for Indian causes.[2] Many tribal women have also chosen to tell or write their life stories for a nontribal readership, giving voice to a wide range of personal intentions and experiences. However, despite the substantial canon of American Indian women's autobiographical publications (Bataille and Sands; Brumble, *Annotated Bibliography*), little attention has been given to these works even by scholars in the field of autobiography and American Indian literatures.[3] In many cases, this is because the works are hard to find, often obscured by misclassification in libraries (anything Indian must be anthropology) or not kept in print by publishers or marketed widely. And, of course, like all women's literature, these texts suffer from marginalization, but to a much higher degree, particularly when they challenge the princess/squaw image of Indian women held so dearly by American culture. As Sidonie Smith points out:

if the autobiographer is a woman of color or a working class woman, she faces even more complex imbroglios of male-female figures: Here ideologies of race and class, sometimes even of nationality, intersect and confound those of gender. As a result, she is doubly or triply the subject of other people's representation, turned again and again in stories that reflect and promote certain forms of selfhood identified with class, race, and nationality as well as sex. In every case, moreover, she remains marginalized in that she finds herself resident on the margins of discourse, always removed from the center of power within the culture she inhabits. (51)

Indian women autobiographers participate in two cultures, tribal and Euro-American, yet reception and recognition of personal narratives by Indian women are rare indeed, because the marginality of Indian women's autobiographies also is complicated by factors unique to their tribal source.

Autobiography is not an indigenous form of literature for American Indian peoples. The traditional literature of tribal peoples is oral in nature and communal in source—myths, tales, songs, and chants performed in ceremonial context or told for the purpose of instructing and entertaining the community. Only since the nineteenth century have Indian people used written forms to record their histories and produce literary works, and until this century only a minority of Indians wrote English, making their production of text very minimal until relatively recently. Furthermore, tribal societies do not value individualism or self-assertion in the Euro-American sense highly, so to relate one's life story is to put oneself forward in a way that may elicit criticism from one's own community. Added to this is the fact that cross-cultural writing requires complex processes to make what is "foreign" accessible to the mainstream of American culture.

To most Americans, Indian culture remains exotic and unknown; moreover, representing Native American experience is further complicated by the fact that Indian culture is not homogeneous but made up of several hundred separate cultures with separate languages and literatures, so cultural and linguistic translations are necessary for a wide readership. And, as in mainstream and other American minority cultures, the female autobiographical tradition is separate from the male tradition. Autobiographies of Indian men tend to focus on public lives; their subjects are figures of historical importance—chiefs, warriors, medicine men—while the autobiographies of Indian women tend to focus on private lives, examining personal relationships and individual growth and concentrating on everyday events and activities.[4]

Finally, the process of Indian personal narrative is often collaborative—a tribal person narrating to a nontribal collector/editor. The intervention of a mediator between the narrator and the reader complicates the issues of voice and reliability enormously since the published narrative is actually a bicultural composition (Krupat, "Indian Autobiography"). Speaking of cross-cultural writing, anthropologist James Clifford states, "Literary processes—metaphor, figuration, narrative—affect the ways cultural phenomena are registered, from the first jotted 'observations,' to the completed book, to the ways these configurations 'make sense' in determined acts of reading" (Clifford and Marcus 4). Even if the intention of Indian personal narrative is not literary, the writing of lives employs culturally defined cognitive processes and narrative techniques that affect cultural representation; the text is both a cultural and a personal interpretation in which the narrator "in a sense, makes or remakes" (Personal Narrative Group 101) her life and its cultural context through language. Moreover, bicultural narrative doesn't simply double the problem of reliability, it multiplies the complexity of interpretation. The relationship between truth and illusion, story and reality is one not only of intimate codependence but of multiple codependences affected by colonialism.

In many cases, tribal people have been interviewed about their lives by historians or anthropologists seeking ethnographic data. Yet even in anthropological writing, as Clifford Geertz points out, truths are only partial—ethnographic fictions (15)—constructs of language and memory that bring to the reader ways of imagining lives and cultures.[5] In every collaborative narrative, the power relationship is unequal and the intended audience is outside the tribal group, so dominant culture forms and interpretations overpower the indigenous narrative style. In some cases ethnographic intent leads to short, episodic narratives collected to illustrate anthropological categories; in others a full life history is presented but with little attention to aesthetic techniques or style, particularly not Native style.

Thus the term autobiography, which is always difficult to define, becomes particularly problematical in reference to American Indian personal narrative since autobiography generally presumes literary intention and form. "Personal narrative" or "life history" (Frank, 72) describes many of these texts more accurately though some Indian narratives are, despite their ethnographic genesis, of recognized literary merit and fit commonly held notions of autobiography (Neihardt; Underhill), and others have been written consciously as literary works.[6] Whether literary or ethnographic, the cross-cultural discourse required to represent the life and culture of a tribal person to a nontribal reader is complex and adds to the already problematical nature of autobiographical process.

And to further complicate the study of Indian personal narrative, three separate traditions of autobiography coexist: composite, written, and multiform. The bicultural composite often described by the terms "as-told-to" or "life history" is characterized by oral narration by the subject, and recording, structuring, and editing by a nontribal person to form an extensive record of the subject's life.[7] This form should not, however, be seen as an early stage in the development of Indian autobiography since it is still being produced today and has coexisted with the written tradition over the past century and a half. The written text, often affected by extensive editing by a nontribal person, may too share, in varying degrees, the bicultural method of composition.[8] The multiform text, a recent innovation by contemporary Indian creative writers, mixes oral tradition, personal narrative, fiction, and poetry into works which might best be described as cultural memoirs composed and controlled by tribal authors.[9]

Autobiographical works by American Indians, because of the variety of forms of discourse used in their production, defy genre categorization and are best examined as processes of personal narration.[10]

Though the three processes referred to are not gender specific, gender must be considered in examining autobiographical works by American Indians, because it not only establishes the public/private contrast in these texts but has impact on the issues of reader reception and critical assessment. Because warriors and medicine men, like Geronimo or Black Elk, have historical recognition apart from their narratives, their autobiographical texts receive far greater critical attention than those written by Indian women who have no public reputation. Hence, female narratives are, as in mainstream literature, marginalized because their content does not seem significant. Indian women, not generally actors in the public arena, create narratives, it is assumed, essentially repetitious of one another, focusing on childhood, puberty, marriage and childbearing, and old age. Readers expect little variety or significance. Even for the purposes of ethnography, women's lives often claim attention only in terms of their generative and male-supporting roles, so in some cases little beyond data supporting representative social roles has been gathered and published. If it has traditionally been a negative characteristic for tribal people to put themselves forward, the woman who narrates her individual experience, particularly if she presents herself as other than representative of tribal norms, calls particularly negative attention to herself. She places herself in double jeopardy, criticized within her tribe and unlikely to find validation for her experience or narration in the world of her nontribal audience either, because it generally upholds male dominated criteria for autobiographical writing and clings to the princess/squaw image tenaciously. As Sidonie Smith says:

Since the ideology of gender makes of woman's life script a nonstory, a silent space, a gap in patriarchal culture, the ideal woman is self-effacing rather than self-promoting, and her "natural" story shapes itself not around public, heroic life but around the fluid, circumstantial, contingent responsiveness to others, that according to patriarchal ideology, characterizes the life of woman but not autobiography. (50)

The American Indian woman who, either through a nontribal collector/editor, or by her own pen, ventures to call attention to her life, whether as representative or, more dangerously yet, as unique risks censure at home, tepid reception in the dominant culture, and indifference from scholars even in the field of Indian studies.

It is a wonder, given this personal and literary peril, that any Indian women have chosen to share their life stories. Some have, in fact, remained anonymous informants for anthropologists, but most of the over one hundred and thirty autobiographical texts by Indian women[11] carry the narrators' names, and many are powerful and eloquent statements of personal and cultural survival.

WRITTEN AUTOBIOGRAPHY

One of the earliest written autobiographies by an American Indian is Sarah Winnemucca Hopkins' *Life among the Piutes: Their Wrongs and Claims,* published in 1883. As the title suggests, this autobiography is not only a personal narrative, but also a cultural history of the Northern Paiute tribe from early contact with whites to the 1880s, and a plea for an end to unjust treatment of her people.

Thocmentony (translated Shell Flower), as she was named when she was born, probably in 1844, in the vicinity of Humboldt Lake in present-day northern Nevada, was the granddaughter of Truckee "who had been a guide to early emigrants crossing the Great Basin" and leader of the Numa, as the Northern Paiutes called themselves (Canfield 4). She was the daughter of Winnemucca, an important antelope shaman who became the leader and spokesman for his tribe upon Truckee's death. Sarah Winnemucca was born into an important family at a time of rapid and bewildering change for her people.

Her first encounter with whites was filled with terror. Stories of cannibalism in the doomed Donner party had filtered into the tribe and become the basis of stories of fierce whites who would eat Numas (Hopkins 11), so Thocmentony did not believe her grandfather's story about the tradition of the white men as prophesied benevolent lost brothers of the Numa (Canfield 6). Frightened by the approach of a party of whites, Thocmentony's mother buried Thocmentony and her cousin to the neck and hid them under sagebrush, leaving them there all day until she could safely return to uncover them. The trauma of this event stayed with the child, making her fearful and timid, especially after one of her uncles was killed by a party of whites (Hopkins 20). She was especially terrified when her grandfather insisted that his daughter and granddaughter and other kinsmen accompany him to California. During the journey, gifts of sugar from white settlers and the kind nursing of a white woman when Thocmentony became ill with poison oak finally dissolved her fear of "the owls," as the Numa called white people because of their bearded faces and light eyes (Hopkins 11–32). In fact, she was so thoroughly taken with her nurse she claims in her autobiography that this incident made her "come to love the white people" (Hopkins 33). By 1858, in fact, Sarah and her sister were living with a white family and learning English rapidly (Hopkins 58). The timid little girl who had been mute, too afraid even to speak her native language around whites, was finding her voice and would soon become an interpreter for negotiations between the army and her people though she was only an adolescent. Her skill as a translator and her position as a member of the most prominent family in the tribe brought her to the very center of her tribe's negotiations with Indian agents and army officers and rapidly led to her role as spokeswoman for her people to white society in western towns and cities and eventually as a lecturer and lobbyist for Indian causes in the eastern United States.

Sarah Winnemucca, as she became known to whites, wrote her autobiography to reach a wider audience than her lectures could in order to convince the white world that her people were not bloodthirsty savages but decent people willing to coexist peacefully with the growing white population in their traditional homeland (now western Nevada, southeastern Oregon, and northeastern California), if only the injustices and corruption of Indian policy could be redressed.

In Elizabeth Palmer Peabody and Mary Mann, the widow of Horace

Mann, Sarah Winnemucca found loyal support; Peabody found her lecturing engagements and Mann volunteered to edit Sarah's book, which she quickly found to be quite a task. Writing about the narrative of this self-educated Indian woman, Mann says:

> I wish you could see her manuscript as a matter of curiosity. I don't think the English language ever got such treatment before. I have to recur to her sometimes to know what a word is, as spelling is an unknown quantity to her. . . . She often takes syllables off of words & adds them or rather prefixes them to other words, but the story is heart-breaking, and told with simplicity & eloquence that cannot be described, for it is not high-faluting eloquence, tho' sometimes it lapses into verse (and quite poetical verse too). I was always considered fanatical about Indians, but I have a wholly new conception of them now, and we civilized people may well stand abashed before their purity of life & their truthfulness. (Canfield 201)

Mann's enthusiasm for the project did not fade despite Sarah's unorthodox writing; in fact, she aided in defraying publication costs by getting subscriptions to underwrite printing. Mann's comments on the project are particularly useful because they verify that Sarah Winnemucca composed her autobiography with relatively little help from Mann, who writes in the preface, "My editing has consisted in copying the original manuscript in correct orthography and punctuation, with occasional emendations by the author, of a book which is an heroic act on the part of the writer" (Hopkins 3).

Sarah Winnemucca's personal narrative fits poorly into the genre of women's autobiography as reminiscence; rather, because of the very public nature of her life, it corresponds more accurately to the memoir style of male autobiography. That her mentors were active in the transcendentalist movement and that she had become quite sophisticated in eastern society suggest that she may well have been deliberately modeling Victorian male autobiographies, though that must remain purely speculation, since no records exist of literary influences on her text. The political nature of her authorial intent must also be taken into account, and so must the nature of her life experience. A pivotal figure in the relations of her tribe with the military and bureaucratic agencies of the United States government,[12] she acted as a scout for the U.S. Army under General Howard's command in the Bannock War (Canfield 141). In the appendix to her autobiography, a letter written in 1878, by R. F. Bernard, a cavalry captain, verifies her role:

> This is to certify that Sara Winnemucca has rendered most valuable services during the operations of this year against the hostile Bannock and Piute Indians. About the commencement of hostilities, she went for me from my camp to that of the hostiles, distant about a hundred miles, and returned bringing exceedingly valuable information concerning their number, location, intentions, etc., and she also

succeeded in getting her father, the Piute chief Winnemucca, with many of his band, to leave the enemy and go to Camp McDermit, Nevada, where they remained during the summer campaign. (Hopkins 259)

Sarah's version of these events is considerably more dramatic:

This was the hardest work I ever did for the government in all my life,—the whole round trip, from 10 o'clock June 13 up to June 15, arriving back at 5:30 P.M., having been in the saddle night and day; distance, about two hundred and twenty-three miles. Yes, I went for the government when the officers could not get an Indian man or a white man to go for love or money. I, only an Indian woman, went and saved my father and his people. (Hopkins 164)

Her vision of herself as a warrior woman dominates this summary and interpretation of her actions. She presents herself as a hero, brave beyond either Indian or white males, yet speaks of herself as "only" an Indian woman, a dramatic contrast that indicates her awareness of her readership who certainly would not expect such bravery of a "squaw."

Winnemucca does not, however, reject the Euro-American stereotype of "princess"; she allows herself to be billed as "Princess Sarah Winnemucca of the Piutes" for her lectures (Canfield 200), perhaps in this case deliberately using the stereotype of exotic royalty to work for her cause.

Sarah Winnemucca is a very self-conscious narrator. At work here are "strategies by which the author seeks to explain or justify her current sense of herself, a need which might be especially strong in a woman who feels herself moving into uncharted waters . . ." (Chevigny 83). She writes her narrative directly to her audience, frequently addressing them in the second person and using genteel language as when she describes the traditional flower festival among her people:

Oh, with what eagerness we girls used to watch every spring for the time when we could meet with our hearts' delight, the young men, whom in civilized life you call beaux. We would all go in company to see if the flowers we were named for were yet in bloom, for almost all the girls are named for flowers. (Hopkins 46)

Note the term "civilized." It is hard to believe that she sees white society as more civilized than her own; she frequently chastises whites for their perfidy in dealing with Indians and portrays her people as trustworthy, gentle, clean, hospitable, and above all, moral—far superior to the corrupt agents who steal their food rations and keep the income from tribal farming for their own enrichment. It is clear who she thinks is really civilized, but she knows how to play her audience and uses her "only an Indian woman" pose to gain sympathy for her cause, just as she uses the image of the exotic "princess" to fill a lecture hall.

Winnemucca takes considerable pains to give details of traditional life, especially the training of young men and women for adult roles as spouses and parents. In her chapter entitled "Domestic and Social Moralities" she also makes it clear that women have power within her tribe. She writes:

The women know as much as the men do, and their advice is often asked. We have a republic as well as you. The council-tent is our Congress, and anybody can speak who has anything to say, women and all. (Hopkins 53)

She continues, giving an account of a woman who takes her fallen uncle's place in battle. Winnemucca, herself, of course, remains the ultimate warrior of her tribe, risking her life to rescue her people and also fighting for her people in the council tents, lecture halls, and even the halls of Congress and of the White House itself, yet maintaining the demeanor of a humble Indian woman when it suits her need for audience reception. Adroit at two techniques, she uses a conventional autobiographical form for her time, and she manipulates her status as an Indian woman in her own favor. She has it both ways—male and female, private and public. Not only does she present herself as a warrior for Indian justice, but she also develops a portrait of a child terrified by white power who, toward the end of her narrative, has become a dedicated teacher of Indian pupils—a version of motherhood.

The fact that she is a woman is a great asset for her in reaching her audience. Male Indian warriors may threaten; look at Geronimo, Sitting Bull, etc., but a woman as warrior, in alliance with the U.S. Army and her own people, is safe—a powerful yet acceptable image, not so very different from Pocahontas after all, especially considering she has a white man for a husband. She ironically fits all the conventions already well established in the American mind and thus gains reader acceptance despite her strident accusations of injustice toward her people. Winnemucca does call very public attention to herself, not so much by writing her autobiography as by appearing as the "princess" in full buckskin dress before audiences on both Pacific and Atlantic coasts, speaking out to whites on behalf of Indians, pointing out the misuse of Indian women by white men, accusing whites of lying to Indians. She also calls attention to herself in her own tribe. As interpreter between tribe and whites, she is particularly vulnerable to criticism if things do not go as promised, if blankets and food are not delivered as scheduled, or land settlements she negotiated in Washington are not implemented. She is an easy scapegoat among her people, and as a highly unconventional representative of Indian women in white society, is also open to scrutiny and occasional barbs, particularly about her liaisons with white men, including two marriages. The first marriage to a drunken gambler who wasted her meager resources was disastrous, and the second, to Louis Hopkins, was stormy and unconventional. In part, the autobiography defends her against gossip about her private life and criticism of her public life; it is a rationale—but clearly not an apology—for the unusual thrust of her life in a period of Victorian sensibilities in white society and confusing social change in tribal society. Sarah Winnemucca's autobiography explains her public life and makes a case for her integrity as a Northern Paiute woman working for understanding and cooperation between tribal people and the dominant society.

The reliability of the Winnemucca text, as with all autobiographical texts, is suspect particularly because she uses her life story to promote the cause of her own personal integrity and the broader cause of tribal justice—she has axes to grind. It is also suspect at another level. Included in the text, in fact dominant in it, lengthy speeches and dialogues highly unlikely to have been remembered and written verbatim are presented in the conventional forms of quoted monologue and dialogue, and thus purport to be accurate. These techniques suggest a considerable use of poetic license, recollections edited with political as well as artistic intent in mind, other voices played through the voice of the narrator, noticeably in the narrator's narrative style. The text is not a polyphony; only the single voice of Winnemucca actually narrates dramatic events and characters. She creates speeches by her grandfather to move a white audience to admire him and the nature of tribal culture. Sarah's dialogues with military officers, white settlers, her family, and others enhance her own stature and her case for justice toward the Paiutes. In the name of justice, she sees manipulation of the past as fair. Her "fictions," as Geertz would put it, however suspect, make the autobiography far livelier than it would be without such dramatic devices.

Sarah Winnemucca places herself at the center of every event and action in the autobiography, from her description of her terror at the first contact with whites, where, actually, she is only a bit player, to her daring rescue of her father and his band, where she is indeed center stage, to her negotiations with congressmen and cabinet members. It is Winnemucca's verve, her certainty of the epic nature of her life, her absolute dedication, despite enormous personal sacrifice, and her genteelly Victorian use of language that work in concert to move the reader and convince the audience of the justice of Indian rights even a century after its first publication.

COMPOSITE NARRATIVE

Almost exactly a century later, another autobiography, *During My Time* narrated by Florence Edenshaw Davidson, a Haida woman, demonstrates the continuing viability of the as-told-to method of Indian autobiography. Collected and edited by anthropologist Margaret B. Blackman, Florence Davidson's life history presents a far more conventional portrait of Indian womanhood than does the Winnemucca autobiography. Davidson was born in 1896, five years after Winnemucca's death, and her life story centers on the domestic activities and family relationships commonly the concern of women's autobiography. As one of the last Haida women to go through traditional puberty rituals and an arranged marriage, she represents the old ways of her tribe. As a Christian woman active in her community on the seaward side of Queen Charlotte Island off the coast of western Canada, she also represents the changing experience of tribal women.[13] Like many other bicultural composite autobiographies, this one presents a woman typical of her time and tribe. As editor Blackman points out, "Despite the social position she has enjoyed as the daughter of high-ranking parents and the esteem she has earned, Florence Davidson views her life as 'ordinary,' in the sense of being uneventful" (Blackman 7). In fact, in one conversation with the collector/editor, she jokingly says, "If only I lied, it could be so interesting" (Blackman 7).

Despite her own assessment of her life, Davidson is an engaging woman living through compelling times. At the time of her birth, reservation life for the Haida was only fifteen years old, and the introduction of Christianity to the tribe only twenty (Blackman 7), so during her lifetime she observes and experiences the dynamic interaction of Euro-Canadian culture and traditional tribal culture.

Davidson's narrative begins, as Indian life stories often do, with a chapter on her family before her birth. In it, she recalls stories handed down to her from her parents about such events as the smallpox epidemic that decimated the tribal population in the 1860s, the potlatches[14] for her grandmother and aunt, her father's ritual tatooing which covered his body, and her parents' traditional marriage ceremony before the coming of the missionaries. She begins her own life story ab ovum, relating that while her mother was in the last trimester of pregnancy with her, her parents journeyed by canoe to Juneau, Alaska, where her father spent the summer carving. They sold the canoe and took the steamer to Victoria, B.C., to buy a treadle sewing machine on the way back home; the old ways begin to pass for her family just as Florence enters the world. But her birth still occasions the traditional rituals for the placenta, piercing of the infant's ears, and a Haida name, Jadal, and name story. But she is also christened Florence by the missionary.

Much of Davidson's narrative focuses on details of domestic life—her father carving, her mother working at a cannery, berry picking, games with playmates, gardening, meal preparation—though some attention is given to the winter dances, recalled as frequent and dramatic because of the masks quickly being bought up by white men. Two events receive much more detailed attention. One is her first menstruation where she was isolated for ten days and was "the talk of the town" (Blackman 92). She recalls that three years later, her younger sister's puberty was not celebrated with a give-away or ritual isolation because, as she puts it, "we became like white people then" (Blackman 92). The second is her arranged marriage when she was only fourteen years old to a much older man, a widower. Still a schoolgirl and adamantly resistant, she was nonetheless married at the village church, though she felt ashamed and refused to recite the vows and felt sad during the feast and dance that followed. Despite her resistance, the marriage was successful and after a period of refusing to let her husband even touch her, she finally gave in and bore many children.

That so much of Davidson's narrative focuses on domestic detail is not surprising, as Blackman explains:

The options open to Haida women of Florence Davidson's generation were few. Most women married young, remained in their village of birth, and bore and reared large families. The main alternative to such a life course was to marry a white man and leave the islands, but few followed this pattern at the time Florence was married. (146)

Not until menopause does Davidson's life story shift from family-centered activities to the community. In her mature and later years, while still maintaining domestic skills and providing a home, not only for family but for boarders as well, Florence asserted herself as an artist, first painting a canoe with traditional designs. Seeing such decorative work as a male form of expression within the tribe, she made the design secretly and painted it during the night, suprising the villagers but receiving praise and recognition. She also began making button blankets and cedar bark baskets, and learning traditional songs, revitalizing traditional arts for her village.

The purpose of this narrative is neither literary nor political; it is anthropological, an attempt to present a representative life, one well within the norms of tribal behavior and values. In that it succeeds. As Blackman says, "Her life history . . . bespeaks her tenacity and endurance, and that of other women like her" (153). Though Davidson is a rebellious bride, she nonetheless goes through with the marriage and becomes a devoted wife and mother, delaying or giving secondary attention to her personal needs and interests. She does not threaten the family or community at any stage in her life, yet she gains an outlet for personal expression in her artistic skills and achieves considerable recognition for them—a common pattern in Indian women's life histories. In some sense, she too has it both ways, not in the dramatic sense that Winnemucca does, but in the private and isolated arena of her own village. She does, in fact, fulfill all the sexual roles of her tribe and time, but she also enters into the male practice of decorative painting. While her breaking of sexual barriers may be a small triumph, it is one she chooses to narrate in detail, suggesting this is an important achievement in her life.

Davidson's narrative is typical of many women's narratives, not only in its focus on domestic life but in its technique. In many autobiographical texts "irregularity rather than orderliness informs the self portraits by women," so their narratives "are often not chronological and progressive but disconnected, fragmentary or organized in self-sustained units . . ." (Jelinek 17). Though Davidson's is chronological in chapter divisions, within chapters it tends to focus on themes and suspend strict sequence of events, collapsing time to serve topics, such as when she talks about her artistic work and ranges from childhood to the present within a few paragraphs.

During My Time is far more unusual for its format than for its subject's life. Anthropologist Margaret Blackman deviates from the usual as-told-to pattern of life story, which generally consists of a brief introduction about the processes of collection and editing and the heavily edited text of the life story.[15] Davidson's actual narrative is only 65 pages of the 162-page text; the remainder is Blackman's interpretative material, including a scholarly discussion of the use of life history in ethnography, a rationale for and discussion of the history of the Davidson project itself, a brief cultural history of the Haida, a biographical sketch of Davidson to establish chronology and fill in omissions in the narrator's text, an analysis of Davidson's text, and a sample of the raw text taken from the interview tapes. Since "autobiography is primarily an art of perspective, an art of juxtaposed perspectives" (Shapiro 437), what comes of all this apparatus is a fully fleshed out life story and a self-reflexive analysis of the process of as-told-to autobiography by the collector/editor. This personal narrative acknowledges the fact that the production of an as-told-to autobiography is "an exchange—a dialogue between a narrator and an interpreter" (Personal Narratives Group 203). The book, then, explores the process of autobiography as much as the life of a Haida woman. It allows the reader to see how such a narrative is decided upon, collected, edited, structured, arranged, and interpreted—a sort of primer on the production of ethnographic life story. This revealing of the process of bicultural compositive autobiography gives a sense of reliability to both narrative voices. Blackman analyzes Davidson's story so thoroughly that the reader develops a sense of trust in it, partly because it is not a controversial or very remarkable story, but primarily because it is a story overtly presented from two perspectives—insider and outsider. As Elizabeth Kamarck Minnich suggests:

Writing the life of another woman requires some of the same qualities or conditions as a good conversation with a friend: mutuality, an interdependence risked, respected and enjoyed; equality guaranteeing the grounds for and so allowing the celebration of difference; familiarity, knowing enough about each other in the various worlds we inhabit to hear what is said and to comprehend what is meant. (287)

Because Blackman is so candid about her methodology throughout the collecting and editing steps, the reader gives him/herself over into her obviously competent hands. Despite the openness and thoroughness of the collaborative work on *During My Time,* the autobiographical writing remains fraught with the complexities of any personal narration, in this case doubled, since two narratives are actually at work; two lives are being created out of language, two intentions and styles are interacting and intersecting to produce a multiple text. The same questions raised by any as-told-to narrative still need attention here, but the search for answers is considerably less frustrating because of Blackman's openness. What disappears, as a result of this form of presentation, is any sense of narrative magic. The artistic sleight-of-hand that produces a sense of literature in works such as *Black Elk Speaks* and *Papago Woman* is missing, and along with it the lyricism that literary collectors/editors bring to their work. The issue is not altogether a scholarly matter, but one of reader taste and need and tolerance for ambiguity; fortunately, the wide variety in modes of presentation of Indian as-told-to autobiography will likely meet interests and needs ranging from strictly ethnographical to those pertinent to scholars of autobiography theory.

MULTIFORM NARRATIVES

Production of autobiographical literature by fiction writers and poets is a long tradition in Euro-American letters, but when American Indian women poet novelists produce multigenre works, the conventional notions of Indian autobiography become expanded and redefined. Laguna Pueblo Indian writers Paula Gunn Allen and Leslie Marmon Silko, both widely published writers of fiction and poetry, have ventured into areas of women's writing radically unlike the forms of autobiography discussed above but which are bicultural in nature and multigenre in form of expression. Like autobiography, written poetry and fiction are not indigenous forms of writing for Indian peoples, but forms they have adapted from the Euro-American tradition of belles lettres and manipulated to serve tribal sensibilities, bicultural personal experiences, and artistic inclinations. These women stand simultaneously outside and inside their own cultures and the events they narrate, profoundly affected by their experiences in non-Native culture, but consistent in their expression of Native sensibilities and stories.

Silko's collection of traditional stories, short fiction, poetry, and photographs, entitled *Storyteller,* is a new kind of autobiographical text. In this work Silko uses fragments of personal narrative to bind together traditional expression of collective cultural memory with her contemporary fictional and poetic versions of those stories central to the identity of Laguna people. Personal reminiscences link past and present in her book, cementing the individual to the tribal experience and memory and elucidating "the way remembrance works" (Bataille and Sands 139). The reader must discover the connections between the photos, stories, poems, and traditional stories. As Silko puts it, "The book shows how directly and indirectly, relying on my past and family, how much my 'autobiography' has become fiction and poetry" (Bataille and Sands 139). If remembrance is the essential activity for initiating autobiographical writing, it is the key term for Silko's *Storyteller;* in the introductory poem about Silko's Aunt Susie, the writer and storyteller who first and enduringly influenced Silko's skill as a narrator, Silko sets out the intention and strategy for her inventive form of autobiographical discourse.

> As with any generation
> the oral tradition depends upon each person
> listening and remembering a portion
> and it is together—
> all of us remembering what we have heard together—
> that creates the whole story
> the long story of the people.
> I remember only a small part.
> But this is what I remember.
>   (7)

In the last two lines, Silko claims all that follows as her own memory and an integral part of her identity as a Laguna woman. She claims that "autobiography gets distilled and comes back in fiction and poetry" (Bataille and Sands 140), and demonstrates this process repeatedly throughout *Storyteller* through her mixing of genres and reshaping of oral into written forms. For example, she narrates an incident that occurs in her own life when she is thirteen. Out hunting with a borrowed rifle, she sees a giant bear "lying in the sun below the hilltop" and stops to wonder if it is dead or only sleeping (77). Knowing that no bears that large inhabit the area, she stops, considers the peril she might be in, the effect that walking the hills in search of deer might have had on the imagination, and carefully walks away. She closes the incident with "I never told anyone what I had seen because I knew they don't let people who see such things carry .30-30s or hunt deer with them" (78). The poem that follows this recollection adds a postscript, referring directly back to the mysterious event:

I walked past the place deliberately.
I found no bones, but when a wind moved through the
light yellow grass that afternoon I hurried around the
hill to find my uncle.
Sleeping, not dead, I decided.
(79)

A prefatory comment connects the traditional story that follows the poem
to the event, explaining that the story was told to her and her sister by
her Aunt Susie on a day when her parents had gone to the mountain of
the bear incident to hunt. The resulting tightly woven web of memory blurs
the line between personal and communal recollection and between oral
tradition and contemporary poetry. It binds the multiple voices and genres
of the book into a single, continuous narrative.

Like more conventional forms of women's autobiography, this work contains fragments of memory and narrative, but unlike conventional autobiography, it makes no claim to be verifiable or to develop a comprehensive history of a life; rather, "its coherence depends upon our rejection of
the differentiation between fiction and non-fiction" (Elbaz 119). It presents
a series of relationships, a variety of personal and communal experiences
and voices, and traditional and innovative forms of narration—another form
of cultural composite, but in this case, wholly controlled by the imagination and voice of an Indian woman.

Paula Gunn Allen in her scholarly study of American Indian women's
worldviews, *The Sacred Hoop: Recovering the Feminine in American Indian Traditions,* draws on her own personal history to examine the Indian
woman's "way of being" (Allen 6). She begins by referring to her childhood and the traditional knowledge handed down from mother to daughter:

When I was small, my mother often told me that animals, insects, and plants are
to be treated with the kind of respect one customarily accords to high-status adults.
"Life is a circle, and everything has its place in it," she would say. (5)

With this traditional knowledge Allen begins to know herself as an Indian
woman. And as her examination of American Indian women continues,
she draws on traditional Laguna stories and her own memories to illustrate
her argument for the gynocratic nature of tribal life. Characterizing the
source and process of her development of ideas about Indian women, Allen
says:

My ideas of womanhood, passed on largely by my mother and grandmothers,
Laguna Pueblo women, are about practicality, strength, reasonableness, intelligence,
wit, and competence. I also remember vividly the women who came to my father's
store, the women who held me and sang to me, the women at Feast Day, at Grab
Days, the women in the kitchen of my Cubero home, the women I grew up with;
none of them appeared weak or helpless, none of them presented herself tenta-

tively. . . . Nowhere in my mind is there a foolish woman, a dumb woman, a vain woman, or a plastic woman, though the Indian women I have known have shown a wide range of personal style and demeanor. (44)

These ideas about female strength serve her well when she ventures into the male-centered white world and is "informed that her people were 'savages' who interfered with the march of progress pursued by respectable, loving, civilized white people" (49). Put in the villain's role, systematically dehumanized by the princess/squaw stereotypes, Allen draws on the oral tradition of her tribe for affirmation of woman's centrality and power, remembering the stories of

Yellow Woman, Coyote Woman, Grandmother Spider (Spider Old Woman), who brought the light, who gave us weaving and medicine, who gave us life. Among the Keres she is known as Thought Woman who created us all and who keeps us in creation even now. I remember Iyatiku, Earth Woman, Corn Woman, who guides and counsels the people to peace and who welcomes us home when we cast off this coil of flesh as huskers cast off the leaves that wrap the corn. (45)

The power and strength of her gender, confirmed by communal memory and her own experience of Laguna women, give Allen a context for personal growth and achievement. She speaks of herself as "Kochinnenako in Academe" (6), a manifestation of a Laguna female deity.

Allen's collection traces the intellectual and spiritual growth she has achieved through the experience and examination of tribal gynocracy. She creates a multigenre work through her personal history as it intersects and meshes with communal tradition and the voices of other tribal women. Her book traces the sources of and defines Indian womanhood in order to counter the ignorance and misinterpretation common in American society. Like Winnemucca, she has a cause, the restoration of dignity and centrality to Indian women, and she articulates that cause by examining personal and tribal mechanisms for achieving identity. She says:

At Laguna Pueblo in New Mexico, "Who is your mother?" is an important question. At Laguna, one of several of the ancient Keres gynocratic societies of the region, your mother's identity is the key to your own identity. Among the Keres, every individual has a place within the universe—human and nonhuman—and that place is defined by clan membership. In turn, clan membership is dependent on matrilineal descent. Of course, your mother is not only that woman whose womb formed and released you—the term refers in every individual case to an entire generation of women whose psychic, and consequently physical, "shape" made the psychic existence of the following generation possible. But naming your own mother (or her equivalent) enables people to place you precisely within the universal web of your life, in each of its dimensions: cultural, spiritual, personal, and historical. (209)

Allen's approach to recovering the feminine in American Indian traditions is non-Western, and her presentation of her life is not a conventional event-focused autobiographical text. The structuring of her text clearly "demonstrates that the writer's gender is relevant to the choice of narrative form" (Personal Narrative Group 100). She engages in "multiplicity of self-representation in a necessarily discontinuous because serial and temporally elaborated form" (Schenck 290). Here is a history of the development of a way of seeing that is woman-centered, a history of an idea as manifested in her own life through modeling on and counseling from tribal women. She expresses that history in a series of essays; she is, after all, a bicultural woman, trained in tribal kitchens and academic classrooms. She reflects on her bicultural approach saying, "So you see, my method is somewhat western and somewhat Indian. I draw from each, and in the end I often wind up with a reasonably accurate picture of truth" (7).

Unlike Silko, who radically manipulates the autobiographical form, Allen uses a conventional form, the personal essay, to express radically feminist ideas drawn and shaped from personal and tribal stories of women's power, but in her hands the essay form itself becomes multiform and polyvocal as it incorporates myths and stories from the past and voices from many generations. Like Silko, Allen pulls experiences out of chronological sequence, sometimes altogether ignoring the distinctions between myth, history, and individual experience, collapsing time and blurring the I/other distinctions in order to expose patterns and meanings. She becomes a manifestation of mythic figures. Her technique parallels Silko's use of mythic figures in contemporary context,[16] both demonstrating the viability of stories and the cyclic nature of tribal experience.

Both authors reject the conventional notion of autobiography as correspondent to some outward reality; instead, they make coherence the issue, the coherence of past and present, the coherence of communal and individual identity, and the coherence of language that has the power to make things happen. They do not simply attempt to "report, duplicate or verify the truth" (Elbaz 9); they make truth by blurring genres and by developing "an imaginative organization of experience for aesthetic and for various intellectual and moral purposes" (Shapiro 425).

Allen and Silko, in dynamic and distinctly tribal and innovative ways, demonstrate the remarkable flexibility of autobiographical writing; it adapts to new needs, accommodates non-Western ways of knowing and expressing ideas, generates new concepts of text, and expands the definition of what autobiography is.

TRENDS IN INDIAN WOMEN'S PERSONAL NARRATIVE

The directions in American Indian women's autobiographical writing are likely to be multiple. As more Indian women become creative writers, it is likely that they will express themselves in innovative ways as creative as those of Silko and Allen. In a recent collection of autobiographical essays by American Indian writers, *I Tell You Now,*[17] several women poets and fiction writers present personal narratives, tracing their interest in writing to family and tribal influences and to deep attachments to landscapes imbued with sacred traditions. These creative women shape their personal histories self-consciously, accustomed to using language to probe the most elusive experiences. For instance, each of these women incorporates poems into her personal narrative. Several juxtapose contemporary events, even newspaper reports, with historical events in their tribes, contrasting the minute-to-minute events with the sweep of history to examine survival despite destruction. For each, history is a living force, a reality to be animated by recollection and revisioned in poems or fiction. For Wendy Rose, autobiography is agonizing. She says, "I don't want to lie to you, but I don't want to tell the truth. The dirty laundry flaps in the wind, yet the alternative is to go on wearing it" (Krupat and Swan 260). She even invents two stories about her youth, brighter, easier histories, but rejects them to examine her struggle for identity as Hopi woman. Joy Harjo gives only the barest outline of her life, telling instead the autobiography of a poem, which is, of course, the autobiography of her creative imagination. The multiplicity of approaches by these professional writers suggests the potential capacity of the autobiographical form to accommodate the growing variety of life experiences available to Indian women.

It is also likely that more Indian women will take control of writing their own autobiographies, simply because the many well-educated Indian women today value their lives as models for younger generations or have Indian causes that might be expressed through personal narrative.

Surely the as-told-to form will endure as long as ethnographers continue to study American Indian cultures, but with the growing interest among anthropologists in the analytical nature of narration, the thrust toward a more humanistic approach to the discipline, and the lively interdisciplinary dialogue concerning the writing of ethnography, it is probable that the level of sophistication in ethnographic autobiography will be significantly raised. It is also probable that Indian women who agree to participate in the collaborative process to produce an autobiographical text will be more assertive in controlling the use of their narratives; they will achieve full partnership too in the collaborative process. It is a possibility that the collaborative process may become exclusively Indian in some instances as Indian men and women become trained in anthropology, oral history, linguistics, comparative literature, and folklore and begin to take an active part in the preservation and publication of all genres of oral tribal material.

As new developments in the process of Indian women's autobiography influence and shape the understanding of personal narrative, new developments in literary and feminist theory may also open up new areas of discourse for interpretation as text. Women-centered mythology and ceremonial roles may receive more attention, and gossip, a powerful narrative tradition among Indian women, may gain legitimacy as a genre. As one anthropologist sees it:

Because of its role in conflict and the constant tension between the desire for privacy and the desire to know about the actions of others, gossip is almost always condemned, but the condemnation itself makes clear its power in social life. (Borker 34)

Silko has already demonstrated the relationship of gossip to myth in her cycle of Yellow Woman stories. In her poem "Storytelling" she writes:

> "No! That gossip isn't true.
> She didn't elope.
> She was *kidnapped* by
> that Mexican
> at Seama feast.
> You know
> my daughter
> isn't
> that kind of girl."
>   (96)

In this brief stanza, the mother places her daughter in the role of Yellow Woman, mythic cultural heroine who, kidnapped by a katchina, ultimately returns to her people with twin sons who become cultural heroes; thus she infuses new blood and power into her culture. The myth provides context for a mother's explanation of her daughter's disappearance which has obviously attracted the notice of the village women. The actions of the daughter and the commentary by the village women create another composite form to consider.

Whatever future forms Indian women's autobiography may take, personal narrative by American Indian women will continue to be one of the few means open to nontribal people in America to learn the realities of life in tribal cultures; their autobiographies present detailed and intimate ways of knowing Indian women that demand that stereotypes be set aside. Unfortunately, those old stereotypes of "princess" and "squaw" have endured tenaciously in the American mind and are not likely to be replaced with accurate portraits or comprehension of the power of Indian women traditionally and today. The dynamics of gender representation and the politics of discourse in America insure the continuance of the princess/

squaw images in popular culture and the mind of the populace, but Indian women are no longer mute. Sarah Winnemucca found her voice, as have dozens of other women who have told and written their stories. And there will be more. The voices of the past and the present verify and vivify the range and variety of experiences and roles in American Indian women's lives. Though it is unrealistic to expect the voices of the next generation of Indian women narrators to radically change popular attitudes toward Indian women, the voices of the future, with new forms and narrative strategies opening to them and with support from feminist theory and scholarship, will continue to give Indian women human dimension—depth and individuality—and perhaps may begin to counter the superficial, flat stereotypes that clutter the American imagination. Indian women know about endurance, about survival under the most difficult hardships, about prejudice, paternalistic romanticism, manipulation. They've survived—by passing stories from one generation to the next—by literally and figuratively generating cultures. They, and the narratives they produce, may remain marginalized in American society, but it is absolutely certain they will endure.

NOTES

1 Rosaldo and Lamphere clarify this problem: "Because men everywhere tend to have more prestige than women, and because men are usually associated with social roles of dominance and authority, most previous descriptions of social processes have treated women as being theoretically uninteresting. Women who exercise power are seen as deviants, manipulators, or, at best, exceptions. And women's goals and ideologies are assumed to be coordinate with those of men" (9).

2 Notable examples are Zitkala-Sa (Gertrude Bonnin), a Sioux woman who wrote three autobiographical essays published in *Atlantic Monthly* in 1900; Ada Deer, a contemporary Menominee woman active in the restoration of her tribe's rights and author of an autobiography, *Speaking Out;* Susette La Flesche, activist for her Omaha tribe and the Ponca tribe in the 1870s and subject of the biography *Bright Eyes* by Dorothy Clark Wilson.

3 American Indian autobiography scholars Lynne Woods O'Brien, William F. Smith, Jr., Arnold Krupat do not include analysis of Indian women's autobiographies in their critical studies; nor do autobiography scholars Estelle C. Jelinek, Domna C. Stanton, Sidonie Smith, or the Personal Narratives Group. Work since the mid-1980s shows some increase in attention to Native American women narrators. H. David Brumble addresses women's narratives in the first two chapters of his book *American Indian Autobiography,* and Hertha Wong briefly mentions Plains quilts and Navajo weaving as forms of women's

autobiography. Helen Carr offers a substantial analysis of two Native women's narratives, *Autobiography of a Fox Woman* and *Autobiography of a Papago Woman,* which reveals the colonial ethnocentricity of the collectors of these texts. Kathleen M. Sands applies new ethnographic theory to a Papago autobiography. Arnold Krupat, in "The Dialogic of Silko's Storyteller," provides a reading of Silko's multigenre collection as autobiography, emphasizing the polyvocal character of the volume and the self-reflexive nature of the discourse as it incorporates traditional stories, voices from the community, and recollection. This essay is useful to compare with my designation of this volume as a multiform autobiography later in this essay. A. LaVonne Ruoff gives a detailed analysis of the Winnemucca narrative useful for comparison with the analysis of the same text given in this essay. Clearly, a great deal more critical work will be required in order to develop critical theory and methodology appropriate for Native American women's autobiographies.

4 See Bataille and Sands, especially chap. 1, for a discussion of the form and content of Indian women's personal narrative.

5 In *The Interpretation of Cultures* Clifford Geertz uses the term "fictions" to describe anthropological writing "in the sense that they are 'something made,' 'something fashioned' . . . not that they are false . . ." (15). James Clifford, in his essay "On Ethnographic Allegory," makes a strong case for the term allegory to describe anthropological field reporting, on the basis that representations of other cultures are convincing or rich to the degree allegories "stand behind the controlled fictions of difference and similitude that we call ethnographic accounts" (101). For an analysis of a Native American woman's autobiography grounded in current ethnography theory, see Sands. Collection and critical analysis of any form of Native text, of course, is an act of colonization and often reveals as much about the non-Native culture as it does about the Native text and culture, since colonization is a matter as much of language as of action, and, as Clifford suggests, may be defined as the continuous replacement of an indigenous allegory by a colonial one. Exposure of the colonial allegory, as it is imbedded in collected versions of Native texts and the critical discourse about them, is being facilitated by the current crisis in ethnography though it is unlikely that any theory or methodology will eradicate ethnocentricity; this crisis will, one hopes, sensitize scholars and generate more incorporation of Native metacommentary in the field of Native American studies. Autobiographies by indigenous women, despite the imposition upon them of Euro-American forms and interpretation, are, as the Personal Narrative Group points out, "particularly effective sources of counterhegemonic insight because they expose the viewpoint embedded in dominant ideology as particularist rather than universal, and because they reveal the reality of a life that defies or contradicts the rules" (7), and question the cultural norms of the dominant society.

6 See Kiowa poet and Pulitzer Prize-winning novelist N. Scott Momaday's *The Names: A Memoir* for an example.

7 Quoting Langness, *The Life History in Anthropological Science,* Susan N. G. Geiger says: "Although the demarcations between types of oral data are not

always clear, a life history is generally distinguishable from other kinds of oral documentation as 'an extensive record of a person's life told to and recorded by another, who then edits and writes the life as though it were autobiography'" (336).

8   For an example of the editorial control of a written autobiography, see the analysis of Anna Moore Shaw's *A Pima Past* in Bataille and Sands 89–99.

9   See N. Scott Momaday's *The Way to Rainy Mountain;* also Leslie Marmon Silko's *Storyteller,* which is discussed later in this essay.

10 For a more complete discussion of sources of and influences on American Indian autobiography, see Bataille and Sands 3–20.

11 H. David Brumble's *Annotated Bibliography of American Indian and Eskimo Autobiographies* and "A Supplement to An Annotated Bibliography of American Indian and Eskimo Autobiographies" include 133 American Indian women and 444 American Indian men.

12 Several biographers call Sarah Winnemucca Hopkins a chief; one, by Dorothy Nafus Morrison, is titled *Chief Sarah: Sarah Winnemucca's Fight for Indian Rights.* As a spokesperson, negotiator, and warrior, she does, in fact, fill the role of a chief though she never bore the title; however in one speech, her father said, "Now hereafter we will look on her as our chieftain, for none of us are worthy of being chief but her" (193), or at least in her autobiography she reports that that is what he said.

13 The United States/Canadian border has little effect on autobiographies by American Indians; though it intersects the traditional territories of many tribes, it does not affect how tribal peoples define their traditional homelands or cultures. Looking at a Canadian autobiography is useful, since the impact of Canadian governmental policies on tribes came somewhat later than in the United States, and the isolation of the island culture of the Haida made contact later than in most tribes in the United States. This autobiography allows some insight into the transitional period that is within living memory for older tribal members. Another as-told-to autobiography narrated by a Native Canadian woman and collected and edited by Margaret Blackman has been published since 1987, when this essay was originally written for this volume; see *Sadie Bower Neakok: An Inupiag Woman.*

14 Potlatches are traditional in Pacific Northwest coastal tribes. They are feasts at which sponsors, demonstrating their wealth and generosity, distribute large amounts of food and goods to those in attendance in order to celebrate some family or community event.

15 The fact that Blackman appears as the author of this bio/autobiography is typical of the as-told-to form and causes considerable confusion in locating copies of such work, since they are usually found under the collector/editor's name, not the narrator's.

16 In her book *Storyteller,* Silko has several Yellow Woman (Kochininako) stories from oral tradition. A short story entitled "Yellow Woman" (54–62) places the central events of the traditional story in the contemporary time period and thematically examines the revitalization of oral tradition by the repetitions of familiar experiences taken up in village gossip—validation of both myth and

individual experience are achieved in this manner. She also gives comic treatment to the myth in a poem titled "Storytelling" (94–98), which interweaves three separate versions of the Yellow Woman story, again demonstrating the recurrence of mythic patterns in contemporary time and narrative.

17 Subtitled *Autobiographical Essays by Native American Writers* and edited by Arnold Krupat and Brian Swan, this collection includes seven essays by American Indian women writers.

WORKS CITED

Allen, Paula Gunn. *The Sacred Hoop: Recovering the Feminine in American Indian Traditions.* Boston: Beacon Press, 1987.

Bataille, Gretchen. "An Interview with Geraldine Keams." *Explorations in Ethnic Studies,* 10/1 (1987), 1–7.

Bataille, Gretchen, and Kathleen M. Sands. *American Indian Women Telling Their Lives.* Lincoln: University of Nebraska Press, 1984.

Blackman, Margaret B. *During My Time: Florence Edenshaw Davidson, A Haida Woman.* Seattle: University of Washington Press, 1982.

Blackman, Margaret B. *Sadie Bower Neakok: An Inupiag Woman.* Seattle: University of Washington Press, 1989.

Borker, Ruth, "Anthropology: Social and Cultural Perspectives." In *Women and Language in Literature and Society,* ed. Sally McConnel-Ginet, Ruth Borker, Nelly Furman. New York: Praeger Publishing, 1980.

Brumble, H. David. *American Indian Autobiography.* Los Angeles: University of California Press, 1988.

Brumble, H. David. *An Annotated Bibliography of American Indian and Eskimo Autobiographies.* Lincoln: University of Nebraska Press, 1981.

Brumble, H. David. "A Supplement to An Annotated Bibliography of American Indian and Eskimo Autobiographies." *Western American Literature,* 17 (November 1982), 243–60.

Canfield, Gae Whitney. *Sarah Winnemucca of the Northern Paiutes.* Norman, University of Oklahoma Press, 1931.

Carr, Helen. "In Other Words: Native American Women's Autobiography." In *Life/Lines,* ed. Bella Brodzki and Celeste Schenck. Ithaca: Cornell University Press, 1988.

Chevigny, Bell Gale. "Daughters Writing: Toward a Theory of Women's Biography." *Feminist Studies,* 9/1 (1983), 79–102.

Clifford, James. "On Ethnographic Allegory." In *Writing Cultures: The Poetics and Politics of Ethnography,* ed. Clifford and George E. Marcus. Berkeley: University of California Press, 1986.

Deer, Ada. *Speaking Out.* Chicago: Children's Press, 1970.

Elbaz, Robert. *The Changing Nature of the Self: A Critical Study of the Autobiographic Discourse.* London: Croom Helm, 1988.

Frank, Geyla. "Finding the Common Denominator: A Phenomenological Critique of Life History Method." *Ethos,* 7/1 (1981), 68–93.

Geertz, Clifford. *The Interpretation of Cultures.* New York: Basic Books, 1973.

Geiger, Susan N. G. "Women's Life Histories: Method and Content." *Signs,* 11/1 (1986), 344–51.

Green, Rayna. "The Pocahontas Perplex: The Image of Indian Women in American Culture." *Massachusetts Review,* 16/4 (1976), 698–714.

Hopkins, Sarah Winnemucca. *Life among the Piutes: Their Wrongs and Claims.* Boston: Printed for the Author, 1883. Photographically reproduced by Chalfant Press, Bishop, CA, 1969.

Jelinek, Estelle C. *The Tradition of Women's Autobiography: From Antiquity to the Present.* Boston: Twayne Publishers, 1986.

Jelinek, Estelle C. *Women's Autobiography: Essays in Criticism.* Bloomington: Indiana University Press, 1980.

Koehler, Lyle. "Native Women of the Americas: A Bibliography." *Frontiers,* 6 (Autumn 1982), 73–93.

Krupat, Arnold. "The Dialogic of Silko's Storyteller." In *Narrative Chance: Postmodern Discourse on Native American Indian Literatures,* ed. Gerald Vizenor. Albuquerque: University of New Mexico Press, 1989.

Krupat, Arnold. *For Those Who Come After: A Study of Native American Autobiography.* Berkeley: University of California Press, 1985.

Krupat, Arnold. "The Indian Autobiography: Origins, Type, and Functions." *American Literature,* 53 (March 1981), 22–42.

Langness, L. L. *The Life History in Anthropological Science.* Boston: Holt, Rinehart and Winston, 1965.

Minnich, Elizabeth Kamarck. "Friendship between Women: The Act of Feminist Biography." *Feminist Studies,* 11/2 (1985), 287–305.

Momaday, N. Scott. *The Names, A Memoir.* New York: Harper Colophon Books, 1976.

Momaday, N. Scott. *The Way to Rainy Mountain.* Albuquerque: University of New Mexico Press, 1969.

Morrison, Dorothy Nafus. *Chief Sarah: Sarah Winnemucca's Fight for Indian Rights.* New York: Atheneum, 1980.

Neihardt, John G. *Black Elk Speaks: Being the Life Story of a Holy Man of the Oglala Sioux.* Lincoln: University of Nebraska Press, 1961.

O'Brien, Lynne Woods. *Plains Indian Autobiographies.* Idaho: Boise College, 1973.

Personal Narratives Group. *Interpreting Women's Lives: Feminist Theory and Personal Narratives.* Bloomington: Indiana University Press, 1989.

Rosaldo, Michelle Zimbalist, and Louise Lamphere, eds. *Women, Culture, and Society.* Stanford: Stanford University Press, 1974.

Ruoff, A. LaVonne. "Nineteenth-Century American Indian Autobiographers: William Apes, George Copway, and Sarah Winnemucca." In *The New American Literary History,* ed. Jerry Ward. New York: MLA, 1991.

Sands, Kathleen M. "Ethnography, Autobiography, and Fiction: Narrative Strategies in Cultural Analysis." In *Native American Literatures,* ed. Laura Coltelli. Pisa, Italy: Servizio Editoriale Universitario, 1989.

Schenck, Celeste. "All of a Piece: Women's Poetry and Autobiography." In *Life/ Lines,* Bella Brodzki and Schenck, eds. Ithaca: Cornell University Press, 1988.

Shapiro, Stephen A. "The Dark Continent of Literature: Autobiography." *Comparative Literature Studies,* 5/4 (1968), 421–54.

Silko, Leslie Marmon. *Storyteller.* New York: Seaver Books, 1981.

Smith, Sidonie. *A Poetics of Women's Autobiography: Marginality and the Fictions of Self-Representation.* Bloomington: Indiana University Press, 1987.

Smith, William F., Jr. "American Indian Autobiographies." *American Indian Quarterly,* 2 (Autumn 1975), 237–45.

Stanton, Domna C., ed. *The Female Autograph.* New York: New York Literary Forum, 1984.

Swan, Brian, and Arnold Krupat. *I Tell You Now: Autobiographical Essays by Native American Writers.* Lincoln: University of Nebraska Press, 1987.

Underhill, Ruth M. *Papago Woman.* New York: Holt Rinehart, and Winston, 1979.

Wilson, Dorothy Clark. *Bright Eyes: The Story of Susette La Flesche, An Omaha Indian.* New York: McGraw Hill, [1974].

Wong, Hertha. "Pre-literate Native American Autobiography: Forms of Personal Narrative." *Melus,* 14/1 (Spring 1987), 17–32.

Zitkala-Sa [Gertrude Bonnin]. "Impressions of an Indian Childhood," "The School Days of an Indian Girl," "An Indian Teacher among Indians." *Atlantic Monthly,* 85 (January, February, March 1900], 31–45, 185–94, 381–86.

CHAPTER 14

Listening to the Secret Mother: Reading John Edgar Wideman's Brothers and Keepers

C. MARGOT HENNESSY

I have a lot to hide. Places inside myself where truth hurts, where incriminating secrets are hidden, places I avoid, or deny most of the time. Pulling one piece of that debris to the surface, airing it in the light of day doesn't accomplish much, doesn't clarify the rest of what's buried down there. What I feel when I delve deeply into myself is chaos. Chaos and contradiction. So how up front can I get? I'm moved by Robby's secrets. The heart I have is breaking. But what that heart is and where it is I can't say. I can't depend on it, so he shouldn't. Part of me goes out to him. Heartbreak is the sound of ice cracking. Deep. Layers and layers muffling the sound.

John Wideman

I think that in the imaginary, maternal continuity is what guarantees identity. One may imagine other social systems where it would be different. . . . The imaginary of the work of art, that is really the most extraordinary and unsettling imitation of the mother-child dependence. [It is] its substitution and its displacement towards a limit which is fascinating because inhuman. The work of art is independence conquered through inhumanity. The work of art cuts off natural filiation, it is patricide and matricide, it is superbly solitary. But look backstage, as does the analyst, and you will find a dependence, a secret mother of whom the sublimation is constructed.

Julia Kristeva

When I first met my husband, I was acutely aware of the fact that he talked very softly, perhaps even mumbled. Several months later I met his brothers and was surprised to find that they too talked very softly and that none of them moved their lips very much when they spoke. It was not until much later that I connected this trait to the fact that their mother was deaf. It was then that Jay told me about how he and his brothers used to sit around

295

the dinner table when they were adolescents and communicate with each other in barely audible mumbles, carefully avoiding moving their lips. This way they could discuss forbidden plans with each other while being sure that their mother could not understand even though she had become an expert lip-reader. When I first heard this story I laughed. It rang to me of many adolescent pranks that we all pulled to get something by our parents, but this story stuck with me and I found myself repeating it now and then when people asked me why Jay mumbled. He and his brothers had formed a special kind of communication which shut out their mother, which allowed them a space to separate themselves from the world of women, and even my reaction saw this as a "natural process." But is it?

Recent feminist psychoanalytic theory has proposed the idea that the female forms her ego based on the similarities between self and the mother, and thus must assert difference in ways not as clearly demarcated as the male way (the phallus). The male, on the other hand, following the oedipal phase, constructs his gender identity based on difference from the mother and separateness; thus he is socially encouraged to embrace autonomy and individuality. This process as illustrated by Nancy Chodorow suggests that the female tends to form more diffuse ego boundaries and to define herself by connection and relation; the male forms those boundaries based on autonomy and the "outside" world of public space and institutions.[1] The ways in which my husband and his brothers defined self by creating a discourse unavailable to their mother would suggest that Chodorow is correct. Yet each of them has said that such a process left them seriously handicapped emotionally. For despite the fact that they had excluded the mother in this discourse, they also had to banish parts of self. Much of the recent work on gender construction looks at the process as it begins in early childhood, but rarely investigates its continuation in adulthood—how does a man reconcile the patrilineal and matrilineal lines that have come to form his own discursive practice? Is there a discourse among brothers, in both the literal and metaphorical senses, that by necessity excludes the mother? Does that discourse allow for difference? How can I, as a woman, be allowed into that conversation?

Sidonie Smith has used much of the ideology of Chodorow and Dorothy Dinnerstein to develop her theory of the poetics of woman's autobiography. Smith has suggested that for the twentieth-century female autobiographer the need to discover and come to terms with the voice of the mother, the need to pursue the matrilineal line in order simultaneously to separate oneself from the mother and to find connection within the matrilineal history, is tantamount. Smith's work makes no claims for examining the ways that the matrilineal line would encode itself in the autobiography of a male writing in the twentieth century. However, this is a much-needed investigation.

of exploring an experience" (Smith 7). The desire to claim a place for the voices of women and the complex production of the female "I" within critical autobiographical discourse leads Smith into a place not unlike that of Schweickart. Although recognizing that her referent is for all practical purposes Anglo-American, Smith still constructs a critical investigation based on the premise of a singularly identifiable women's *aute* and *graphia*. This singular attention to gender ignores the interaction of multiple and heterogeneous subjectivities which are constructive of the "I" of autobiography.

I am not devaluing the importance of Smith's or Schweickart's efforts; I am in fact suggesting that it is within these paradigms that I can begin to investigate the importance of the multiplicities of identity within the autobiographical acts of construction and reception. However, to bracket off the "female" or woman's experience from other possible variations of identity seems to suggest a particularly logocentric version of the reading and writing perspective. To establish gender as THE organizing principle only endorses stratification of the "other" categories which go into the construction of identity. It automatically requires that I say I am first woman and then I am white and then I am middle class, etc. I am required to bracket off all the other forces and agencies which go into my construction of the speaking "I" and the reading "eye."[2]

It is in fact the interaction of these multiple subjectivities that specifies the "I" and that creates its connections to various constituencies. In this variousness the issue becomes not how can I create or perceive self as the all-important individual, but instead how am I connected to the speaking voice within the autobiographical text and how is that voice speaking to me. Schweickart suggests that the male text is an "enemy or a symptom of a malignant condition": does this mean that all texts which construct the speaking subject (the postmodern protagonist) as male are thus enemies? Are there some texts which are more malignant than others? Are there some texts which by their process and investment, perhaps characterized by the "I's" own interrogation of unity and autonomy, speak to the "woman" reader more than do others? Are there some situations where the text, encoded with a multiple subjectivity which is yet male, can reveal to us more about the process of gender encoding than others?

If we say "yes" to male texts as enemy and "yes" to the real need to distance and control the definition of self as other in the face of a fictional text that posits male experience at the center, then the subsequent dismissal of all male autobiography would necessarily follow. I am not prepared to do this. Calling upon Fredric Jameson's thesis that "the effectively ideological is necessarily utopian," Schweickart suggests that the "male text draws its power over the female reader from authentic desires, which it rouses and then harnesses to the process of immasculation" (42). The out-of-hand acceptance of Jameson's construction here, which Schweickart takes unabashedly out of context, is problematic. The process by which narratives become documents of effective ideology is not explored, and this allows us once again to see the reading experience as one which is singularly identical no matter what the specificities of the individual text. For Schweickart, in the final analysis, our responses to texts are characterized by how that text is gendered: is it male or female? But at no point does she investigate the categories upon which the gender of the text is determined. What is it that codifies one text as female and the other as male? Is it simply the gender of the "author"? What role does the reader play in the engendering of a text? Is that voice male because I call it so? Or does some inherent characteristic make it so? It is these questions that this discussion would like to explore within the rubric of the autobiographical voice.

As Sidonie Smith has pointed out, shifts in critical discourse have found their way into the criticism of autobiography. The current generation of critics has challenged the notions of referentiality and the confidence in the authenticity of the self. For these critics,

the autobiographical text becomes a narrative artifice, privileging a presence, or identity, that does not exist outside language. . . . Such challenges both to the concept of a speaking subject and to the belief in language's transparency have shattered the epistemological certainties and ontological legitimacy of what the French theorists call the "master narratives" of the West, autobiography among them. As notions of an authoritative speaker, intentionality, truth, meaning, and generic integrity are rejected, the preoccupations of autobiography critics—the nature of its truth, the emergence of its formal structures, the struggle with identity, even the assumptions of a motivating self—are displaced by a new concern for the *graphia*, "the careful teasing out of warring forces of signification within the text itself." (5–6)

Within this discourse the question of the engendering of a text becomes much more problematic. The question no longer is the "sex" of the author but in fact: what are the forces within this discourse which we call female and what are those we recognize as male? In such an investigation the question is no longer, is the male text an enemy or does it represent a malignancy of culture? but rather, where does it reveal itself to be gendered and why? Within the signifying process is the "war" won by the resolution offered within the text or is it provided by the methodology of reading itself?

The ways in which Smith carves out her "critical fiction" of twentieth-century female autobiography require that she center her discussion on the relationship of the female to the center of phallocentric discourse. Yet her discussion of the female working from the margins and embracing or rejecting the dominant discourse clearly holds implications for "other" groups marginalized in the "dominant culture." Thus, I would argue that in many ways what Smith has called the poetics of women's autobiography may indeed be more aptly titled the poetics of the marginalized autobiography.[3] For a feminist reader it becomes equally important to investigate the ways in which the male autobiographer "negotiates the imperatives of 'paternal' and 'maternal' fictions," and I propose to do this with particular attention to the marginality imposed upon a speaker who is black as well as male, and who in the long run, I will argue, embraces the "voice of the mother outside time, plural, fluid, bisexual, de-centered, nonlogocentric" (Smith 58).

Weaving throughout this discussion, then, are two concerns: a concern with the singularity of subjectivity suggested by the critical paradigms of Schweickart and Smith, and a concern with the ways in which such paradigms lead to facile and reductive notions of gendering within the action of a text itself. I propose a view beyond this by investigating the ways that engendering and the codifications of identity within an autobiographical text affect the process of reading that text as a woman. If I reject Schweickart's notion of controlling the male text so as not to be controlled by it, then is another relationship possible between the gendered female and the male autobiographical text? Perhaps a unique relationship exists predicated upon difference, or perhaps there is a process of recognition conceived of within the paradigms of self being constructed within the action of the text.

II

At one moment when reading John Wideman's *Brothers and Keepers,* I became acutely aware of myself as reader, and perhaps this discussion is an investigation into that process. If James Olney is right when he suggests that the desire to write about autobiography mirrors the autobiographical impulse—then perhaps this moment was for me an enactment of the process of self-reflection and consciousness that characterizes much of the autobiographical works being published today. Or is it that Wideman's work is really the representative voice of the "other" squared? He is A Black Man. I am A White Woman. How does this narrative speak to me? All the work I have done is an effort to find a way that the female voice speaks from the margins and permeates the phallocratic discourse that is Western culture, and here I was mesmerized by a text which has no clear configuration of me as white or me as woman within it. Or does it?

The discursive style and power of *Brothers and Keepers* struck me almost immediately. Perhaps it was also the situation Wideman is illuminating—a brother in prison, he a successful writer and teacher; how did they each get where they are? If I were to succumb to Sidonie Smith's belief that the gender of the speaker determines the "gender" of the text, then I would have been put off by the obvious "masculinity" in some parts of this text. Upon describing entering the prison to visit his brother, Wideman writes blatantly about his desire to protect his "people," his "women," from the imminent danger of the eyes of the prisoners. However, it is passages like this very one which display the complexities of gender encoding in the light of marginality.

They're with me. I'm responsible. I need to say that, to hang back and preside, to stroll, almost saunter, aware of the weight, the necessity of vigilance because here I am, on alien turf, a black man, and I'm in charge. . . . And that posture, that prerogative remains rare for a black man in American society. (44)

Wideman's expressed need "to say that" is in fact a response to the white society which denies him the "role" of male as it is venerated in the phallocentric universe. Thus, the desire to call himself male and call himself powerful is not unlike that of the female autobiographer who enters phallocentric discourse and at first attempts to "call it her own." I am not suggesting that the powerful embrace of masculine metaphors and behavior within this text should be ignored, but I am suggesting that the position Wideman occupies in relation to the centered dominant discourse reveals a gap, a split, in his unity of male selfhood. It is here perhaps that I as woman reader begin to recognize self, not in the desire to be protected, but in the desire to be empowered in order to protect.

Much of the emphasis of recent autobiographical criticism has shifted to the reader as producer. This shift comes out of the poststructuralist challenge to the authenticity of the "speaking subject." Thus, for some, "writing is the inscription within an existing literary code, either in the form of appropriation or rejection," and autobiography becomes a manifestation of a prior act of reading on the part of the author, who rereads literary and cultural conventions. Such a paradigm, reminiscent of Harold Bloom's "anxiety of influence" theory, ignores that for many voices of autobiography the "literary and cultural conventions" which are predominant in our culture do not represent any aspect of self. These conventions privilege a white, male, middle-class canon of Western literature, and the relationships that writers such as John Wideman have with that canon are full of conflict. Also, such a configuration suggests that the autobiographical act is most significant when it is an enactment of the emergence of a "literary" voice on the part of the author. Such a vision of the autobiographer as a reader of "literary and cultural conventions" limits the specificity of each text and requires that we see each work as a "child" of all those works preceding it: in fact, it enforces the vision of history as patrilineal, chronological, and centered in white Western experience.

For other critics of autobiography who focus on the reader, the "fictive" reader becomes central to the act of production and assumes prominence. Thus the reader becomes the actual producer of the text, and by inscribing the text within his or her own conventions transforms it into her own, creating a confrontation between reader and author. What if a work presented thwarts our ability to locate it; or as one of my students put it, "I have no place to put it"? Does this suggest that a reader must perform psychological gymnastics in order to fit the text into the conventions which that reader knows? Such debates fall prey to what Schweickart has discussed as the tyranny of the reader or writer in much of reader-response criticism. However, Janet Varner Gunn departs from such singularity by situating "her theory of autobiography in both moments of reading — by the autobiographer who, in effect, is 'reading' his or her life; and by the reader of the autobiographical text, who is also . . . rereading his or her own life by association" (Smith 6). In such a paradigm my "reading" of *Brothers and Keepers,* and John Wideman's reading of his life as text, come together at the scene of my reading, and both acts of reading become constitutive of meaning within the text. Then the question for the reader of autobiography is: Where do I find recognizable parts of self within this process and where is the discourse defined by its difference from self? In a self-conscious narrative such as this work, the process of reading is enacted within the text. Thus I am conscious of Wideman's reading his own memory and experience and simultaneously conscious of my own acts of reading. And for me those acts are somehow characterized by a sense of otherness and yet recognition. I am other in that I am white and I am other in that I am a woman, yet within his discursive pursuit of his "history," his "blackness," and a language that intersects with the master narrative yet deviates from its conventions to speak from the margins, I recognize self.

The act of creating autobiography is not a simple telling of one's life story. It "is not a hypostasizing of fixed grounds and absolute origins but, rather, an interpretation of earlier experience that can never be divorced from the filterings of subsequent experience or articulated outside the structures of language and storytelling" (Smith 45). Thus it is the act of writing that assigns significance and meaning to the "experience," and this process necessitates a series of omissions and choices that undermine the impression of a full and complete picture of one's life. The autobiographer is seduced into the process that makes her both creator and the creation, writer and that which is written about. However, such an "adventure" has its dangers, and "the very language she uses to name herself is simultaneously empowering and vitiating since words cannot fully capture the full sense of being and narratives explode in multiple directions on their own" (Smith

46). Thus the autobiographer is forced to create a "fictional" unity of "I" which in no way represents the multiplicity of experience. This sometimes, especially in the postmodern universe, results in the author's presenting several different representations of self, voices and stories which call attention to this impossibility of language. Wideman's narrative often erupts into passages which lament the inability of language to express—"But what that heart is and where it is I can't say"—and the work moves through a series of voices and techniques never comfortable with the unity of meaning implied by one form.

Smith characterizes female autobiography according to its pursuance of the patrilineal and matrilineal lines within the construction of self. It is accepted, but perhaps unspoken, that as a "master narrative" autobiography is "male," and thus the male, whatever his own marginality, has access to its realm, and his enactment of self in the autobiographical contract will be along the lines familiar to us as "male." Yet the uneasy relationship between the black man and that "master narrative" cannot be ignored. The autobiographical form has been one that the black male literary tradition has in many ways grown to call its own. Much of this comes out of a desire to be "representative" as Toni Morrison has pointed out:

The autobiographical form is classic in Black American or Afro-American literature because it provided an instance in which a writer could be representative, could say, "My single solitary and individual life is like the lives of the tribe, it differs in these specific ways, but it is a balanced life because it is both solitary and representative." (339)

The tradition of black autobiography is very different from that of the Anglo-American white autobiography to which Smith is referring in her work.[4] It is a form which depends upon connection and community, a form which is not defined according to the logocentric notions of the individual as central and omnipotent. Such an assertion holds well for Wideman's book, as displayed even within the title; the effort of this book is connection and communion. Wideman's expressed intent is to get beyond self to be able to hear Robby's story:

The hardest habit to break, since it was the habit of a lifetime, would be listening to myself listen to him. That habit would destroy any chance of seeing my brother on his terms; and seeing him on his terms, learning his terms seemed the whole point of learning his story. (77)

This desire is also articulated in the frequently second-person address within the text: we are invited to participate in a conversation between two brothers. Such a participation implies a movement beyond the self as subject. The status of this work as both autobiography and biography creates a tension. Here the speaker is both subject and object, and this is so for both speakers, Robby and John, as they talk about themselves and each other.

These are a few of the many ways in which this work radically challenges the form of the autobiography as it is articulated within Western tradition. The specificity of this text's desire to go beyond the self is categorically different from what has been defined as the "necessity of autobiography" by George Misch, who has suggested that "it is chiefly the self-assertion of the political will and the relation of the author to his work and to the public that show themselves to be normative in the history of autobiography" (quoted in Smith 7). Wideman's expressed desire to get beyond self, suggesting a negation of the solitary individual and his relation to the public, is problematized in much the same manner as that which Smith sees as the female's. His access to the public space has been "severely proscribed," and "male [read white] distrust and consequent repression of female [read black] speech have either condemned her [him] to public silence or profoundly contaminated her [his] relationship to the pen as an instrument of power" (Smith 7). All of this is further supported by Wideman's desire in this narrative to speak not his own story of success within the white world, but the story of his brother's life, which in no way accords with the dominant culture's vision of success.

So this hip guy, this gangster or player or whatever label you give these brothers that we like to shun because of the poison that they spread, we, black people, still look at them with some sense of pride and admiration, our children openly, us adults somewhere deep inside. We know they represent rebellion—what little is left in us. . . . Even if I had struck it rich in the life, I would have managed to throw it down the fast lane. Or have lost it on a revolutionary whim. (57)

In much the same way as a woman speaks the male language of the dominant group, a black speaking implies a black man entering the dominant white male discourse. This is not to suggest that the encoding of gender is subservient to the encodings of race, but in fact that it is impossible to see them as separate, and thus impossible to assert that one stands in binary opposition to the other.

Wideman's pursuit of both the patrilineal and matrilineal lines of his construction of self and of Robby indicates a dualistic vision of the construction of voice. Although clearly for both of these characters the pursuit of the patrilineal line would seem to be "natural," it is in fact the father who disappears from this narrative first. Does this indicate a rejection of the father as a sign of rebellion? or a need to assert self over and beyond the towering figure of the patriarch? Wideman's own memories of the fam-

ily arrangement he and Robby experience recalls the community arrangement of the African village, a far cry from the Western nuclear family:

None of us knew how traditional West African families were organized or what
values the circular shape of their villages embodied, but the living arrangements
we had worked out among ourselves resembled the ancient African patterns. (79)

Important to the analysis of this text, however, are the ways that Wideman presents a history of the family which originally seems to be patrilineal, and thus representative of the Western vision of family. We get the
"history of the family" in patriarchal terms in the early part of the narrative, and such a "history" is notable for its emphasis on the male relationship to landscape and accomplishment:

I think of grandpa high up on Bruston Hill looking over the broad vista spreading
out below him. He's young and alone; he sees things with his loins as much as
his eyes. Hills rolling to the horizon, towards the invisible rivers, are breasts and
buttocks. Shadowed spaces, nestling between the rounded hills summon him. . . .
This city will measure his manhood. (22)

Such a passage is reminiscent of the voice of the male in much of American literature—the landscape as woman to be conquered, a woman through
whom he will prove his manhood. It is a "melodrama of beset manhood,"
as Nina Baym has said, and it rings of Nick's conclusion to *The Great
Gatsby:* "the fresh, green breast of the new world." But the world to be
conquered is not the frontier; it is instead the city, a city built by white
men, a city that in many ways does not welcome Wideman's grandfather
at all. The history of the patrilineal line for Wideman is one which is inscribed with poverty and struggle, and his desire to attach it to the American myth of selfhood is clear: "the strong survive. The ones who are strong
and *lucky*" (23). Yet there is no real recognizable self within the cultural
conventions that Wideman is reenacting here. And not unlike Smith's female
autobiographer, he tries on the cultural fiction of self, and rejects it. This
meditation leads him to questions, not to a neat acceptance of the myth.
History is not finally for Wideman the chronological, straightforward story
that has been told to us by the white patriarchy; instead it is a series of
accidents: "Accidents like the city poised at the meeting of three rivers, the
city strewn like litter over precipitous hills" (24). Wideman's forage into
the cultural myths of history and family allows him to recognize that the
"real" stories of his people do not fit into that prescribed myth. He, like
the woman autobiographer, has to investigate the silences of culture in order
to inscribe the story of his people: "Did our grandfathers run away from
the South? Black Harry from Greenwood, South Carolina, mulatto white
John from Culpepper, Virginia. How would they answer that question?

Were they running from something or running to something?" (24). It is indeed this question which starts Wideman on his real quest for a voice with which to speak to Robby and about him.

As John Wideman begins this narrative searching for a place within the symbolic realm of literature, a place occupied by white males, as he tries to tell "his" and Robby's story with the literary language that is the language of the patriarchy, he discovers the impossibility of that language. His position in the margin makes the symbolic language of American history and literature unfamiliar, inappropriate, unable to encompass textually any recognizable "I." Unable to work within those institutional expectations, he moves to narrative forms which defy singularity of meaning—dialogue, musing, questions, memory, and a variety of voices. Such a narrative technique more closely approximates what Kristeva has called the realm of the semiotic, Cixous the "écriture féminine"; it is a technique which problematizes the possibility of self-present meaning; challenges the possibility of conveyance.

Yet as Kristeva has pointed out, the attempt at recreating the semiotic cannot take place outside of the symbolic of language itself; thus despite the fact that we have changed the form, we are still unable to communicate without the aid of symbolic formations. What Wideman's narrative succeeds in questioning is the efficacy of language's ability to "fictionalize" meaning. The point in the text where such a recognition becomes visible is when he encounters his mother's dilemma.

If it is true that this text rejects the conventions of autobiography in its rejection of the assertion of the individual, then it is also true that it rejects the patrilineal line as a singular basis of the construction of identity. For John the narrative attempt to connect with Robby is in fact enacted through the "woman" in his life. As we look backstage, invited there by John himself, we do in fact find a "dependence, a secret mother upon whom the sublimation is constructed" (Kristeva 14).

It is here that my discussion turns to a configuration of a woman's hermeneutics of autobiography. I do not read this text as simply a woman, or even as an immasculated woman; I read it with an eye toward recognition. If it is true that the reader of autobiography "naturally" encodes self into the text, then perhaps I am performing an act of imposition, but more to the point I feel I am performing instead an act of re-cognition. It is a recognition of difference and sameness within the articulation of the "story" of these two brothers, and it is by looking at the women within the text that I begin to get a sense of backstage happenings. Yet it is not only the relations between these two men and their women which strikes the chord of recognition, but the ways in which both of them contain within their speaking voices aspects of that which has been called the "feminine," and how it is indeed these aspects which lead them toward an understanding of each other.

One of the very first memories which John presents to us of Robby is on the night of Daddy John's death, when he is babysitting for Robby, who was "just home from the hospital." Illustrating the nurturer's need for nurturance, John's fears are held at bay by the presence of the baby in the room—"I'd snatch you up and walk the floor. Hold you pressed in my arms against my heart like a shield. Or if the night cracks and groans of the house got too loud, I'd poke you awake, worry you so your crying would keep me company" (26). These early memories come easy, memories of closeness and comfort. Yet the distance between the brothers grows as they get older, and it is characterized by John's need to reject all that the previous relationship has suggested—closeness, blackness, ancestry. In order for John to succeed, he had to take on the trappings of a white patriarchy—"I'd made my choices. I was running away from Pittsburgh, from poverty, from blackness. . . . One measure of my success was the distance I'd put between us" (26–27). For John, not unlike the binary choices that encage the woman autobiographer, the choices were simple, "either/or. Rich or poor. White or black" (27). "To succeed in the man's world you must become like the man" (27–28). Yet this discursive attempt to escape the binary refuses easy categories, and fails to subsume one world within the other. This strategy becomes an embrace of that which is other, not white, not dominant, and by definition not "male." Wideman's discourse enters the realm of the "semiotic, and maternal continuity" (Kristeva xii).

Such continuity is established very early in the narrative, as John recounts Robby's visit to him while on the run and Robby's introduction to his new niece, Jamila. It is Jamila's birth that shatters complacency in John and that brings him to the realization that "things didn't have to be the way they were" (17). It is Robby who recognizes their mother in Jamila's eyes— "My God, she's a little picture of Mom" (17). Jamila becomes the measure of their "new" connection and also becomes the measure of their "old" connection with her likeness to their mother. Jamila becomes the link between past and present, the new and the old, the representation of "other" possibilities inextricably linked to history.

As soon as Robby made the connection, its rightness, its uncontestability, its uncanny truth hit me. Of course. My mother's face rose from the crib. I remembered a sepia, tattered-edged, oval portrait of Mom as a baby. And another snapshot of Bette French in Freeda French's lap on the steps of the house on Cassina Way. The fifty-year-old images hovered, opaque, halfway between the crib and my eyes, then faded, dissolving slowly, blending into the baby's face, alive inside the new skin, part of the new life, linked forever by my brother's words. (17–18)

Later Jamila becomes the measure of Robby's time in prison, and her visits to the prison allow both men to weigh the time that Robby has been behind bars. In an early characterization of Jamila, John notes her seductive powers and her curious liking for graveyards. Jamila makes friends with one gravestone, Vass—"Jamila picked this buddy by reading his name on a large headstone visible from the road and greets him cheerily whenever we drive past the clutter of tombstones abutting the fence on Fifteenth Street" (37). It is also important to note that it is Jamila's premature birth that first alerts John to the fragility of life and awakens in him, perhaps for the first time, real parental desires—at least for the first time since he left Homewood. Jamila's connection to the dead further underscores her position in the narrative as a function of the maternal continuity within the text. She is of both the past and the present, life and death within the workings of the narrative. It is important that she is the only child who has a significant place within the text; she is the daughter and the granddaughter.

The maternal continuity which makes it possible for the narrative to establish a connection between these two men, these two worlds, is represented within the figure of Jamila on one end and that of her grandmother on the other. Both serve to incite inside of the brothers the need to connect, to listen, to speak to one another within this text. It is Jamila who leads us up to the visit in prison, and it is the pursuit of the maternal in their history which leads John to the space where he can listen.

John's discussion with his mother about Robby is a text which is presented in the narrative as a site of recognition. Following Robby's first narrative recounting of the death of his friend Garth—"'It all started with Garth dying'" (66)—John tells us of his conversation with his mother concerning Garth's death. The positioning of this recounting within the text operates as a signpost to John's increasing ability to recognize and listen.

My recollection of details was vague at first but something about the conversation had made a lasting impression because, six years later, hearing Robby say the name *Garth,* brought back my mother's words. (66)

Therefore, in many ways the recollection of this discussion suggests a change in John as reader and a change in the reader's experience of John. It is also here that we get the only other first-person voice outside of Robby and John; we enter the voice of their mother. John's fiction-making skill has not been rooted out, as he calls for later, but here serves to move him into a position of the mother—to enter her discourse, to recreate the discussion, in order really to hear it. The scene of writing becomes synonymous with the site of recognition.

Here we enter an open dialogue between different aspects of self in John, as well as between Robby and John and other expected listeners. The text moves away from the "image of self-present meaning" and begins to question its own workings within this movement. By recognizing this point in the narrative as important, I recognize that it is through a real engagement with his mother, both textually and in memory, that John is able to begin to break away from the cultural constrictions of the patrilineal form. This important section of the text reveals the backstage sublimation—the mother upon whom the text is constructed.

We all construct our mothers within a rubric of cultural conventions and sometimes do so with a striking lack of attendance to the "person" behind our own need. The mother becomes a space, a maternal space which needs to remain obscure and "other" in the patriarchal world. Yet John's decision to enter that space and try to characterize his mother's conflict offers another picture of mother and son. No longer fictionalizing but investigating, John begins to see how Robby's "troubles" affect his mother. He begins to notice a change in her. The injustice of the treatment of Garth brings home to her many years of trying to come to terms with the oppression and subordination that have been hers. Yet the change in his mother becomes a textual enactment of the change in his vision of his mother and possibly himself. No longer a patient and long-suffering tolerant woman, she has become angry and bitter. The process by which a change occurs in his mother is not quick but takes place over years and exemplifies the specificity of the position of the black woman.

The focus in modern feminist theory as well as in a century of Freudian psychoanalysis on the mother as a figure much adored but left behind in "healthy" male development structure, which leads to the important oedipal moment when the son turns outward toward the father and the institutional world of autonomy and action, has failed miserably to characterize the mother as a person, an individual, not simply an objectification of desire. In Sidonie Smith's appraisal of the need of the female autobiographer to encode the silent history of the mother and the matrilineal line within stories of self, the need is seen as part of the psychoanalytic structure whereby a female identity is formed based upon continuity and identification with the mother. Thus women are more likely to have more diffuse ego boundaries, and to value connection and continuity. Despite the efficacy of such a proposal, and the implicit valorizing of things female, such a paradigm in no way accounts for the male's vision of the mother in adulthood. When the male autobiographer, especially a black autobiographer working outside the singularity and privilege of language as it is given to the white male, tries to encode the matrilineal line, tries to investigate the mother as a person—what then? John Wideman's inclusion and, in fact, enactment of his relation with his mother suggest that this process is not for him a negation of self in difference, but instead a recognition of self within the experience of his mother, her changes, her anger and her conflicts. John's narrative reenactment of his mother's process in fact points to an understanding of the need to listen, a need culturally encoded as feminine, and an ability that in this narrative makes the "I" dissolve into an "eye."

The long meditation on his mother takes place over twelve pages in the text and is fraught with familiar images of "Mother"—"Mom could let it all hang out, but most of the time she radiated a deep calm" (69); "Gentleness styled the way she thought, spoke, and moved in the world" (70). Yet each of these characterizations carries with it the additional weight of racial oppression and poverty—the sense that the private world of Freeda French is her realm and within that realm she approaches problems with extreme intensity and vigor; those problems "outside herself" she accepts with the same "resigned alert attention she paid to roaches or weather or poverty . . ." (70). It is the crashing together of those two realms, the private and the public, the inside and the outside, that "radicalizes" John's mother, that sends her into "bitterness" and anger. Yet our vision of this change is still cloaked within the narrative recreation of the autobiographer, the constructed "I," and it is John who sees the complexity of his mother's changes as reduced to binaries—"On one side there were the stark facts of his crime: robbery, murder, flight; her son an outlaw, a fugitive; then a prisoner. On the other side the guardians of a society, the laws, the courts, police, judges and keepers who were responsible for punishing her son's transgressions" (71). Those binaries are representative of a world, a text, that is not written by the mother, yet one within which she must make her decisions: "She didn't invent the two sides and initially didn't believe there couldn't be a middle ground" (71). Yet forced to operate within the patriarchal codes of "justice" and other abstractions, his mother chooses to find her place in that which is connected to experience, to her sense of reality—"on the side of the crime and its terrible consequences she would find room to exercise her love" (71).

In so many ways his mother's process in this section prefigures and echoes the process of the narrative itself. The narrative begins with a sense of the inability of John to understand the reality of Robby's crime and imprisonment, and moves quickly toward an attempt at an understanding that represents a middle ground, a place where the "reality" of the choices offered is denied. In memory, the experience of Robby is one that is clearly connected to John's blackness and his history. Yet in his late adolescence there were two choices—rich or poor, white or black. Choosing to move outside Homewood and enter the "white" world means a denial of those moments and that history—a denial of Robby. Moving into the white center allows

John to escape, at least marginally, the poverty of choices offered to blacks; yet it also means that he must deny a culture and a self that exist there. His private successes are not necessarily encumbered by the public institutions which have oppressed him. The turning point in the narrative is the point at which the poverty of choices confronts John, where the encodings of white versus black, rich versus poor, and right versus wrong no longer hold up. For John's narrative as for his mother's sense of being:

Accepting the version of reality encoded in *their* rules would be like stepping into a cage and locking herself in. Definitions of her son, herself, of need and frailty and mercy, of blackness and redemption and justice had all been neatly formulated. No need here for her questions, her uncertainty, her fear, her love. (71)

In the textual space where the symbolic formations of logic and the linguistic assurances of the conveyance of meaning no longer hold up, John Wideman finds his Mother. In the place where the prevailing cultural myths about importance of abstractions and institutions are questioned, the "I" finds another form—perhaps the semiotic. The reality of the margins is affirmed in the movement of this narrative on several levels, in terms of race, and in terms of gendered experience. There is no place for this "I" within the patriarchal discourse, within a patrilineal line of white men; searching out new discourse, another sense of history and happening, sends Wideman contextually and textually to the experience of his brother's imprisonment as it is related through his mother. Searching for a means by which to connect passages of time and memory to reach a connection with Robby and Robby's sense of reality, John first must get to a place where connections are possible:

her sense that things like good and evil, right and wrong bleed into each other and create a dreadful margin of ambiguity no one could name but could only enter, enter at the risk of everything because everything is at stake and no one on earth knows what it means to enter or what will happen if and when the testing of the margin is over. (71–72)

It is at this point in the text that we are sent into the interrogation of the validity of the speaking "I" and the ability of that "I" to convey meaning outside its accepted symbolic function—the "fiction-making self." The confrontation with the maternal, with the mother, with the margin, leads Wideman to a reconsideration of his own interpretive process and how that process affects the constitutive process of language and more specifically of the linguistic action of creating an autobiographical "I," the "I" that is simultaneously the subject and the object of the text, the "I" that is impossibly self-conscious, the "I" that must assert and yet deny its own validity constantly.

The conflation within the text of both Robby's and Freeda's experiences of Garth's death sets up the narrative turning point that this entire section represents. The beginning of this section of the book, called "Our Time," signals a shift in narrative style and in concern. Up until this point the narrative has been controlled by John, his memory, his voice, his "fictional" recreations of the happenings leading up to Robby's arrest. Yet the opening of this section brings us to John's first aborted attempt to "capture" Robby's experience:

Garth looked bad. Real bad. Ichabod Crane anyway, but now he was a skeleton. Lying there in bed with his bones poking through his skin, it made you want to cry. (59)

We begin with a representation of Robby's voice, for one paragraph, but the "fiction-making self" kicks back in and the rest of the story is related in the third-person omniscient point of view—"Ever since Robby had entered the ward, he'd wanted to reach over and hide his friend's arm . . ." (59). This leads John to his memory of the conversation with his mother, and eventually, as suggested above, back to a real confrontation with his discursive practice and the image of the unity of the speaking "I." The entire first seventy-five pages of the book have enacted John's process of "root[ing] my fiction-making self out of our exchanges" (77). And it is not until he has narratively enacted his mother's process that he can begin to confront his own.

And even if I did learn to listen, wouldn't there be a point at which I'd have to take over the telling? Wasn't there something fundamental in my writing, in my capacity to function, that depended on flight, on escape? Wasn't another person's skin a hiding place, a place to work out anxiety, to face threats too intimidating to handle in any other fashion? Wasn't writing about people a way of exploiting them? (77).

This is perhaps the real challenge to phallocratic discourse within this text: the effort to learn to listen and to tell about people without exploiting them—and for Wideman it is this that he must accomplish before he can effectively portray the experience of his brother and allow Robby to tell his story. The effort here is one that encompasses an implicit challenge to the discursive exploitation of all that is different and other, a movement beyond a vision of autobiography of self as central subject and object, an embracing of the warring forces of signification, and a recasting of them not as oppositions but instead as parts of a contiguous and fragmentary "I" and "you" represented within the act of speaking, telling.

In her characterization of "critical fiction" about twentieth-century woman's autobiography, Smith suggests that the female's need to engage self-reflexively with the language of the dominant group is then replaced by an embracing of an "alternate tongue," one that would be perhaps called the "language of female desire" (13). Citing the French feminists Cixous, Irigaray and Kristeva, Smith sees that the female autobiographer might develop a sentence or language that most approximates the "pre-Oedipal realm of the semiotic," which finds its voice in alliance with the mother and "her milk, her body, her rhythmic and nonsensical language" (13). Yet for Smith the assumption is that the text is clearly gendered by the "sex" of the author, but for these French feminists "biological sex" and the language used by a speaker are not necessarily related. Cixous, in her embrace of the Derridian paradigm of interrogating the binary oppositions imposed by Western logocentric discourse, is careful to qualify her use of the terms masculine and feminine:

I am careful here to use the *qualifiers* of sexual difference, in order to avoid the confusion man/masculine, woman/feminine: for there are men who do not repress their femininity, women who more or less forcefully inscribe their masculinity. The difference is not, of course, distributed according to socially determined "sexes." (93)

For example, Cixous cites the French writer Jean Genet as one of the best practitioners of *écriture féminine* (98). This would seem to suggest that Smith's characterization of the autobiographical voice of the female as that which embraces the semiotic is too dependent on the Anglo-American desire to equate sex with a gendered representation in language. Thus it is only within the female autobiography that you will find this feminine embrace of that which is nonlinear and semiotic. However, within the text of *Brothers and Keepers,* we do encounter a voice that might approximate the "feminine" as it is defined by Cixous, both in its linguistic activity and within its contextual concern.

Within John Wideman's work *Brothers and Keepers,* we have a postmodern autobiography which challenges the transparency of language and the image of self-present meaning. Such a challenge suggests the need to listen to language while being aware of the specificities of the discourse you are entering. John has "lost his Homewood ear" at the start of this narrative, and it is only after regaining it that he is able to conceive of the significance of Robby's story:

People in Homewood often ask: You said that to say what? The impacted quality of an utterance either buries a point too obscurely or insists on a point so strongly that the listener wants the meat of the message repeated, wants it restated clearly so it stands alone on its own two feet. (76)

Thus the reader must develop her Homewood ear also, and this sets up a new way of reading, a reading which is conscious of its own process and of the textual production which is a reproduction of the author's memory and a conflation of experience at the scene of writing. We become aware of what is being said and of the way that it is being said. That act of reproduction of the author's experience allows us to consider gender within the text in very different ways. It is no longer simply a case of how the female is represented or not represented within the text, but more how the ways of telling enact a process which encodes gender within it.

I feel that the ways in which gender is encoded within the text of *Brothers and Keepers* on one level is very clear. The narrative is filled with sexual imagery of possession and conquering. However, when we begin to ask, "You said that to say what?" the emergence of Kristeva's "secret mother" becomes very important to the narrative. That mother, although represented in the "actual" characterization of John and Robby's mother, Freeda French, is more complexly revealed in the action of the narrative itself.

In a lecture at Boston College (November 21, 1988), Kristeva spoke extensively about one of her own cases. The patient, Paul, was a five-year-old boy who was unable to speak. After quickly discounting the possibility of a traditional oedipal conflict, Kristeva began searching for other ways of dealing with Paul. Her eventual therapeutic treatment depended upon a process of what she termed "mother listening." Noticing that he and his mother were able to communicate quite well without the aid of linguistic formation, Kristeva was able to construct a mode of communication which, although rooted in the symbolic, found its conveyance in the permeation of the symbolic by the imaginary. Thus, central to such a treatment is the idea that the two realms are not necessarily separate and inaccesible to each other. Paul refused to enter the symbolic world of linguistic configuration because it meant abandoning the maternal space of continuity and fluidity—termed the "semiotic" in earlier work by Kristeva. Kristeva was able to get him to speak by discovering a way in which Paul could enter the linguistic realm, and thus the symbolic order, while not abandoning the imaginary completely—through the use of music and operatic phrases.

Such a treatment suggests two important things for the process of textual production: the desire to create an image of self in language is constitutive of both the symbolic and the imaginary; thus Wideman needs to find a voice that allows the imaginary to permeate the linguistic and symbolic configurations which are language. To succeed in this process, he tries on various literary forms and conventions which are constitutive of the literary forms of autobiography: linear temporality, paternal lineage, and the clothes of the fiction maker. Each of these methods falls short, because they do not allow for the voice of the other; they do not allow for any kind of listening; and they assert the importance of the self above all others. Therefore, he must move beyond literary conventions of autobiography and try to recapture that childhood imaginary realm where he and Robby first encountered each other.

This process begins with a recognition that the "object" of such an endeavor is not simply to tell, but to learn to listen—a kind of listening not unlike Kristeva's mother listening—a listening which forgets the autonomy of "I" and focuses on continuity and connection. It is a listening which moves beyond his own desire to escape into the symbolic and hide in another person's skin.

It is the confrontation with his own process which allows John to break free of convention and blast open the narrative into ambiguity that overturns the oppositions which have up to now defined the narrative: rich/poor, white/black, John/Robby. The two voices become united in a process of listening: John listening to Robby's story and reproducing it narratively for the reader to "listen" to as well.

This process begins with John's memory and enactment of a conversation with his mother—a relistening through the telling—and it reaches its peak with his confrontation of his own process: "wasn't writing about people a way of exploiting them?" It is here that John must perform for Robby what Kristeva performed for Paul, a kind of "mother function":

You were encouraged to deal with as much as you could on your own, yet you never felt alone. The high wall of the family, the collective, communal reality of other souls, other huts like yours eliminated some of the dread, the isolation experienced when you turned inside and tried to make sense out of the chaos of your individual feelings. No matter how grown you thought you were or how far you believed you'd strayed, you knew you could cry *Mama* in the depths of the night and somebody would tend to you. Arms would wrap round you, a soft soothing voice lend its support. If not a flesh-and-blood mother then a mother in the form of *song or story or a surrogate* [emphasis mine], Aunt Geral, Aunt Martha, drawn from the network of family members. (79)

This passage enacts what the narrative itself must provide in order for Robby to tell his story. Such an arrangement—a familial community—encompasses both realms: the individual and the community, the public and the private, the imaginary and the symbolic. Wideman couches his characterization of this in "aesthetic" terms:

Since we all benefit from the larger pattern, let's compromise, conform to some degree on the materials, the shape of each unit. Because symmetry and harmony please the eye. Let's adopt a style, one that won't crimp anybody's individuality, one that will buttress and enhance each member's image of what a living place should be. (79–80)

This passage enhances the idea that such a space is both social and *textual*. It is within a reproduction of this familial space narratively that John is able to "listen" to Robby, and Robby is able to break through his own series of oppositions and tell his history. John has created for Robby narratively and textually "arms [that] would wrap round you, a soft soothing voice lend[ing] its support," that mother in the form of a song or a story that allows Robby's voice to be born:

Robby backtracks his story from Garth to another beginning, the house on Copeland Street in Shadyside where we lived when he was born.

> I know that had something to do with it. Living in Shadyside with only white people around. You remember how it was. Except for us and them couple other families it was an all-white neighborhood. I got a thing about black. See, black was like the forbidden fruit. (84)

From this point, the two voices merge in a litany of choral conversation, trading memories and temporalities back and forth. And shortly we are brought textually to Robby's birth, and John's textual enactment of the birth of Robby's voice is complete: the responsibility for Robby's birth falls both literally and textually on John:

I named Robby. Before the women hustled my mother out the door into a taxi, I jumped down the stairs, tugged on her coattail and reminded her she'd promised it'd be Robby. No doubt in my mind she'd bring me home a baby brother. . . . I liked the sound. Robert was formal, dignified, important. Robert. And that was nearly as nice as the chance I'd have to call my little brother Rob and Robby. (93)[5]

III

The idea of a women's hermeneutics in terms of both autobiography and fiction does not necessarily depend, as Schweickart has said, upon "controlling" the impact of the text, on refusing to give in to the signification of self as other, but depends instead on looking for ways that the text reenacts processes which are perhaps female, but more likely signs of difference. Autobiography depends upon the reproduction of experience, and within such a reproduction a secret mother may emerge. Such a mother is not by any means necessarily biological or even necessarily female, but one who performs a "mothering function," as Freeda does for John and John does for Robby. Despite the obvious dangers of using such a construction, if we shift the emphasis of "mother" from noun to verb, perhaps we can begin to reconceive of the possibilities for the maternal not as a metaphor but as a process. Domna Stanton has argued convincingly for an interrogation of the metaphoricity upon which the French feminist vision of the maternal must stand.[6] Suggesting that the maternal metaphor is too often bound up with the traditional metaphoric structure of "standing for" something else, she suggests a move toward metonymy.

Because it does not cross the bar to truth . . . metonymy underscores the desire for the other, for something else/somewhere else, a desire extended along an indefinite chain of signifiers by substitution, by a displacement that wanders off the subject. (175)

There may be many other aspects of difference which are at work in *Brothers and Keepers,* and our reading of the autobiography must take a stand away from metaphor (this life stands for my own) toward metonymy (this life is different from my own, displaces my own, substitutes for my own). A recognition of the "mother listening" which John learns to perform alerts us to the limitations of a definition of the maternal based upon biology or even previous cultural conventions of "Mother" or "mothering." We need to refocus our attention on the activity which we might call "mothering" within the individual text, and not assume that gender is the primary qualification for the performance of this "function" or that the maternal process is continuous and identical in all circumstances. We need to reject images of control such as Schweickart presents and install images of investigation:

Is there a matrilineal story within this text?
Is the birth of the voice within this text an act of reproduction?
Do the language and movement of this text operate within or outside the
    critical fictions of autobiography which are "male" and "master" narrative configurations—configurations which deny the voices of a host
    of Others including those not white, not middle class, and not heterosexual as well as those not male?
If so, what are these new configurations and how do they relate to gender
    as well as other categories of identity?
Where do I recognize aspects of self encoded both within and across differences in this text?

It is not simply, do I "identify" with the protagonist, as Fetterly and Schweickart have suggested, but within the postmodern world where the speaking voice becomes protagonist, how is that *voice* gendered? Or how is gender encoded within the textual practices of that voice? This is a question not simply of identifying, as Cixous does, the male speakers who challenge the dominant discourse and heralding them as writers of *écriture féminine,* but instead of challenging our ability or the attendant need to explain away difference in neat categories such as gender. In fact the process I have charted in Wideman's autobiography may be closer to the process in Maxine Hong Kingston's *The Woman Warrior* than Kingston is to Elizabeth Cady Stanton. Does that mean that Stanton writes like a man and Wideman writes like a woman? Such categories which are transhistorical and transcultural lead us back to a process of totalizing which invites the rejection of difference and other and leads toward exploitation. Thus I am not prepared to go as far as Cixous and suggest the existence of a voice specifically "feminine," nor am I prepared to suggest that all that is "other" or different is female. However, it is within works that challenge the traditional literary conventions—which are admittedly male yet also Western, middle class, and white—that we may begin to discover gender encoded in different ways, and perhaps develop a hermeneutics that operates on the principles of recognition, not identification or appropriation; strategies which do not depend upon misogynistic and racist methodologies.[7] If within these works, written by both men and women, we begin our search for the "secret mothers," we may discover a different kind of discourse among males, between brothers—a discourse that is continuous and fluid, a discourse which depends upon connection, which belies oppositions and embraces difference.

NOTES

1 There have been numerous critiques of Chodorow's theory of gender construction which recognize its inability to account for difference in class, race, historical period, and political climate. For more detailed discussions of Chodorow and race and class, see Nicholson and Fraser, chap. 4.

2 The conflict in feminist theory about the privileging of gender as a category of experience and identity has a strong and complex history, particularly in the work of black feminist critics in the United States. For more comprehensive discussions of this conflict, see bell hooks, *Ain't I a Woman;* Angela Davis, *Women Race and Class;* Barbara Smith, "Towards a Black Feminist Criticism"; Gloria Hull, *All the Woman Are White, All the Blacks Are Men, But Some of Us Are Brave;* Anzaldua and Moraga, *This Bridge Called My Back: Writings by Radical Women of Color;* Elizabeth Spelman, *Inessential Woman: Problems of Exclusion in Feminist Thought;* Henry Louis Gates, Jr., *Reading Black, Reading Feminist.* These suggestions are by no means exhaustive, as this is an issue which continues to occupy, and rightly so, center stage in debates and dialogues in feminist theory today.

3 This is clearly a rather clumsy phrase, and in fact it may be even more accurate to suggest that Smith's theory for a poetics of women's autobiography is in itself impossible. The notion that there exists a stable category called "women" and thus a consistent genre called "Women's Autobiography" speaks to a set of assumptions about identity which fails to consider difference, and, as Vicki Spelman and others have pointed out, presupposes that "woman" equals white middle-class women. Aren't all autobiographies about the desire to reconcile differences within identity—to produce a fiction of wholeness?

4 For more detailed discussion of the tradition of autobiography in African American literature see Roger Rosenblatt, "Black Autobiography: Life as the Death

Weapon," and John Paul Eakin, "Malcolm X and the Limits of Autobiography"; Houston A. Baker, "The Problem of Being: Some Reflections on Black Autobiography"; George Kent, "Maya Angelou's *I Know Why the Caged Bird Sings* and Black Autobiographical Tradition"; Elizabeth Schultz, "To Be Black and Blue: The Blues Genre in Black American Autobiography"; Sidonie Smith, *Where I'm Bound: Patterns of Slavery and Freedom in Black American Autobiography*; Albert E. Stone, "After *Black Boy* and *Dusk of Dawn*: Patterns in Recent Black Autobiography."

5 I have dealt here almost exclusively with the first hundred pages of *Brothers and Keepers*. This is not to discount the importance of the remainder of the text, but instead to demonstrate the process which the narrative represents within the writer at the scene of writing up to a point of recognition. There is a great deal more to be said about Robby's story which cannot be addressed in this article, but I look forward to continuing the discussion at a later time.

6 Stanton's article, "Difference on Trial," critiques the notion of difference between genders as the primary focus of feminist investigations in both the United States and France, and is admittedly limited in its scope because it focuses on works by Kristeva, Cixous, Irigaray and Chodorow to the exclusion of several other French and American theorists who have taken up this question. Although I think that Stanton's argument is useful and incisive, her notion of difference is not analogous to what I am suggesting in this last section. I am arguing for difference as a sign of multiple and complex aspects of "identity" and culture which cannot necessarily be viewed in isolation, both culturally and historically. Thus, John Wideman's maleness is not the sign of absolute difference for me, and cannot be discussed outside the constructions of race and class in late-twentieth-century ghettos in the United States. I am also aware that within this context difference is not a constant category, but a shifting trope, which allows for moments, as I have argued, of recognition across boundaries. Therefore John is able to hear Robby only when he has allowed for the differences their experiences represent—when he has learned to listen and not project. It is the process of "rooting out the fiction-making self," of "mother listening" which creates moments of recognition within the text.

7 I am presently at work on a longer discussion of this process in terms of fiction and particularly the fiction of women of color within the United States. This project includes examining the recently articulated yet tenuous relationship between postmodern theories of identity and feminist politics, looking specifically at the works of Morrison, Naylor, Bambara and Kingston.

WORKS CITED

Anzaldua, Gloria, and Cherrie Moraga, eds. *This Bridge Called My Back: Writings by Radical Women of Color*. New York: Kitchen Table: Women of Color Press, 1981.

Baker, Houston A. "The Problem of Being: Some Reflections on Black Autobiography." *Obsidian,* 1 (1975), 18–30.

Cixous, Hélène. "Sorties." In *New French Feminisms,* ed. and introd. by Elaine Marks and Isabelle de Courtivron, 90–98. 1979; New York: Schocken Books, 1981.

Davis, Angela. *Women, Race & Class.* New York: Vintage Books, 1983.

Eaken, Paul John. "Malcolm X and the Limits of Autobiography." In *Autobiography: Essays Theoretical and Critical,* ed. James Olney, 181–93. Princeton: Princeton University Press, 1980.

Gates, Henry Louis, Jr., ed. *Reading Black, Reading Feminist: A Critical Anthology.* New York: Meridian Books, 1990.

hooks, bell. *Ain't I a Woman.* Boston: South End Press, 1981.

Hull, Gloria, et al., eds. *All the Women are White, All the Blacks are Men, But Some of Us are Brave: Black Women's Studies.* New York: Feminist Press, 1981.

Kent, George. "Maya Angelou's *I Know Why the Caged Bird Sings* and Black Autobiographical Tradition." *Kansas Quarterly,* 7/3 (1975), 72–78.

Kristeva, Julia. *The Kristeva Reader.* Ed. Toril Moi. New York: Columbia University Press, 1986.

Morrison, Toni. "Rootedness: The Ancestor as Foundation." In *Black Women Writers (1950–1980),* ed. Mari Evans, 339–45. Garden City, NY: Doubleday, 1983.

Nicholson, Linda, and Nancy Fraser. "Social Criticism without Philosophy: An Encounter between Feminism and Postmodernism." In *Postmodernism/Feminism,* ed. Linda Nicholson, 19–38. London: Routledge, 1990.

Rosenblatt, Roger. "Black Autobiography: Life as the Death Weapon." In *Autobiography: Essays Theoretical and Critical,* ed. James Olney, 169–80. Princeton: Princeton University Press, 1980.

Schultz, Elizabeth. "To Be Black and Blue: The Blues Genre in Black American Autobiography." *Kansas Quarterly,* 7/3 (1975), 81–96.

Schweickart, Patrocinio P. "Reading Ourselves: Toward a Feminist Theory of Reading." In *Gender and Reading,* ed. Elizabeth Flynn and Schweickart, 31–62. Baltimore and London: Johns Hopkins University Press, 1986.

Smith, Barbara. "Towards a Black Feminist Criticism." In *The New Feminist Criticism,* ed. Elaine Showalter. New York: Pantheon, 1985.

Smith, Sidonie. *A Poetics of Women's Autobiography.* Bloomington: Indiana University Press, 1987.

Smith, Sidonie. *Where I'm Bound: Patterns of Slavery and Freedom in Black American Autobiography.* Westport: Greenwood Press, 1974.

Spelman, Elizabeth. *Inessential Woman: Problems of Exclusion in Feminist Thought.* Boston: Beacon Press, 1987.

Stanton, Domna. "Difference on Trial." In *The Poetics of Gender,* ed. Nancy K. Miller, 157–82. New York: Columbia University Press, 1986.

Stone, Albert E. "After *Black Boy* and *Dusk of Dawn:* Patterns in Recent Black Autobiography." *Phylon,* 39 (1978), 18–34.

Wideman, John. *Brothers and Keepers.* New York: Penguin, 1984.

Index

abortion, 194
Adams, Elizabeth, 8
Adams, Henry, 238
Addams, Jane, 15, 189, 240
Addis, Patricia, 5
Addison, Joseph, 6
affliction, in women's lives, 59–67
African Americans: women's autobiographies of, 4, 7, 8–9, 11, 13, 14, 15, 22, 24, 90–102, 218–31; critics, 91–92, 160; Gertrude Stein's comments about, 162; women preachers, 191–92; attitudes toward, 234; and culture studies, 298; autobiography, tradition of, 304; and John Edgar Wideman's *Brothers and Keepers,* 301–21; autobiography, in contrast to Anglo-American, 314. *See also* race; individual authors
"Africans," 91–92
African Studies, 298
agency, nature of, 3, 4
agoraphobia, 236–37, 246
alcohol, dependence on, 236, 238
Allen, Paula Gunn, 26, 282, 284–86, 287
American Dream, 133–34
American Indian, 5, 25
American Studies, 298
Anderson, Margaret, 18
Andrews, William, 92–93, 95, 96, 101, 192
Angelou, Maya, 8
Anthony, Susan B., 87, 88, 120, 121
Anthony, Susanna, 57, 58, 60, 67–68, 71
anthropology, 271, 287, 290n5
anti-utopian visions, 23, 128, 131, 141–46, 147
Aquinas, 81
Asian American writers, 25, 247–50, 252–

67. *See also* Chinese American writers; individual authors
Atlantic, 128, 136
Atwood, Harriet. *See* Newell, Harriet Atwood
Augustine, Saint, 4, 51, 81, 189
Austin, Mary Hunter, 13, 18
authority, 3
authorizing, 4
"autobiographical pact," 7
autobiography: studies, 3; theory, 3; criticism as, 3, 26; gender and, 6–8; race and, 6–8; defining, 18, 272; truth/fiction in, 18–20, 157, 179; self-knowledge and, 19–20; metaphors of, 21; spiritual, 24, 32–56, 185–217; reader of, 26, 92, 147, 297–303; history of, 32; nineteenth century, 75–110; self in, 253; not indigenous for Indian peoples, 270; composite, 272, 278–82; multi-form, 272. *See also* women's autobiography
autonomy, women's, 67

Bailey, Abigail, 19, 57, 58, 59, 60–63, 66–67, 70, 71
Baker, Ella, 227, 230
Baker, Louise, 6
Bakhtin, M. M., 171–72
Barker, Francis, 76
Barney, Natalie, 159
Barthes, Roland, 9, 175–76
Bataille, Gretchen, 269, 270
Batterham, Foster, 196, 198, 210
Baudelaire, Charles, 196
Baym, Nina, 306
Beauvoir, Simone de, 9, 80
Belfrage, Sally, 220, 221, 225, 226, 227, 229–30, 231

323

Marian Anderson
My Lord, What a Morning
Introduction by Nellie Y. McKay

American Women's Autobiography: Fea(s)ts of Memory
Edited by Margo Culley

Frank Marshall Davis
Livin' the Blues: Memoirs of a Black Journalist and Poet
Edited, with an introduction, by John Edgar Tidwell

Joanne Jacobson
Authority and Alliance in the Letters of Henry Adams